Writings on Glass

For Magdalena Salvesen

Writings on Glass

Essays,
Interviews,
Criticism

Edited and Introduced by
Richard Kostelanetz

Assistant Editor
Robert Flemming

UNIVERSITY OF CALIFORNIA PRESS
Berkeley · Los Angeles · London

University of California Press
Berkeley and Los Angeles, California

University of California Press, Ltd.
London, England

Copyright © 1997 by Schirmer Books

Published by arrangement with Schirmer Books
An Imprint of Simon & Schuster Macmillan

First Paperback Printing 1999

Printed in the United States of America

1 2 3 4 5 6 7 8 9 10

Library of Congress Cataloging-in-Publication Data

Writings on Glass : essays, interviews, criticism / edited and introduced by
Richard Kostelanetz ; assistant editor, Robert Flemming.
    p.   cm.
Originally published : New York : Schirmer Books, 1997. With updated
list of works and discography.
Discography: p.
Includes bibliographical references (p.   ) and index.
ISBN 0-520-21491-9 (alk. paper)
    1. Glass, Philip—Criticism and interpretation. I. Kostelanetz,
Richard. II. Flemming, Robert.
ML410.G398W75   1998
780'.92—dc21   98-7976
                                                         CIP
                                                         MN

CONTENTS

PART THREE: PLAY (MUSIC FOR THEATER AND FILM)

PART FOUR: ENDGAME

PREFACE

Initially regarded as a renegade, Philip Glass has become one of the most popular serious composers of our time, writing symphonies, operas, ballets, film scores, music theater, music for dance, and songs. He has made more than thirty compact disks and albums. An active performer, he presents on average over seventy-five concerts a year. In 1998, his score for the Martin Scorcese film, *Kundun*, won the best music award from the Los Angeles Film Critics Association and was nominated for both a Golden Globe and an Academy Award for best original score. With its sparing use of dialogue, this film about the early life of the fourteenth Dalai Lama relies heavily on images complemented only by music to evoke an emotional response. The use of actual Tibetan instruments combined with the essential Eastern underpinnings of Glass's musical style effectively convey the mysteries of the Tibetan culture. And like the earlier films for which he has written music, *Koyaanisqatsi* and *Powaqqatsi*, *Kundun* addresses a subject that has profound social and cultural importance for our time. Glass has been a visionary leader from the beginning of his career and now popular culture is coming to reflect his aesthetic.

There is perhaps no better time to take a careful look at the work of the musician Philip Glass. The essays in this book trace his development from his entry into the music scene in the 1960s, a time of interest in experimental forms in all the arts. Glass, along with contemporary avant-garde composers like Terry Riley, Steve Reich, and others, created repetitive modular music that was similar to visual structures employed by Sol LeWitt, Carl Andre, and other Minimalist artists. The connection between art and music at the time is underscored by an illuminating conversation between the sculptor Richard Serra and Glass. Edward Strickland's essay "Minimalism: T" studies the development of Minimalism and its aesthetic characteristics. Strickland points out that both Glass and Reich performed at the "Anti-Illusion" show at the Whitney Museum, an important Minimalist/Post-Minimalist exhibition.

Tim Page's essay on Glass's seminal *Music in Twelve Parts* (1974) describes the work as a "conscious encyclopedic compendium of some of the techniques of repetition the composer had been evolving since the mid-60s." Calling it "both a massive theoretical exercise and a deeply engrossing work of art," Richard Kostelanetz in his essay analyzes its structure, examining both its novelty and its resemblance to Bach's *Art of the Fugue*. He shows how the similar *Changing Parts* was designed, in Glass's words, to be deliberately "intentionless," and concludes by describing Glass's musical grammar as a psycho-acoustical phenomenon that demonstrates experientially the relationship between music and human physiology.

The *Tricycle* interview with Helen Tworkov and Robert Coe allows a rare glimpse into Glass's spiritual practice and its impact on his work. Beginning with his finding his first yoga teacher in 1962 by looking under Y in the yellow pages, Glass traces his journey from reading about Zen in John Cage's writings and learning Indian musical forms from Ravi Shankar in Paris. This interview will enable readers to see that Glass's success is to some extent a reflection of his acceptance of a synchronistic chain of being and his ability to maximize its potential. In retrospect, Glass's involvement with Eastern forms and practices can be perceived as a chain of serendipitous events that, taken together, have a profound logic and inevitability and that have shaped his work.

Writings on Glass follows Glass's work as it became more multivalent and more content-oriented in the 1970s. The work began to move beyond purely musical issues when he undertook a series of collaborations with Robert Wilson, Lucinda Childs, Constance DeJong, Richard Foreman, Doris Lessing, Robert Coe, Allen Ginsberg, and others that can be seen as the vanguard of what is being called the new opera. Most intriguing is Paul John Frandsen's essay about *Akhnaten* in which he points out similarities between Glass and his subject and shows how Glass, like Akhnaten the ancient Egyptian religious reformer, resorts to convention to make himself understood. Analyzing and describing *Akhnaten* scene by scene, Fransden identifies Glass's unique musical structures and musical notation, the opera's plot and its use of Egyptian mythology, all from an Egyptologist's perspective. Glass even inspires his critics. Thomas Rain Crowe's inventive review of *Hydrogen Jukebox* is written in the spirit of the music, using a repetitive structure similar to Glass's own compositional techniques. Crowe in effect collaborates with Glass, combining his own spontaneous notes taken in the theater during the performance with sections quoted from Ginsberg's libretto and excerpts from a pre-show interview with Glass. Using three different typefaces, Crowe interweaves these different points of view into a new text produced in response to the original.

Recently, Glass completed his operatic trilogy based on the works of Jean Cocteau: the chamber opera *Orphée* (1993), an opera for film *La Belle et la Bête* (1994), and the opera ballet *Les Enfants Terribles* (1996). Glass wrote a new operatic score for the classic 1946 Cocteau film *La Belle et la Bête* (*Beauty and the Beast*) using words from the original film and synchronized his music precisely frame by frame with the original film. The live singers act as a visual counterpart to the characters on screen and in a deliberate layering or mirroring one character is sometimes played by two persons. This doubling emphasizes the duality which Cocteau himself uses as an allegory for the creative process and which Glass reinvents on stage. The result is one of the most moving and innovative works he has ever done.

Les Enfants Terribles (*Children of the Game*), the final opera of the trilogy, premiered on May 18th, 1996 in Zug, Switzerland. A collaboration with American choreographer Susan Marshall, *Les Enfants Terribles* is not properly an opera but is called a "dance-opera spectacle." Subdivided into 27 scenes, the music is scored for three electronic keyboards played by members of the Philip Glass Ensemble with Glass among them and directed by Karen Kamensek. It is adapted from a Cocteau novel about the tragic story of four children who live in a self-made narcissistic fantasy world and are incapable of escaping from it as they grow up. The setting is a room that the children turn into a private sanctuary, a place of mystery and magic that only children can comprehend and enjoy. Juxtaposed to this mythical world, over which no one seems to have control, is the actual world in which they live and reluctantly must face.

Heroes, Glass's fourth symphony, is the second part of a trilogy and is based on the 1977 album by David Bowie and Brian Eno. (The first Bowie/Eno/Glass collaboration was the *"Low" Symphony*, and *Lodger* is planned as the third.) Recorded by the American Composers Orchestra under the impeccable direction of Dennis Russell Davies, *Heroes* was released in 1997 on Point Music. Twyla Tharp created a ballet for the piece which toured during the fall of 1997. Glass describes his record label, Point Music, as representing "a kind of new classical music out of which good music can appear anywhere whether it be techno, classical, or popular." The Japanese CD edition of *Heroes* included a bonus CD single with a remix of the first movement by the British techno artist Aphex Twin with samples of Bowie's original 1977 vocals track.

Called a "digital opera in three dimensions," *Monsters of Grace*, the latest major opera by Robert Wilson and Philip Glass, premiered at Royce Hall at the University of California Los Angeles campus on April 15, 1998 as a work in-progress. "Version 1.0" is scored for live amplified voices, woodwinds, keyboards, Macintosh computers, MIDI interface, and electronic keyboards using sampling of traditional Persian and other Middle-Eastern string and percussion instruments. The libretto is based on fourteen poems by the thirteenth-century Sufi mystic, Jalaluddin Rumi.

Utilizing advanced digital technology developed by Silicon Graphics and first made famous in the movie *Jurassic Park, Monsters of Grace* melds high art and high technology to achieve a multi-platform conceptual and aesthetic benchmark. Seven of the thirteen scenes were presented as three-dimensional computer-generated images projected onto a large screen in 70mm stereoscopic film format. For these portions audience members wore special polarized 3-D glasses so that the slow moving and at times abstract visual elements appear sometimes as close as arm's length and at other times as far as the eye can see. The other seven scenes had live performers. With substantial sponsorship and a touring schedule to include over thirty cities through the spring of 1999, *Monsters of Grace* is intended to be another landmark in twentieth-century theater and a model perhaps for the twenty-first century. A CD ROM version of the work is planned and the web site can be visited at www.extremetaste.com. *Monsters of Grace* reflects Glass's ongoing effort to establish new agendas for the future of opera.

Robert Flemming
New York City
May 1998

INTRODUCTION

Philip Glass has become the most visible sometime-avant-garde composer of his generation—the genuine successor to Aaron Copland, nearly four decades his senior, and the precursor of John Zorn, sixteen years his junior. Some of his compositions have earned him a secure place in the history of innovative modernist music; others have been heard over radio around the world. With an abundance of works complementing innumerable public performances, he has made his initially innovative music widely heard.

He determined early in his career that he would be his own best spokesman, and so it is not surprising to find that many of the following articles (as well as shorter pieces not reprinted here) depend upon personal interviews with him. One contribution distinguishing this book is the initial publication of the fullest interview known to me (who has read scores of them, including several unpublished ones in Glass's own archive)—the one given to Ev Grimes in 1989, commissioned by the Archive of American Music at Yale University. Many remarks there appear in other interviews, usually in different forms; some statements there appear nowhere else. The other interviews here have been chosen to reflect different stages and ambitions in his career. The discussion broaching the heart of his esthetics is the conversation with the American sculptor Richard Serra (born in 1939 and thus two years Glass's junior). One recurring theme is his own articulateness in an age when composers have become unashamedly inarticulate.

The rest of this book contains major extended essays in English (I resisted the temptation to translate). Likewise lacking are Glass's notes on his own work, such as his much-reprinted essay on *Einstein on the Beach* that has accompanied recordings of that work. After a general profile written by the music critic Tim Page, one of many he has written over the years, and the Ev Grimes interview on Glass's professional origins, this book follows the development of his instrumental music from the truly austere minimal pieces of the early 1970s through *Music in 12 Parts* (1974), perhaps his masterpiece, to later works. There are two chronicles by reviewers, Tom Johnson and Art Lange, who frequently returned to Glass's works. The second half of the book focuses on Glass's work for films and theater, in roughly chronological order. In both sections are essays that survey several works, along with those that concentrate, often at length, upon a single Glass piece. This book concentrates on those Glass works about which much can be said (for not everything of his satisfies his minimal critical criterion).

I'm grateful to Philip Glass for allowing me access to his archives and giving me permission to reprint his words here; as well as to his archivist Jeri Coppola for making appointments and skillfully organizing Glass's files. This book is meant to supplement *Music by Philip Glass* (Harper, 1987; Da Capo, 1995), which deals primarily with his first operatic trilogy, and his forthcoming book on his Jean Cocteau–related compositions. *Writings on Glass* is also meant to celebrate his 60th birthday (31 January 1997), coincidentally the 200th anniversary of the birth of Franz Schubert (1797–1828).

I want to thank numerous authors and publishers for granting me reprint permission; Richard Carlin at Schirmer Books, for commissioning this volume and for his and his associates' vigilance; Robert Flemming, an aspiring visual artist/composer, who used this book to satisfy in part his internship for a B.F.A.; Michael W. Sumbera for his necessary proofreading; and Richard Kassel for his sophisticated copyediting.

Richard Kostelanetz

New York

Part One

Metamorphosis

(Overview)

PHILIP GLASS (1989)
TIM PAGE

One two three four
One two three four five six
One two three four five six seven eight

From this unpromising beginning—a succession of numbers chanted by a small chorus beneath a stage flooded with light at the opening of *Einstein on the Beach*—has grown the most successful opera career of any composer within recent memory.

Consider. In the past dozen years, Philip Glass has created four major operas—*Einstein on the Beach* (1976), *Satyagraha* (1980), *Akhnaten* (1984) and *The Making of the Representative for Planet 8* (1988). He has also composed several chamber operas—*The Photographer* (1982), *The Juniper Tree* (with Robert Moran, 1986) and *The Fall of the House of Usher*, heard in Cambridge, Massachusetts and at Louisville's Kentucky Opera in May and June. In addition, he contributed the Cologne and Rome sections of Robert Wilson's opera *the CIVIL warS: a tree is best measured when it is down*. Most recently, he has been commissioned by the Metropolitan Opera to write *The Voyage*, a celebration of the 500th anniversary of Columbus' discovery of America.

Moreover, Glass is a genuinely popular composer. Opera companies are notoriously timid, and most modern works are studiously ignored; when a composer is lucky enough to get a production, it is usually at a small house, and after the first run, the work vanishes from the

ut Glass's operas rarely play to an empty seat, and there have
al separate productions of *Satyagraha* and *Akhnaten*, with a
ion of *Einstein on the Beach*, directed by Achim Freyer, promised
Stuttgart Opera this October.

Glass and his performing ensemble now present some ninety concerts a year and are capable of selling out Carnegie Hall one night and a Midwestern rock club the next. Conservatory students diligently analyze the composer's unusual orchestration, while their more hedonistic contemporaries are content to blare Glass albums from dormitory stereo systems.

Not surprisingly, Glass's commercial success has not sat well with some of his more conservative colleagues. ("Glass is not a composer," one of them told me. "That's all. He's simply not a composer.") Nor has his music been hailed universally by the critics. "[Glass' operas] stand to music as the sentence 'See Spot Run' stands to literature," Donal Henahan wrote in the *New York Times* after the first New York City Opera performance of *Akhnaten*.

And there have been some important critical reversals along the way. Andrew Porter of *The New Yorker* wrote rapturously of *Einstein on the Beach* and *Satyagraha* when they were new, dismissively thereafter. ("My own responsiveness to minimalism in opera—to minimalism of all kinds—soon diminished," he explains in a connective passage after a reprint of his paean to *Satyagraha* in his latest book.)

Others have felt very differently indeed. "One listens to the music and, somehow, without quite knowing it, one crosses the line from being puzzled or irritated to being absolutely bewitched," Robert Palmer of the *New York Times* has written. "The experience is inexplicable but utterly satisfying, and one could not ask for anything more than that."

I count myself an admirer. More so, perhaps, than any other composer of our time, Glass has fashioned his own inimitable aesthetic. Those who disdain Glass's work for its seeming simplicity miss the point. Of course it is simple. But it is not easy, and it is very difficult to imitate. What may impress one as a banal chord progression at the beginning of the piece grows increasingly interesting as the work progresses, and as we examine it from each new vantage point that the composer presents to us. This sort of musical alchemy is what sets Glass apart from his many followers.

Glass himself doesn't care what the critics say. "Don't tell me whether the review was good or bad, tell me how much space the paper gave to the event," he said one afternoon while relaxing in the basement of his elegantly funky town house in Manhattan's East Village. He had been up since five in the morning and working since dawn to fulfill his quota of music for the day. Yet he was full of energy and seemed ready to reminisce, gossip, and philosophize.

"Only a few people read reviews through, you know, and only a few of *those* people really care what the reviewer thought," he continued. "I had a vivid demonstration of this. A cousin of mine in California sent me a long review of my work in a local paper. And the letter said, 'I was so pleased to see this review, and I'm so proud of you, Cousin Philip.' And it was one of the worst reviews in history, just nothing good about it at all. So I wondered what she could have been thinking of, sending it to me, and then I realized she hadn't read it and was just happy to see me on the page. That was all that mattered."

Glass is amiable, articulate, unpretentious and funny, with a hint of defiance towards the musical establishment. "We're getting ready for the fourth production of *Akhnaten*, which is going to take place in Brazil," he said. "You just wait, this is the opera that everybody is going to want to do, despite the initial response. I'd really like to have it performed in Egypt, like *Aida*, among the pyramids"—*Akhnaten* is the study of an eighteenth-dynasty pharaoh—"and we were close to making some progress. But no luck. They'll wait 100 years, and then they'll get around to it."

Though he loathes the term, Glass is often classified as a "minimalist," along with such fellow composers as Steve Reich, Terry Riley and John Adams. His mature music is based on the extended repetition of brief, elegant melodic fragments that weave in and out of an aural tapestry. Listening to these works has been compared to watching a modern painting that initially appears static but seems to metamorphose slowly as one concentrates. Compositional material is usually limited to a few elements, which are then subjected to a variety of transformational processes. One shouldn't expect Western musical events—sforzandos, sudden diminuendos. Instead, the listener is enveloped in a sonic weather that twists, turns, surrounds, develops. Detractors call it "stuck-record music" and worse, but Glass has brought an excited new audience into the opera house.

*   *   *

Born in Baltimore in 1937, Glass began his musical studies at the age of eight. At fifteen he entered the University of Chicago, where he majored in philosophy but continued what had already become an obsessive study of music. After graduation, he went the route of many other young music students—four years at the Juilliard School in New York, later work in Paris with the legendary pedagogue Nadia Boulanger, who had taught Aaron Copland, Virgil Thomson, Roy Harris and other American composers. During his time in Europe, Glass also was exploring less conventional musical venues, working with Ravi Shankar and Allah Rakha. He acknowledges non-Western music as an important influence on his style.

In 1967 Glass returned to New York City, establishing himself in the blossoming downtown arts community. "At first, my compositions met with great resistance," he said. "Foundation support was out of the question, and the established composers thought I was crazy. I had gone from writing in a gentle, neoclassical style that owed a lot to Milhaud into a whole new genre, and the timing wasn't right."

So Glass worked as a plumber, drove a cab at night and spent his spare time assembling an early version of the Philip Glass Ensemble. The group, which consists of seven musicians playing keyboards and a variety of woodwinds, began concertizing regularly in the early 70s, playing for nothing or asking for a small donation. "People would climb six flights of stairs for a concert," Glass remembered. "We'd be lucky if we attracted an audience of twenty-five, luckier still if half of them stayed for the entire concert." Then as now, audience response was mixed. Some listeners were transfixed by the whirl of hypnotic musical patterns the ensemble created, while others were bored silly, hearing only what they considered to be mindless reiteration.

But slowly, very slowly, the concerts gained a cult following, and then suddenly *Einstein on the Beach*, a collaboration with the austere theatrical visionary Robert Wilson, made Glass famous. *Einstein* broke all the rules of opera. It was five hours long, with no intermission—the audience was invited to wander in and out at liberty during performances. Glass's text consisted of numbers, solfège syllables and nonsensical phrases by Christopher Knowles. The Glass-Wilson creation was a poetic look at Albert Einstein: scientist, humanist, amateur musician—whose theories led to the splitting of the atom. The final scene depicted nuclear holocaust: With its Renaissance-pure vocal lines, the blast of amplified instruments, a steady eighth-note pulse and the hysterical chorus chanting numerals as quickly and frantically as possible, this was a perfect musical reflection of the anxious late 70s.

Einstein was presented throughout Europe, then at the Metropolitan Opera House for two performances in November 1976. But Glass lost a great deal of money on the production. "In the winter of

1976–77, what we had come to refer to as the 'Einstein debt' seemed a huge weight that could never be rolled away," Glass recalled in his book, *Music by Philip Glass*. So he returned to driving a cab while working on his next opera, *Satyagraha*, produced in Europe in 1980 and at the Brooklyn Academy of Music in 1981.

Satyagraha, a metaphorical portrait of Gandhi, was completely different—closer to religious ritual than entertainment, to mystery play than to traditional opera. While *Einstein* challenged all received ideas about what opera, even avant-garde opera, should be, *Satyagraha* fit Glass into the mainstream. Where *Einstein* had broken the rules with modernist zeal, *Satyagraha* adapted the rules to the composer's aesthetic—a much more difficult task.

Akhnaten was another step in the same direction. Here there were genuine set pieces—duets, ensembles, choruses and one long, challenging aria for countertenor—and the work was scored for a more or less conventional orchestra. Though it sold out all performances at the Houston Grand Opera and New York City Opera, it was widely considered a failure, in part because of an ugly, pretentious production that resembled a *"Saturday Night Live"* sketch, along the lines of "The Coneheads Go to Egypt." (A recording has been issued since, to better press.)

Still, it was an unusual work—the language was ancient Egyptian, and the only English in the score was narration. As with *Einstein* and *Satyagraha*, there was little drama in the sense that Verdi or Puccini might have understood it. Which suits Glass fine. "I don't really take opera composers as models," he said. "Isn't that the point? I like to listen to the same works that everyone likes to listen to—Mozart, Rossini, Verdi, Wagner and the rest. But it never occurred to me to write like any of them, any more than it would to put on the clothes of a nineteenth-century Italian. These works occupy a world of their own, and it is a beautiful world, one that enriches us all. I am a devotee of museums, but I don't want to live in one."

Glass names Virgil Thomson as one of the predecessors he most admires. "He's a friend of mine. We were talking not long ago, and he said, 'People like us'—I was flattered that he included me—'People like us, we're theater composers. We might write an occasional piece of abstract music, but we're really theater composers.' And he's right. I consider my three—now four—big operas my most important works.

"I'm not so interested in relating a story in the traditional sense of the word. Even *The Fall of the House of Usher*—you know, you can tell the plot in a few sentences. A brother and a sister are living alone in the ancestral home. A friend visits. The sister, quite ill, dies, or so it seems. She is buried in the vault, prematurely as it turns out. She comes back and murders the brother. The visitor runs from the house as it collapses. That's it. But for me it is a story that gives scope for an emotional examination of Poe's world. My score is eighty-five minutes of musical atmosphere with a simple tale at the bottom of it.

"In my theater pieces I like to leave some passages in which the eye can wander. In *Usher* there is a six-minute scene with only three lines. Not much happens. One person hears a voice, and a butler brings in chairs. But the music and the staging should keep the spectator's attention."

Glass is particularly excited about *The Making of the Representative for Planet 8*. "It's my first big opera in English," he said. "Like the others, it's an opera of ideas. The plot is simple. It's the story of a planet that is entering an ice age through what Lessing calls a 'cosmological disaster.' It's basically about a race of people who are about to die, about a planet that is losing the heat of the sun. It's one of the saddest stories you can imagine, and a lot of people have treated the book as if it were science fiction, but it is really an allegory.

"The power of allegory is that we can talk about things that are difficult to talk about, things that are close to us objectively. You know, it really isn't happening here, but on Planet 8. If we actually set the story on Planet Earth, it would be too depressing to think about. Nothing much really happens in the opera. People face their death, the death of their species. But there are many different ways of dying. An allegory, really, almost like a Biblical story.

"The emphasis of my work has been on collaboration throughout, whether with Bob Wilson or Doris Lessing, whether in music theater, film or dance. I'm convinced that this is one of the major reasons that I followed a path different from other composers. There was always input from another person."

Glass expounds on this in his book:

> For the most part, [the standard] operas in the Italian and German traditions were the work of one man with one vision (the contribution of librettists notwithstanding). The opera houses of the past simply produced these works and did not function as workplaces where artists from different fields collaborated on joint projects. Most modern operas written for present-day opera houses are conceived in exactly the same way. It is not so odd, then, that music theater works coming from a new and very different tradition should be greeted with surprise

and even alarm—when they are acknowledged at all—by most producers of traditional work.

Still, I feel very positive about our inherited and changing world of music theater. New works not modeled on the past are being created, producers are beginning to appear in cities and countries all over the world, and the public for these new works is very much there. When new works can outsell classics of the Italian and German repertory, as is actually happening all around us, it is hard not to sense a growing momentum towards a new and revitalized future for the music theater of our time, and I think this will have the proper effect on our opera houses. I don't doubt that the world of traditional repertory opera will eventually be dragged—probably screaming—into the twenty-first century, and that will be a whole new story.

Glass's current projects include the score to *Powaqqatsi*, a sequel to the acclaimed film *Koyaanisqatsi* by Godfrey Reggio; a ballet for Molissa Fenley; a science-fiction music drama with David Henry Hwang, *1,000 Airplanes on the Roof*; and a new opera with Robert Wilson, *The Palace of the Arabian Nights*, which will receive its world premiere at the Théâtre du Châtelet in Paris next December.

Beyond that lies *The Voyage*, Glass's major project for the Met. When the commission was announced in March, its fee of $325,000 was called the highest ever paid for an opera. Glass notes that "A lot hasn't been decided yet," but he does cite the theme he has chosen, "the idea of the great explorers at different times in our history. There's fantasy and history in it. By the time I get done with it, it will be a pretty good tale." He is scheduled to deliver the score in 1991 for production the following year. The Met management, which has been criticized both for essaying so few new works and for offering any at all, discounted the current vogue for Glass as a determining factor. General manager Bruce Crawford said, "The synopsis caught both Jim [James Levine] and me and produced our enthusiasm," though the composer's popularity "didn't hurt" and showed his capability to deliver a viable score.

*   *   *

Glass is a resolutely cheerful man. He now lives with his girlfriend, the artist Candy Jernigan, in a guacamole-colored house on a particularly seedy corner of the East Village. Glass has two children from a former marriage: Daughter Juliet is off at college in Oregon, son Zachary is living at home, studying music. "He's not interested in my stuff at all right now," Glass said with a grin. "It's probably healthy."

Jernigan's art, on prominent display, is good-humored and allusive, occasionally gently punning (a drawing on the wall features the labels of several varieties of canned Spanish beans, straight from the shelves of a local *bodega*; it is called "Homage to Goya"). There are books by the photographer Robert Mapplethorpe on the table, also a volume of illustrated Talking Heads lyrics to which Jernigan contributed. There's even something called *The Wonderful Private World of Liberace*, a coffee-table pictorial celebration rather than an exposé. The phones ring constantly. A cat lies on the counter. The atmosphere is friendly and informal. Glass bought his house in 1984 and, when he is in New York, he leads a quiet, strictly disciplined existence. "I work best in the early morning," he said, "so I get up around five or six and compose until noon or so. . . . Occasionally I will have to write really quickly. I once wrote and recorded forty-five minutes' worth of incidental music in a week—*literally* a week. The guys in the studio were working three hours behind me. I'd finish a movement, and they'd learn it and record it. I do compose quickly, you know, but nobody likes to work *that* fast. Still, I liked the incidental music enough to fashion a twenty-minute orchestral suite from it. It's not bad at all.

"Just recently, somebody asked me how long it took me to write one of my pieces he'd just heard. And I said about forty years. I know it sounds like a cynical answer, but I've been working at this business of composing since I was eight. And everything adds to the whole—everything I've learned influences the music I write.

"I deal with business matters in the afternoon—recording, auditioning, the *real world*. Giving interviews, too. I decided long ago that I was my own best spokesman, and I made it a point then and there to talk with anybody. I'm rather proud of the fact that I've spent as much time talking with reporters from high school newspapers as I have talking with *Time* magazine. Kids grow up, you know, and these same folks who are now at high school newspapers or college radio stations have a habit of becoming music professionals. It's not just that I like to talk with young people—which I do, and sometimes they are better prepared than professional critics—but it's good business as well." Evenings are reserved for friends, for family, an occasional party, even a concert or two.

Of course, Glass isn't home very often these days. He spends much of the summer in Nova Scotia, where he devotes himself to a strict regimen of composing. And then there are the tours. "I cross the country twice a year with the ensemble," he said. "I play all over the place. I've played in six cities in Montana. Did you *know* there were six cities in Montana? Do you know the population of Laramie, Wyoming? I do. I know where the pizza places are. I know both of the hotels."

Glass leaned back and grinned. "You know, it's just like I always thought it would be. When you start to be well-known, you get to play all the really *small* places."

INTERVIEW: EDUCATION (1989)

E V   G R I M E S

Edited by *Philip Glass and Richard Kostelanetz (1996)*

EV GRIMES: TELL ME ABOUT YOUR EARLIEST MUSICAL MEMORIES WHEN YOU WERE A LITTLE KID. WHAT KINDS OF THINGS WERE YOU HEARING AROUND THE HOUSE?

PHILIP GLASS: My father had a record store with an interesting history. He actually began as an automobile mechanic in the early '30s and at one point someone got the idea of putting radios in cars. So he learned to fix the radios. As long as he was fixing the cars, he fixed the radios, too. So, eventually he got rid of the cars and kept the radios. Actually in the '30s he had a radio store and radio repair store, and he began putting records in as a sideline to the radios [laughs]. Eventually the radios ended up being the small part of the business while the records grew to be an enormous part of the business, ending up with a record store. . . . He sold classical records and popular records and what they used to call—at least in Maryland—"hillbilly" music, which is now called Country Western music. You could never call it hillbilly music today—you'd be run out of town [laughs] for doing that—but actually that's what it was, Maryland is right across the line from West Virginia and Virginia. In those days there was a lot of country music coming into Maryland from that way and on the radio. That was the music he sold, and he built up a personal record collection consisting mainly of records he couldn't sell. If he couldn't sell it in the store, he would bring it home. Right? [laughs] That's a funny story.

So he ended up with a lot of modern music, because no one bought it. You know, he would have a recording of a Bartók piece or Hindemith; people didn't buy that in Baltimore. Somehow, some salesman had sold him this record, and he got stuck with it. They were all 78s, don't forget, and he would bring this music home. We heard all the esoteric pieces. We even had all the modern music that was then recorded. . . . Also, other music that didn't sell, which was the very esoteric in those days it would seem, was chamber music. The Beethoven quartets didn't sell well, you know, Schubert piano trios didn't sell well. He ended up with a very refined collection.

He told me later that he listened to these records to see what was wrong with them. He wanted to figure out why they didn't sell. That was his motivation, because he was a practical guy. In the course of doing that he became a great lover of chamber music, mostly chamber music but very little symphonic music, which usually sells very well, you know. I didn't hear the Beethoven Fifth Symphony until I was in my late teens simply because it never was at home. Right? [laughs] The so-called "war horses" I discovered much much later. I never heard those when I was a kid.

I began taking music lessons when I was six. Greg Sandow said I began when I was eight. What is true is that I began at the Peabody when I was eight, but I began in the elementary school where I went. It was one of those music programs in the school where everyone got a violin, but not today like the Suzuki method. We sawed away at the violins, you know; it was quite awful really. But I did that for a while and then when I was eight I went to the Peabody. Baltimore was very fortunate in having a very good orchestra. . . . Don't forget that in the '40s a lot of refugees had come over from the eastern European countries. Baltimore had a fair share of refugee musicians who had survived the concentration camps or had come over before, so that Baltimore ended up with a very good orchestra. There was a guy who conducted—very few people would remember his name— Reginald Stewart, a Canadian conductor. Later there were other conductors. Because there was a good orchestra in Baltimore, the Peabody had a very fine faculty. That's all it takes, really. Wherever there's a good orchestra, you'll find a good music school, obviously. But if you don't have a good orchestra, it's hard to find good teachers, because they aren't there to teach, they're in some other city. . . .

I began studying the flute, and I also took Saturday classes. . . . They had something they called the Preparatory Division in Baltimore at the Peabody, but there wasn't anyone teaching flute there. So, I had to become a student at the Conservatory. They're actually different buildings. The Preparatory building was a smaller building somewhat down the street in a part of town called Mount Vernon Place. The Preparatory Division had its own building, which was devoted to music education for children. It had classes on Saturday in theory and in percussion and different . . . and I took those classes, but in order to study flute, I had to study at the Conservatory, so I became the youngest student there.

I take it they found you particularly talented to let you in.
I don't think I was particularly talented. I think they'll take anybody in who's interested in music and whose parents will pay a little of the tuition. It's not hard to get into a music school. Music schools are always looking for kids, you know. Music educators love to teach music. I was what in those days we called an inner-city kid. We grew up in those row houses in Baltimore that have the white marble steps in a mixed neighborhood. This was before the days of suburbs. I'm talking about the years during the Second World War and immediately after that. We didn't talk about ghettos in those days, I don't know what we called them. Anyway, we had our own house, but we lived in a very mixed neighborhood in a kind of lower-middle-class part of town. My lessons weren't so far away—maybe fifteen minutes by streetcar. By eight or nine years old I was taking that ride by myself once or twice a week. I had a very good teacher, a guy named Britton Johnson. He was a student of William Kincaid's, the great flutist from Philadelphia, and was a very good flutist himself. All of Kincaid's students were good flutists and they all had a particular sound to them. You find them around—if you look around in different orchestras—they're dying out now, but you hear it even in the students of his students. It was like Juilliard, where there would be great violin teachers like Ivan Galamian, you know his students would have a certain sound and Johnson's students had Kincaid's sound. It was a very round, very warm sound—not the modern flute sound you hear with someone like James Galway but a bit more different, much more defined in a way. Anyway, I studied there, and then I began to participate in concerts at the schools that I went to. I played in my high school band; the school also had an orchestra that did musicals, a marching band, and different kinds of things that I did. By the time I was ten, I also played in some of these church orchestras that would put on Bach masses and things like that.

Did you have any interest in popular music at all?

Well, I did, but you have to remember that in 1945 or '46 the popular music of the time were the crooners—people like Frank Sinatra and Perry Como. Popular music as we know it today didn't exist—there was no rock and roll. There was rhythm-and-blues, but that was considered, in the store where I worked from a very early age, what we called "race" records. Can you imagine using that description today? "Race" records— my God. Actually what you had—you had "hillbilly" records, "race" records, popular music, and classical music—that was it. You know, this was in the '40s. Don't forget Baltimore was a segregated city. Baltimore was a city where if you had a black friend and you were white, there was no restaurant you could eat dinner at, there was no movie you could go to; you couldn't go swimming together and you couldn't play golf, even. Baltimore was a typical southern town. With the renaissance of Baltimore, this has been forgotten. During the years I grew up I worked in places where the washrooms in the work places were segregated, you know, and the drinking fountains—the whole bit. Bethlehem Steel had a big steel plant outside of Baltimore, and I worked there too. There was a separate dressing room and washrooms and toilets for the black guys. I know, it's amazing, isn't it? Well, that was Baltimore right up until desegregation in 1962. So as a result, in the town I grew up in, the music was segregated as well.

Now, at one point, my brother and I ran a record store for my father in East Baltimore. What we sold in that store was mostly black music. That music would never have been bought by the clientele that bought in the regular downtown store. Very few white people bought black music. You know, Elvis Presley was really the guy that took black music and made it—well, popular is really the best word. . . . I knew a lot more about popular music than most of my friends did because I worked in the store and besides that, I worked in the stores that sold black music, so I knew a lot more about it than other people did. I daresay very few of my friends had heard the music that I heard. Then I went to the University of Chicago when I was very young, I was fifteen, and there I discovered there was a lot of black music in the form of jazz.

Then you graduated from high school two years early?

No, I didn't graduate, I just left high school; it was not necessary to graduate. The University of Chicago had a program that was initiated by this guy Robert Maynard Hutchins. He's an educator who began the Early Entrance Programs at the University of Chicago, and the University provided an entrance exam; upon completion of this exam you became eligible to go to the University; graduation from high school was not a requirement. I took the test when I was around fourteen, but it wasn't a very difficult test. Most people could have passed it, really. The thing is that very few people thought of taking the test. . . .

When I arrived in Chicago in 1952, I discovered a whole world of black music, which was not what existed in Baltimore. On Fifty-Sixth Street in the part of Chicago called Hyde Park, where the University was located, there was a club called the Beehive. Charlie Parker and Bud Powell used to play there. I heard Billie Holiday sing at the Cotton Club, actually, it was called the Cottage Grove—Ben Webster and people like that. I heard them sing and play there. Downtown in Chicago there was a place called the Modern Jazz Room where the early Gerry Mulligan Quartet with Chet Baker used to play, you know. And all those guys would play there—Dave Brubeck. You see, even then the Modern Jazz Room played mostly white musicians—Warne Marsh, Lee Konitz. The black guys played on the south side of Fifty-Third Street or thereabouts. White guys didn't play down there. But I became educated about jazz in Chicago. . . .

What was it about jazz? What were you hearing?
Well, first of all it was a technique that I didn't myself ever acquire any confidence in at all. I never was an improviser. I wasn't drawn to it as a player. So, I really couldn't say that it inspired me in any direct way. I just liked the music. In a way, you might say it was the first form of truly contemporary experimental music that I had ever heard, if you want to look at it that way. After all, jazz is a form of experimental music in the sense that it's a musical language which is still in the process of being created. That may be less true today, but that was certainly true in the '50s—early '50s—when Miles Davis was still a very young man. Ornette Coleman hadn't even begun to play when I was there; John Coltrane was evolving his own style. What you were witnessing in 1952, '53, '54, '55, and so forth was the transformation of the world of jazz from the big swing bands and the big jazz bands; bebop was still fairly young in 1952, five or six years old. It really dates back from the late '40s, and even then it was not very well understood. So that what I was seeing was a language that was in the process of transforming itself, which was not true for classical music, which was done. That was a language in which Schubert wasn't going to write any more quartets—that was for sure.

In Chicago at that time there were some contemporary composers, but I didn't know them. Alexander Tcherepnin was there. He taught at De Paul University, a refugee Russian composer, certainly not on the level of Stravinsky or even Rachmaninoff. I don't think very many people know his music today. Later I met another guy named Lopatnikoff in Pittsburgh. There were a fair amount of these refugee composers who got sprinkled around the States because of the war. Later on, people like Alan Stout settled in Chicago. He was from Baltimore, by the way; I knew him, we went to the same high school. Then you had people like Easley Blackwood and Ralph Shapey, who came to Chicago in the '60s. When I was in Chicago in the early '50s, they weren't there. The University of Chicago's music department was basically run by a guy named Grosvenor Cooper. It was basically a musicology and music history department with very little to offer anyone interested in composition. You couldn't really study with them.

So, you knew by the time you were fifteen, sixteen—
I was already writing music by the time I was fifteen. I took harmony lessons with a guy in Baltimore named Louis Cheslock, who was a local composer, and I think he had some pieces played in Baltimore. . . . maybe one of the few we had at the time. There may have been some people writing educational music, but Cheslock wrote symphonic music and piano music, which was known in a very small circle.

I went to Chicago. I was no longer at the Peabody and so I didn't continue flute lessons. I began taking piano lessons with a young friend of mine, an ex-Juilliard student named Marcus Raskin. Marcus works now in a place in Washington called the Institute for Policy Studies, which is, you know, kind of an independent think tank, definitely left-of-center. Marcus had been to Juilliard; he was the first person I'd met from Juilliard. He had been a prodigy there, a young pianist, but had given it up and gone to study law in Chicago. I began taking piano lessons from him. I think it was through him that I became aware that there was such a thing as a contemporary form of concert music. . . . I remember in his repertory he played the Alban Berg Sonata.

The school had a good music library, so I could look at scores. I studied contemporary music through scores. There wasn't anyone to teach it or anybody who played it, and there weren't any recordings in 1952 or '53. There was a company called Dial Records, which had recorded Webern's *Bagatelles* and Berg's *Lyric Suite*—things of this kind. The twelve-tone school was somewhat represented on Dial. I think Marcus must have explained some of the principles to me because, in fact, my first pieces were twelve-tone pieces; that's the only contemporary language that I knew in terms of concert music.

Now, see, we're talking now about a tradition of notated music. I always worked in the tradition of notated music, whereas the jazz music I listened to was a tradition of improvised performed music that wasn't notated. Phil Russo had a big band in Chicago, and taught there, but I didn't study with him. I knew some of his students; through them I heard things like the Stan Kenton Band and this kind of thing. These guys wrote "charts" as we call them, but you didn't find notated music in the world of jazz, really. So that working in the field of notated music, I began working in the only contemporary music that I was aware of, which was twelve-tone music. Very shortly after that I came across Charles Ives's music, that was also in the library, and then a little bit later some of Aaron Copland, Roy Harris, and William Schuman. Ultimately that led to my going to Juilliard because that was where that music, as I understood it, was taught.

So, while you were in Chicago, you didn't have a composition teacher?
No, I was on my own. I had a piano teacher, and I wrote music, but there was no one to even show it to. I could have found somebody, but you have to remember that I was also going to the University and I was also working part-time, so I didn't really have the time to pursue composition. . . .

Were you a music major?
No, I wasn't. To be a music major there I would have to be a musicologist.

So what were you studying instead?
Well, it was just an ordinary, general education course leading to some kind of bachelor's degree. It wasn't anything special, except it was the University of Chicago, which was a very highly academic school, very much the way places like Reed are now. . . . They had no real majors. I think it changed somewhat in '56, '57, when Hutchins left, and you no longer could really do that. I think now that that course exists as a kind of optional feature, but it was the only thing you could do. So they didn't encourage people to do majors anyway. So, I went to Juilliard after I graduated from there. I was about nineteen.

So, you're off to New York?
Yeah, but not right away. I had to spend a half-year in Baltimore working at Bethlehem Steel.

What were you doing?
I ran a crane—I worked at the steel mills. . . . I made enough money to come to New York. First I stayed in Chicago after I graduated. I graduated in the spring of '56 and I stayed into the fall, and I went to New York in the winter of '56-'57 and I did take some courses there. They had an extension division . . . anybody could take a course there . . . I wrote some pieces there, but they were not really formal enough to submit, so I went back to Baltimore in the summer of '57 and I worked until sometime the next winter. I probably had about twelve hundred dollars when I got back to New York, which thirty years ago was enough money to live on for the rest of the year.

What were your early pieces like?
Oh, they weren't much, really. They were just music like everybody else wrote.

Was it twelve-tone or was it—
No, they didn't do that. The twelve-tone days were over for me. All the twelve-tone music I wrote was in Chicago. At that time William Schuman was the head of Juilliard, and Vincent Persichetti, Vittorio Giannini, and William Bergsma were teaching there. They all wrote in a tonal school derived from the Copland/Harris/Schuman school. . . . If you wanted to study European twelve-tone style music, then you had to study at Columbia or Princeton. Juilliard didn't pay any attention to it, or very slightly. I'm talking about the first half of the '60s. Juilliard specialized in what it thought was American music. Of course, it all changed after a while.

Everybody wrote very tonal music, and they could have been slightly dodecaphonic. I mean our music could have gotten to something like Hindemith, but not anymore. . . . Everyone wrote the same music, really. I can't say it was very distinguished, but I don't think anybody's was. But, music students don't really . . . I mean, there are not many people who write interesting music before they're thirty. People like Mendelssohn, Schubert, and Mozart . . . are rare events. Most people write the music for which they're known in their late twenties—they begin then. . . . If you listen to the early works of Rachmaninoff, Stravinsky, Bartók, Hindemith—that's not very interesting.

When you were a teenager and in your early twenties and writing music, were you aware of the fact that your music wasn't there yet?
Oh, sure. I realized that I didn't have a distinctive voice in my music. But,

looking around, I saw very few people who did, and it wasn't a cause of much anxiety on my part. On the other hand, I was winning prizes all over the place. Juilliard had its own music, its own system. There were only about eight or ten kids in the composition department at any one time. It was a fairly small school, like the College at the University of Chicago. There could have been six hundred students at Juilliard—enough for a couple of orchestras, sixty or seventy pianists, an opera department, a dance department, a handful of composers, and a handful of conductors. The conductors and composers were very few. Jean Morel taught the conducting students, and he maybe had five or six students. When I say twelve composition students, that was a high number. . . . But they had a lot of prizes in composition, so you almost couldn't help but win a prize. It was very easy to win prizes at Juilliard, because once you were in the composition department they had to give them to somebody and there wasn't anybody else there.

I didn't get into the composition department right away. After about a year of working I went back in the 1957–58 year, I registered for their Literature and Materials course, and Composition. In the spring of '58 I submitted my pieces for the first time to the composition department and I was accepted as a student for the next year. My first teacher was William Bergsma, and I studied with him in 1958–59 and 1959–60; then I studied with Vincent Persichetti for two years after that. I think I was there four years altogether—five, if you count the preparatory year. Then there was the half year that I spent working for Bethlehem Steel. So I was about twenty-four when I got done there.

What was it that you actually learned at Juilliard?
Not much, you know [laughs]. You don't learn much at Juilliard. What they do at Juilliard is they have a very hard entrance examination and a very easy graduation examination. It's a good theory because the idea is that you get really talented kids and you put them in a good environment and you wait. They have good major teachers, but then nothing much else happens. They spend time together, they grow up. Their natural talent and the energy of youth accounts for a lot. Juilliard was not a very organized school when I went there. For example, I remember there were pianists who studied with Rosina Lhevinne. I didn't have to take academic courses, obviously, because I had taken them before. The ones who had to often did not go to their classes. When the academic teachers threatened to fail the students, Rosina Lhevinne would threaten to resign, at which point these students found that they had somehow marvelously passed their courses. So, you see, the major teachers had their pet students, and the

school simply did whatever the teachers wanted them to do. So many talented people came out of Juilliard; but the thing to remember is that they were talented when they got there [laughs]. They may have learned something from the teachers, but Juilliard was a system where you had a major teacher—it was basically a guru-student type thing. . . .

There were valuable experiences there—singing in the chorus happened to be one of them, actually. There wasn't anything else there, but you met interesting, talented people that you would know for the rest of your life. As I chose to live in New York after that, I've come across people all the time whom I knew at school. So, Juilliard, after all, is a local music school. There are two or three others, Manhattan and Mannes, real trade schools. The academic schools weren't trade schools, Columbia and even Princeton further away aren't real trade schools. . . .

I must have written something close to seventy-five pieces during the years I was there. Virtually every one was played. I would say every piece I wrote during my years at Juilliard was performed and often recorded. . . . One of my part-time jobs was working at what they called the Acoustics Department. There was a recording studio, mostly set up so that kids could record recitals and prepare applications for Fulbrights. They also recorded new music that was played; the music department had a budget for performing the work of the young composers. What they or our faculty did was to prepare reading sessions throughout the year with designated ensembles. These would be, let's say, a string orchestra session, full orchestral session, string quartet, or whatever. For these reading sessions, our fellow students were hired; they were paid out of the budget and brought into the recording studio to play our music. Besides that, we organized concerts. We had to do that ourselves.

The thing that Juilliard emphasized was composers being actively involved in writing music and having it played. They didn't encourage us composers to play the music, which was rather an odd thing, but not really when you think about who was there. After all, though I was a flutist, Paula Robison played my flute pieces, I didn't have to play them, so why *would* I play them, right? I mean, this was the problem, actually. If you could play the piano, why play your own piece when Jerry Lowenthal or someone of that caliber could play it? These were all young people and it was a very friendly school in the sense that it was easy to know everyone. Basically, the reason that it was a friendly school was that it had a good cafeteria. So you spent a lot of time in the cafeteria talking to people [laughs]. If they didn't have a cafeteria they wouldn't have had a friendly school. This is my theory.

I met the dance department there and I began writing music for them. . . . It was not that hard. Because there were so few of us composers, I could find conductors to do my work. Arthur Weisberg would conduct pieces of mine or play pieces of mine and other people did. The point is that Juilliard was a tremendous place from the point of view of access to other musicians and performances. When I say I wrote seventy-five pieces at Juilliard, it's easy to imagine what happened—in five years there, I wrote about fourteen to fifteen pieces a year. I was literally writing a piece every two or three weeks and getting it played.

So, what did I learn at Juilliard? Well, I learned mostly by doing there. I think this was, generally speaking, a good idea. The people who graduated when I was there were people like Richard Peaslee, who makes his living writing—he does work for Martha Clarke, he does a lot of Broadway straight plays, music for shows, films. Peter Schickele, whom everybody knows, was another student there. Conrad Sousa was there; he's an opera composer who lives on the west coast now and has a long association with the Shakespeare Theatre in San Diego. Actually, it was through Conrad that I began to write theater music, really. He was also writing music for the McCarter Theatre in Princeton. When Conrad had more scores to write than he had time for, he would give me a score to do. That's how I began writing theater music.

Another thing about Juilliard was that it had no courses in music education. That meant that you could not get a teaching certificate at Juilliard. If you travel around the country, you will find that most music schools are giving out education degrees; and when their students graduate, they become teachers. At Juilliard, you were not qualified—you could not teach in New York State. . . . You could become a teaching assistant at Juilliard, but you couldn't teach in a high school or in any grade schools in New York. I think you could probably teach in the universities.

You see, when I said that Juilliard was a real trade school, I meant that its students were prepared to work in the world of music, not in the world of academia. That's all they did, and as a result very few of the composers became teachers. I ran into Leonardo Ballada, who teaches at the University of Pittsburgh, and Dorothy Klotzman at Brooklyn College. They were both there in those years, and there may have been a few other teachers—Peter Dickinson [the American] teaches in England. Most of the students that came out of Juilliard did not expect to teach, and some of them did, of course—instrumentalists—but, they were being prepared as players and conductors, and the composers were not trained to do anything but write music.

We were trained in this rather odd way where they simply threw you into these situations time after time after time. For example, there was no course given called "Scoring for Films." . . . What the composition department did was this: the faculty got together, and they announced there would be a project for that semester involving scoring a film. Who would like to volunteer for it? I was one of the people who volunteered. Then they would rent a movie from the Museum of Modern Art and three of the students scored the film. Then they hired an orchestra, and we went into the studio and recorded it. . . . They also tried to recreate, as much as they could, the conditions that would be the kind of conditions you would really come across in the professional world. Perhaps on a Friday they would announce that this project would begin on the following Monday, and the whole thing would be due in two weeks. So in two weeks you had to write the whole score and do all the parts yourself. Two weeks from the day it began, you were expected to walk into the studio with the music ready to play. In fact, I was one of the students that did that particular assignment. When I walked in that day with my music, before Bergsma even looked at the music he said, "Congratulations," meaning, of course, that just getting it done was good. I fulfilled the terms—I got the music done, I had the parts copied in the two-week period. In fact, that's exactly what happens. Someone calls you up and says they expect a commercial to be done in three or four days, or a band arrangement, sometimes overnight. . . .

When you say, "Well, what did you learn?" Well, you learned a lot at Juilliard, but you learned it because of the conditions of the school. The school was set up as a kind of machine that, if you got involved with it, taught you how to write music or how to play in an orchestra or how to do a lot of things. But in order to take advantage of it, you had to work all the time. To write seventy-five pieces in five years means that you're literally writing a piece all the time. You don't ever spend any time not writing music. The composition lessons were mainly to see whether you were getting your work done, and if you got stuck, they could help you get over your stuck period. However, courses in harmony and counterpoint, which I later learned from [Nadia] Boulanger, hardly existed at Juilliard. You took this kind of general course in music theory, but the practice of harmony and counterpoint wasn't really taught in a systematic way. So it was an odd kind of education.

How did your music change over the time you were there, or how did your thoughts about your music change?
It didn't change much. I got more skillful at doing it, but I didn't really have any ideas. . . . I wrote everything, violin concertos, string quartets—

but my ideas about it didn't change much. I didn't have any ideas to change. Juilliard wasn't an ideologically oriented school. It didn't have a theory about music history and music composition as some schools did. Some schools had very clear ideas about what people should be writing or the direction the history of music should be taking. Juilliard didn't have that. You pretty much wrote whatever you wanted to. As long as you wrote enough of it, no one bothered you too much. That's literally true. It was a funny school, not a bad school though; it was not a bad way to do it, in a way. . . . There are a lot of ex-Juilliard students around, working in the music business, and they tend to be very good.

What about Darius Milhaud?
I stayed with Milhaud one summer, the summer of 1960. He gave composition lessons and courses, but he didn't teach harmony or counterpoint either. He taught analysis a bit, and analyzed a little; they did a little bit of that at Juilliard, but not much. . . . Well, he taught at Aspen, and he had a large class of maybe twenty students, which was very unusual for me. Don't forget you had private lessons at Juilliard, with maybe one other student in the class. . . . Milhaud didn't do it that way. You were kind of crowded into the living room of his house. People played their music, and he insisted that the music be played, which I thought was a good idea. The interesting thing about the Milhaud class was meeting other students from other parts of the country.

He was in a lot of pain. He was very old then—this was 1960— and he was in a wheelchair with arthritis of a very extreme kind. His wife Madeleine used to take care of him. He would have students over for dinner now and then, and we would talk. I was mostly interested in the people he knew in Paris in the '20s and '30s. I had been to Paris myself one year. I think it was in 1954. I spent the summer in Paris studying French. I was interested in Paris, and I asked him about what it was like then and he talked about it. He reminisced a little bit, I liked the stories. He also taught at Mills College every other year, and he brought with him from Mills his real students and they were very close to him. I'd never come across this before, the kind of teacher who had a very devoted following. They were very close to him, and they were a bit, well, standoffish, or even downright mean to the students who were just the summer students. We **were** considered not serious because we weren't the real students. You know how kids are, they play these little games with each other; but they were children just like we were. When I say children I mean people around the age of eighteen, nineteen, twenty, twenty-one. These kinds of little things were going on, but I don't think it affected Milhaud very much. He treated everyone very seriously, I thought. I learned some things from him. I don't know exactly what.

I remember Copland came to one of our classes, and he was his guest there. I had written a violin concerto that summer, and I was showing my piece and he said, "Oh, this orchestration isn't going to sound well," and I said, "I'm sure it would." I was sure that it would. He said, "Oh, you'll never hear these trombones and these French horns," and I said, "Of course, you'll hear them." We got into a big argument. He didn't like me very much. I kind of told him that I thought he was wrong. Don't forget, I was twenty and he was about sixty, and I think he was completely shocked that I even talked back to him. . . . By the way, the concerto was played at the end of the summer, and it turned out I was right. The orchestration was absolutely hearable. Well, he wasn't around for the performance, but I did see, and I was right.

Milhaud kind of watched this conversation taking place, but he didn't say anything. I don't know what he thought of that—I didn't mean to get noticed, but I kind of got noticed because of this little ruckus. It was very minor, but, you see, you weren't supposed to say things like that. But, at that age, I had already heard my orchestral music, you know. I wasn't a theoretical composer—I never would write something you couldn't hear. . . . That's true for the music I write today. The thing that's common to the music I write today is that everything I write is playable and listenable. I don't write ideological music or theoretical music. And that was true then as well. Even today, I wonder what Copland meant by that remark. He was a very good orchestrator himself. His music is superbly written, but he just didn't see what I was getting at, I guess. It wasn't that hard.

At any rate, the piece I wrote that summer was the *Violin Concerto*, for a woman named Dorothy Pixley; she later graduated from Juilliard, and married a man named Rothschild. I think she was the concertmistress of one of those Lincoln Center groups like "Mostly Mozart." She died a number of years ago of cancer, when she was a fairly young woman. I wrote that concerto for her, and a couple of string quartets, even some pieces later on. That very often happens with composers—they'll meet an instrumentalist and they get into writing for that person if they're lucky. I was lucky, because Dorothy was the person I wrote for. After she died, I began writing for Paul Zukofsky, who was, in fact, a student of the same Juilliard teacher, Ivan Galamian. There was a style of violin playing that was nurtured by this one teacher, that you'd hear in the students, and I always was attracted to that sound. It wasn't a very sweet sound. It had a very clear, precisely defined tonality, and the timbre was a bit hard, but it's the kind of playing that I liked.

Milhaud saw that concerto as I was writing it. He didn't say much. He made one comment—I remember we were looking at the third movement, and he was looking at the violin part. I think he was playing a joke. When I was playing it on the piano, he took his little finger and he drew an imaginary line over the violin part and said, "You missed the flute line" [laughs]. That was pretty surprising, and I said, "What?" and he said, "There's a flute line here," and he traced it with his finger. It was interesting that he could do that. He was able to hear things—he could look at a score and hear music in it. Not that many people can do that. In point of fact, very few people really hear music. Milhaud could hear it, Persichetti could hear it, Boulanger definitely could hear it. . . .

After Juilliard you were off to Pittsburgh?
There were a couple of years there I spent writing music for schools. It was an interesting program run by the Ford Foundation. About ten or twelve graduating composition students a year were assigned to music departments in high schools. I went to Pittsburgh, but some people went to Louisville, Los Angeles, Buffalo; they went all over the country. The idea was that you were a composer-in-residence at the school. In Pittsburgh I think we got paid about five or six hundred dollars a month. I stayed for two years, and by the end of that time, I had somehow saved two thousand dollars. I could make any schedule I wanted to there, and Pittsburgh was an easy city to live in, because I could get to New York—in eight hours I could drive there. I made the kind of schedules that I used to have at the steel mill, where you worked ten days on and four days off. I would stay there for ten days, and I would go away for four days, and it didn't matter whether it was a weekend or not—that's just the way I did it. . . . I wrote, in the two years, about twenty pieces, for everything from orchestra and string quartet to woodwind quintet and trio. I wrote a lot of choral music, a brass sextet, even a band piece. There was a guy there named Stanley Levine who was in charge of instrumental music for the city of Pittsburgh. . . . Stanley would put together all the best—he would make up a string quartet of the best students from different schools. I don't doubt that many of those kids have become professional musicians—they went from there into music schools. It wasn't really much different from what I had done at Juilliard, you see. The players weren't quite as accomplished, but the enterprise was very similar. Basically, I was writing music all the time for specific concerts, for specific ensembles, and I did that for two years.

At the end of the first year I applied to study with Nadia Boulanger and I was accepted as a student of hers. At the same time, Stanley asked me if I would stay another year in Pittsburgh. I was nervous about that. I was afraid I wouldn't get the Fulbright again, but I was more or less told not to worry about it. I think very few people turn down those Fulbrights, especially the ones to Paris, but I did, that's why I was nervous about doing it. I thought, "Well, if I don't go, they won't let me go the next year." Unofficially, there wasn't much to worry about—stay another year and apply again. In fact, this turned out to be the case.

You have to remember the faculty of Juilliard also sat on those committees. You know, for example, I won the BMI Award for Young Composers, I think in 1960. It was a very prestigious award; I shared it that year with Mario Davidovsky, who had just come from Argentina. The year that I won it I remember showing a string quartet to William Bergsma. He said, "Why don't you submit this to the BMI Award?" I said, "Well, do you think it's a good idea?" He said, "Yeah, I have a feeling that this is the time to do it." Well, of course, he was on the award committee, you know, that's how he knew that. Or I would say to Persichetti, "I think I'd like to go to Paris," and he'd say, "Well, why don't you apply for a Fulbright? I think you've got a good chance." Well, I had a very good chance, he was giving them out. That's how those things worked. I think it must have been very tough for even a very good student at a small music school in Alabama or Louisiana applying for a Fulbright; they're not truly competitive. . . .

When I went to New York, I didn't really realize that so much of the power base was in New York. . . . The advantage of going to school in New York is that, when you get out of school, you don't have to go to New York; you're already there. It's very traumatic for kids from even really good schools—big midwestern universities like Illinois, Indiana, or Michigan that are turning out terrific students—to come to New York. It's much easier to graduate in New York. You don't have to look for an apartment; you've already had one for four years. That's what I mean when I say that Juilliard was the local music school, along with Manhattan and Mannes. Generally speaking, the kids who graduate from those schools have jobs when they graduate. A horn player would be told that there was an opening at the Metropolitan Opera and to go audition. Well, their teacher is first chair. You know that guy or girl has a very good chance of getting that position. So a lot of those New York orchestral jobs go to the students of the teachers.

We're talking about Pittsburgh. At the end of that time, I gave a concert of six or eight pieces of chamber music, not the orchestral music or choral music, which I wrote quite a lot of. I think all of the music I wrote got published at that time, which wasn't really such a great thing, but I didn't really know any better. Vincent Persichetti was, at that time, the editor of a company called Elkan-Vogel, a small publishing company that later became part of Theodore Presser. When I was a student of Persichetti's in my last year at Juilliard, he would say, if he liked a piece of mine, "Gee, this is a nice piece, why don't I take it down to Philadelphia and show it to Presser and see if they like it?" Well, of course, he was the guy publishing it. He basically was saying that he was the editor—if he liked it, it got published. So he published three or four of my pieces, even as a student. He did that for Peter Schickele, too, and a few of the other students. He was always doing things like that. I discovered how much money was involved with publishing years later, when I started my own publishing company [Dunvagen]. But Vincent wasn't trying to deprive me—he was actually trying to help me get my first pieces published, which he did, and a number of the pieces got published from the days in Pittsburgh too—I guess about twenty pieces altogether. Many of those pieces are still in print and still kicking around, and the reason I've tried to withdraw them, sometimes unsuccessfully, is that they don't really represent the music I write. I was still very much in the mode of writing a kind of generic contemporary music that was not distinguishable, really, from dozens of other composers with similar backgrounds. So, it's a little misleading to perform those pieces today. I acquired my own voice as a composer when I was older, when I was twenty-eight.

Were the Pittsburgh pieces any different from what you'd been doing?
Not much. Technically easier. I knew a lot about writing for instruments, because growing up at Juilliard I knew the wind instruments to begin with, and I spent a lot of time with Dorothy Pixley on string music—I even took violin lessons from her at one point. We were encouraged to do that. So, I knew how to write for instruments, and I simply wrote easier parts so that the students could play it. I was aiming for something a little harder than what they wanted to play. . . . but not too difficult, otherwise the piece couldn't be done.

It didn't change much. As I say, it was a kind of generic music that young people in their early twenties from that kind of background would write. Perhaps I did it better than other people, but I'm not even sure that I did. I was well-placed coming out of New York and Juilliard. I worked hard at what I did, and I accomplished it reasonably well. I don't think any of the music is distinguished by anything particular, if I look back on that music.

I discovered at Juilliard that there was a brilliant, brilliant young man who was a student of Jean Morel. His name was Albert Fine, and he was a conducting student. What I found out was that he was the most accomplished musician at the school. He was very young, about twenty-three or twenty-four. I remember I was having dinner with him once—we spent a lot of time together—and William Schuman came up to us. He was writing something and he wanted to talk to Albert about a bass clarinet part he was writing. Another time I was at Albert's house, and I saw Persichetti's new symphony there, number four or five, and I said, "What's that doing there," I said, "What are you doing with Vincent's new symphony?" He said, "Oh, he wanted me to look at it because it's going to be published, and he wanted me to check it through." I said, "Well, what did you find?" He said, "Well, as a matter of fact, I found a mistake. In one movement Vincent inadvertently transposed a melody and wrote the notes in the wrong order, and I found it." So, I was twenty-one, he was twenty-two or twenty-three, and I discovered that my teachers were taking their music to him.

So I said, "Well, what would it take to have lessons from you?" and he said, "I'll teach you. But you have to do the work that I give you. If you don't do the work, I won't give you any lessons." By the way, he had one other student, the soprano Shirley Verrett. We were super-private students—no one knew about it. These lessons were outside of the school. I would take my lessons at his house and Shirley did also. We didn't pay him. I studied with him for several years. I said to him at one point, "Where did you learn this?" He said, "I studied with Nadia Boulanger," and I formed the idea that this was where I should go after Juilliard. It was clear that Albert had a depth in his training that no one else I knew had; even my teachers knew it. It was not hard to figure out that the thing to do was to go and study with the person he studied with. He wrote a letter to her introducing me as one of his students—although in fact I was practically the same age as he was—and I went to study with her. She never asked very much about Albert, though it was clear that what I had been studying with Albert became developed in my lessons with her. So in a sense, you see, my work with her had already begun. I had been working with Albert two years before I went to see her. In between was the hiatus of Pittsburgh.

Albert's dead now. He didn't have much of a career. He was one of those funny people who just couldn't get along very well with other people, and that, of course, is terrible if you're a conductor. . . . Musicians were offended by his manner. He was an extremely difficult teacher and an extremely difficult conductor. If people played out of tune or they played wrong notes, it almost killed him, and he almost killed them. Well, of course, that's okay if you're Toscanini—perhaps you can get away with it—but if you're a twenty-two-year-old kid, no one is going to listen to you. Basically, he couldn't find anyone to work with; he finally left music entirely. . . . He once described his career this way: "I began to compose when I was nine, began to play the clarinet when I was eleven, began to conduct when I was fifteen; I stopped composing when I was seventeen, stopped playing the clarinet when I was nineteen, stopped conducting when I was twenty-one." It's very sad in a way.

Boulanger wasn't interested in the music I had written. She looked at it and wasn't very interested. I began studying first-species counterpoint with her again. Now, mind you, I was twenty-six at the time, so it was very difficult to do that in a way; but in fact I studied counterpoint and harmony with her for over two years. . . . By about 1965 or '66 I left for India. So, I was with her '63–64, '64–65, while '61–63 I was in Pittsburgh. Something like that. I don't remember, I'm not good at years.

What were her lessons like?
Well, she had a variety of techniques that she was teaching. They included score reading, counterpoint, harmony, figured bass, and analysis. You spent the whole week preparing for that class. She had an assistant called Mademoiselle Dieudonné, a *répétiteuse*, who gave the other lesson. She did the ear training and the score reading. Between these two ladies, it was easy to spend six or eight hours a day doing basic music practice. With Boulanger, nothing was theoretical; it was all practical. The rules of harmony she could describe in a few sentences, but you could spend years writing it, because to her the difference between technique and theory was that technique is practice. Harmony is practice, counterpoint is practice—neither is theory. So, what she was interested in was harmonic practice of a certain period and contrapuntal practice of a certain period.

You took three classes with her a week. One was the private class; the second was the class you took with Mademoiselle Dieudonné, which was also private. Then there was a third class called the Wednesday Class, which was a general class of all her students who were there at the time. There could be forty people of all ages, because her students who lived in Paris continued to stay with her all of their lives. So in that class there would be people in their thirties, forties, fifties, and sixties. And that Wednesday class would have a project for the year, like all the Mozart piano concertos, or the first book of the Bach *Well-Tempered Clavier*. Every year it would be a different project, and that class was devoted to analysis of that large extended work, whatever it might be. So I took a private lesson with her, and a Wednesday class with her. Then she had the Black Thursday class—that was a special class.

Black Thursday?
That was the class where you were asked to come to that class; you couldn't request it. She put together six or eight students and basically that was quite an interesting class. It would begin at nine o'clock and would go till noon. The subject of the class was usually announced at the beginning, and we rarely accomplished it. I remember one class where we went to the piano. I had already begun some of that with Albert, so I wasn't completely out of my depth. On that particular day there would be a melody written in tenor clef, and she would say, "Well, before we get to the main subject for today, let's warm up by doing the harmony for this." Of course, that was, in fact, the main subject. We never got to anything else. So, first she would say, "Daniel, come here." So Daniel would sit down, and he would play the first chord, and she would fly into it . . . and she'd say, "Oh, that's completely wrong. How can you even think of doing it that way?" Go to the next person—he would play the harmony of the first note, until finally we found the exact disposition of the voices she wanted. Then we would go to connecting that note to the second note. Well, this took three hours to do, and finally we had realized a four-part harmony exactly the way she wanted it. Then she would say, "Well, I really thought this would only take a few minutes and after all," and then she would whip out Beethoven's second violin and piano sonata, and point to the slow movement and say, "You see."

Basically all she had wanted us to do was simply the exact harmony that Beethoven had done. That's all [laughs]. Well, of course, had we *known* that piece, we might have been able to do it; but she always picked a piece that no one knew or found something so obscure. It could be anything. She had a different project for every class. I guess I don't have to tell you why we called it the Black Thursday class. When we left the class, we would sit in the café across the street. No one would say anything; we would have our coffee or a beer, then we would part until we got together the next week. No one would say anything. It was totally demoralizing in one way. We all knew that we were either her best students or her worst students, but none of us knew which ones we were. It was impossible to tell; it was probably a combination.

The Wednesday class, the class with Dieudonné, was mainly *solfège*, and that class also consisted of score reading and Paul

Hindemith's *Basic Musicianship* book. Of course, that's a sly title. If you've gone through the book, it's far from basic. If you can get through that book, you've gotten through everything. I got through the book. It took about a year to do the book with Dieudonné. When you get through the book the first time, you go back and you do it again. The second year you do it, she adds exercises to those already there. For example, if there's a passage that you're supposed to sing, the second year you have to transpose it into a different key and play a different counterpoint with it; or sometimes you'll come up with a three-four rhythm and sing a part in four-four—that would be normal for her. That would be the second year. She expected you to clap, sing, and tap your feet in three different rhythms. That was what you ended up doing, if you could, and you learned to do it. So, the Hindemith book, again, was something of a pretext that became an adventure for her to figure out ways to make music difficult. She gave you plenty to do. I spent at least two hours a day working on her exercises. . . .

In the years when I was there, don't forget, Boulanger was still a young vigorous woman of seventy-six—she died at ninety-two—she hadn't lost anything. . . . Another exercise she used to do was to write down a tenor part and then say, "Okay, Eric, sing a soprano part that goes with the tenor part." So, we all had to listen because this would not be written down. Eric would sing a soprano part that satisfied the voice-leading requirements of correct eighteenth-century harmony and counterpoint. Then the next person would have to sing an alto part that would fit in with the soprano part that Eric had just sung. It wasn't written down either, mind you. Then came the last lucky—and not lucky—person. The bass part wasn't really that hard to figure out; but you had to remember the other three parts. Well, you could see the tenor part; it was written down. So, if you were smart, as soon as you saw the tenor part and you heard the soprano part, you began to think about what the bass part would be. You were already working on it because you knew that inevitably your turn would come [laughs]. And then with the alto part, which wasn't hard to do, the hidden fifths began appearing, and immediately Boulanger could hear them. This was one of her more advanced exercises, but it was something you were expected to do.

Each day began with a Bach chorale: by the end of the week, I had completely mastered a chorale in open score, that is, in four clefs. I could sing any part and play any of the other three parts without any problem at all. Every week I had to bring a Bach chorale to my lesson. Even though Boulanger might not ask to hear it, she would say, "And did you learn your chorale this week?" I would say, "Yes, would you like to hear it?" And often she would say no, but often she would say yes. So you always had to have it ready. Once she was sure that you were doing it, she never asked, but every once in a while she would ask you and then you had to do it. In the more than two years I was there with her, I got through the first book of the chorales—they're published in two books. At least I got through that.

The chorale was the warmup; I would spend twenty minutes on that. For the next thing you had to do, she had devised a formula, an exercise where from any note you would sing a cadence. Any note would become the beginning of a cadence. Whether it was the third of a chord, the fifth of a chord, or the root of a chord, it would depend on what key you were in and on what form of the cadence you were using. This usually took about thirty minutes. I used to be able to do it. You didn't just play it; you had to sing it. You usually had to sing the four parts from the bottom up and go through that. This could take a while to do [laughs].

You'd already spent an hour getting warmed up and then you started your counterpoint exercises. They had to be done perfectly. I was thrown out of classes when I had a mistake. She would just tell me to leave, but Albert had done the same thing. When I had studied with Albert, if I came to the lesson with something not prepared, he said, "Well, that's the end of the lesson." They were free lessons, but that meant that I didn't have a lesson that week. Boulanger was a little tougher than Albert. You know the rules of counterpoint are very exact in a certain way. Of course, you can't have parallel octaves with parallel fifths. They're out; but the hidden ones are difficult—they can sneak in sometimes. I've literally been thrown out of her class—out of my private lesson for having a mistake. As that was your lesson for the week, you didn't want to miss any lessons. What you did was not make any mistakes.

So, how do you not make mistakes? She didn't give me any hint as to how to accomplish this. I had to figure out a way to bring in an exercise with no mistakes. I finally figured out how to do it. First I would write out the exercise, and then I would write above every note the intervals to the notes above. So, if it was in root position, I would write 1, 5, 3, 5; or 1, 5, 3, 1; or 1, 1, 3, 5, or whatever. If it was an inversion, it would be 3, and so on. If you did that, I discovered that you could then *visually* see if there were any parallel fifths. You could just see hidden fifths right away. So, once I figured that out, I never had any mistakes in my harmony after that. However, she never made any comment about it. She never said, "Well, I was wondering whether you would figure that out," or "That's a clever way to do it," or "Well, you really don't need to do it that way." She said nothing. I brought it in with all the numbers on there and at that point my harmony exercises looked like advanced arithmetic. She looked at it and said nothing. She could glance at a page and find a mistake. Pages that would take me hours to prepare would be checked in matters of seconds, literally.

After that, I began the counterpoint exercises, and that would last until the late morning. I had begun at seven. It was still dark outside. I had to turn a light on—Paris is dark in the winter, you know. Then it was eleven or twelve, and I did the Hindemith, which took a while. Then I might have lunch. Four of the seven days, I would have a class that day, either a private lesson, the Wednesday class, the Dieudonné class, or the Black Thursday class—one of those. So, I had to do that as well. I was also expected to learn one piece a week, usually one of the Bach preludes. I wasn't a very good pianist at the time, but I was supposed to analyze and learn how to play one prelude a week. It took all day; these two ladies kept you busy all day long.

I didn't write any new music those two years and didn't really mind. I had written so much music by then it didn't really matter—oh, that's not true—I did write some music, but not at the rate I used to write. Before that, I had been writing virtually a piece a month, if not more. At that point, I wasn't writing at that rate anymore, one or two pieces a year at the most. I wrote some theater pieces for the Mabou Mines. I wrote a string quartet. There was no time to show her that music; the lessons were full. She didn't really teach composition; she taught technique. That's the only way to describe it. She didn't teach theory. It was only at the very end of my lessons with her that I actually began to understand what she was teaching. By the end of my second year, I was doing an exercise and she kind of upped the ante. I began doing exercises then, and they were starting to be wrong again. I said, "They can't be wrong." I was sure they couldn't be wrong, and I remember bringing her harmony exercises and she said, "Well, the resolution is incorrect." I said, "But, Mademoiselle Boulanger, there are no mistakes. I've analyzed it and I've written it. There are no mistakes," and she said, "It's wrong." Then I recited the rules; finally, I said, "These are the rules that you have given me. There are no mistakes," and she said, "It's wrong." . . . Then she would find the Mozart piano sonata and she would say, "See, this is what he did," and he had simply done it differently. The first time she did this I was flabbergasted. I said, "Well . . . [laughs]." What can you say?

She merely wanted me to write in the style of Mozart. That's why

I say she upped the ante. It was no longer enough to do the rules. I knew how to model my results against the best results of Beethoven or Mozart; Bach didn't come in too much. I thought if she could find a better resolution—a better solution—to that exercise in a classical model, then it was the right one. The difficulty, of course, was that she knew that music backwards and forwards.

But then I understood that she wasn't teaching technique, she was teaching style. Style is a special case of technique. In other words, to put it in terms of logic: given a particular harmony exercise, there's a class of incorrect solutions and a class of correct solutions. I no longer offered her incorrect solutions—that wasn't possible—but in the class of correct solutions there would be a best solution among the correct solutions. And the best one would be in the same style as Mozart. As far as I could tell, that seemed to be the standard, though she never exactly said that. Now, when you say the best solution, it's not really the best solution; it's just the one that Mozart did. But it becomes clear then that personal style is a special case of technique. So that, for example, if you take a passage of Rachmaninoff or a passage of Mozart, they sound very different within seconds. Within two or three chords, you instantly know which is Rachmaninoff, you know which is Mozart. But what is it that you're hearing? Why is Rachmaninoff particularly Rachmaninoff? The reason is how he has chosen to write. Let's say his predilection for voice-leading and harmonic writing is of a certain kind, and he almost always does it that way. But Mozart does it another way. I call it a predilection, a tendency, an inclination, or even habit in a certain way. I would say that a personal choice comes into it. Within all the possible technical solutions, Rachmaninoff will always pick the ones that always sounds like him, or— to put it another way—the ones that he picks always sound like Rachmaninoff. Mozart would always pick the ones or the solutions that we consider Mozartean. So, someone else using the same rules will sound like Rachmaninoff or sound like Mozart.

After you got through the first couple of years of Boulanger, then she got into this next stage . . . where you were meant to find out for yourself that technique forms the basis of style, that style was a special case of technique. From her point of view, there's no point in teaching style without a technical basis. In other words, there *is* no style without technique. You can't even discuss it. That's basically what she taught. I learned that lesson in something between two and three years. I'm not saying that's the only lesson that she taught; I left after that. I was twenty-eight or twenty-nine, and I was sick of school.

Was that a useful lesson for you?

Of course. Because what I later discovered was that my own personal style was a special case of technique. I began to gravitate towards specific uses of my own technique. They became the recognizable style. People say to me, "We can always tell it's your music." Even I can do that and sometimes I don't even know what the piece is. The other day I was in Los Angeles and we turned the radio on. There was a piece of mine. I was with a friend of mine. He knew the piece before I knew it; I knew it was my piece, but I didn't know which piece it was. I could tell right away that I had written it. I can tell right away people who think they sound like me, but they don't. It's hard to truly create a replica of someone else's style; you might as well try to walk like them, talk like them, or sign your name like them. It's very, very hard to do. You can study someone and you can mimic the walk of a particular person or the cadence of their language. Personal style emerges from personality—that's where the word comes from—but it's where personality and technique come together. You have to have them both to have style; you can't have one without the other. . . .

A lot of things I learned later. If you look at my music now, the voice-leading is very, very—to use a funny word—accurate. There is no sloppy voice leading in my music, even if it's complicated opera like *Akhnaten* or a string quartet. If I write in a particular way, there are no accidents in any of the parts. It's because that's how I wanted it to sound, because the technique is being used for a particular kind of effect. Of course, there's always room for accidents and inspiration. That's what one counts on. But, I can go back at my music and as I'm writing it, I don't have to correct it in terms of wrong notes. I learned that from Boulanger in a way, if you can imagine years of that kind of drilling that I described to you. You don't write carelessly, and you don't write notes that don't belong. One of the things that's characteristic of my music today is that every note has a place in the music. There are no extra notes in the music; there are no notes that don't belong. There are only the notes that I need.

Part Two

Music with Changing Parts

(Instrumental Music)

PHILIP GLASS AND STEVE REICH: TWO FROM THE STEADY STATE SCHOOL (1974)

JOAN LA BARBARA

La Monte Young, Terry Riley, Steve Reich and Philip Glass have been linked together in a school of composition based on repetition and exploration of minimal amounts of material. In tracing their roots one naturally encounters John Cage, most directly in Young's anti-traditional-music word pieces. Once Cage had paved the way towards all-sound-is-music and Young, George Brecht and the Fluxus group had fully investigated the verbal concept pieces the air was cleared of traditions to fight. Into this open space came the experimenters—what I call the Steady State school. Having severed ties with European traditions they were free to acknowledge the values of non-western musics and mold what they found into a new sound experience, a fusion of western harmony and eastern stretched-time sense.

Riley and Young began their association in the late 50's at University of California/Berkeley while Reich and Glass studied composition at Juilliard School in New York. Leaving New York for California, Reich worked with an improvisation group (1962–63, including Jon Gibson, Paul Breslin and Gwen Watson) producing a "third stream" piece for jazz ensemble as his Mills College Masters thesis. During 1963–64 Reich wrote a voice and kazoo piece for the San Francisco Mime Troupe's production of *Ubu Roi* and also produced his first tape collage piece, using crowd noises from sport events, for Robert Nelson's film *Plastic Haircut*.

In 1962 Glass received his Masters degree from Juilliard and a Ford Foundation grant (renewed for 1963–64) to be composer-in-residence with the Pittsburgh public school system. He produced a number of pieces for various ensembles which were published by major music houses. Through listening to a tape of *Haze Gold* (for a cappella chorus, 1962) I discovered an early indication of Glass' attraction to steady rhythmic foundation; a slow eighth-note ostinato figure, first in the alto and later in the tenor voices, forms the base over which a melody is floated.

On the west coast Reich and Gibson had begun working with Riley, Young and Terry Jennings doing repeated figures. Their activities culminated in 1964 with the first performance of Riley's monumental *In C* in which performers move at their own musical discretion through 53 repeating melodic phrases, related in modal character, against a steady eighth-note pulse.

In 1964–65 Reich worked in conjunction with the San Francisco Tape Music Center, producing *Livelihood* (a collage based on sounds collected during his cab driving experience), *Oh Dem Watermelons* (a voice tape piece for a Robert Nelson film) and *It's Gonna Rain* (his first tape phase piece). Inspired by his work with Riley on repeated figures and his own interest in found sound Reich recorded the voice of black preacher Brother Walter and made identical tape loops of a section of the talk, using his natural pitch inflection and speech rhythms as the basic "musical" elements. The two tape machines running at slightly different rates of speed caused a gradual shift in the phase relationship of the material. The result of emphasizing this effect in *It's Gonna Rain* and *Come Out* (NY, 1966) is a gradual flow of sounds as words slowly metamorphose into other words, rhythmic accents shift and the extra elements of tape noise, street and room sounds blend and beat, creating many colors out of a small amount of material.

In 1964 Glass won a Fulbright scholarship and spent two years in Paris studying harmony and counterpoint with Nadia Boulanger. Early in 1966 while helping Ravi Shankar notate film music for western-trained musicians, Glass discovered a system he thought to be the basis for Indian music. Combining this with the Boulanger-learned techniques he produced four separate pieces using cyclic structures. The first, music for a production of Samuel Beckett's *Play*, was written for two soprano saxophones each having two notes to be played in the same key, at the same tempo but in different meters. The second, *Talking Piece* (for two voices and 6 instruments) had two movements of serial writing and two movements based on repetitive structures and steady pulse with abrupt starts and stops, and no dynamic changes. The third (for winds) had parts dropping out and re-entering with new material so that the cycle kept changing. Glass considers the fourth, a *String Quartet* in which each instrument has only one or two notes per section, to be the most successful. Its characteristics form the basis for all his music since that time—constant eighth-note foundation, repetitive and cyclic structures, overlapping rhythmic patterns, harmonically stable with no change in volume or tempo and it just starts and stops. My diagram below illustrates Glass' strict mathematical and structural logic and attention to balance in this germinal effort. From this *String Quartet* in which dotted bar-lines broke the musical flow into arbitrary 4/4 measures Glass moved to a notational system in which the bar lines indicate the duration of a repeatable phrase, more clearly representing his music's elongated nature.

In 1966 Reich wrote his first live performer phase piece. In *Reed Phase* Jon Gibson pre-recorded the melodic pattern on soprano sax, later phasing ahead of the original pattern, creating new relationships between the two lines. Continuing to pursue this aspect of the phasing task Reich and Art Murphy began working against tape loops of keyboard patterns. In 1967 Reich produced *Piano Phase* for two keyboards with both performers taking turns at phasing, and *Violin Phase* in which Paul Zukofsky played against several pre-recorded loops of a 12-beat figure, first going through the phase shifts and then emphasizing some of the patterns that result from the interlocking phrases.

Glass left Paris in 1966 and spent eight months studying in Asia and India before returning to New York. His 1967–68 compositions dealt with several ideas. One was an extension of the Indian "tal" (a rhythmic cycle of a fixed number of beats on which a piece is built), letting the cycle repeat only after a long period of time. He also dropped harmony completely, concentrating on monophonic solo music with a steady pulse. Trying to alter the traditional staid concert situation, he wrote scores which made shapes and had performers move around a space to follow a score. *Strung Out* (8/67) included all these ideas besides amplifying the violin, fixing the sound source and allowing the performer to move without the audience experiencing a volume change. Following this Glass produced *Head On* (violin, cello and piano, 10/67), /\ *for Jon Gibson* (soprano sax, 2/68), *In Again Out Again* (2 pianos, 3/68), *Music in the Shape of a Square* (2 flutes, 5/68) and the fascinatingly simple *How Now* (for piano) in which an 18-beat cycle is divided several different ways and the

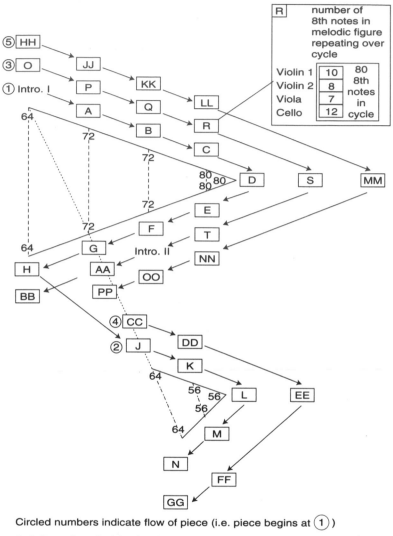

Circled numbers indicate flow of piece (i.e. piece begins at (1))

2-digit numbers inside triangles are number of 8th notes in cycle

boxed letters B indicate sections

dotted lines ---- connect identical sections

arrows ——→ show direction of piece

sum of 8th notes in cycles of △HH MM PP = sum of 8th notes in cycles of △ J L N + △ CC EE GG

Example 1: Graphic Analysis of Glass' String Quartet No. 1 (1966)

Music with Changing Parts

order for playing the eight repeatable figures is a mirror image, using the 4th figure for rotation of the other figures and the 8th figure as the pivot point of the mirror structure.

Glass then decided to write pieces which extended beyond the physical endurance time of one performer and formed an ensemble of keyboards and saxophones (including Murphy, Gibson, Reich, Dickie Landry and James Tenney). *600 Lines* consisted of 600 single lines of music each equal to 16 beats (cycle of "tin tal"), played in unison, with performers dropping out to rest when necessary over a two hour period.

In November 1968 Glass wrote his clearest and simplest additive piece *1 + 1 for One Player and Amplified Table-Top* based purely on rhythm, combining two rhythmic elements in continuous, regular arithmetic progressions. From the monody of *Two Pages* (2/69) which the group played in unison, two lines a fifth apart in *Music in Fifths* (6/69), two lines moving in exact mirror images in *Music in Contrary Motion* (7/69) to four lines in *Music in Similar Motion* (11/69) all the writing is harmonically and rhythmically stable, based on constant eighth note movement and additive process. In analyzing *Fifths* I found two main sections, the first having three rhythmic units, a + b + c, with emphasis on increasing the "c" unit, the second was based on the fragmentation and repetition of the "c" unit in an additive extending process. Beginning at figure 19 the numbered "measures" are divided in two halves, indicated by melodic direction (up in the first, down in the second) with identical numerical increases on each side and at figure 26 with identical tags.

During 1968–69 Reich worked on several electronics oriented pieces. In *Pendulum Music* 4 microphones swung freely over 4 speakers, tweeting and fluttering from feedback and finally resting directly over the speakers, producing a steady sound. He also conceived of a device called a Phase Shifting Pulse Gate (physically realized with the help of Bell Laboratories) which had 8 gates, producing a pulsing chord, repeating broken chord or melodic pattern depending on the phase position. Reich abandoned the box due to a mechanical difficulty and its limitations as a performance-related instrument. It did lead him in January 1970 to write *Four Organs*, using maracas to beat a steady pulse against which the gradual change from one chord to a second is measured.

Phase Patterns (2/70) is a return to phasing using the paradiddle, a rudimentary drum stroke, played first on four organs, then while one remains stationary a second moves ahead gradually to a new phase relationship and the remaining two reinforce the resulting patterns. (Reich's group of musicians at that time included Gibson, Murphy and Steve Chambers.)

During the summer of 1970 Reich traveled to Ghana to study with a master drummer of the Ewe tribe. In 1971 combining his African studies with phasing techniques he produced the 90-minute work *Drumming* (first performed at the Museum of Modern Art, New York, 12/71) scored for 8 tuned bongo drums, three marimbas, three glockenspiels, three singers and piccolo, and all based on one 12/8 rhythmic figure. The voices precisely imitated the sound of the instruments while singing resultant patterns after each phase shift. Jay Clayton, Judith Sherman, and I spent several months listening to tape loops of the marimba sections, singing melodies we heard in the interlocking patterns which Reich notated and organized into duets and trios.

In his music from late 1972–73 Reich abandoned the gradual phasing process in favor of "substitution," i.e., inserting beats for rests, building a pattern one note at a time in a new phase relationship to the stationary pattern. *Clapping Music* and *Music for Pieces of Wood* (claves) simplified both his amplification and instrumentation to the barest. *Six Pianos* uses this substitution process with two keyboards also playing resulting patterns. *Music for Mallet Instruments, Voices and Organ* uses substitution in the mallet instrument, augmentation (gradual lengthening of note duration as in *Four Organs* in voices with organ), and resulting patterns (voice-marimba imitation as in *Drumming*). Reich's studies in Balinese Gamelan are reflected in this work and his most recent effort, orchestrated similarly in its first draft but adding more voices and replacing the organ with strings.

In 1970 Glass expanded his writing from four to eight parts in *Music in 8 Parts* and then further to include modulation and long tones, generated by the rippling eighth notes, in *Music with Changing Parts*. His instrumentation shifts slightly as new members enter the ensemble. (The first version of *Changing Parts* used violin and trumpet and upon my entrance Glass added the names of the notes, in the solfeggio system to change the trumpet line to a voice part.)

From 1971 to '74 Glass worked on a four-hour composition using cyclic structure and additive process in which each of 12 parts had a distinct melodic shape over one rhythmic phrase. *Music in 12 Parts* (first performed at Town Hall, New York, 6/74 by Glass and his present ensemble: Gibson, Landry, Richard Peck, Kurt Munkacsi—who created a complete sound system to fit the needs of the music—Bob Telson and myself) is the culmination of Glass's musical investigations to date. Part 10 begins in similar motion then combines the mirror-image lines (*Contrary Motion*) with figure fragmentation and repetition (*Fifths*). The combination of additive process and cyclic structures is most clear in Part 5 where a two-note melody is set over a 6-beat cycle and each arithmetic addition is in direct proportion to this cycle. Parts 11 and 12 show a new direction in Glass's music. Part 11 has quick (in Glass's extended time sense) harmonic progressions, while Part 12 explores a new structural idea. The repeating measure is divided in two parts each with its own distinct harmony and separate melodic figure; the first has a moving chromatic bass line, lengthening as the piece unfolds, while the second combines fragmentation and ornamentation to slowly expand the melodic figure from 32 to 214 notes.

Perhaps most interesting from the audience stand-point about the music of both Glass and Reich are the extraordinary results. In Reich's music the phasing process stands out, creating a form of excitement during that period of transition from one interlocking relationship to the next. In working with melodic units over a fixed cycle and steady pulse Glass leads the ear and body to hear and sense strong accents, felt in different places according to the point of augmentation or diminution of the melodic unit, while relaxing the mind through pure order.

DIALOGUE WITH PHILIP GLASS AND STEVE REICH (1980)

T I M   P A G E

TIM PAGE: *How did the two of you get to know each other?*
STEVE REICH: *I met Philip at the Juilliard School of Music twenty years ago, in 1958. We were both composition students, and both had come from an undergraduate background in philosophy, strangely enough; Philip at the University of Chicago and I at Cornell University. I studied at Juilliard from 1958 through 1961, at which point I left to go to California to study with Luciano Berio. In 1965, I returned to New York City and began performing with my first ensemble. At that point it had no name. It was simply myself and Art Murphy (who was a friend of Philip's and mine at Juilliard) and Jon Gibson, a woodwind player who presently plays with Philip, and whom I knew in California. So many of these paths cross!*
PHILIP GLASS: We met again after I returned to New York from Paris, where I was studying with Nadia Boulanger. We met on the occasion of Steve's concert at the . . .
REICH: . . . *at the Park Place Gallery.*
GLASS: That was a very famous concert in its day. We each had been developing our own music in our distinctive ways. When I met Steve, I discovered that there was another group of musicians working in a way similar to the way I had begun working. For a number of years immediately after that, we spent a good deal of time together. We showed our music to each other. There was a very active dialogue going on.

This was a very small world we're talking about. A lot of these people know each other . . . Jon Gibson has played with Terry Riley, La Monte Young, Steve, myself, and with his own ensemble. Ten or twelve years ago, this phenomenon was so underground that it was really our isolation from everyone else that threw us together. It was the isolation and real hostility and/or indifference that created a kind of community.

From that point of view, it was a very healthy and exciting period.

It's interesting that people always seem to lump your names together, whereas in reality, your paths have diverged from what were somewhat similar beginnings. How do you feel about this continued pairing of your names?

As our paths continue to diverge, it becomes easier for us to be in situations like this dialogue. It's so clear we are dealing with two different personalities. Ten years ago, when you had something like *Music in Fifths* on the one hand and *Four Organs* on the other, there wasn't an awful lot of other music around to compare it to except [Charles] Wuorinen's music and [Mario] Davidovsky's music. So, in that context, we looked like Siamese twins.

Ten years later, with not only ourselves but a whole new generation of people, it's very clear—as it was always clear to Steve and me—that our personal ways were very distinct. I don't think we were ever particularly worried about that.

There are obvious similarities. But anyone living in a particular period of time in the world, in the same general geographical area will probably give off a similar response if their receptors are in order.

I think one of the most important things about the effect the two of you have had on young composers is the way you've liberated an entire generation from having to go the old post-Webern route, which was becoming so institutionalized.

Can you believe that was true when we were students twenty years ago?

As a matter of fact, they hadn't gotten to that yet. While we were at Juilliard, the blooming aesthetic was "Americana." Elliott Carter's quartet—I think it was his second—was premiered while we were there, and it was considered very questionable by some members of the faculty. Some liked it, some didn't, but it was on the edge of respectability. And if you were composing twelve-tone pieces . . .

I think a lot of the reasons for our many problems with the music world were economic. Funds for new music in America are still so limited that as soon as people begin to appear who can challenge the funding—or the *tra-*

ditional funding of new music and raise questions about it—these people become the "young turks" and they are very threatening to other people.

I think you're right. There is also a psychology involved: there are bound to be deep first impressions involved with our music, particularly among people who make up the faculties of music departments at various universities. This music might have struck them as really alien to what was an accepted norm in the late 1960's—which was a toss-up between European serialism and a certain sort of American aleatory music, both of which came out sounding atonal and non-rhythmic. This music is very rhythmic and very tonal. I think this must have struck certain people as being psychologically threatening. It has taken a long time for this music to gain acceptance. But music is a pretty slow moving art field as opposed to, say, movements in painting and sculpture which—at least during the 1960's—were very rapid. On the other hand, there seems to be a little more permanence in the field. Once something seems to gather the interest of other musicians and composers, there is a possibility that they will remain interested in it.

It must have taken a good deal of courage to play this music in a time when the prevailing attitudes were so diametrically opposed to it.

I remember when Michael Tilson Thomas and I played Four Organs *on an otherwise normal Boston Symphony program at Carnegie Hall in 1973. The subscribers came to hear the other music—C.P.E. Bach, Mozart, the Bartók* Music for Strings, Percussion and Celesta, *and the Liszt* Hexammeron. *There was a pretty full house and, after my piece, I would say well over three-quarters of the people were not booing, but were* really *enraged—shaking umbrellas so loudly during the piece that, on stage, we began to lose count.* Four Organs *is a piece that calls for a lot of concentration on the part of the performers. There was so much active feedback from the audience during the performance that we got lost while playing. Michael Tilson Thomas had to yell out numbers so that we knew what bar we were in. When the piece was over, a small crowd was bravoing and a much larger crowd was booing as strongly as possible. And the reactions of the press! "Primitive" was one word bandied about a lot.*

Like the Rite of Spring *all over again.*

We've all had our own "Rites of Spring." It is very interesting that one can still write music that causes this kind of reaction. However, that's hardly been the purpose of this music. One of the things that motivates this type of reaction is the audience's thinking that, for some reason, you are trying to make a fool of them. That's what really gets them upset. And, of course, the furthest thing from my mind is to bait an audience in that way.

I think the way you relate to your audience is very interesting. You have revived the composer-performer tradition.
It wasn't entirely a dead tradition. Stravinsky conducted and played a lot of his music and made much of his living that way. Aaron Copland is a conductor. Béla Bartók was primarily a concert pianist. It is true that we both believe in performing our own works.

You also have very different attitudes towards the publication of your music. Steve, you once told me there were going to be a number of your works published entirely by Universal Editions in the spring of 1980, whereas you, Philip, are very reluctant to part with any of your works.
I don't want to talk for Steve, but my motivation has been mainly economic. We both make a living as performers of our own music. I'm unwilling to let pieces go one at a time. I want some publisher to take the whole ball of wax; when I make a deal, I'm going to make it with one company for everything.
At this point, I have decided to publish only pieces that can be done relatively easily. Something like Clapping Music *can be performed a lot more easily than a piece like* Drumming. *I'm not going to release a piece which would interfere with the living I make as a performer, but some of the pieces Universal is going to publish are now out of my repertory—something like* Four Organs, *for example. I would like other musicians to continue playing these pieces, even if I am not doing so.*
If I'm the only one who owns the music, then anyone who wants to hear it has to hire me to play it. That's what it comes down to. In England— where I did a tour after a number of years bickering with various sponsor groups—I was able to organize concerts for the simple reason that there was no other way for the British to get my music. They would have been much happier performing it themselves, but they couldn't get the scores. So they had to hire the ensemble.
I would say that the largest source of my income is—and has been for a number of years now—European. We couldn't live here without it—and yet I have no desire to live there.
Yes, I calculate that 90% of my income is made in Europe. There is much more government support of the arts. Nothing like that exists here.
Well, let's give credit where credit is due. There is a New York State

Council on the Arts and a National Endowment for the Arts. *I have been to a lot of premieres that wouldn't have been possible without them. So I certainly want to give them the credit. I just think they stand alone.* They do their best with what they have, but they work with a very limited budget.

Should there be a budget strictly allotted to "minimal" music?
I want to say right away that that is a misnomer. It is *not* "minimal" music. I think that word should be stamped out! To call it "minimal" is just a mistake. This technique is capable of supporting music of richness and variety. If you are talking about *Music in Fifths*, okay. If you want to talk about *Violin Phase*, okay. But if you want to talk about the works which have continued these ideas, it's not at all an appropriate term.

But nothing seems to be a suitable term! What do you call it?
That is a problem that has plagued all of us for years. If there had been a good name, we would have leapt on it long ago. For that reason, one talks around it in various ways. I talk about music that's based on process. I talk about repetitive structures. I think this comes closer to it than anything else. Anyone who wants to talk about this music seriously is going to have to talk about repetitive structures—both harmonic and rhythmic. The minimalism idea is only a rather short-lived stylistic period of this music. *I don't think these questions are answered, historically, by composers. For instance, Arnold Schoenberg wanted to call his music "pantonal." He desperately wanted to call it "pantonal." But everyone else called it atonal music, and that was that. He also insisted that there was no such thing as atonality. He used to rant and rave about "atonal." But finally the decision wasn't in his hands. I think the various media—whether they be scholarly journals, newspapers, or somewhere in between—really make the decision. Philip tries to convey information and I try to convey information about the music when we talk about it. But I don't think that this is what makes for catch-all titles in music. That's left to other people.*

Recorded at WKCR Studios, New York City

CHRONICLE,
1972–1981
(1989)

T O M   J O H N S O N

Philip Glass's New Parts (April 6, 1972)

One of the most important new trends in music is the area I like to refer to as "hypnotic music." It has a hypnotic quality because it is highly repetitious, and employs a consistent texture, rather than building or developing in traditional ways. Usually pieces in this genre are rather long, and they can seem tedious until one learns how to tune into the many subtle variations which go on underneath the sameness of the surface. Then very new and exciting musical experiences begin to happen.

Philip Glass's work for the past couple of years has been at the very center of this new trend, and his *Music with Changing Parts* is one of the finest pieces of this type which I have heard. It is an hour-long piece, in which electric organs ripple along in little repeated patterns, while sustained notes in viola, voice, and wind instruments fade in and out. The music uses a simple white-note scale, and most of the rhythms are also relatively simple, but the patterns shift constantly in subtle, unique ways, and enough of them are going at any one time to keep the ear more than occupied.

Glass's latest piece, *Music in 12 Parts*, is a continuation of this style, the main difference being that it uses a different structural format. It is divided into sections, or "parts," which are about half an hour long, and quite different from each other in character. Parts IV, V, and VI of the new work were presented at Village Presbyterian Church on March 26, as part of the Spencer Concerts series. Two organs were used through the evening, and the four wind players worked with various combinations of flutes, saxophones, and trumpet.

One hardly notices that Part IV is actually a labyrinth of rhythmic complexity, so smooth is its flow. Usually at least three simultaneous patterns are distinguishable, each independent of the others. Without stopping, the performers made a rather abrupt transition into Part V, which is built on a simple waltz rhythm and maintains interest through melodic shifts, particularly in the saxophones and trumpet. After intermission, they played the last half of part VI, which features quick patterns in two flutes, and many metric shifts.

In some ways, *Music in 12 Parts,* or at least these three sections of the work, is less successful than the earlier *Music with Changing Parts.* The transitions from part to part are somewhat jolting, and seem to go against the hypnotic character of the music, although that may have been just a performance problem. And sometimes the variation procedures do not seem as intricate or subtle in the new piece, especially during Part V.

But that is just quibbling, because both pieces are really wonderful in so many ways. The loud textures are extremely rich and sensual, and the organs and other instruments are so well blended that it is sometimes difficult to tell which instrument is playing what. The music has a sensitivity to subtle differences between modes, which can only be compared to the Indian raga system. And such finesse informs the details that the music is always interesting, although it never moves outside a small confined area. Finally, it conveys a mood which is overwhelmingly joyous. Although the music does not resemble anything by Bach, it sometimes lifts me up the way a "Brandenburg" Concerto does.

Philip Glass in Twelve Parts (June 13, 1974)

After three years of work, Philip Glass has finally completed his *Music in 12 Parts,* and it is a major accomplishment. The work, which was presented in its entirety for the first time at Town Hall on June 1, contains four hours of music altogether, and there is no padding. It is rather complex music, extremely rich in ideas, but also strong in its direct emotional impact. And the ensemble of Jon Gibson, Dickie Landry, Richard Peck,

Bob Telson, Joan La Barbara, and Glass sailed through the long taxing evening with apparent ease. I have already written about the rich blended sound Glass gets with electric organs, amplified winds, and an occasional female voice, and about the static or minimal or hypnotic style of his music, which ripples along on endless eighth notes. But I have never emphasized the complexity of his work, because only now, having heard all 12 parts of this piece in a single evening, can I see the degree of inventiveness and the variety of the intricate techniques which he has found within the severe restrictions of his style.

Only toward the end of Part V did I ever lose interest in what was going on, and even there the problem could have been my inability to latch onto things, rather than any lack of ideas on the composer's part. In general, the music constantly uncovered new possibilities and constantly challenged my ear and brain. And it never became dull or repetitious, despite all the repetition.

Sometimes the interest lies in gradual fluctuations between modes, like a shift between a kind of major key sound and a kind of minor key sound.

Sometimes the focus is on polyrhythms, with little contests between, say, the three four figures and the six eight figures.

Sometimes the music is simply unison melodies, but with small variations in individual instruments.

Sometimes unison melodies become parallel fifths, often so subtly that one hardly realizes the shift is going on.

In some sections, at the whim of the performer, sustained tones creep in and out, having strange effects on the moving parts.

Sometimes syncopated rhythms simply wind around each other in cycles. But if the cycles are repeated 15 or 20 times, as they often are, it is only because it actually takes the listener about that long to figure out what is going on.

Frequently figures repeat over and over, gradually adding notes and becoming longer, or gradually omitting notes and becoming shorter. In the more recent of the 12 parts, the music sometimes alternates between two kinds of material. Both sets of material go through independent variations as the antiphonal music shifts back and forth. Another technique common in the recent parts is the sudden modulation. At unexpected moments, the music suddenly pops into a new key, making it hard to remember where you just were or to figure out how you got where you now are.

There are constant fascinations, and they always happen on a level of subtlety where you can't quite figure out what the hell is going on. Glass may be avant-garde in many respects, but he apparently respects the age-old art of concealing art as much as any past master.

One of the pleasures of Glass's music is his joyous optimistic tone. No gnashing dissonances, no eerie sounds, no melancholy moments, no downs. It just keeps chugging away toward some ultimate high. I'm not sure that's necessarily a good thing, as most of the music which has lasted in our culture is music which contains liberal doses of the bitter along with the sweet. But I'm certainly not complaining. A little musical optimism is a refreshing contrast to the dark expressionistic shadows of Schoenberg, Berg, and Bartók, which still hang over so much contemporary music.

As I was sitting in Town Hall that night I couldn't help thinking of a letter which had been in the *Voice* that week. Someone named Matthew Paris had written about how he usually stayed home and listened to records instead of going out to concerts, because he felt that concerts seldom offered anything he could not get on records. I doubt that Paris bothered to attend Glass's concert, but if he had, the experience might well have turned his head around.

If and when *Music in 12 Parts* does come out on records, I imagine it will be a six-record album, and it will probably come to five or six times the price of a ticket to this concert. And even with a relatively luxurious home stereo set-up, Paris will never be able to reproduce this music as vividly as the live performers can produce it on their own superb sound system.

Like a lot of music being created these days, the effectiveness of Glass's subtle textures depends quite a bit on hearing them at the right volume and with just the right balance of voices. Even Kurt Munkacsi, the group's sound man, can't always get things exactly right for all parts of a hall, but he comes a lot closer than anybody's home stereo system will.

Rehearsing Einstein on the Beach: *Philip Glass and Robert Wilson (January 26, 1976)*

There hasn't been much in the papers about Robert Wilson since *A Letter for Queen Victoria* and *The Dollar Value of Man* last season, but his Spring Street studio is as busy as ever. From 10 in the morning until 7 at night every day, a company of 26 has been preparing a new work, tentatively called *Einstein on the Beach*. The first performances of the work, in Germany and France, will not begin until August, so it is far too early to say anything final about what it will be like. But since theater is a new genre for Philip Glass, who has already spent about a year composing the music for *Einstein*, it seemed worthwhile to drop by one afternoon and find out what is going on.

Glass's approach in the new piece turns out to be a fairly predictable outgrowth of the work he has been doing during the past few years with amplified winds and organs, and his regular ensemble will be carrying much of the show. In fact, the piece that the group premiered last spring, under the title *Another Look at Harmony*, is included in this score. But in addition there will be sections for solo violin, others with vocal solos, and others featuring a 12-voice chorus. The five hours of music will be divided into a number of shorter segments, generally alternating between large ensemble pieces and smaller groups. Much of the music will be carried by the chorus, which will apparently be onstage playing roles most of the time.

The vocal lines in Glass's choral music employ the same kind of rhythmic modules as his instrumental parts. The little melodies repeat over and over, shifting to slightly new patterns maybe once every 10 to 30 seconds. The only lyrics are "do re mi" and "one two three," which are used simply to articulate the melodies. Most of the time the music is diatonic, though there are a few chromatic passages. It's hard work for 12 singers to keep together on such fast rhythms, but judging from what I heard, and considering that they have several months of rehearsal time left, they just might be as crisp and unified as Glass's regular ensemble by the time the production begins its European run in August. The curious thing about this chorus, however, is that Glass has selected thin, relatively untrained voices for his group, despite the plans to perform in a large hall without choral amplification. The singers were barely holding their own against the loud electric organ Glass was playing at the rehearsal, and knowing the kind of high volumes he normally uses in concerts, I couldn't imagine how he was going to achieve a balance in this piece.

Glass says that he is interested in the natural resonance of the voice, and wants to avoid soloistic qualities, since he rarely writes solos. He went on to explain that trained voices, working with supported tone and nominal vibrato, never blend very well. I asked him if he had heard any groups like the Robert Shaw Chorale or the Gregg Smith Singers lately, and he said he hadn't. In any case, the composer was quite confident about his group, and assured me that they would be producing two or three times their present volume by the time the show opens.

Glass's way of working with Wilson appears to involve the same kind of give and take which one normally finds in collaborations where both artists respect each other, and neither is determined to dominate. But it was curious to learn how they got started when they first began working together about a year ago. Glass told me that Wilson did a lot of preliminary sketches of what he expected various scenes to look like, and that Glass began working out musical ideas based largely on these visualizations.

I was not surprised to learn this, because it had always seemed to me that Wilson is basically a visual artist, and that his feelings for the exact placement of people and objects on the stage, his color sense, and his sets are the most fundamental aspects of his work. His scenes always become animated paintings for me, and I have the feeling that if we ever have any really useful criticism of Wilson's work, it is going to come from an art critic, or at least someone who really understands surrealism, Hopper, O'Keeffe, and so on.

Meanwhile, back at the rehearsal, the group was completing a short physical warm-up, and Glass was asking me if I would like to sing along on a section they were about to rehearse. I jumped at the chance. I'd been hearing Glass's pieces for some time and had often wondered what it would be like to try to read one of his parts. It is obvious just from listening to the long repetitions and quick pattern shifts that there has to be a lot of counting involved. But what kind of counting? Is it tricky, difficult counting that requires heavy concentration? Is it dull drudgerous counting that bores the hell out of you? Is it the kind of counting that can alter your consciousness, as in so many yoga and Zen exercises?

It's really none of the above, though it's a little like each. Let's say we're working on pattern number 65, and our part is something like "fa si la si." And let's say that there is a little "4" off to the right side, meaning that after we've sung "fa si la si" four times we've completed one sequence. And let's say that there is another "4" above the music, meaning that we have to sing four sequences before going on to pattern 66.

If you followed that, you're probably thinking, as I did, "Glass, can't you multiply? Why didn't you just say to do it 16 times instead of going through all this four times four stuff?" And if you are pretty headstrong about your opinion, as I was, you would decide to do it your own way, and the downbeat would come, and everyone would start charging through their quick little patterns, and everything would be fine until you discovered that you weren't sure whether you were on the 12th repetition or the 14th. And meanwhile the music would be going by so fast that every time you tried to figure it out you would just become more confused.

I decided I'd better try it Glass's way the next time around, and for some reason it was a lot easier. It still took a lot of concentration, but somehow the challenge seemed fun, a little like keeping track of how many times the runners have gone around the track, or something like that. It felt good as the sequences went by, feeling the fours within the fours, or the twos within the eights, or whatever, and getting ready for the next shift. And sometimes I could make it through three or four patterns without losing count.

The problem is that a single segment might involve 10 or 20 patterns, and there are an awful lot of choral segments in *Einstein on the Beach*, all of which Glass expects the singers to memorize. But of course, every time I started thinking about something like that, I lost the count again.

I enjoyed the challenge of the whole thing, and I guess I was doing all right, because during the break Glass offered me a job. I figured he was kidding, but by the time he'd mentioned it three times, complimenting my sightreading and complaining that they really did need another good musician on the tenor line, I decided I really ought to consider the prospects.

The rehearsal atmosphere seemed quite pleasant, the money would be adequate, and the months in Europe wouldn't be hard to take. But then I started thinking about how I'd have to do the four sequences of the three-note pattern four times and the eight sequences of the four-note pattern two times, and about how it would all have to be memorized, and I realized that I'd probably never be able to muster up the kind of dedication the task would require.

Maximalism on the Beach: Philip Glass
(February 25–March 3, 1981)

I had long preferred Philip Glass's *Music with Changing Parts* and *Music in 12 Parts* to the more recent Glass works I have heard. The earlier pieces seemed more disciplined, more careful, more focussed, and more closely allied with the principles of minimalism, the later music seemed flabbier, and I was comfortable with that opinion for quite a while. But since I hadn't heard Glass's ensemble live for some time, and had never heard *Einstein on the Beach* in its complete form, I decided to attend the recent performance at Town Hall. *Dance fi 3* and *Dance fi 5* still seemed flabby to me, but when we got to *Einstein on the Beach*, I had to revise my opinions quite a bit. It now seems clear that *Einstein* is much stronger than any of the music he first wrote for his ensemble. The technique is more skill-ful, the insights are deeper, and the style is more personal. And after rehearing the earlier pieces, I am finally beginning to understand that Glass was probably never really a minimalist in the first place.

What is fascinating about *Einstein on the Beach* is how much Glass's style broadened as he approached the operatic stage. Traditional techniques that the composer scrupulously avoided in earlier works are rampant here. Many segments are wrapped up in neat A-B-A forms. The unaccompanied violin music sounds a lot like Bach's. The piece moves in and out of its basic tonal center, D minor, very much the way a 19th-century piece might. There are even some organ figures that sound like those Alberti basses Mozart loved so much. Perhaps the most drastic difference between *Einstein* and *Music with Changing Parts*, however, is the pacing. Between 10 o'clock and 11:15 I counted 14 completely different sections, including an organ solo, a violin solo, a soprano solo, some a cappella choral music, some accompanied choral music, an ensemble section so loud I had to put my fingers in my ears, an organ solo so soft that I almost forgot I was listening to amplified sound, a section of unison scale patterns quite different from anything I had ever heard from Glass, a wide variety of tempos and meters, and a section in which I hardly felt a beat at all. Clearly, any piece that can use up this much contrasting material in a mere hour and a quarter is not even trying to be minimalist, at least not in any very meaningful sense of the term.

But after listening again to *Music in Similar Motion* and *Music with Changing Parts*, I'm not convinced that Glass was terribly interested in restricting his materials even then. When these pieces were new I remember thinking of them as very simple, and I remember how a lot of people said they were simple-minded. In a way, however, it didn't make a lot of sense to call Glass a minimalist even in 1971, and I can understand why Glass doesn't like to be associated with the term. His music, even then, had little similarity with the unadorned rhythmic patterns of Steve Reich's *Clapping Music*, the electronic drones of La Monte Young and Alvin Lucier, or the meditative chants of Pauline Oliveros, not to mention Philip Corner's *Elementals*, which probably makes the most extreme state-ment of all, as well as providing a theoretical base for that whole way of musical thinking. There is a surface simplicity in *Music with Changing Parts*, and the piece does develop rather consistently, simply by adding and subtracting notes from little repeating figures. Yet as I listened once again to those additions and subtractions I realized that they are actually rather whimsical. Composers like Frederic Rzewski, Robert Moran, Louis

Andriessen, and William Hellermann have written such sequences with much greater rigor. By comparison, Glass is not a reductionist at all but a romantic. Nor are Glass's textures as simple as they may seem. Even *Music with Changing Parts* is covered over with several layers of subjective sensuality. The organ colors change frequently. The saxophones become so mixed up in the amplified texture that it's often difficult to separate one from another. Someone is always singing or playing a sustained high note, producing complicated acoustical interactions with the natural overtones in the music. Sometimes improvised saxophone lines weave whole knots of intricate counterpoint into the texture, while many additional complications are added electronically as the instruments are blended, separated, mixed, rebalanced, reverberated, panned, and filtered.

This may be minimalism in a kind of sociohistoric sense, but it has little to do with the purer minimalism of other composers, or with the spirit of reductivism so widely practiced in the visual arts. Of course, that leaves us with the problem of finding another label for Glass, and I really can't figure out what to call him other than a good composer. But just as I was pondering this question, a press release arrived regarding the bass trombonist David Taylor who, we are informed, "has worked with such contemporary popular musicians as Duke Ellington, Thad Jones, Steve Reich, Barry Manilow, Frank Sinatra and The Rolling Stones." So maybe that makes Glass yet another "contemporary popular musician." But I expect that Glass might be even more unhappy to be linked with Barry Manilow than with Philip Corner.

FORM AND PROCESS (1981)

W E S   Y O R K

Preface

Much controversy has surrounded the work of the American composer, Philip Glass. Although his compositions have been performed with critical and popular acclaim in Europe and America, in such auspicious institutions as Carnegie Hall and the Metropolitan Opera, there have been few efforts to understand the structure of this music and there seems to have been little, if any, serious analysis of the work to justify praise or criticism. Many questions remain to be asked:

——— *Is there any underlying structure creating and support-ing the shapes we hear?*

——— *Does the opening of the piece have any special signifi-cance in relation to the rest of the piece?*

——— *What purpose does the process of repetition serve?*

——— *What motivates the minimalist nature of this music?*

This paper attempts to answer these and other crucial questions through a detailed analysis of Glass's *Two Pages* for electric organ and piano (1968) and perhaps throws some light on the larger body of works which the composer has produced since 1968.

As is true of many of his pieces, it becomes immediately apparent that Glass makes his statement through the shaping of a minimal number of musical materials. There are no dynamic changes, no new pitch materials after the initial five pulses, no changes of instrumentation, and no juxtapositions of sound and silence. Rather, and stated most simply, contexts of up to five pitches are continually shaped and re-shaped as they articulate an even and unchanging pulse. Ultimately, the structure of *Two Pages* can be understood as first, the exposition and juxtaposition of two sets of opposing processes, and then, the coordination of all shapes which both emerge from, and reflect back on, those processes. Thus, the emergence of formal relationships occurs through the interaction of the various processes themselves. Regarding this emerging form, it becomes apparent that the symmetrical arch shape pervades the entire piece.

A) Preliminary Considerations

Before proceeding to the analysis itself, a brief discussion is in order with respect to three important factors: first of all, terminology; second, the types of processes at work in the piece; and finally, the particular graphic-analytic method employed in the analysis. After these preliminaries, the structure of the piece will be discussed in some detail.

Reproduced on the following two pages is a transcription of the Shandar recording (#83515) of *Two Pages*.[1]

Terminology

The work is comprised of five parts. Each of these parts is subdivided into several sections: *Part I - three sections; Part II - three sections; Part III - two sections; Part IV - two sections; Part V - three sections.* Each section, in turn, includes one or more measures and each measure contains a number of repetitions of a single melodic pattern. For example:

m. 1

Once again, a measure includes the pattern with all its repetitions.

TWO PAGES

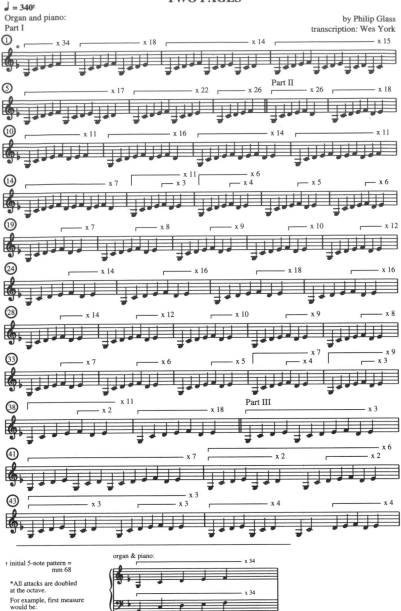

© 1968, Dunvagen Music Publishers, Inc.
Reprinted by permission of Dunvagen Music Publishers, Inc.

Music with Changing Parts

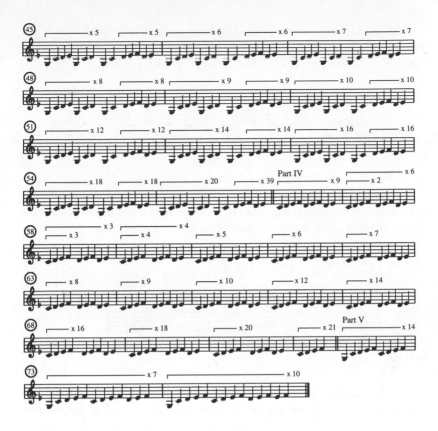

Processes

With respect to the various processes at work, one finds two types which are responsible for creating all motion and change within the composition. One of these is a subtractive process; the other is additive.

The process involved in moving from pattern to pattern, shown in the example below, can be understood as a subtractive process. The five-note group becomes a four-note group by the subtraction of one note. This subtractive process will be referred to as process A.

mm. 1–2

The other process involved in moving from pattern to pattern is an additive one. In the example below, a five-note pattern is expanded into six notes. This additive process will be referred to as process B.

mm. 7–8

In addition, there are two processes involving repetition—external repetition and internal repetition. All external repetition involves the repetition of an entire pattern. As may be seen in measure 1, in such a case, the number of repetitions is external to the pattern. This procedure will be referred to as process Alpha:

m. 1

In contrast, internal repetition involves the repetition of only part of a pattern. As such, the number of repetitions is internal to the pattern. Measure 20, shown below, is an example of a pattern with such internal repetitions, which will be referred to as process Beta.[2]

m. 20

Finally, one should note that, at certain points, external repetitions are superimposed on a pattern with internal repetitions.

m. 15

In the graph below, all measures of the composition are notated in terms of pulses (one pulse equals a quarter note in the transcription). Successive measures are plotted along the horizontal axis, numbers of pulses along the vertical axis. There are three lines shown. The broken line represents the number of pulses per pattern (without external repetitions). The dotted line shows the unfolding of the repetitions of process Alpha. Finally, the solid line connects points which represent the total number of pulses per measure: this is the number resulting from the multiplication of the number of pulses of a particular measure with the number of external repetitions of the pattern of that measure (process Alpha). The significance of this graph will emerge in the analysis which follows.

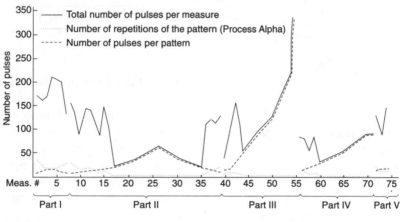

Graph 1

B) Analysis

The following chart outlines the overall formal plan of *Two Pages*:

PART I		
Section 1	Section 2	Section 3
mm. 1–3	mm. 4–6	m. 7

PART II		
Section 1	*Section 2*	*Section 3*
mm. 8–16	*mm. 17–35*	*mm. 36–39*

PART III	
Section 1	*Section 2*
mm. 40–43	*mm. 44–55*

PART IV	
Section 1	*Section 2*
mm. 56–59	*mm. 60–71*

PART V		
Section 1	*Section 2*	*Section 3*
m. 72	*m. 73*	*m. 74*

Part I (measures 1–7)

Part I consists of seven measures. In it the composer employs both processes A (subtraction) and Alpha (external repetition) which interact to expand those patterns and measures into three larger groups, to be called sections 1, 2, and 3. As was mentioned earlier, the motion from the pattern of measure 1 to the pattern of measure 2 provides the first example of process A. Process A is continued until measure 4, the midpoint of part I, where it reaches its furthest extrapolation:

Process A is then reversed through measures 5 and 6, and in measure 7 returns to the opening pattern. Thus, part I outlines an arch-shaped motion. (This is reflected in the symmetrical arch-shape seen in the broken line of the graph 1 which, as mentioned earlier, represents process A.) Process Alpha (the dotted line) then may be understood as superimposed onto the ongoing pattern-to-pattern motion of process A.

Next, it should be noted that the intersection of process A with process Alpha creates three groups of measures, three different plateaus each consisting of measures with a similar number of pulses (ca. 170, ca. 200, ca. 130) and, therefore, a similar duration. These three groups of measures will be referred to as sections 1, 2, and 3. Significantly, none of these sections are articulated by process A alone (the broken line) as process A is continuous and uninterrupted. Likewise, none of the sections is articulated by process Alpha alone (the dotted line) which is also a continuous unbroken progression lacking any internal subdivisions. It is, however, when these two processes are superimposed that the three sections of part I emerge with vivid clarity:

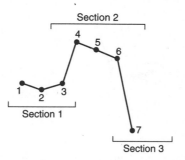

Solid Line (Graph 1)

Closer examination of relationships found among the various parameters in part I shows the symmetrical relationship and the proportion 4:5 to be of primary importance. Significantly, in terms of the former, one may note that musical space itself is proportioned symmetrically. The five pitches are organized as two perfect fourths (G-C and C-F), the first of which being a leap and the second being filled in symmetrically. These five tones comprise the complete set of pitches for the entire piece and are exposed immediately as the pattern of measure 1:

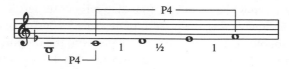

The symmetrical organization of pitches maintains an ambiguity as to which is the stressed tone. If, for example, the F were an F#—breaking the symmetry—a less ambiguous, and perhaps less interesting, situation would result. (Over the course of this analysis it will become clear that the concept of ambiguity is indeed central to the entire composition.)

The perfectly symmetrical arch of part I, unveiled by calculating the number of pulses per pattern, has already been noted. However, there are also several symmetrical relationships to be found among the total number of pulses per measure (the solid line of Graph 1). As might have been expected, measure 4, the central measure, is the highest point on the curve. Comparing this central measure with the first and last measures of this first part, one finds that, in terms of duration, the point representing measure 1 is exactly midway between those points representing measures 4 and 7, respectively, the highest and lowest of part I:

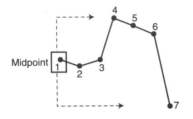

Such symmetry is not only apparent in the disposition of pitches employed, but is also apparent in the temporal structure of part I. As the following chart demonstrates, there exists a virtual symmetry, with respect to the total number of pulses around the central measure:

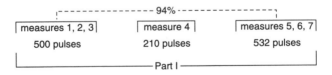

In addition to such symmetrical relationships, the proportion 4:5 (80%) is reflected on several levels. Initially, it was noted that the pattern of measure 1 exposed a gesture of four step-wise notes inside a gesture of five notes. Following this, the pattern of measure 2 consists of a gesture of four notes following a gesture of five. In addition, the proportion of total pulses in measure 1 to total pulses in measure 4 is 4:5, as is the relationship of total pulses in measure 7 to those in measure 1. In fact, throughout part I the proportion 4:5 seems to permeate the arrangement of total pulses per measure:

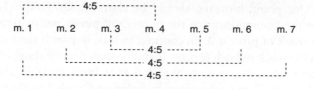

In summary, the final shape of part I and the most significant proportions found therein are brought about through the interaction of process A and process Alpha. As we shall see, this mode of unfolding formal relationships is of central importance to the piece as a whole.

Part II (measures 8–39)

Part II is in three sections: section 1 (measures 8–16), section 2 (measures 17–35), and section 3 (measures 36–39). In it, a new process, additive, is introduced:

mm. 7–8

Each new measure from 7 to 15 adds one new note. Then from measures 16 through 22, each bar adds three new notes: F-D-E♭, which will be referred to as the "tag" of the pattern. From measures 23 through 26 two statements of this tag are added. Consequently, beginning at measure 8 there is a steady accumulation of pulses per pattern, until a climax is reached at measure 26, in which one finds a total of 58 pulses comprising one pattern.

After measure 26 the music proceeds essentially through a mirror image of what has just been described. Of course, this type of symmetrical motion was also observed in part I. In this instance, however, the listener is not brought back all the way to the initial pattern (i.e., to measure 8). The return, in contrast, arrives only at a reiteration of measure 9, which enables the composer to preserve the tag ending intact as part II concludes:

One point, however, should be clarified. On Graph 1, the arch shape of the line representing the number of pulses per pattern of part I was the result of process A. In contrast to this, in part II the similar arch-shape is the result of both process B and process Beta. It should be emphasized that process Beta evolves in part II as an intensification of process B, and that process Beta is, therefore, included on Graph 1 as contributing to this arch.

Next, it should be noted that process Alpha is also operative in part II. Referring to Graph 1, it may be observed that process Alpha (the dotted line) descends from measures 8 through 17. Then, from measures 17 through 35, there is only one statement of each pattern. Finally, from measures 36 through 39, the dotted line ascends. Thus, with respect to process Alpha one finds, for the first time, a long section in which there are no external repetitions. As will be shown, this shape, first exposed in part II, will recur in parts III and IV.

Referring now to the progression of total number of pulses per measure in part II, (represented by the solid line) it is obvious that, as in part I, the interaction of two quite continuous processes, B and Beta (represented by the broken line) with Alpha (represented by the dotted line), results in the articulation of three distinct sections:

————Section 1 - measures 8–16

————Section 2 - measures 17–35

————Section 3 - measures 36–39

Specifically, section 1 is characterized by the gradual formation of the tag; section 2, by the addition and subtraction of successive statements of the tag; and section 3, the gradual removal of all internal repetitions. Incidentally, the resulting concave shape of the solid line on Graph 1 occurs because of the absence of process Alpha in section 2.

It should be noted that it is in section 1 of part II, during the gradual formation of the tag, that we have the first hint of process Beta:

m. 12

Measure 12 contains the first multiple statement of the tag ending, F-D-E♭, and thus, the first instance of internal repetition.

One significant by-product of the additive process in part II is the gradual lessening of the stability associated with the notes G-C as established in part I. Concomitant with this increasing instability is the growing expectation for a return to the G-C as it is denied for longer and longer periods. The interesting corollary to this development, however, is the subtle and steady establishment of F-D-E♭ as a more potent center unto itself. As such, there seems to be a growing sense of polarity between a G-C cell and an F-D-E♭ cell.

Part III (measures 40–55)

Overview

Part III is in two sections: section 1 (measures 40–43) and section 2 (measures 44–55). Thus far in the piece, part I introduced processes A and Alpha, and part II introduced processes B and Beta. In contrast, part III combines all the processes from both previous parts in a *tour de force* which constitutes the central passage of the entire piece.

A brief examination of measure 43 will immediately reveal this combination of processes:

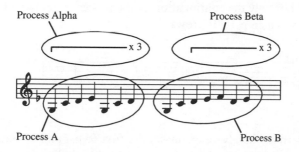

Referring to the two patterns above, it is clear that the first half of the measure is borrowed from part I and, of course, represents a pattern from process A (subtractive). Opposing this, the music comprising the second half of this measure is borrowed from part II and represents a pattern from process B (additive).[3] In addition, the entire seven-note pattern which constitutes the first half of the measure is repeated three times, representing an example of process Alpha (external repetition). In contrast, in the second half of the measure, only part of the pattern is repeated. Thus, the repetition is here internal to the pattern and so represents an example of process Beta.

Referring now to Graph 1, a comparison of the above-mentioned pattern-to-pattern motion (broken line) of part III with those of parts I and II reveals a most significant difference. In parts I and II, the broken line rises, reaches a peak, and returns to, or quite near to, where it began. In contrast, the shape of part III rises to a peak, but then, instead of returning where it began, abruptly ends.

As was the case in parts I and II, in part III process Alpha is superimposed upon the pattern-to-pattern level referred to above. When the basically continuous evolution of processes A and Beta are combined with the similarly continuous motion of process Alpha, a rather dramatic division into two sections emerges (measures 40 through 43, and 44 through 55), illustrated in Graph 1 by the striking break in the solid line representing the total number of pulses per measure.

In summary, then, several important events take place in part III. Most significantly, there occurs a juxtaposition of the processes from part I with those of part II. In addition, the shape of the pattern-to-pattern motion, which described an arch in parts I and II, is quite different in part III. Finally, the superimposition of processes articulates two distinct sections.

A Closer Look at Part III

The logic of the first pattern of part III is impressive. The pattern holds within itself not only the continuation of the process from part II but also the seed from which part III grows:

mm. 39–40

As can be seen in the above example, the first four notes of measure 40 could represent a continuation of the process concluding in part II as it removes three more notes, the tag, from the previous pattern.

Indeed, the pattern of measure 40 represents, in microcosm, all of what is to come in part III. Every measure which succeeds it bears the same basic internal structure:

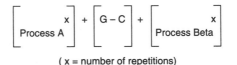

(x = number of repetitions)

The pattern of measure 42, for instance, is created by superimposing process Beta onto the pattern of measure 41. A subtle junction is thus made between the gestures labeled A and B, below. A question arises. Does one hear:

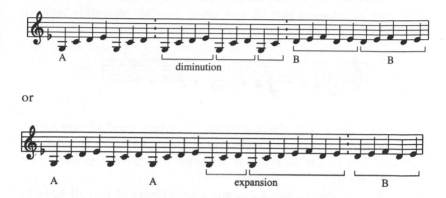

or

The answer, of course, is that one can hear either or both. The middle G–C can be understood as the end of a subtractive process or as the initiation of the process of building the new tag. The pattern of measure 43, however, clarifies the ambiguity, as it here becomes clear that the true structure consists of, first, repeating the seven-note gesture and then, adding five-note tags to G–C:

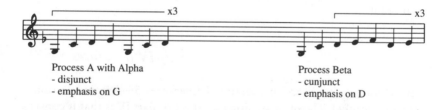

Process A with Alpha
- disjunct
- emphasis on G

Process Beta
- cunjunct
- emphasis on D

In attempting to integrate these two gestures, the listener might perceive an element of instability in the first half of the measure in that there is no F. As such, when the note F occurs in the second half of the measure, there is a certain sense of completion. However, an unstable quality then seems to develop in the second half of the measure, by the complementary absence of G which is resolved when the G is heard again in the first half of the next measure.

Process Beta now unfolds as it did in part II—adding, at first, one more internal repetition per pattern, and then, eventually, two internal repetitions. Once again, however, unlike parts I and II, part III is not constructed as an arch-shape. As can be seen in Graph 1, part III ends at the furthest working out of its processes.

Curiously, as a result of the extensive simultaneous development of the two processes of part III, one senses a certain separation between the two halves of each measure:

In addition, along with this separation, a certain sense of expectation develops. With the continued repetition of the tag (in which D is the central pitch), one awaits the return of the seven-note gesture (in which G is the central pitch).

It must also be noted that the final measure of part III adds 19 extra internal repetitions of the tag, creating an added sense of expectation for a new event—the return of the note G. As we shall see, in the next measure (the first of part IV), this expectation is denied. Significantly, the number of pulses in measure 55 is the highest of the entire piece. It is interesting, too, that process Alpha (external repetition) is not involved in this central passage of the piece. It is the juxtaposition of processes on the more fundamental pattern-to-pattern level of form that articulates this focal point.

Part IV (measures 56–71)

Part IV contains two sections: section 1 (measures 56–59) and section 2 (measures 60–71). The most significant aspect of part IV is that it consists primarily of process Beta reversed. One might recall that Beta is that process which involves adding internal repetitions at the end of the pattern. Now, in part IV, the internal repetitions occur at the beginning of the pattern, as can be seen in the example below:

m. 57

Thus, the pattern-to-pattern evolution of part IV involves successive additions of the first gesture, while the second gesture remains constant. Specifically, in each succeeding pattern of part IV, one more internal repetition is added until a total of ten repetitions is reached. At this point, two internal repetitions are added per measure until twenty repetitions are reached. This basic motion would seem to duplicate that heard in parts II and III. However, it is significant to note that this motion does not mirror back on itself as it did in parts I and II. Rather, it recalls more the motion of part III since it also reaches a point of furthest extrapolation and then ends.

Referring to the pattern-to-pattern motion of this fourth part (the broken line of part IV on Graph 1), one finds a shape similar to that of part III: the continuous working out of the single process at hand. Although this process (shown by the broken line) begins at about the same number of pulses for both parts III and IV, in part III it rises to 336 pulses in the same number of measures in which in part IV it rises only to 85 pulses. In other words, the process in part IV is evolving at a much faster pace since its 16 measures unfold more rapidly (i.e. contain many fewer pulses) than do those of part III. Thus, because of the more rapid evolution after the dramatic central passage of the piece, one might begin to feel a certain compelling force moving toward the completion of the composition.

In addition, process Alpha operates in part IV. The presence of external repetitions in the first four measures retards the movement of the pattern-to-pattern process. The use of such repetitions only in the first four measures helps create two sections. As has been mentioned, section 1 begins at measure 56, and section 2 at measure 60. Curiously, as in part III, the very last measure contains some extra repetitions. However, these serve a very different purpose than the final repetitions in part III, where the repetition of D-E♭-F-D-E♭ builds expectation for a return to the note G. In contrast, the repetitions of C-D-E♭-F at the end of part IV give the central note C more weight. Supporting this is the fact that C is now the lowest tone of the pattern. It might be added, however, that although the note C acquires local emphasis, the pitch layout of measure 71 is, once again, symmetrical and, therefore, still basically ambiguous.

One final point: looking again at the pattern-to-pattern motion (the broken line) on Graph 1 and comparing the connections between each part, one sees a minor change of direction in the line between parts I and II, and between parts II and III. But, in contrast to this, between parts III and IV there is a leap which spans practically the entire depth of the graph. Significantly, this dramatic leap in the number of pulses per pattern is accompanied, as previously mentioned, by a denial of the expectation of the return to the note G.

Part V (measures 72–74)

Part V consists of the final three measures of the piece and, as we shall see, is comprised of three sections—each measure, in this case, being one section. Thus, in part V each point on the solid line of Graph 1 seems like a small plateau unto itself. Indeed, the difference between each successive point on the resultant line of part V is equal to or greater than the distance which creates sections 1 and 2 in part I, thus enabling one to perceive a formal articulation.

Primarily, part V consists of process A inverted. Previously, process A always involved successive subtractions of one note from the top of the basic pattern. Contrasting with this, in part V these successive subtractions are taken from the bottom:

m. 74

Part V seems to recall many ideas from the first part of the score. In fact, the three patterns which comprise part V are directly analogous to those from measures 2, 3, and 4 of part I, although, as mentioned above, process A is now inverted. Specifically, as with the first part, the line representing the pattern-to-pattern process (broken line) in part V seems part of a convex arch, while the line representing process Alpha seems part of a concave formation. Indeed, the resultant line (solid) is basically an inversion of the general convex shape of that of part I, as the processes of part I and V are both inversions of one another. Moreover, shapes from several other previous parts seem to be in evidence in part V. Referring to Graph 1, it may be noted that the pattern-to-pattern evolution of part V unfolds in a manner which is quite similar to parts III and IV since there is no mirror return.

Finally, in reference to repetition process, as in part I, only process Alpha is operative here. There are, however, fewer external repetitions in part V than in part I, with the result that the measures of part V progress much faster than the analogous measures of the opening.

The Piece as a Whole

With the foregoing information, the essential characteristics of the entire five-part form may now be revealed. First of all, considering the total number of pulses in the entire piece (its duration), the midpoint of the work occurs in the very last measure of part II (measure 39). It may be recalled that the first two parts were expository in nature. As such, the piece divides precisely in half between exposition of materials and their further working out.

In contrast to this bipartite plan is the inherent symmetry of the composition's five-part scheme:

PART I	PART II	PART III	PART IV	PART V
Process A	*Process B;*	*Process A;*	*Process Beta*	*Process A*
	Process Beta	*Process Beta*	*(as intensification*	*inverted*
			of B) reversed	

Understood in these terms, the work seems to articulate a tripartite form in which parts I and II function as exposition, part III as development, and parts IV and V as a varied return. Turning once more to Graph 1, it becomes immediately apparent that this symmetrical, ternary form is also reflected in the succession of arches which constitute the overall shape of each individual part:

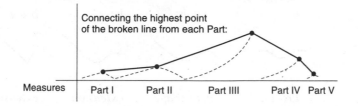

The chart below represents an encapsulation of the entire analysis.

In summary, one discovers in *Two Pages* a compelling compositional framework. The piece concerns itself not with one single process, but with the interaction of several processes. In this interaction, ambiguities of several kinds act to propel the working out of the various processes toward the ultimate resolution.[4] Together, these factors provide for one listener a rich aural experience.

SUMMARY OF ANALYSIS

Exposition		*Juxtaposition*	*Varied Return*	
Part I	*Part II*	*Part III*	*Part IV*	*Part V*

1) Pattern-to-Pattern Process:

Process A— subtracting from the top	*Process B— adding to the end, beginning is static*	*Process A— with Process Beta*	*Process Beta— reversed*	*Process A— inverted, subtracting from the bottom*

2) Type of Repetitive Process:

Process Alpha— external repetitions	*ProcessBeta— internal repetitions*	*Processes Alpha and Beta*	*Processes Alpha and Beta*	*Process Alpha*

3) Shape of Entire Part—Solid Line, Graph 1:

arch	*inverted arch*			
a	*b*	*a + b*	*b*	*b + a*

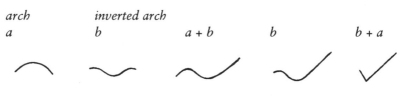

Process moves faster at ends	*Process moves slower at ends*	*new shape*	*extension*	*extension*

4) Shape of Pattern-to-Pattern Process—Broken Line, Graph 1:

arches　　　　*arches*　　　　*extends*　　　　*extends*　　　　*extends*

5) Note Given Emphasis:

G *(C also*　　D　　　　G + D　　　　C　　　　F
has some　　　　　　*juxtaposed*
weight)　　　　　　　*as opposing*
　　　　　　　　　　　centers

Notes

1. In conversation (January 1980), Mr. Glass has mentioned that his score, as originally conceived, included two measures which were removed from the Shandar recording. These two measures, 23 and 24, were interpolated into the transcription of the recorded performance. Moreover, there may be further differences between the original score and the piece as represented by the Shandar recording. However, since, as of this writing, the score is not available, Mr. Glass has agreed to a reprinting of the present transcription.

2. Process Beta might well have been called process B^1 since it is introduced in part II as an intensification of process B, and also (and more importantly), it always functions in the same manner as processes A and B. However, since it is heard, I believe, as a repetition, we will identify it as process Beta.

3. It is important to note, however, that process B is not actually operative here, although, as shown in the second pattern of measure 43, it is explicitly quoted.

4. Ambiguities already discussed include the symmetrical layout of pitches as well as ambiguity in the flow of gestures (for example: Is measure 2 heard as five pulses followed by four or the reverse?). Further, the mechanical evenness of attack maintained by the organ heightens the sense of ambiguity. Finally, line 5 of the chart on the last page ("Note Given Emphasis") shows that emphasis rotates to every note except E♭. The composer thus avoids the only tone with a half-step (leading tone) below itself, thereby assuring ambiguity in terms of "tonal" orientation.

GLASS AND SNOW (1970)

RICHARD FOREMAN

Composer Philip Glass and filmmaker Michael Snow are in the vanguard of a small group of artists who have been building upon that contemporary aesthetic which sees the work of art as primarily a structure articulating its "mode of being-present."

> The painter or sculptor is making an object which is clearly "placed" at each encounter—placed contextually within the going contents of the brain, the perceptual fringe, the memory overlay, the ideological overlay.

To a greater or lesser extent, it forces a recognition of at least certain areas of consciousness. The power of these minimal, systemic, primary structure space objects lies in the confrontation of the purely *present* (the art-object) with the consciousness mechanism of the spectator, which is no longer purely present as it is encrusted with a web of associational conditioning. As a result, the art-object is unavoidably "object," "other," a realm of "elsewhere," no matter what strategies the artist resorts to in the attempt to create a work that exalts the fact of its presence in the here and now. The viewer's basic task as a "consciousness" is to choose, to say "yes" or "no," to make decisions as to whether or not the newly encountered object-of-presentness has created a unique and valuable experience in his consciousness.

The music of Glass, the films of Snow, do not evoke this same degree of implied "ego-centeredness" as the fulcrum and pivot of the art-experience.

Philip Glass's compositions are all based upon the premise of a performing group of five to eight musicians. All amplified instruments (electric organs, viola, cello, soprano saxophones) play in unison throughout each piece. Only one of his pieces has had to be written up in parts; in every other, each player plays exactly the same notes at the same time, or an intervalic displacement of those notes. In *Music in Fifths* a simple phrase is played by all the musicians in unison; the phrase has a bottom and a top line, identical but for the fact that a fifth separates each simultaneous note. The phrase is repeated in performance between two and eight times—Glass plays and also conducts—depending on the tightness of unison playing and the overall length of the piece. At the point when he feels the group is ready to change, Glass cues the ensemble to proceed to the next section, in which an additional few notes are added to the end of the original phrase. This second phrase is repeated until the performers have again attained the same tightness of unison playing, whereupon new notes are added to this second stage form, and so on through perhaps thirty or so phrases of addition. The piece itself may last from twenty minutes upwards. In recent pieces, such as *Music in Similar Motion* and *Music in 8 Parts*, the introduction of intervalic displacement of some parts leads to a treatment of musical texture in terms of the overall structure. But the method is constant in Philip Glass's music: simple addition allowing for the expansion and contraction of musical phrases, and simultaneous unison playing.

I would relate the "additive" nature of Glass's structure to his own growing vision of his music as primarily a kind of "performance piece" rather than a disembodied sound phenomenon that stands by itself. The compositional exploration of addition and unison playing leads directly to a consciousness that the performers themselves are cellular units who maintain their identity, just as the musical phrase is added to but never manipulated and reshuffled. Unison playing reveals each player as a unit "added" to the next, contrary to the normal situation where performers intertwine their musical lines in such a way that they lose their identity in the service of a composition that exists as a kind of transcendental structure.

This method of composition then is a total rejection of serial method, for process here is the subject rather than the source of the music. The web of lucidly clear, reiterated yet slightly "shifting" sound created by Glass is not to be understood as a disembodied "force" of sound, snatched by the artist out of some normally "unheard" level of sound "elsewhere." The few commentators who have so far written of Glass's music err in linking it to Eastern music (which might indeed be thought of as a sound continuum snatched from elsewhere). Though there is a certain similarity in the texture of shifting sound, Glass's compositions are rather to be understood as performance situations in which musicians (and spectators) put themselves in a certain "place," located through the coordinates of the specific phrase. Then this place—which is not an evocative composed "elsewhere" but rather the here-and-now of a chosen method of procedure—slowly opens, becomes slowly filled and informed with the shared "space" of consciousness which is founded at each moment as the spectator "allows" the piece to exist.

Michael Snow's films are all basically the exploration of a given "idea of presentation" set to work on a particular object. The black-and-white *New York Eye & Ear Control* examines all the compositional variations available in the placement and manipulation of a positive and negative silhouette of a walking woman in various scenic and social environments; an opposition is created between these basically static images and an intense dynamic sound track. *Wavelength* is a single, slow, forty-five minute zoom down the length of Snow's studio. The light, color and textural variations of the image serve as filmic events on an equal basis with several events involving people. All these events briefly punctuate, at five or ten minute intervals, the unceasing zoom, which ends on a photo of the ocean tacked to the wall at the far end of the studio. An electronic sine wave rises in pitch as the film proceeds with a synchrone sound (street noises, conversations). In *Standard Time* the camera has been set in the center of a room, and it proceeds to pivot, filming the room in smooth circular sweeps. There is some variation in the length and speed of the sweeps, and toward the end a cat, a girl, and a turtle are briefly glimpsed; all of this against a sound track of a radio discussion fading in and out in counterpoint to the sweeps of the camera. In *One Second in Montreal* a series of still photos of Montreal covered with snow (A pun? There are flashes of wit in all Snow's films, for all their rigor and shattering intelligence.) fill the screen for a subtly varying period. In the silence one watches what is alive, *now*, in the presented film (the image gently shakes, dirt flashes lightly against each frame . . .), as opposed to other films where one watches that life pictured and alluded to "elsewhere." As each cut to the next photo is anticipated, one watches the anticipation modulating one's watching. In ↔, perhaps the most powerful of Snow's films, the camera has been set up in a classroom. Four windows look out upon trees and houses. The camera pans back and forth through approximately 180 degrees with the continuous machine sound in accord with the varying speed of the camera movements, and with a "clunk" at the limit of each pan. The speed of the back-and-forth movement increases, and, within the panning, there are sometimes jump cuts to pop people into the frame. Sometimes these people disappear after a few frames, sometimes they remain longer and the camera pans back and forth across some ongoing activity in which they are engaged. The camera pans get faster and faster until the image itself blurs, and the pure motion of the pan takes over and becomes the available visual material. At top speed, the pan suddenly becomes an equally fast vertical camera motion, and, as that motion is slowly reduced in speed, we see the camera filming the same room—up and down, up and down. At the end the camera is motionless, and after the titles appear with a brief coda of superimposition of the various camera movements, the film ends with a mysterious blue-white blur.

As in Glass's music, Snow is working in these films not to re-create the image of an intuited or sensed reality that is normally unavailable to consciousness; rather he is taking the material (the view of the room, in Glass's case the musical phrase) and subjecting it to a series of reiterated manipulations in which its elements are held in unchanging relation (there is no cutting in the camera motion, the notes from the phrase are not rearranged). The changes that are slowly introduced respect the integrity of the found image or structure and are specifically designed to show how they sustain themselves under the impact of *time*. Going back and forth over the image or the musical, time is a heavy truck knocking them a little this way, a little that way . . . repeatedly impressing a bit of dirt from the road.

As time rolls over the musical phrase or the selected image, it is also rolling over the spectator; it is a "process" selected as a rule for composition and perception. The initial moment of the spectator's encounter with this art is perhaps not unlike the encounter in spatial art, where consciousness feels the necessity to give a "yes" or "no" to the work. In most previous time-art the work begins and the spectator decides to hold his "yes-no" decision in abeyance. He sees the work is going to develop in time and that development is crucial to a final determination of exactly what the work has done to his consciousness. Glass's music and Snow's films generally succeed in establishing a different kind of relationship to the work of art. The spectator very soon intuits that these structures are *not* developing in the usual way. He is *not* going to be gratified by a series of modulations which will so manipulate and exercise the range of his feeling-tone resources that he will be reawakened to the full range of his "savoring." This function of stimulating the spectator to "flex his feeling apparatus" is the source of gratification in most Western art; our "yes" or "no" is really determined by whether or not our "feeling" center has been momentarily "re-presented" to the consciousness so that its boundaries can once again be reached.

Glass and Snow have created works which, in a sense, baffle our attempt to derive pleasure in the name of that characterological configuration which is "myself." Rather than creating images of an "elsewhere" that asks our sense of emotional self to wake up and go for a moment to its frontier, their art makes its *process* rather than its resultant object into the mode of "being-present." The reiteration of process is always in the now, and we do not confront its occurring in the same way that we confront an object. We rather test ourselves, our own consciousness continuing in time against the piece's continuing in the same shared time. The only object that is "elsewhere" is the self which experiments with creating different modes of its own problem of "doing something with the attention" as it confronts the on-going structure of the work.

The capacity that the work's process of "being-present" brings to consciousness is not the capacity to "feel," to experience a variation of an internal "yes" or "no"; but rather a capacity of attention in which the internal "noticing" seems cleansed of the need to constantly check whether or not it is pleasure or pain. The noticing of process itself becomes exhilarating—the matching of one's internal on-going time with the piece's "suffering" of a time which is the common possession of piece and spectator.

To clarify this, one should not overlook the importance of the slight variations which occur within the repetitions of this art. Those who claim that Glass and Snow are creating an art basically hypnotic in intent are missing the point. The spectator discovers his consciousness as a nonsubjective faculty—as a Hegelian "spirit" behind all being rather than as a means of being his exclusive self—precisely as he registers the matching and slight mis-match-composition as the piece "drifts" precisely onward in time. Exposure to the piece makes present the factors of memory lag and overlap, a feeling for the slow distortion of process by the time alone, and a kind of tuning to the truth of quantum theory as a basic organizational principle; Glass's music seems to "prove" that change is but the biological or spiritual "blooming into the next stage" after a certain optimal fulfillment of a previous form has been achieved (that is, change when the ideal of unison playing has been attained). In Snow's ←→, it is as if the initial premise of the back and forth camera motion is a means of letting both the spectator and the room photographed be open to energies which—reflected in the continual *alterations* of speed, etc. that impinge upon the initial movement—are the secret energies of growth and transformation.

Whereas most of the advanced art which has led to the moment of Philip Glass and Michael Snow has created Zen-like moments of confrontation between the impenetrable object and "what we are now," the art of Glass, Snow, and perhaps a few others (composers Steve Reich, La Monte Young, Terry Riley; filmmakers Ken Jacobs, Joyce Wieland, Ernie Gehr, Hollis Frampton; and also Yvonne Rainer in dance, Ken Kelman and myself in theater) is rather a setting into motion of a process that vibrates in such a way that what grows in us is not greater knowledge of the self and its resources but the capacity to let the universe of consciousness (the non-I consciousness) work through us, to be more attuned to the ontological truths and categories.

Most art of the West has taken the form of objects that channeled our consciousness into work . . . encouraged it to read into the work, to project into it what we are as individuals and "persons" in the full Christian sense of the word. Recent advanced spatial art has put a stop to that; we run into the surface of such work and are thrown back upon ourselves. But in a sense, the work is then a mirror that still returns us to the self that has just "suffered" (in the best, wisdom-giving sense of the word) a collision. The new time-art of Glass and Snow, because it does go on in time and because the drift of regular change built into the work keeps us from settling back to use the work as a mere reflecting-glass (useful as that might be in itself) opens a new dimension in art. No longer images and relics brought back by artists from the spiritual "beyond," it is the building of a house within which the spectator, in order simply to *notice* the work itself, *must* replace himself so that he is no longer confronting an object, but putting "himself-as-self" elsewhere, so that naked presence is the mode and matter of the artistic experience.

CHRONICLE, 1977–1980

ART LANGE

The Ancient Avant-Garde Music of Philip Glass (1977)

It seemed that three-quarters of the audience attended out of curiosity and the rest out of a desire for chicness. For while Philip Glass has built a solid if ambiguous reputation on the East Coast, precious little of his music preceded him to Chicago. His recordings are available only on his own Chatham Square label (I doubt if more than three stores in Chicago stock them) and certainly no radio station around would touch his music. A mixture of fact and rumor filtered in ahead of his visit, of his four-and-one-half hour score for the opera *Einstein on the Beach*, of five-hour marathon concerts in New York that consisted solely of three repeated chords, of inane music that went on and on until you were ready to climb the walls or reach Nirvana, depending upon whom you talked to.

For his two Chicago performances Glass brought along an ensemble of six performers and one sound technician whose job it was to balance and blend the various instrumental and human voices through the ten speakers that all but surrounded the audience. These speakers allowed for some antiphonal effects, but mainly they were used to place the audience in the middle of the wash of sound produced by the three organs, one keyboard bass, two saxophones, one flute, and voice.

One interesting aspect of the music of Philip Glass is that despite its supposed "avant-garde" modernity, it utilizes elements that have been around for over a thousand years. Almost all of Glass's compositions employ a ground bass, a series of unchanging bass notes upon which are stacked a variety of short melodies and scales. The ground bass evolved out of the "cantus firmus" used in Gregorian Chant and was characteristic in Baroque music. The antiphonal effect (the alternating back and forth of sound from one side of the room to the other, or from one speaker to the other on home stereos) was developed to a great extent by Giovanni Gabrieli's use of a divided choir in late sixteenth- and early seventeenth-century Venice. The continual use of repetition within melodic contours can be traced far back to pre-Christian African, Buddhist, and Tibetan chanting, which often drones on for hours. And the close, overlapping harmonies that Glass employs often echoes the sixteenth-century English madrigalists.

Glass and his cohorts, seated in a semi-circle, used all these elements to create a sort of ritual: a dramatic structure that the listener must penetrate (almost physically, due to the heaviness of the total sound) if he is to get anything out of this music. Listening to this is like wandering through a maze: no one knows how long it will go on, and suddenly you turn a corner and find yourself out in fresh, quiet air.

The first part of the performance opened with five pieces from Glass's newest (and most readily available) recording, *North Star*. These short (two to ten minutes in performance) pieces were written by Glass for the film *Mark Di Suvero, Sculptor*. All of them are built basically from the same materials: three organs playing left-hand ostinato bass patterns; right hands playing simple song-like melodies or running up and down a particular scale; horns and voice riffing the same simple melody or breaking open and articulating the notes in the bass chord progressions. All of the melodies used by Glass are exceedingly simple, ranging from one reoccurring note to eight-note florid phrases. He uses simple, tonal, close harmonies both in the organs and in the overlapping reeds, thus achieving a loud, tight, bright, thick ensemble sound. When the music cuts off suddenly, the silence is a shock to the ears. By adding extremely subtle dynamic changes (alternating the various individual voices from loud to soft) and by alternating stress and emphasis within the phrasing of the melodies, he creates a continuously shifting kaleidoscope of sound which, unless you get "into" it, seems basically the same from piece to piece. The faster tempos are infectious and jazzy, and the occasional use of upper-register reeds and flute gives a shimmering effect. Through the introduction, voice by voice, of new phrases and fragments, a layered texture is created.

The second half of the performance featured parts one, two, and three of Glass's *Music in 12 Parts*. That entire composition lasts some four hours; these three excerpts lasted 35 minutes. There is the same use of patiently repetitive bass progressions contrasted with upper-register simple figures and riffs, but here the outstanding ingredient is that of highly charged, electric, ever-changing rhythmic patterns. The first section began in 8/4, then alternated 8/4 and 6/4, then moved into a passage alternating one bar of 3/4 with one bar of 8/4 and one bar of 6/4. The result was a highly dramatic sensation of tension and release; of pushing forward, then pulling back. The second section began as a fast 4/4, then sprang into 6/4, 2/4, and 3/4 passages to give off a bouncy, syncopated movement with a seamless texture. The third section held 2/4 against 3/4, with the vocalist here seeming to sing first "snow-ing" and then "lump-ing."

The music of Philip Glass is demanding, charming, and, in the sense of ritual and drama, mysterious. It is a synthesis of sound, mind, and body achieved by placing equal importance on tone or timbre of instruments, harmonies, and rhythm (like that of a heartbeat). Glass's use of imitation, of repetition, of consistent body rhythms, strikes a responsive chord in the human unconscious, an inner voice that we carry along with us. The music sings in a manner that seemingly need never stop, and actually it never does.

RECORDS: *Steve Reich:* Music for 18 Musicians *and Philip Glass:* Einstein on the Beach (1979)

It's been variously labeled "pulse music," "minimalist music," "phase music," "trance music," "modular music," and "music to climb the walls by." It can be boring or illuminating, expressive or shallow, invigorating or oppressive. It is obviously based on repetition, but it allows for a great deal of subtle development and momentum. It is a music the likes of which have never been heard before, yet it often takes its rhythmic inspiration from sources as archaic and diverse as Balinese gamelan music, Indian ragas, African polyphonic drumming, the medieval European organum, and American jazz. Its two chief practitioners are Steve Reich and Philip Glass.

Reich and Glass met in the 1960s, when they and Terry Riley and La Monte Young hung out together and compared notes. Each had come, through an individual path, to be interested in the same sort of musical expression—one that used simple (nearly banal) melodies and melodic fragments, grade-school harmonies, and obsessive rhythmic ostinatos in a revolutionary fashion. The four worked closely on each other's projects for a few years, and then split up to develop their individual syntaxes in the minimalist language: Young's static exploration of timbres and intonation, Riley's incorporation of improvisation, Reich's layered phrase juxtapositions, and Glass's additive combination of rhythmic cells. What's interesting about these two new recordings, besides the inherent three-way successes of composer's intent, performer's interpretation, and engineer's aural re-creation, is the fact that despite all the aesthetic theories and claims to the contrary, the music on these two records sounds quite the same—but only in the way that Haydn's and Mozart's, or Ravel's and Debussy's, music sounds the same, which is to say only from a distance, and not at all when put under the microscope. Reich and Glass share certain structural sensibilities, but each masks these similarities with a timbral palette and emotional ambiance unique to his own inner ear.

To anyone who is familiar only with Steve Reich's earliest pieces, say the electronic modifications of *Come Out* or the monochromatic, maniacal poundings of *Six Pianos*, *Music for 18 Musicians* is going to come as a breath of fresh air. The music is still repetitious, built around a regular, unchanging pulse upon which a series of melodic patterns and rhythmic relationships is layered. But there is a new breadth audible here, obtained through expanded instrumentation (adding to Reich's usual mallet instruments and pianos, winds, strings, and voices) and less reliance on mechanical-sounding activity. Instead of rigidly following the dictates of a predetermined methodology, *Music for 18 Musicians* actually sounds as if there is a human being inside it searching for beautiful textures and melodies. Though the music does follow a strictly structured and labyrinthine series of chords and is precisely delineated through purposely ambiguous rhythmic patterns, Reich has softened the former severity of sound by adding a rainbow-like bouquet of instrumental color. Further, the 11 key modulations on which the music is based come quickly and unexpectedly, hit-and-run fashion, as opposed to the snail's-pace variation of, say, *Drumming*, where each episodic section lasts some 20 minutes.

There are a great many things to admire in *Music for 18 Musicians*: the initial shimmering texture; the intriguing use of bass clarinet (suggesting the composer's familiarity with the music of Eric Dolphy); and the snappy, swinging syncopated reed riffs, reminiscent of those the Count Basie band played to back Lester Young's flights of fantasy. But there is danger here too—the insistently buoyant pulse and overwhelmingly lush texture threaten to lull one into a complacent stupor, which is not at all the state of mind needed to follow the music's intricate circuitry.

Compared to the relaxed evolution and cumulative legato flow of Reich's sonic vegetation, Philip Glass's music is more aggressive, more fragmented, less flexible—partially because of the emphasis on electronic organs, which are loud, thick, and inhuman sounding, and partially because of the way Glass stacks short, jerky motifs up against one another, in building-block fashion. This style of composition, adapted from Glass's study with Indian musicians Ravi Shankar and Alla Rahka, consists of the addition or subtraction of beats from phrases of predetermined length; in conjunction with Glass's extremely close triadic harmonies and unison passages of themes, it contrasts greatly with Reich's polyphonic flowering of phrase. The weight of these repetitious rhythmic riffs and varying accents is similar in effect to Stravinsky's *Le Sacre du Printemps*, and every bit as engaging.

While Glass's music for *Einstein on the Beach* picks up where his previous works *Music with Changing Parts* and *Music in 12 Parts* leave off, there is an added sense of theater to be considered. *Einstein on the Beach* is actually an opera, though it would never be recognized as such by Puccini lovers; it was performed for two sold-out nights at the Metropolitan Opera House. The complete work contains solo vocalists and chorus (though their texts limit them to singing the notes of the scale and counting the beats out loud); three narrators (who recite passages of a Gertrude Stein-like design having to do with trains, the breezes necessary to sail boats, a paean to Paris as a tourist delight, and a brief description of a love affair); dancers; actors; and a solo violin (played on this record by the virtuoso Paul Zukofsky) which takes the otherwise mute role of Einstein. Evidently there is no sung story line or comprehensible plot in the music, so one must assume that the "meaning" of the music is explained through the scenery, dance, and actors' activity—all of which, naturally, are impossible to experience on records. Thus Robert Wilson's entire contribution to the opera, his abstractly manipulative mise-en-scène, is lost except for a few frustratingly evocative photographs in the accompanying booklet. In effect, this recording is little more than a sound track, and we only can deduce a semblance of the work's drama when the music is at its most programmatic—when, for example, Glass's churning rhythmic motifs imitate a speeding train, or when the soothing, church-organ chords and chanting chorus create the dreamlike trial scenes or whenever the violinist appears; since we know Einstein played the violin to relax, we tend to think of him whenever we hear its simplistic scalar passages.

The major problem with *Einstein on the Beach* is that without a plot to follow, Glass's music fails to reveal any theatrical continuity or structural development. Over the opera's three-hour length, we hear a sequence of 20-minute episodes that vary attractively in texture, mood, and phrasing, but they need not be heard straight through from beginning to end. When one does listen from start to finish, one realizes that the parade of fragmented motifs heard over such a length of time tends to alter one's perception of the music's contours and details; but it's just as easy and possibly much more enjoyable to dip into *Einstein* a little at a time and concentrate on individual pieces, such as the sizzling momentum of the prison scene, or the rigorous and rambunctious choral interlude entitled "Knee 3."

Both the Reich and Glass recordings are performed by their composers' regular working ensembles, and the familiarity and nearly superhuman concentration and virtuosity they bring to these difficult and rewarding scores is truly phenomenal. ECM has captured the mosaic intricacies of *Music for 18 Musicians* in a warm, lucid, vibrant ambiance, and Tomato Records has done no less for the cumulative power and iridescence of *Einstein on the Beach*.

Not-So-New Waves (1980)

A "New Wave" nightclub might seem to be an incongruous site in which to encounter both Chicago's foremost experimental duo and a New York pioneer in pulse, pattern, or whatever-you-want-to-call-it music. But don't forget . . . Philip Glass, in addition to producing an album by the New Wave band Polyrock, numbers Brian Eno, David Bowie, and an amazingly large cross section of jazz, classical, and rock listeners among his fans.

Glass's music has become surprisingly popular over the last few years, considering it isn't the sort of thing you're apt to hear on Top 40 radio. It could be called hypnotic, since its relentless repetition lulls the listener into a disarming sense of false familiarity, and yet the propulsively aggressive attack and mercilessly loud volume, thick texture, and static harmonies are not really conducive to meditation. If you wanted to, you could boogie to this music; the beat is always evident and the sound is completely enveloping—pea-soup dense yet airy, like six layers of burlap. The Glass Ensemble consists of two organists (Glass and Michael Riesman, who together are Farfisa's most visible advertisement since the Dave Clark Five and ? & the Mysterians), three reed players, and one vocalist who doesn't sing lyrics but abstract sounds and notes ("Do, re, mi . . . "). They're balanced by one ever-present sound technician.

Experienced in person, their sound comes at you in waves: rolling and cresting, breaking and submerging, defying you to ignore the music's simplicity, exuberance, and power.

The music is built from economical means, but don't let that fool you. Glass uses extremely simple chords . . . arpeggiated and ornamented with passing notes, but layered and repeated so cunningly that Glass suggests locomotive forward movement without actually developing any of this material, creates periods of tension and relaxation by teasing the listener with the motion of those few chords toward a tonic resolution. The arpeggiated chords result in riffs as insistent as Count Basie's million-dollar horn section's, usually syncopated and soaring over feverish bass lines that bubble in ways wicked and sassy and almost inhuman. The intensity of the music makes severe demands on the performers, requiring incredible stamina, concentration, and dexterity (Riesman and Glass both seem to have left hands that anyone but Fats Waller would envy).

Glass has been writing and performing music of this nature for years now, and the only concession he's made to his new-found popularity is to shorten the length of his exhilarating, occasionally exasperating pieces. *Music with Changing Parts*, for example, is an older score that lasts some two hours without pause. The first three pieces Glass performed on this evening, however, were from his score for the film *North Star*, and none of them exceeded seven minutes in length. All the familiar Glass trademarks were there, but they seemed to have been abbreviated and cut off before the listener could find his place in the intense action and follow the music's devious circuitry. The next two pieces found the perfect length, however—approximately 20 minutes—short enough not to become physically exhausting but long enough to allow us to revel in the meticulously controlled flux. *Dance no. 3* was a particular achievement. Initiated at a gallop, with exquisitely brief seconds where the organs dropped out leaving horn chords hanging in the air, the scalar patterns prompted a number of echoes of bizarrely divergent musics I've heard elsewhere—incandescent flashes of Van Morrison's "Gloria," Fauré's *Requiem*, some salsa and polka rhythms in the horns, and even, I swear, "Over the Rainbow." I don't know if this was the result of temporary insanity or ecstatic satori, but Philip Glass's music can do that to you.

LISTENING TO GLASS (1974)

JOHN HOWELL

In writing about any fully realized art, "significance" often threatens to undercut the complexity of the actual experience. Performances are particularly susceptible to this treatment, since the event itself exists for only a brief time. Comments by performers, scripts, and outlines are evidential forms which emphasize a largely verbal and always fragmentary aspect of the whole. The most clearly didactic statements, methods, and moments tend to be singled out and developed to confirm the meaning or "importance" of a work. These approaches eventually risk a distortion of original context and intentions in the name of some inclusive theoretics. On the other hand, simple documentation of a performance delivers an equally imperfect replica. Even "mere" description involves a dimension of selective choice by the writer which qualifies it as only another version.

The possibility does exist for a critical interface, one which allows channels of reflective thought and external fact to inform each other in a continuous exchange. Insights depend on a constant adjustment between the work's integrity and the inevitable desire to locate its consequences. This writing about performance would be a reasonable facsimile of a substantive yet absent subject.

*   *   *

Phil Glass's recently completed *Music in 12 Parts*, like any original art, subverts limiting rhetoric. The work and his presentation allude to singular positions in music and performance modes but they derive from varied concerns that evade reductive categorization. And while no descriptive comments could be more lucid or to the point than those Glass provides in program notes, the phrases about specific techniques and musical bases do not seem to indicate the full implications of the piece. For example, the notated score contains few clues to the music's considerable sensuality.

These observations raise questions about the need for any critical writing; at the same time, they present occasions for an exploratory analysis. That *Music in 12 Parts* is a radical extension of ideas which have occupied Glass since 1968 offers a further opening for this kind of critique.

In terms of fundamental structure, the principal device remains additive process ("alteration of a melodic figure after a number of repetitions by adding or subtracting one or a group of related notes"). These figures are organized around principles of cyclic structures that create a densely textured music; this "richness" derives from a complex series of shifting relationships between note choices, patterns, and rhythms.

Written over a period of three years (1971–74), *Music in 12 Parts* demonstrates a large vocabulary within the tight limits of this basic process. All of Glass's previous music exhibits a homogenous structure; this piece is divided into distinct "parts." Generally speaking, these Parts divide into three sections of concerns, and 10-12 (ornamentation). Although internally consistent, each Part is sharply differentiated from the others by a variety of techniques. The broad parameters of these concerns result in a pluralistic framework, one which allows for structural elaboration within a particular method.

But this method conveys only an indirect unity throughout the 12 Parts—no superficial uniformity is really attempted. The Parts show no "narrative" connections to each other, they are simply adjacent. Transitions between them consist of "abrupt modulations" or complete breaks. A strict juxtaposition makes for a clear reading of the unique procedures which characterize individual parts; contrasts between textures which result from different concerns are heightened.

Texture is the quality of *Music in 12 Parts* most resistant to definition. Glass has said that note choices give emotional color. The note-on-note relationship and rhythmic movement provide what might be called "feeling" aspects to the piece. The diversity of structural methods used in this work present several textures from various combinations of density, melody, and movement. Occasionally, specific intentions seem apparent, including, for the first time in Glass's music, a definite humor.

However, the Parts do not "mean" in any adjectival sense. These colorations depend on the composer's musical sensibility and the listener's reception of it. Glass's "expression" is ultimately the entire phenomena of the music.

Listening to Glass (1974)

In *Music in 12 Parts* this dimension resides in an emphatic but also elusive interaction. The effect of the music is clearly more than that of a demonstration of certain techniques. Neither does it seem merely a style of inducing "hypnotic" states. The structures which produce such evocative textures use form as a process that creates its own meanings as it develops. Here form serves as a method for discovering new notions of musical content.

A proper appraisal depends on recognizing the music's proposals for unique modes of listening. Its "essence" lies in a specified style of perception in performance.

Glass's presentation defines the particular locus. The placement of speakers around and outside the grouping of both musicians and audience puts everyone at the center of the sound. Released throughout the space rather than projected into it, the music fills its situation with a pervasive aural mix. Presence derives from an activation of the entire performance area, including the audience as a resonant element of that sound.

This location is developed by playing *Music in 12 Parts* at a very high volume. The low distortion quality of the amplification system eliminates most unintended sounds. "Clean" volume enhances the sensual density of the music to allow psycho-acoustical effects (tones inherent in the music, but not written) to emerge. Such tones are clearly heard but remain intangible products of musical and auditory processes.

The resulting presence denotes a kind of relation that does not traditionally exist between performers and audience. As performed, the music draws its "reality" from an interaction with the physical space occupied by the listener, who is thus literally put *in* the music. That is to say, the music proposes a state of "active listening" for its completion—in a very basic way, the listener participates in the final invention of the work.

*   *   *

Like all of Glass's previous work, *Music in 12 Parts* exhibits this kind of presence as a crucial aspect in perceiving the music. However, a shift in emphasis occurs throughout this piece, from a primary focus on sound qualities to a concern with the musical scale or time of their duration. The composition is a lengthy cycle of music; the average time of each Part is around twenty minutes, comprising a total music of some four hours.

Such an ambitious scale provides the frame for the "extended time sense" Glass uses.

Time within the Parts is a "non-narrative" temporality. Glass's structures create sequences which negate a past and prevent a future. The music simply proceeds from moment to moment, its continuity supported by the progression of small but integral units, not by any musical flow of statement and elaboration. A steady eight-note beat makes for a musical time which does not decay or accelerate—it is a perpetual "present."

This constant present tense, combined with essentially cyclic frameworks, subverts typical conceptions of time as a continuum with definite starts and projected endings. Parts do not begin or end in the common understanding of those terms. The stunning silence that occurs at the finish of the music is a function of immersion in this present.

The Parts follow each other as units of "presence" which *almost* replace each other; it is the sheer accumulation of such musical experience that serves as the unifying element to support sustained perception. The listener can then exercise another mode of listening to perceive the entire work as an extended "pure medium of sound."

Clearly, *Music in 12 Parts* requires its own conditions at basic perceptual levels. These displacements of aural and temporal sense have concrete yet finally indefinable effects. What they might "mean" can only refer the listener to the subjective experience of the music.

MUSIC IN 12 PARTS (1993)

TIM PAGE

Music in 12 Parts, written by Philip Glass between 1971 and 1974, is a conscious, encyclopedic compendium of some techniques of repetition the composer had been evolving since the mid-1960s. It holds an important place in Glass's repertory—not only from a historical vantage point (as the longest and most ambitious concert piece for the Philip Glass Ensemble) but from a purely aesthetic standard as well, because *Music in 12 Parts* is both a massive theoretical exercise and a deeply engrossing work of art.

Glass wrote Part I in early 1971. "The first movement was originally intended to stand on its own and the '12 Parts' in the title referred to 12 lines of counterpoint in the score," he explained in 1993. "I called it *Music in 12 Parts* because the keyboards played six lines, there were three wind players involved, and I had originally planned to augment the ensemble to bring in three more lines, for a total of 12. I played it for a friend of mine and, when it was through, she said, 'That's very beautiful; what are the other 11 parts going to be like?' And I thought that was an interesting misunderstanding and decided to take it as a challenge and go ahead and compose 11 more parts."

By this point, some new music for the Philip Glass Ensemble was needed, and needed badly. *Music with Changing Parts* (1970) had proven the epical possibilities of Glass's new musical language and the very early pieces were slowly being phased out of the repertory. Some of these—titles such as *How Now, 600 Lines,* and *Music in 8 Parts*—are tantalizingly obscure, known only to the most fervent and superannuated Glassian, having been out of the repertory for more than 20 years. Other early pieces—*Two Pages for Piano and Organ*, *Music in Contrary Motion*, *Music in Fifths*, and *Music in Similar Motion*—are available on a Nonesuch reissue.

The Glass Ensemble, after a rather freewheeling beginning during which visiting composers and players would simply drop by and join in rehearsals and performances, had now been formalized and had begun to tour. (By the early 80s, it would be playing almost 100 concerts every year.)

"When I started the first Philip Glass Ensemble in 1968, it was easy to find people to rehearse with me every Thursday night because nobody had anything else to do anyway," Glass recalled. "But I wanted to make this a professional organization. When you are creating a new musical language, you need a new technical way of playing it and to develop this, I needed to have a consistent ensemble."

"My strategy was to play enough concerts every year that I could pay the musicians 20 times a year and provide them with unemployment and health benefits," he continued. "To organize our first tour, I sent out something like 120 letters and got six responses. We played in Tacoma, St. Louis, Minneapolis, and a few other places. We loaded our van, unloaded it, played the concert, loaded up the van again and drove on. Presenters put us up in their homes. But, by the mid-70s, we were starting to establish ourselves."

Indeed, by the time of *Music in 12 Parts*, the Glass Ensemble had solidified into an aggregate of three electronic keyboards (Farfisa organs in the early years), wind instruments and voice, amplified and fed through a mixer by Kurt Munkacsi, who was considered in every way a full member of the group.

In the past, Glass vociferously objected to being called a "minimalist" composer. ("That word should be stamped out!" he said in a 1978 interview.) He now grudgingly accepts the term—with the distinction that it only applies to his earliest pieces, those up to and including *Music in 12 Parts*.

Glass prefers to speak of himself as a composer of "music with repetitive structures." Much of his mature music is based on the extended repetition of brief, elegant melodic fragments that weave in and out of an aural tapestry. Listening to a piece like *Music in 12 Parts* has been compared to watching a challenging modern painting that initially appears static but seems to metamorphose slowly as one concentrates. A listener quickly learns not to expect Western musical events—sforzandos, sudden diminuendos—in such a composition. Instead, one is immersed in a sort of sonic weather that twists, turns, surrounds, develops.

Music in 12 Parts (1993)

The world premiere of *Music in 12 Parts* took place at New York's Town Hall in 1974 and lasted more than four hours (there were further New York performances in 1981 and 1990). The first eight parts were taped by the Glass Ensemble in 1974 and 1975; this writer presented their radio premiere in 1978 on Columbia University's WKCR-FM. Parts I and II were briefly issued on LP 1975, on the Caroline label, but the entire work (most of it recorded in the mid '70s) was not available on disc until 1989. And so this new interpretation represents not only a radical improvement in electronic technology but the accretion of 20 years thought and experience playing *Music in 12 Parts* as well.

There are many beauties in the score, but Part I—the original *Music in 12 Parts,* from which the other eleven sprung—remains some of the most soulful music Glass ever wrote. And yet it is also one of his most determinedly reductive compositions: at any place in the music, reading vertically in the score, one will find both a C sharp and an F sharp being played somewhere in the instrumentation. Through skillful contrapuntal weaving, Glass creates what is, paradoxically, a drone that is not a drone—an active, abundant, richly fertile stasis.

Part I leads directly to Part II, which introduces a different key, a faster tempo, greater rhythmic and melodic variety and the human voice (the soprano, as was customary in early Glass works, sings only solfège syllables). Andrew Porter, writing about *Music in 12 Parts* in 1978 for *The New Yorker,* described these transitions well: "A new sound and a new chord suddenly break in, with an effect as if one wall of a room had suddenly disappeared, to reveal a completely new view."

Part III, one of the few movements that is entirely self-contained, is a gurgling study in fourths, and the shortest, at 15 minutes, of the 12 parts. Part IV is extraordinary: after a brief introduction, it becomes a lengthy examination of a single, unsettled chord that sweats, strains and ultimately screams for resolution until the musicians suddenly break into the joyous, rushing catharsis of Part V.

Part VI is another example of how Glass can take what initially seems a standard chord progression and gradually build considerable interest on the part of his audience as he presents it to us, again and again, from different rhythmical perspectives. Part VII clearly derives from *Music in Similar Motion* (1969) which is, in 1993, the oldest piece in the ensemble's active repertory. But the development is much more swift than that of the earlier work and it is infinitely more virtuosic (the soprano, in particular, must do her best to avoid tongue-twisting and sibilance in the exposed, rapid-fire melismatic passages). And the close of Part VIII prefigures the "Train" scene in *Einstein on the Beach,* with its irresistible forward motion and sheer, "boy-with-a-gadget," fascination with a systematic augmentation and contraction of the soprano line. (For whatever it's worth, Glass used to refer to those occasions when the ensemble got lost in the middle of a piece as "train wrecks.")

"I had a specific didactic purpose in mind when I set to work on *12 Parts*," Glass said in 1990. "I wanted to crystallize in one piece all the ideas of rhythmic structure that I had been working on since 1965. By the time I got to Part VIII, I'd pretty much finished what I'd started out to do. And so the last movements were different. Parts IX and X were really about ornamentation." Part IX, after a lithe, bouncing, broken-chord introduction, becomes a study in chromatic unison while Part X begins with a blaring, aggressively reiterated figure in the winds that is eventually softened—cushioned—by the addition of complementary figures in the bass.

Parts I–X had each been based on stable, unchanging harmonic roots that had remained constant throughout the movement. Part XI is just as rigorous in its application of an antithetical approach: the harmony changes with every new figure. In Part XI, which is essentially an aria for soprano and ensemble, there is more harmonic motion than in all of the mature works Glass had composed in the previous ten years put together; here, once again, is a clear prefiguration of what is to come in *Einstein on the Beach*.

Music in 12 Parts ends with a quodlibet—a "musical joke"—that will be especially amusing to those who remember the musical politics of the 60s and 70s. Like most young composers of the time, Glass was trained to write 12-tone music; unlike most of them, he rejected the movement entirely. And yet, in the bass line of Part XII, toward the end, the careful listener will discern a 12-tone row, underpinning this riot of tonal, steadily rhythmic, gleeful repetition—underpinning, in other words, all the things that textbook 12-toners shunned.

"It was a way of making fun not only of other people but also of myself," Glass said in 1993. "I had broken the rules of modernism and so I thought it was time to break some of my own rules. And this I did, with the shifts of harmony in Part XI and then in Part XII, where, for the first and only time in my mature music, I actually threw in a 12-tone row. This was the end of minimalism for me. I had worked for eight or nine years creating a system, and now I'd written through it and come out the other end. My next piece was called *Another Look at Harmony* and that's just what it was. I'd taken everything out with my early works and it was now time to decide just what I wanted to put back in—a process that would occupy me for several years to come."

THE TOURING COMPOSER AS KEYBOARDIST (1980)

ALLAN KOZINN

The years of struggle are finally paying off for composer Philip Glass. His recent four-record set of music from *Einstein on the Beach*, the five-hour opera on which he collaborated with avant-garde theater wizard Robert Wilson, garnered rave reviews from the major rock, jazz, and classical music publications. The opera itself, when it was presented at the Metropolitan Opera House in 1976, attracted a great deal of critical praise and won Glass and Wilson an Obie award—although it left them in a financial hole $120,000 deep.

In May, 1979, the world premiere of a cycle of songs by various composers, including Glass, commissioned by Chicago classical music station WFMT, was taped, and has since been syndicated nationally via that station's new satellite system. Largely ignored by the classical music establishment through much of his career, Glass has made a couple of Carnegie Hall appearances in the last two years. He's had a string of commissions from the Netherlands, including a solo organ work for the tenth anniversary of the Doelen Hall organ in Rotterdam, and his current magnum opus, an opera called *Satyagraha* based on the life of Mahatma Gandhi, which is to be premiered by the Netherlands Opera in 1980. And while Glass maintains the sole right to perform his music, reports had it that progressive rock guitarist Mike Oldfield (*Tubular Bells*, etc.) spent part of his summer last year in the recording studio cooking up a disco version of one of the pieces from Glass's *North Star* set, a project that Glass has apparently made no move to oppose.

Suddenly, it seems that Glass and the idiom that he, along with Steve Reich, Terry Riley, and La Monte Young, founded in the late 1960s—the so-called minimalist, repetitive, or hypnotic school—are very much in vogue. Why all this attention lately?

"Do you think it could be just 12 years of good, hard work?" he suggests. "I think that's a big part of it, but also, there has been a feedback from the popular music world. I used to tour Europe extensively in 1970, 1971, and I had an influence on a lot of people who were just kids then and who were starting their own bands. Today, when people listen to popular music on which I've had an influence—Kraftwerk, Bowie, the list goes on and on—my music not only becomes more accessible to them, but they begin to see me as a classical counterpart to, say, the Who.

"Yet, I've always thought of my music as concert music. I've never tried to do popular music, and I've never tried to popularize the music I do. Perhaps the seriousness with which I have always taken my work has had a slowing effect on its acceptance. But at least partly as a result of the feed-in and feedback with pop music, my work has gone from being obscure and abstract to being an idiom which is fairly current."

Glass's recent success at the age of 43 seems to have changed neither his basic lifestyle nor his compositional language, although he seems to be branching out somewhat from his five-player/one-sound-technician band format to works like the new opera, which calls for a full orchestra. In New York compositional circles, Glass and his experimental colleagues are referred to as "downtown composers," a reference to the fact that, with the exception of an occasional foray north to Carnegie Hall, most of their compositional and performance activity is centered in the lower Manhattan district called SoHo. In SoHo, the conventions of concert-giving—things like tails and ties, organized seating, and the physical/psychological separation of the audience and the performer—do not apply.

Yet Philip Glass's background is more formal than that of many of his "downtown" colleagues. Something of a prodigy, he enrolled at the Peabody Conservatory, where he studied flute, at age 8, and at the University of Chicago at 14. Later on, he went to Juilliard, where he majored in composition. Like most composition majors of the late '50s and early '60s, Glass turned out piece after piece of atonality, a musical language he now regards as too theoretical and not really communicative. Nevertheless, his works struck a responsive chord within the Juilliard faculty, and he began winning prizes, getting grants, and publishing his music in his early twenties.

After completing his studies at Juilliard, he won a Fulbright fellowship that allowed him to travel to Paris to study with Nadia Boulanger. Boulanger, he says, "was the best teacher I had. She was thorough and conscientious, and had us study composition by studying only Bach and Mozart. She rarely looked at new works. I don't teach, myself; I just don't find it a convenient situation. But if I did, I might work the way she did: there would be lots of counterpoint, harmonic analysis, and very hard work. It would be very disappointing for people who want to learn the secrets of my music—the techniques of additive process, cyclic rhythm, amplification. Those things can only be learned by working with them.

"When I was at Juilliard," he continues, "I was an 'A' student, and so I was rewarded: I had grants, then, and I was able to live on those for about five years after I graduated. Then, when I was about 30, I began to write music in the manner that I'm writing now, so those money sources dried up. My music was not the logical continuation of Western concert music. The logical continuation is the twelve-tone school, the school of extreme serialization of all aspects of composition. And because I stopped doing what I was supposed to be doing, the music establishment of ten years ago became very upset, and so I was punished. How? By not being asked to play at music schools, for instance. It wasn't until 1978 that I had my first music school invitation, and that was from Harvard. But it didn't really matter, because if the music departments at some of the major schools wouldn't have me, I'd play there as a guest of the art department. Other punishment, of course, was a denial of the kinds of grants that are given to so-called serious composers."

Among the forces behind Glass's defection from the serialist camp was his discovery of Eastern music. He first came into contact with it while vacationing in Africa, and his interest was further whetted when, in 1967, he collaborated with Ravi Shankar on a film score. After further investigating Eastern techniques, he decided to work in an idiom in which structure, as such, was a product of melodic and harmonic evolution, rather than the other way around. He disowned his old published works ("I could," he says today, "in all fairness say that those were written by another person. They were errors of my youth.") and began writing pieces constructed of simple melodic ideas which would slowly unfold into long, often rhythmically complicated structures. To have the music performed, he formed his own ensemble using fairly unconventional instruments. A Farfisa organ, for instance, has become a trademark of the Glass sound.

"When I started my ensemble, my first players were Jon Gibson and Dickie Landry, on winds, and two keyboard players: Arthur Murphy, who was a wonderful keyboard player, and Steve Reich, who was an *erzatz* keyboard player—really more of a percussionist. We used to practice in Arthur's loft because he had a piano. So I needed a portable keyboard to use at rehearsals, and to tell you the truth, I opened the *Buy Lines*, and answered an ad placed by someone up in Queens who had a club basement with knotty pine walls, and underneath the stairwell was a Farfisa. I still have that original one. Since then, I've found three more—all in Queens, in knotty pine club basements, under stairwells. They all cost about $150. Some years later, I brought them to Italy and had them refurbished at the factory in Alcona. Nothing special was done at the time, although my engineer, Kurt Munkacsi, rebalanced the lines on them so that they mix more easily with other instruments. They also sound a little cleaner, although that high whining sound that is special to the Farfisa is still there, especially when you have two or three of them.

"When I started using Farfisas, everyone said to me, 'Why are you using that instrument? It sounds so lousy!' But I *like* that sound; it's a very nasty, penetrating, sharp sound. Of course, it's important to find the right speakers to put them through. We started with Altec and did some experimenting with Bose, but we didn't like them. We eventually settled with JB Lansings. We've also done some experimentation with microphones for the wind players, but they aren't as important to me as the sound of the Farfisas."

Among the other keyboards Glass uses are a Yamaha double keyboard organ ("I forget the number. It has a pedal—I've lately taken to writing myself pedal parts.") and an EMI electric piano. Recently, he has acquired an ARP Explorer, which his band's other keyboard player, Michael Riesman, uses, according to Glass, as a bass extension.

"I've really never used a synthesizer as a synthesizer," Glass admits. "I did take lessons for a while, on the Buchla synthesizer, which I think was a good choice. However, I got to a point in my lessons where I was making a piece and I ran into trouble. So I began talking to my teacher—Suzanne Ciani, it was—about various possibilities, and I found that to get a particular effect I would have to get in touch with Donald Buchla, in California, who she said might be able to build the piece of equipment I needed in three months. It occurred to me then that the limitations of the synthesizer were not the limitations of my imagination, but of Buchla's ability to project what I might want to do."

Of course, the same thing can be said about the piano or the organ.

"Perhaps so," Glass agrees, "and perhaps I'm being a bit unfair. I did, by the way, meet Don Buchla some years after I stopped learning the instrument, and I was impressed with his own work. You see, Buchla is a composer who built a synthesizer around *his* needs. What I do now is just use the synthesizer the same way I would use a piano, as just another keyboard. And what I've done over the years is surround myself with different keyboards so that I have all the flexibility I need."

Glass began using amplification partly because the Farfisas required it, but also because amplification gave him a way of controlling the balance of several keyboards playing at once. He found, of course, that once he amplified the keyboards he also had to amplify the winds, opening the door to microphones, mixing boards, and speakers, all controlled by Kurt Munkacsi, who, as the engineer, is an integral member of the ensemble.

"What I found happening when we amplified," Glass explains, "was that we were getting psychoacoustical effects—overtones and things that would happen as a result of repetitive structures played rapidly at high volume. You actually hear sounds that nobody is playing, a shiny top to the music. [Composers] Charlemagne Palestine and La Monte Young have done some wonderful experiments along these lines with acoustic pianos, but you don't really hear the overtones the way you do when the instruments are amplified.

"Ultimately, I found that the band, after playing together seven or eight years, and doing concert after concert, had developed a sound and an identity of its own. And that was largely because Kurt had developed a sound system specific to the needs of this band. We had invested thirty to forty thousand dollars on that system over that eight-year period, and when we travel we take 27 cases that come in at something over a ton. We bring everything including power transformers for when we're in Europe. If there's one thing we learned from being on the road all those years, it is that if you bring everything with you, there's a *chance* of uniformity of quality from concert to concert. The few times we've rented equipment, it's been near disaster."

At the moment, Glass and his ensemble have exclusive rights to the music they play, and Glass steadfastly refuses to make his scores available to other performing groups—except, of course, in the case of works that demand larger forces.

"I don't allow others to play my works for financial reasons," he explains. "Even though I am the sole publisher of the music, the fact is that I can make a better living as the sole performer of it as well. If, for example, I wanted to put together a tour of New Zealand—and I would like to play there—and there was a band similar to mine that played my music, then why would they have to bring me and my whole ensemble and our 27 cases over?"

It was suggested that there is some value to having the composer present, and that his argument was akin to saying that since the Beatlemania companies now put on mock-Beatles performances, the real Beatles would not find a waiting audience if they decided to regroup.

"Well," Glass concedes, "all that may be changing now that more people are paying attention to us. But all that was certainly true for the last ten years. And everyone knows that composers make precious little from the rental of their scores. And of course, having played this music together for so long, we can have a much greater impact than a group that just picks it up and plays from the music. I have been considering making available works that the band no longer plays on tour. My opera, naturally, will be published and will be available to any opera company that wants to do it. Of course, it will have to be a company that has 60 or 70 good musicians and a chorus of 40—it's not the kind of thing you'll be able to rustle up that easily; it's a multi-hundred-thousand-dollar project to present that work. The problem in the past, though, was that I was making my living as a performer more than as a composer. If I was a teacher and had a guaranteed $25,000 a year, I might not have worried about it quite so much."

Even if the music does eventually become available, though, don't let the minimalist label or the fact that Glass is a flutist rather than a keyboard player by training fool you. He has developed his own kind of keyboard technique, and the works he plays are not particularly easy.

"My keyboard technique," he says, "is built around my music. I have played other people's music, too, although very rarely. What I have done in composing for the keyboard is to take advantage of my own idiosyncracies. Things that fit my hands well are things that tend to come up frequently in my writing. For me, practicing is sheer drudgery, and I won't do it unless I have to prepare for a concert. But Michael Riesman, who plays keyboards in the group, has developed special exercises of his own, and another player, George Adoniadis, who is on the *Einstein* album, tells me that Hanon and Dohnányi exercises help. I've been working on the Dohnányi book myself.

"The difficulties in my music are in the metrics. You have to be able to play in five in one hand and four in the other. Or, what regularly happens in my music is that I'll set up a recurring meter of three in one hand and a cycle of meters of three in one hand and a cycle of meters in the other, so that against the three you'll have nine, eight, six, five, four, three, four, five, six, eight, nine, and twelve, all worked out so that they fit the basic cycle of three, but nevertheless require a good rhythmic feeling to carry them off.

"What I've found, though, is that like with any other kind of practicing, if you start off slowly and gradually build up speed, you'll be able to do it. The thing is, the music must be played with a musical feeling, a feeling of naturalness, or else it won't work. Your hand has to be pretty strong, and your fingers have to be independent. You need strength simply because the pieces are so long. It's not uncommon for us to play at rapid-fire tempo for an hour and a half, so our strength, in the band, is a question of sheer endurance. And the independence of parts has to do with being able to feel all the different meters together. Remember, this is basically a chamber group, even though it looks different and it's amplified. The compositional thinking is, in certain ways, the same as you find in chamber works, with lots of interweaving parts integrated into the whole musical sound."

If there can be said to be a good side about being an obscure composer, it must be that you can develop freely without any thought about whether your growing audience will or will not accept changes in your style as you continue along the creative path. Under the pressure of success, one can become forced either to stagnate and keep giving audiences what they've liked in the past, grow more conservative under the temptation to make the audience an even larger one, or, as Glass has done, just continue along as if his recent recognition and near canonization never happened.

"Part of the reason I find my music so hard to teach," says Glass, "is that I'm still discovering it myself. And one of the reasons I'm still discovering it is that I've never stopped to teach it. I wonder whether, had I been forced to codify my music for students or other people, that would have slowed the process of change. It is, after all, the process of change in my music that keeps me writing. Every piece presents itself to me as something I haven't done before. When I find I'm repeating myself, I invariably stop. That's not to say that the pieces don't resemble each other, but in any piece there will be some feature that will not be in any other piece. I can't get interested in doing pieces that are modeled after other pieces. So, to avoid that, I have adopted a method of composing by which my writing is a process of solving problems that I have not solved before. This isn't generally apparent. Nor does it need to be. The music makes the impact it does for *other* reasons, not for the compositional processes involved. I don't care whether someone understands how the music is constructed. I'd much prefer that they just really *like* it. That's why the response of the general audience is so meaningful for me. I don't need an elitist audience to be satisfied that I'm going about it in the right way."

PHILIP GLASS (1979)

RICHARD KOSTELANETZ

Back in 1971, Philip Glass realized that his music was too advanced for commercial record companies; so rather than restrict the performance of it to increasingly popular chamber concerts, he joined a sympathetic art dealer in founding a personal record label named *Chatham Square*, after the principal intersection in New York City's Chinatown. The first record issued by Chatham Square Productions, Inc., was Glass's own *Music with Changing Parts* (1970), which soon became an underground classic that graced the collections of everyone interested in advanced American art and music.

The year that *Music with Changing Parts* was originally written, Glass was moving out of one compositional phase and into another. His initial music of distinction—a sequence of pieces that included *Strung Out* (1967), *Music in Similar Motion* (1969), *Music in Contrary Motion* (1969), *Music in Fifths* (1969)—was monophonic. These compositions have lines of individual notes, with neither harmonies nor counterpoint, conceptually resembling Gregorian chant. These pieces are tonal without offering melodies; they are pleasant and accessible without being seductive.

Nonetheless, such music seemed unacceptably radical at the time, as it avoided the principal issues that nearly all contemporary composers discussed through the sixties—issues such as chance and control, serialism and atonality, improvisation and spontaneity. Indeed, given how different these works were, it is scarcely surprising that they were mostly performed not in concert halls or in the music conservatories but in art galleries and in art museums and sometimes in churches.

Initially, the audience for Glass's music consisted largely of people connected to the New York avant-garde art world. Later, especially in Europe, his audience would include pop musicians like David Bowie and Brian Eno and, still later, music students. To this day, American music conservatories and university music departments regard Glass as an errant ex-student, and only recently have some of the latter come to sponsor his concerts. "Even then," he mused recently, "the students come, while the professors stay away." Every step of his career, Glass won his own audience of people not prejudiced by fashionable ideas of what should or should not be thought interesting in contemporary music. By now, he has the kind of loyal, expanding following that every independent artist envies.

With *Music with Changing Parts* Glass introduced music that moved progressively from monophony, in its opening moments, to a greater polyphonic complexity and then, toward its end, into the kinds of modulations that would inform his next major work, *Music in 12 Parts* (1974), an exhaustive encyclopedic piece that epitomizes Glass's music in much the same way that *The Well-Tempered Clavier* (1744) epitomizes J. S. Bach. Glass also remembers that *Music with Changing Parts* was the first piece of his that was long and weighty enough to fill an entire concert program too; it was the first ever to receive a favorable review—from Alan Rich in the *New York* magazine.

Music with Changing Parts was also the first Glass to be recorded, and through that process the composer learned about the special advantages of audiotape mastering. "I began to see that it was a completely different medium from a live concert," he says. "The record doesn't sound like what we were playing. It's a sixteen-track recording, which means that at the end of *Changing Parts* we're listening to eight flutes, five organs, two voices and a piccolo. We have on the record something I can never play in public with an ensemble of six or seven musicians. So I decided to exploit the new medium and do things that I couldn't have done before. I wrote some new parts that I overdubbed. The tapings took about twenty hours, but three of us spent over two hundred hours mixing. That was the most crucial part, and it took us all winter. When it was finished, I said to a friend, 'Maybe someone can do better, but I can't.'" . . .

The handwritten, photocopied score of *Music with Changing Parts* has eight lines of eighth notes, equally distributed over four staves, two in the treble (G) clef and two in the bass (F) clef. These lines are divided into eighty-eight numbered modules (or "figures" or "phrases") which vary in length from eight to twenty-four eighth notes. Two parallel vertical lines separate each section from its predecessor and successor. At several points above the vertical lines are the letters *CF*, which indicate that at these points the figures (or parts) change drastically. There are no other markings on the score—nothing about interpretation, nothing about instrumentation, not even any indication about how long each section or the entire piece might be.

"It is an open score," Glass explains, reminding us of Bach's *Art of the Fugue*; "I assign the parts." At the beginning of a performance, the group customarily plays only one and then two of the six lines; but as more of the scored lines are incorporated into the playing, the musical texture gets thicker. While the keyboards are playing the notated lines, the horns and the singer either duplicate the keyboards' riffs or improvise harmonically appropriate sustained tones for as long as possible. (That accounts for the long unwavering notes that are almost continually audible.)

Everyone *repeats* his part until Glass as the organist-conductor silently nods his head, indicating that the current section must be repeated two more times before everyone goes on to the next notated module, which usually differs only slightly from its predecessor. (The exceptions are, of course, those modules following the *CF* notation.) Since Glass's nods are determined largely by how the piece feels in each performance, *Changing Parts* can vary enormously in total length—from an hour and ten minutes on the record to an hour and forty-five minutes in live performances.

Glass has been known to speak of this early piece as "intentionless music," by which he means that it does not program "a calculated effect. It does not paint a picture." One could also describe it as *pure music*, much like abstract painting is pure, in representing nothing other than musical sound itself, existing primarily as sounds in euphonious combination. This explains why this music is nonrepresentational and nonsymbolic and also why Glass's titles are characteristically more descriptive than evocative.

However, one crucial difference between *Changing Parts* and the earlier monophonic work is that the composer is, as he says, "less interested in the purity of form than in the psychoacoustical experiences that happen while listening to the music. Music is able to create emotional content because of the ways in which the language is built," he continued, rephrasing his idea for emphasis. "Emotional content is built into the language of music. Musical grammar has always been responsive to physiology."

Part of this emotional impact comes from the fact that, in concert, Glass's music is customarily played at high volume, and one member of the ensemble, Kurt Munkacsi, sits in front of the group, facing them, much like the conductor in conventional music. Actually he is "playing" the knobs of his electronic board to ensure that the group's sound is both loud and free of distortion. Glass recommends that his records also be played loudly, or be heard over earphones. "It brings out the psychoacoustical phenomena that are part of the content of the music—overtones, undertones, difference tones. These are things you hear—there is no doubt that you are hearing them—even though they may not actually be played."

In the past decade, Glass has since progressed on to other music—not only *Music in 12 Parts*, but the score for the great contemporary opera, *Einstein on the Beach* (1976), and more recently the music for the opera *Satyagraha* (1980), which is based upon Mahatma Gandhi's early years. His current major project is a third opera, which he regards as completing the trilogy begun with *Einstein*. Just as the titles of his works are now different in kind, so his latest music represents a departure in style. "I'm now more involved," he explained succinctly, "with dramatic music that paints a picture that is overtly theatrical."

A slender, almost wiry man of medium height, with a familiar face and unusually close-cropped hair, Glass presently lives sparely with his young children in the Gramercy area of New York. His living room contains not couches or coffee tables but rugs and a piano, a harpsichord and an electric organ. Most of his composing is done in his stocking feet on that organ, which is connected to the record player's amplifier. His house has remarkably few records, fewer books and even fewer scores. The truth be known, Glass is not particularly interested in contemporary music and hears little of it, aside from rock. "The composers I studied with Boulanger are the people I still think about most—Bach and Mozart."

MINIMALISM: T
(1992)

EDWARD STRICKLAND

By the time the term Minimalism had been (re)introduced in the visual arts in 1965, the best of Minimalist painting had long since been done. By the time the term was affixed to the music, the period of strict Minimalism was long since over and the composers had evolved in distinctly non-Minimal directions. In print the term had first been applied to music—and then not directly but by extension—by Barbara Rose in her 1965 "ABC Art" article, with specific reference only to [La Monte] Young's *Dream Music*, and a nod to the restrained dynamics of Morton Feldman.

Art critic John Perreault's 1968 article on Young also referred in passing to Young's focus on "sounds in isolation or within minimal non-relational sound contexts" [29]. In his negative review of the premiere of *Four Organs*, Donal Henahan wrote, "Mr. Reich is still obsessed with taking his minimal art as far as it can be taken, and without diluting its abstract purity. His music, therefore, is all pattern and no color, which seems unnecessary" [May 9, 1970, 15]. Henahan thus extended Rose's analogy to music other than Young's and did so more specifically than Perreault's relatively casual adjective, though still not in a specifically denominative manner.

When Emily Wasserman interviewed Reich for *Artforum* (May 1972), she first asked him about the relationship between his work and the "Conceptual art" of his friends Michael Snow, Bruce Nauman, William Wiley, Richard Serra, and Sol LeWitt. Reich then discussed analogies between his music and the "process" art of Serra and Snow. When Wasserman asked him about LeWitt, Reich replied, "There is some relationship between my music and any Minimal art" [48] but proceeded to focus on LeWitt's precompositional conceptualism rather than his Minimalism per se.

It is worth remembering that the Whitney "Anti-Illusion" show during which both Reich and Glass first performed uptown was not concerned with Minimalism but with post-Minimal process and conceptual art, as emblematized by Rafael Ferrer's ice melting on leaves at the entrance to the museum. Reich's first major essay/manifesto, entitled "Music as a Gradual Process" and published in the "Anti-Illusion" exhibition catalogue, clearly aligned his music to art going by the same name. The piece opens, "I do not mean the process of composition, but rather pieces of music that are, literally, processes." What distinguished Reich's processes from Serial and Cageian processes was their audibility: "What I'm interested in is a compositional process and a sounding music that are one and the same thing." The conceptual connection is apparent in his statement, "Though I may have the pleasure of discovering musical processes and composing the musical material to run through them, once the process is set up and loaded it runs by itself" [Reich 9–10]. Reich uses the noun "process(es)" no less than twenty-nine times in a seven-hundred-word statement.

Reich has suggested on occasion, followed in print by at least two critics, Dan Warburton and Jonathan Bernard, that Michael Nyman might have coined the actual phrase "Minimal music," while Glass has attributed it to Tom Johnson. Warburton (who prefers the term "solid-state music") writes that "despite persistent efforts to find out, it is still unclear who first coined the term. A BBC interview with Michael Nyman [in autumn 1983 on Radio Three's 'Music in Our Time'] proudly proclaimed Nyman the originator, though he has since refused to commit himself on the matter, understandably not wishing to be the target of the pent-up wrath of many of his fellow composers," [141] even more understandably since he did not originate the term.

As far as I can determine, it was first applied explicitly and directly to the music as a movement or shared style in 1972 by Johnson. In the *Village Voice* (September 7, 1972) Johnson began his article "Changing the meaning of static" with "I've heard people refer to the 'New York Hypnotic School' several times now, and have been trying to figure out if it is a good term or not." As already noted, he had in fact begun his review of Glass at the Spencer Concerts five months earlier by noting, "I like to refer to [this kind of music] as hypnotic music" [April 6, 1972], so Johnson himself is clearly a man of the "people." The odds seem further stacked in favor of the term since "New York Hypnotic School" has already appeared as the underlined super-title of the piece, and indeed Johnson now finds himself "beginning to think it is valid."

The adjective had appeared as early as April 1969 in the review of Terry Riley at the Electric Circus by the distinctly unhypnotized Harold Schonberg, and of the "hypnotic or boring—depending on one's reaction to that sort of thing"—characterization of Glass at the Guggenheim nine months later by the obviously bored Peter [G.] Davis. Johnson balks at including Frederic Rzewski, Philip Corner, and David Behrman under the "Hypnotic School" rubric with Young, Riley, Reich, and Glass, and excludes Gavin Bryars ("it's a little difficult to consider him part of a New York school since he lives in England"). He also omits "a number of other composers writing hypnotic music . . . because they have not yet attracted . . . significant public attention. And there are no doubt many others that I don't know about."

Johnson describes the differences among the four composers, then their "same basic concern, which can be described as flat, plastic, minimal, and hypnotic." "Flat" is applied to their form, "static" to their pitches and rhythms (not their dynamics). "Minimal" is applied to "the very small range of contrasts within their pieces," despite "hundreds or thousands of variations [that] may occur. People frequently try to equate minimal music with minimal painting, but the two are actually quite different, even though the word 'minimal' seems appropriate in both cases. A minimal painter employs only one idea—a straight line, for example. The material itself is minimal. But these composers employ a great many ideas or variations. It is the degree of contrast between them which is minimal." What is uncertain here is whether Johnson is inventing the phrase "minimal music" or repeating it, whether he has heard "people frequently" use the phrase or merely compare the composers with the producers of "minimal art" (e.g., Wasserman or her readers in the four months since her article was published).

In any case, no sooner had Johnson inked the term that was to go down in history than he implicitly dismissed it. The next sentence in his article reads, "'Hypnotic' is probably the best word for this music, because it comes closest to describing the effect that it has on the listener." Had a consensus developed around Johnson, I would be citing him as the critical originator of the term "Hypnotism" generally applied to the leading Hypnotists Young, Riley, Reich, and Glass—which in itself explains why the phrase never caught on and one had to be borrowed, quite belatedly, from the plastic arts.

An equally valid candidate to preserve the analogy with those arts would have been "process[ism/ists]," which unfortunately sacrifices in euphony what it gains in accuracy, at least vis-à-vis Reich (phasing, radical augmentation, systematic hocketing) and Glass (additive/subtractive structure) and some of Riley (the tape and time-lag works, possibly even *In C*) and Young (the frequency tuning, drift studies, etc). "Minimalism" was a more inclusive term insofar as the rest of Young's work and Riley's then-current keyboard improvisations would have proven less amenable to labeling under "process."

As things worked out, they were not subject to it. Nyman, now an established composer in his own right, and one strongly influenced by both Reich and Glass, had begun writing on the two in 1971 for the *Musical Times*. The seventh chapter of his book *Experimental Music: Cage and Beyond* was entitled "Minimal music, determinacy and the new tonality." It was published in England by Studio Vista and in the U.S. by Schirmer in 1974 and as publishing schedules go, probably completed a year or so earlier. (The most recent works of the group discussed directly in the chapter are the 1971 *Drumming* and *Music with Changing Parts*, though at one point he alludes to Reich's work "until 1973" [131]). Nyman writes of "Young's minimal alternatives," "minimal process music" [119], and, less denominatively, the "quite minimal" rules of Riley's scores [125].

John Rockwell had referred casually to "the minimal allure" of Reich's *Clapping Music* in the August 1973 *Musical America* [MA 32] and on May 26, 1974 repeated the adjective in the [*New York*] *Times* in referring to the "minimalist fascination with cool lucidity and sparse understatement" shared by Reich and Glass, and to the latter's hitherto "austerely minimal aesthetic" [21]. In the January 31, 1974 *Village Voice* Johnson referred to Charlemagne Palestine's tape-music as "perhaps the most extreme form of musical minimalism I have yet encountered" [44]. In the June 13 issue he then reviewed the Town Hall performance of *Music in 12 Parts*, noting, "I have already written about . . . the static or minimal or hypnotic style of his [Glass's] music" [55]. None of these terms had been used in his review of the Philip Glass Ensemble at the Kitchen in the March 14 issue, while their performance at Max's Kansas City the previous June 19 had led him to apply his still-favored phrase, "hypnotic music," in the July 5, 1973 *Voice*.

Johnson, Rockwell, and Nyman's use of the word—seven years or more after Rose's, remarkably—did not cause either a terminological or musical revolution largely because the music itself had yet to attain mainstream acceptance as classical music, despite greater "respectability" along with wider exposure.

As Young had earlier won an unlikely place in *Vogue*, Reich made its English edition in February 1972 as the subject of an article by the ubiquitous Mr. Nyman. His music had also been the subject of a *Times* feature by Donal Henahan in October 1971 (now less confidently dismis-sive than earlier), in advance of a performance of *Phase Patterns* by Steve Reich and Musicians in a Boulez/New York Philharmonic-sponsored concert series, and of another article by Reich himself in September 1973. Even when Nyman interviewed Reich again for a 1976 *Studio International* piece in which the focus was on analogies between music and visual art, Minimalism was still referred to in passing, with greater reference to "process painting."

It was not until after the success of the 1976 debut of *Music for 18 Musicians* (Town Hall, April 24) and the sensation of *Einstein on the Beach* (Metropolitan Opera House, November 21) that mainstream critics began looking in earnest for a label for this strange enterprise, and Minimalism overtook the runner-up, Robert Palmer's "trance music," and slowly became a household word, at least in more progressive households. Even at this point, however, the label was up for grabs, although Peter G. Davis's "neo-primitive" seems to have lasted as long as his 1970 review. Although the coverage increased exponentially from 1977 to 1981, almost a dozen years after his Guggenheim review, Davis managed to retain a remnant of condescension in his 30 November *New York* article entitled "Simple Gifts," which found Glass "on the verge of romanticizing his minimalist vision" [77]. By this time several critics had already dismissed "Minimalism" as inaccurate, Joan La Barbara first and most forcefully in 1977: "the term not only no longer applies, but is purely laughable to describe such rich and complex music" [MA 14].

In 1982, when Reich, Glass and their colleagues were featured in the largest national news magazines, the case still remained somewhat uncertain, though this year marked the clear tipping of the scales in favor of "Minimalism." The February 1983 *High Fidelity/Musical America* delineated "An Outburst of Minimalism" from erstwhile Glass-basher, now true-believer Robert T. Jones just after *Time* magazine's "Best of 1982" listed *Tehillim* as its representative of "the year of Minimalism" [January 3, 1983, 80]. By then, predictably, articles on the composers had begun to concentrate almost equally on their Minimalism and their remoteness from the Minimalist aesthetic. The scales may have been tipped with Michael Walsh's *Time* article on Glass on August 10, 1981, also identifying Reich and Riley "in the minimalist camp." On October 25 Robert Coe's feature on Glass followed in the *New York Times Magazine*.

Back in 1966 Carman Moore had compared Reich's tape pieces to "watching sea waves; only so much can happen, fascinating though it be" [June 9, 1966]. The cover of Reich's Shandar disc in 1971 featured a photograph of sea waves. Writing for Columbia University's *Spectator* in November 1978, Tim Page tried out different metaphors to describe the ECM recording of *Music for 18 Musicians*, concluding with the similarly elemental "Steve Reich has framed the river" [November 2, 1978]. Three years later, he resurrected the metaphor, extending it to the Minimalists as a group, in "Framing the River: A Minimalist Primer" for the November 1981 *High Fidelity/Musical America* [64–68, 117]. Along with Walsh's and Coe's, Page's insightful article helped bring Minimalism to the masses and also served to indicate that it had developed into an ongoing tradition by featuring the work of John Adams (born 1947); it nonetheless set, along with Walsh's piece, an unfortunate precedent in relegating Young to the fringes of the movement (asking "whether or not La Monte Young was a true Minimalist" is like asking whether Schoenberg was a true dodecaphonist). Many subsequent articles on the subject, to their discredit, mentioned Young in passing or not at all.

Page called "minimalist music" "the most popular, if not the most apt, label for this style" [64], while mentioning "pulse music," Palmer's "trance music," "modular music" (Richard Kostelanetz), "space music" (predictably popular in California), and "stuck-record music" (similar terms had appeared in *Stereo Review* and the *Penguin Guide*). On December 6 Donal Henahan took note of the craze, comparing it to the vogue for insipid Baroque thirty years earlier, and suggested yet another alternative to "Minimalism" in his title, "The Going-Nowhere Music and Where It Came From." The two senior *Times* critics of the era scorned the music—four years later Harold Schonberg, by then serving as cultural correspondent, continued to treat it as a fad that offered the listener "nothing" in "Plumbing the Shallows of Minimalism" [February 21, 1985]. John Rockwell, joined for a time by Robert Palmer and Tim Page on the paper, continued to support the music. On March 14, 1982 Rockwell delineated "The Evolution of Steve Reich," mentioning "the similarly minimalist composer" Glass, noting that, "Starting in the late 60's, both . . . emerged as leading exponents of what has variously been described as 'minimalist music,' 'trance music,' 'pulse music,' 'steady-state structuralist music,' or any number of equally unsatisfactory terms."

Two weeks later Annalyn Swan's "The Rise of Steve Reich" appeared in *Newsweek* [March 29 56] with a photo of the composer captioned "Reich at Rehearsal: Up from Minimalism" and a description of freedman Reich as "along with Philip Glass . . . the leading composer of stripped-down, hypnotically repetitive, so-called 'minimal' music." Swan informed us that "For a 'minimal' work, *Tehillim* is remarkably varied," as the terminological cart began to be placed almost invariably before the musical horse.

Rockwell's "Evolution" had quoted Reich to the effect that "minimalism may be long gone. . . . 'If you want to say minimalism as a movement is dead, I'd say 'hear, hear, but *I'm* not dead.' If you're tied to a movement you go down with that movement" [II, 24]. Despite similar mild disavowals and even disdain from the composers, this anachronism was convenient for them as well as for the journalists insofar as it is easier to gain exposure as part of a movement, however arbitrarily or even erroneously defined. In the court of high-cultural consumerism, not having heard of an individual composer may be punished as a misdemeanor but ignorance of an entire *movement* is clearly felonious.

Tom Johnson's "The Original Minimalists" appeared in the *Village Voice* on July 27, 1982, and the jaded, borderline-sarcastic tone of the piece, compared with his earlier enthusiasm, adumbrates his departure from New York the next year. Ironically, the point of the article is to offer "a more valid list of original minimalists" [69] than the "Riley/Reich/Glass" of the popular press (he notes that Young has already been somehow excluded)—ironically insofar as in the article in which he had popularized the term he only included under the rubric "Riley/Reich/ Glass" and Young, a selection which enjoyed the precedent of the first sentence of Daniel Caux's liner notes for the Shandar *Four Organs/Phase Patterns*.

Johnson argued that "For several years the pieces Reich has been turning out aren't really minimalist. There is relatively little repetition in his recent scores, and he has left those simple minimalist scales for a much fancier harmonic language." Glass is similarly dismissed, albeit on the exaggerated claim that "One of the main characteristics of minimalism, perhaps the most essential one, is that the music is supposed to go on over just one chord, or even just one pitch." More dubiously, he suggests that "Riley's style has not changed much for at least 10 years, and it seems unlikely he will drift very far beyond the general boundaries of minimalism"—a judgment that may have been based on the recent Columbia issue of Riley's keyboard *Shri Camel* but not on the string quartets he had been composing for two years by the time of Johnson's article, which Johnson had most likely not yet heard.

By the time Michael Walsh's more extensive *Time* article, "The Heart is Back in the Game" (the title quotes Riley), appeared on September 20, the battle was pretty much over. "The style goes by many names: 'trance music,' 'process,' or 'system' music, 'steady-state structuralist' music and, even less flatteringly, 'going-nowhere' and 'needle-stuck-in-the-groove' music," Walsh observes, but these ostensibly once-competitive terms have now been sent to the sidelines. The head of the article reads, "Hypnotic and infectious, minimalism is emotional in its appeal" [60]. "Art-Rocker Brian Eno, whose own music has been influenced by the minimalist aesthetic," observes Blake-like, "Minimalism sees the world in a grain of sand" after we learn that "Reich's style of music" is "called minimalism," which is identified as "a joyous, exciting—and sometimes maddening—amalgam of influences as disparate as African drumming, the Balinese gamelan, and new wave rock."

The (now new-wave) cart is again placed before the (now Minimalist) horse. Minimalism had influenced rock as early as the mid-sixties when Young's drones were transmitted via John Cale and others to the Velvet Underground, thence to a host of punkers enamored of their belatedly fashionable nihilism. The drones descended from the eternal music of the spheres through "Heroin"'s repeated tonic/dominant-*cum*-drones-on-the-common-tone to the Ramones' "Gimme Gimme Shock Treatment." Minor-mode Minimalist repetition, on the other hand, appeared opposite Krzysztof Penderecki's anguished microtonality in the 1973 score of *The Exorcist* in the form of Mike Oldfield's "Tubular Bells." Riley's influence was felt there, and his second Columbia album proved eponymous to the group Curved Air, while, contrariwise, the leader of King Crimson, Robert Fripp, was to rechristen Riley's time-lag system, without undue humility, "Frippertronics"—fifteen years or so after its birth. The influence was not all in one direction, however, since Glass's ideas of amplification from the late sixties derive more from rock than any classical source. Tom Johnson, in fact, issued a complaint back in 1974 that is still echoed: engineer Kurt Munkacsi "as usual" cranked the sound up too far, adding "a freak-out 60s veneer which actually contradicts the sensitive harmonies and the highly controlled playing" [March 14, 41].

Ironically, some of the most pretentiously arty "art-rock" had Minimalist roots, including a day-trip by erstwhile "glitter-rock" performer and chronic trendie David Bowie in the 1977 *Low* (symphonized by Glass in 1992). By then Tangerine Dream was borrowing its style from Reich and Glass as clearly as Curved Air was borrowing its name from Riley, taking repetition to a further level of techno-freakishness with the automatic replication of harmonies and rhythms at the touch of a button. Reich remarked to Page years later, "I should be receiving royalties for the theme to 'Adam Smith's Money World,' and the whole soundtrack to the film 'Risky Business,' supposedly by a group called Tangerine Dream, was an out-and-out ripoff of *Music for 18 Musicians*. I should have sued" [June 1, 1986 II, 24].

By the 1980s, swarms of musicians American and European, innovative and clueless alike, had latched on. [Wim] Mertens mentions in passing Nyman and Gavin Bryars in the U.K., Louis Andriessen in Holland, Richard Pinhas and Urban Sax in France, Peter Michael Hamel and Michael Fahres in Germany, Karel Goeyvaerts, Frans Geysen, and Dominique Lawalrée in Belgium, and, among European rockers, Klaus Schulze, Kraftwerk, XTC, Public Image Ltd [11], the Third Ear Band, Soft Machine, and "the Berlin-based Agitation Free [which] included . . . *In C* in its repertoire" [16]. In the U.S., the disco phenomenon, ironically, may have paved the way for acceptance of the new wave music that represented its initially cultish antithesis or antidote. After the inhumanly steady bass-heavy beat of disco the relentless mechanics of Minimalist-influenced rock were less shocking. The latter, however, managed to present themselves as the antithesis of disco by adapting the mechanical repetition to higher registers in vocal phrasing and guitar riffs, offering themselves as the cool (and smart) alternative to hot (and stupid) disco. Most significantly, Talking Heads had employed the motoric repetitiveness of Glass to impressive effect.

Classically trained, a composer of disavowed symphonies in the early seventies, crossover (in media as well as marketing) artist Laurie Anderson accompanied her vocal on "O Superman" with a single repeated tone marking each beat and worked frequently elsewhere in repeating lines. The influence is present throughout the occasionally inspired, often merely gimmicky, music of Jean-Michel Jarre and much of so-called "New Age music," a category which as of this writing may be vanishing along with any hope for a New Age. This form of highly commercial mood music arose, significantly, with no identifiable advent of any new age other than the encroaching *middle* age of the youth-worshiping generation born after World War II. It domesticated Minimalist repetition to such an extent that it is difficult to say whether New Age music represents the Mantovani or the Sominex of baby-boomers. Its utterly specious claims to expand consciousness, while inducing *un*consciousness, represent the last gasp of countercultural ideals for refugees to the same suburbs they once fled in youthful derision.

*　　*　　*

In the 1970s numerous musicians working in a classical vein were drawn to the style, including several members of the Reich and Glass ensembles, such as Richard Landry and James Tenney, and, most notably in this context, Jon Gibson. Gibson began working in tape seriously after working with Reich and Riley, and from 1968 to 1973 gathered natural sounds for "A 16-Track Multi-Textured Environmental Soundscape" entitled *Visitations*. Featuring overlaid percussion, flutes and synthesizer, it was described by Tom Johnson as "some of the densest music I have ever heard" [December 20, 1973, 45]. The genre has since been overdone, but Gibson's early experiment remains musically engrossing. The same may be said for *Cycles*, a 1973 pipe-organ piece whose pedal and overtone mix now seem like a bridge between those of Young, with whom Gibson had played in 1970, and the ambient music of Brian Eno and later New Age knockoffs.

While instrumental or found-sound long-tones and drones pervade *Visitations* and *Cycles*, Gibson was led in the direction of process and repetition in *Untitled*, the flip die of *Cycles* on his album *Two Solo Pieces*, released like *Visitations* on Chatham Square. He played alto flute in this piece, more allied to Reich and Glass, exfoliating a melody through repetition for eighteen minutes. His wind-playing proved generally more impressive than some of the reductivist percussion he examined in the self-describing *Single Stroke Roll on Drum* he premiered at Paula Cooper in December 1973, almost five years after the premiere of *Cymbal* at the Los Angeles Municipal Junior Arts Center in January 1969, in which a similar technique had been applied to a suspended cymbal. At the Kitchen in January 1972 he presented *Voice/Tape Delay*, taking off from Riley and Reich, and *Untitled Piece for Cymbals, Bells, Drums, Flutes, and Oscillators*, later called *Fluid Drive*, a live version of *Visitations*. In the fall he experimented with two amplified flutes playing from opposite ends of Seagram Plaza during a festival sponsored by the company.

Tenney had composed atonally but with repetition of lines as early as the 1959 *Monody* for solo clarinet, and worked with tape as early as the 1961 collage *Blue Suede*. He was a leading figure in the Tone Roads group in the late sixties, while playing in the ensembles of Reich and Glass. In 1969 the anomalous *For Ann (rising)* was about as minimal as it gets, consisting of a single tone gradually and almost imperceptibly ascending, while other works in the late seventies took off from Reich and Glass.

Former collaborators of Young and Riley also worked in the same vein. Terry Jennings and Dennis Johnson were mentioned earlier as Young's first followers. Jon Hassell, who played trumpet in the Theatre of Eternal Music and on the Columbia *In C*, composed under that joint influence as early as the 1969 *Solid State*, and during Young's April 28–May 5 1974 Dream House at the Kitchen presented his own music one night while performing with the Theatre of Eternal Music. By that time he had also begun to explore large-scale outdoor musical environments. David Rosenboom, the violist on the Columbia *In C*, for a time wrote pieces derivative of that work before immersing himself in assorted varieties of process music. Daniel Goode, clarinetist and leader of the ill-fated April 1973 performance of *In C*, was by then composing in a similar vein himself. In the early seventies Yoshi Wada employed electronic and wind drones in a manner derived from Young, also adding voices on occasion.

Maryanne Amacher, Rhys Chatham, and Ingram Marshall—three young composers working in the New York University Composers Workshop directed by Morton Subotnick in the early 1970s—were to contribute in very different ways to the evolution of later Minimalism. Amacher experimented not only in extended durations but in long-distance concerts, once informing the audience assembled at the Kitchen that the music was being played in Boston and they would have to concentrate in order to hear it. Chatham, who was named music director of the Kitchen at the age of twenty-two, was an associate of Young and incorporated the influence of rock as well as drones. In his score for Robert Streicher's solo dance *Narcissus Descending* he set a single electronic drone-pitch and varied the overtones dynamically. He followed Young into gongs with his 1973 *Two Gongs* and in a Paris performance of Young's *Poem for Chairs, Tables, Benches, etc.* served as concertmaster and "first chair." Marshall explored *musique concrète*, and his live/tape compositions in particular, at once austere and grimly lyrical, have a humane quality absent from much Minimalism, combined with an aversion to sentimentality unshared with some of its later offshoots. Inspired by the Reich tape works in 1973, he created the text-sound piece *Cortez* and others. In the late seventies he began to integrate with telling effect his interests in both long-tone and repetitive Minimalism, electronic music, European Romanticism, and Indonesian music, which he had studied *in situ* in 1971. His 1976 *The Fragility Cycles* is one of the finest post-Minimal compositions and matched by subsequent works like *Fog Tropes*, *Gradual Requiem*, and *Hidden Voices*.

Charlemagne Palestine has maintained that he developed his piano technique without ever having heard Young play *The Well-Tuned*

Piano (or any piano), but his repetitive strumming of the piano in the early seventies in a search for overtones—also present in his vocal work—shows similar interests, as does his use of drones (e.g., tape pieces with sustained chords or sustained tones fluctuating microtonally). While still in his teens, the prodigious Palestine (né Charles Martin in Brooklyn) was appointed bell-ringer at St. Thomas Church down the street from the Museum of Modern Art, and developed into a virtuoso carillonneur—which would naturally have provoked further exploration of sustained tones and harmonics in any case, and are directly linked to the tubular bells he worked with in the early 1970s. His vigorous "strumming" technique was applied to both Bösendorfers and harpsichords, and his keyboard music grew wilder as the seventies progressed. There are similarities to a Young piece like the "1698" realization of *arabic numeral* in his *The Lower Depths: Descending/Ascending*, in which Palestine virtually assaulted the keyboard for an hour with preternatural endurance. This primal expression was foreshadowed in some of the voice and body pieces in which he ran around galleries or banged his head against floors/walls while wailing or sustaining tones. There is something of Yves Klein in all this, but more proximately it developed concurrently with a performance art that included in its more infamous forms Vito Acconci masturbating and Rudolf Schwarzkogler castrating himself piece by piece (and killing himself in the process, proving less was not necessarily more).

Palestine also took up the experimentation in drone intervals and drift originated by Young. In 1974 Lizzie Borden described "recent performances" given by Palestine that "have begun with an electronic sonority of one interval of a fifth (C/G) reinforced twice, and ten minutes later another reinforced fifth one major third higher (E/B) realized on an electronic synthesizer. The speakers are placed differently for each concert. In a recent performance at the Sonnabend Gallery, they were secreted in a closet, a stairwell, and in a room closed to the audience, so that the sound was filtered by these containers. The sonorities create a space of complex wave shapes with many overtones, of densities varying from place to place" [49].

In the early 1970s Philip Corner, who had been active in both Fluxus and Tone Roads and had provided the music for dance performances by Yvonne Rainer, experimented with economy of means in pieces such as one involving blowing into jugs in front of microphones, before turning his interest primarily to Indonesian (-influenced) music. Phill Niblock, a filmmaker and a self-trained musician, began an ongoing series of pieces in which he clipped off the attacks of vocal or instrumental sustained tones, spliced them in multi-track stereo, and played them loud in marathon concerts at his Centre Street loft, which he has also offered as a performance space to other musicians over the years. His tapes have often been accompanied by live performers mixing with the audience while harmonizing long tones. In its monodynamic sustenance, if not its dissonance, his work offers an interesting variation on Young.

Tom Johnson's own *The Four-Note Opera* premiered in May 1972, the titular heroes being A, B, D, and E—real naturals all. The next month, in a review of Buffalo's SEM Ensemble at the Kitchen, he noted, "I hear a lot of long static pieces these days, and when they are done well, the results can be quite moving. But when they are not done well, they are just long and static" [June 15, 1972, 37]. His advocacy was never undiscriminating. His 1982 list of "Original Minimalists" includes "Maryanne Amacher, Robert Ashley, David Behrman [excluded in his 1972 article], Harold Budd, Joel Chadabe, Philip Corner [excluded in his 1972 article], Alvin Curran, Jon Gibson, Daniel Goode, William Hellerman, Terry Jennings, Garrett List, Annea Lockwood, Alvin Lucier, Meredith Monk, Charlie Morrow, Gordon Mumma, Max Neuhaus, Phill Niblock, Pauline Oliveros, Frederic Rzewski [excluded from his 1972 article], Steven Scott, Richard Teitelbaum, Ivan Tcherepnin, Yoshi Wada" and Young himself [69]. In addition to composers listed earlier, others mentioned by Page in "Framing the River" as influenced by Minimalism include Beth Anderson, Laraaji, Jeffrey Lohn, and David Hush.

Jay Clayton, who has sung for years with Reich, and Laura Dean, who has lived and worked with him, have both subsequently composed in a Reichian vein with Glass affinities. Pauline Oliveros, a classmate of Young and Riley in Berkeley who performed in the premiere of *In C*, worked at the San Francisco Tape Music Center and became its director when it moved across the Bay to Mills College in 1966–67, has employed modality, sustenance and repetition in works scored for unconventional ensembles (e.g., twenty-two accordions and percussion in *The Wanderer*). This 1975 composition carried on the tradition of "instructional" concept art; its original score read, "Sustain a tone or sound until any desire to change it disappears. When there is no longer any desire to change the tone or sound, then change it." Oliveros has become best known for her use of environmentally created drones and delays, which might be called site-specific music after the sculptural term—playing and recording in such locations as an underground reservoir in Köln, and the bombproof concrete cistern at Fort Worden, Washington, to exploit their otherworldly reverberation. Young's influence is again manifest.

The multi-talented Meredith Monk is with Oliveros the most significant of the female composers popularly associated with the Minimalist style, though she not only dislikes the label but finds it inaccurate. Monk was probably best known as a dancer and choreographer in the sixties and early seventies, during which time she in fact resisted what she perceived as the somewhat doctrinaire polemics of dance colleagues associated with reductive style. The Minimal tag is affixed to her music because of her reduced instrumentation and its typical relegation to drones and repeating modules, which are closely allied, respectively, to Young's *Tortoise*, and early Reich and Glass. The crucial difference is that they serve Monk primarily as accompaniment for her anything-but-minimal, virtuosic, semi-improvisational, extended-vocals, whereas in Young the similarly wordless chanting is restricted to predetermined sustained intervals and in early Reich and Glass the modules *constitute* the piece. Monk has, furthermore, worked primarily in additive rather than reductive multi-media (even her first composition in 1966 had the emblematic title *16 Millimeter Earrings*), notably in the operas *Quarry* (1976), the "apocalyptic cabaret" *Turtle Dreams* (1983), and the recent *Atlas* (1991).

In the discography to Chapter Four, "Meet the Minimalists," of his valuable 1987 survey *New Sounds*, John Schaefer lists another thirty composers postdating the area of our discussion of Minimalist origins. By then the voice of the people had clearly been heard; it is unlikely that the author lost a moment's thought on entitling his chapter "Meet the Modularists" or "Meet the Steady-State Structuralists."

In addition to "intentionless music," Glass once said he preferred "music with repetitive structures" [Page 1981, 64]; Reich has similarly opted on occasion for "structuralism" and "*musique répétitive*," but "basically I wouldn't go with any [term]." Riley describes himself as "probably the last person to ask" about vestiges of Minimalism in his work. Young is the only one of four who acknowledges that he is a Minimalist, adding, "but that's only one of the things I am" [AC 45, 123, 69].

All four proved to be lots of other things. If their work had ended in May 1974 like Minimalism proper and this survey, the term would be a footnote in music history, something like Fluxus, and the survey would not exist.

Y   [Selected] Bibliography

This bibliography lists all works cited in the text in brackets by page number, except for unpaginated and single-page works, and with additional identification when necessary for clarity. *"AC"* indicates my book *American Composers.* Quotations without corresponding references derive from conversations with Terry Riley (1987, 1991, 1992), La Monte Young, and Marian Zazeela (1991, 1992); and John Cage, Jon Gibson, Philip Glass, Robert Morris, Steve Reich (all 1992).

Caux, Daniel. Liner notes to Steve Reich, *Four Organs/Phase Patterns.* Shandar SR 10.005, 1971.

Coe, Robert. "Philip Glass Breaks Through." *New York Times Magazine,* 25 October 1981, 68–80, 90.

Davis, Peter G. "3 Pieces by Glass Probe, the Sonic Possibilities." *New York Times,* 17 January 1970, 22.

Henahan, Donal. "Steve Reich Presents a Program of Pulse Music at Guggenheim." *New York Times,* 9 May 1970, 15.

———. "Reich? Philharmonic? Paradiddling?" *New York Times,* 24 October 1971, 11, 13, 26.

———. "The Going-Nowhere Music and Where It Came From." *New York Times,* 6 December 1981, II, 1, 25.

Johnson, Tom. "Music for a Joy-toned Trance." *Village Voice,* 6 April 1972, 42.

———. "Music." *Village Voice,* 15 June 1972, 37.

———. "Changing the Meaning of 'Static.'" *Village Voice,* 7 September 1972, 45.

———. "Music." *Village Voice,* 5 July 1973, 38–39.

———. "Getting Fogbound in Sound." *Village Voice,* 20 December 1973.

———. "Meditating and On the Run." *Village Voice,* 31 January 1974, 44–45.

———. "Music." *Village Voice,* 14 March 1974, 41.

———. "Chugging Away to an Ultimate High." *Village Voice,* 13 June 1974, 55.

———. "The Original Minimalists." *Village Voice,* 27 July 1982, 68–69.

Jones, Robert T. "An Outburst of Minimalism." *High Fidelity/Musical America,* February 1983, 26.

Kostelanetz, Richard. *On Innovative Musicians.* New York: Limelight Editions, 1989.

La Barbara, Joan. "New Music." *High Fidelity/Musical America,* November 1977, MA 14–15.

Moore, Carman. "Music: Park Place Electronics." *Village Voice,* 9 June 1966, 17.

Nyman, Michael. *Experimental Music: Cage and Beyond.* London: Studio Vista; New York: Schirmer, 1974.

———. "Steve Reich: Interview." *Studio International* 1976, 300–307.

Page, Tim. "Steve Reich's *Music for 18 Musicians* finally gets a good treatment on vinyl." *Columbia Spectator*, 2 November 1978.

———. "Framing the River: A Minimalist Primer." *High Fidelity/Musical America*, November 1981, 64–68, 117.

———. "Steve Reich Approaches 50." *New York Times*, 1 June 1986, II, 23–24.

Perreault, John. "La Monte Young's Tracery: The Voice of the Tortoise." *Village Voice*, 22 February 1968, 27, 29.

Reich, Steve. *Writings About Music*. New York: New York University Press, 1974.

Rockwell, John. "What's New." *High Fidelity/Musical America*, August 1973, MA 7, 31–32.

———. "There's Nothing Quite Like the Sound of Glass." *New York Times*, 26 May 1974, II, 11, 21.

———. "The Evolution of Steve Reich." *New York Times,* 14 March 1982, 11, 23–24.

Rose, Barbara. "ABC Art." *Art in America,* October/November 1965, 57–69.

Schaefer, John. *New Sounds: A Listener's Guide to New Music*. New York: Harper and Row, 1987.

Schonberg, Harold C. "Music: The Medium Electric, the Message Hypnotic." *New York Times*, 15 April 1969, 42.

———. "Plumbing the Shallows of Minimalism." *New York Times*, 21 February 1985, C18.

Strickland, Edward. *American Composers: Dialogues on Contemporary Music*. Bloomington: Indiana University Press, 1991.

Swan, Annalyn. "The Rise of Steve Reich." *Newsweek*, 29 March 1982, 56.

Walsh, Michael. "Melody Stages a Comeback." *Time*, 10 August 1981, 63.

Wasserman, Emily. "An Interview with Composer Steve Reich." *Artforum*, May 1972, 44–48.

Part Three

Play

(Music for Theater and Film)

PHILIP GLASS ON COMPOSING FOR FILM AND OTHER FORMS: THE CASE OF KOYAANISQATSI (1990)

CHARLES MERRELL BERG

Philip Glass is a man of many musical hats. He's a prize-winning composer. He's also a concert performer whose electronic keyboards are an integral part of his theatrical and concert performances. And, as leader of the Philip Glass Ensemble, the acclaimed musical group he formed in the 1970s to play his own works, he's a highly successful entrepreneur.[1] Glass is also a visionary whose basic concepts of artistic creation are centered in collaborative dynamics, a process standing in marked contrast to the Romantic tradition's emphasis on solitary creation by an individual genius, a notion still very much alive in such premises as cinema's auteur theory.[2] Glass, as I will suggest, can also be thought of as a member of the vanguard of contemporary performance artists.

The positioning of Glass as a performance artist is based in large part on Philip Auslander's seminal article, "Going with the Flow: Performance Art and Mass Culture,"[3] as well as a brief consideration of Glass's prolific and multifaceted career, and most significantly, in terms of the interview which follows, an examination of Glass's involvement with *Koyaanisqatsi: Live*, the multi-media performance event featuring Godfrey Reggio's 1983 film and Glass's "live music" score which toured throughout the United States in the Fall of 1987.

Auslander, in linking performance art to the postmodern and

interactive worlds of media and popular culture, provides a virtual taxonomy of *au courant* attributes which inform and largely define the variegated and illusive phenomenon of contemporary performance art and, by extension, much of the work of Philip Glass. Auslander's basic tactic is one of comparison, the compilation of a veritable balance sheet of performance art premises from the 1960s/1970s, set in apposition to those of the 1980s, and by implication, the 1990s. At the risk of oversimplifying Auslander's compelling analysis, I would like to focus on several key elements which, as Auslander argues, have emerged during the transition from the first generation of post-war conceptual performers to today's media-aware generation of experimentalists, elements which help establish Glass's credentials as a performance artist.

Central to Auslander's presentation is his positing of performance art's general movement away from the margins and into the very vortex of popular culture. It's a trend that has been facilitated by the enthusiastic embrace of all media, by all manner of performance artists, from Laurie Anderson to the Living Theater. And though at one time such "co-optations" were regarded as expedient, as the means of financing one's "real work," today, with only few exceptions, performance artists actively seek the attention and, indeed, the varied rewards afforded by the rapprochment of performance and entertainment.[4]

The move from marginality to marketability, from self-styled esoterica to commodity art, is one that, not surprisingly, has offended performance purists such as Linda Frye Burnham who sees mass culture as "hegemonic" and only vanguard art as "counterhegemonic," and therefore subversive.[5] Auslander discounts such claims by suggesting that mass culture itself has taken on the potential of being "a site of possible resistance to the mainstream."[6] Drawing on the work of a number of contemporary media theorists, Auslander urges a rethinking of performance art based not just on microtextual studies, but, more significantly, on intertextual approaches such as Raymond Williams' notion of "flow."[7] In the process, Auslander challenges such notions as "high art" and the presumed superiority of "live" vs. "mediated" performances. And in citing Andreas Huyssen,[8] he reminds us that it was the culture industries, not the avant garde, which succeeded in radically transforming everyday life in the twentieth-century. Auslander concludes that "postmodern art does not position itself outside the practices it holds up for scrutiny. It *problematizes*, but does not *reject*, the representational means it shares with other cultural practices."[9]

How does Philip Glass tie-in to Auslander's ideas on post-modern performance art? First, Glass exemplifies the embrace of media and other high-tech means of artistic production. For example, the sound-generating equipment used by Glass and his Ensemble is nothing short of state-of-the-art.[10] His conscious decision to break out beyond the confining walls of the concert hall through collaborations with filmmakers such as Godfrey Reggio and Paul Schrader, as well as with other multi-media artists, is another indication of his desire to reach larger audiences through artistic exploitations of the media.[11] Related to such projects is his very active recording career and his "exclusive composer" contract with CBS Records (a distinction shared only with Igor Stravinsky and Aaron Copland), which further points out his success in establishing a stature as a "serious composer" as well as a potent box office draw.[12] Indeed, Philip Glass is a perfect exemplar of Auslander's notion of the rapproachment between performance art and entertainment.[13]

In the case of *Koyaanisqatsi*, one can clearly read the film as having a politically subversive message, as embodying a critique of the destruction of Spaceship Earth by modern man and his polluting technologies.[14] But, aside from its status as a clarion call for environmental action, one can also "read" the 88-minute, non-narrative film as a "head movie" for people ranging from, as Michael Dempsey puts it in a recent article in *Film Quarterly,* "unconstructed hippies to New Agers, who like blissing out to lulling music and pretty pictures and don't care about 'meaning.'"[15]

As for intertextuality, *Koyaanisqatsi* exists in several forms. First, it is a feature film that was released in 1983 with great critical and box office success.[16] It also is a highly profitable video release, as well as a top-selling musical recording available in compact disc, long play and cassette tape formats.[17] Along with its conspicuous success as a multi-textual commodity, it is also a concert piece in the repertory of the Philip Glass Ensemble, albeit in highly excerpted form.[18] And finally, *Koyaanisqatsi*, at least during the Fall of 1987, can be regarded as a mass mediated performance event with its musical score performed "live" by the Philip Glass Ensemble.[19]

The following interview with Glass was recorded on the morning of November 11, 1987, following a sold-out evening performance of *Koyaanisqatsi: Live* presented on November 10, 1987 at the University of Kansas in Lawrence. Glass is bright and articulate; he's also quietly confident, especially about his own views and working methods. And, in spite of his huge critical and popular success, he's gentle, even humble and somewhat self-deprecating. He is also inquisitive. During our conversation, for example, he asked as many questions as I did. He wanted to know about how people responded to the performance. And he wanted to know more about film and film music theories, areas that he freely acknowledged he knew little about.[20] Still, when sharing his views or discussing his working methods, Glass speaks with calm assurance. The interview, while alluding to many of the points discussed by Auslander, also raises an aspect of performance art that has received little formal attention, collaboration. Indeed, Glass's concern with collective rather than individual visions, is one of the hallmarks of his work as both composer and performer.

Berg: Tell me about your relationship with Godfrey Reggio in the production of Koyaanisqatsi.[21]

Glass: Well, we don't have a relationship in the sense that one has a relationship with a collaborator, say, in theatre or dance. Film, as you know, is peculiar in that the music is usually done at the end of a project. But, I've been somewhat fortunate. When I first started work with Godfrey, he'd only shot about sixty percent of *Koyaanisqatsi.* That was also the case, I might add, when I worked with Paul Schrader on *Mishima* [directed by Schrader; released in 1984]; there, I became involved before we started shooting. Actually, I guess I don't really like to work on films, but if I do, it has to be with some participation.

So genuine collaboration is the key for you?
Yes.

What about the film's subject, its style?
Well, as you know, it's very hard to tell what a film is really going to be like. Therefore, when people tell me about film projects, they all sound wonderful. So if I'm trying to make a decision about a commitment, I look at who the director is, the other artists to be involved, and the overall working conditions; the subject matter is important, of course, but only in a general way. For instance, the subject of *Mishima* appealed to me because I had read all of Yukio Mishima's books that had then been translated.

Then, I read the Schraders' script [*Mishima* was co-written by Paul and Leonard Schrader], and I liked it. So I decided to do the film. But even then, I really couldn't predict that the film would turn out so well. But, as Paul and I looked through the script, he encouraged me to put music where I thought it should go. He did indicate several places where he thought music was needed. But, essentially, he left it up to me. So, in a way, I ended up writing to the script rather than to actual images.

Working with that process, I recorded a work tape from which Paul made the first cut. I then had to go back and rephrase the music to fit specific cuts. Some of the cuts, in terms of the music, were a bit arbitrary. In other words, if he wanted a scene shorter, he simply cut it; that meant, of course, that he had simultaneously cut the music. He'd then say, "You figure out how to end it here."

In effect, I really ended up writing the score for *Mishima* twice. First, I wrote the initial score, the work tape. Then I had to go back and recalculate the music to fit the actual cuts of the final print. Instead of using a composite sound track with dialogue, music and sounds, we used twenty-four separate tracks of sound in the final mix. The producer was a bit nervous about it because of the added expense. So we had the visuals turning as well as each of the twenty-four sound tracks. It got pretty complicated. But, it allowed us to be much more subtle in the mix. For example, when we got to places in the picture where the dialogue begins, instead of just cutting or fading the music out, I could cut off, say, just the first and second violins, thereby leaving only the violas. In other words, I could tailor the music to the real sounds of the film instead of simply having the whole ensemble go either completely in or completely out.

Mishima, *of course, is a very different film than* Koyaanisqatsi *in that the music for* Mishima *had to be choreographed with the interplay of other audial elements such as dialogue and sound effects.*
Yes, the work on *Koyaanisqatsi* with Godfrey was much more of an equal collaboration in that we conceived the film as a real symbiosis of music and image.

Because Godfrey was aiming for a world-wide audience, the film had to convey its point entirely through these two universal, international languages of image and sound. *Koyaanisqatsi*, in fact, has been shown all over the world. The point is that there was nothing that required translation. But this meant that we had to work out a process of structuring the elements in a very close way.

When I first met Godfrey and we began to talk about the project, he had shot only about sixty percent of the film. The first thing that we did was to divide up his images into what he called subject-roles. There was one category for "clouds." Another was called "vessels" for planes and cars, and that sort of thing. But then, after working out the subject-roles, we developed a dramaturgical plan. In other words, the structure of the film became a sequence of the subject-roles which produced a kind of consecutive line of thought, rather than a traditional narrative.[22] At the opening of the film, we start in Monument Valley, then we go to the city. Later, we witness the destruction of the city and the failure of the urban environment. So it becomes a progressive sequence of dramatically structured subject-roles. It seems to work, so I'm glad we did it that way. But actually, at another level, this consecutive thought process is just as narrative in nature as any Hollywood story-film.

Koyaanisqatsi doesn't have a clear-cut beginning, middle or end. Actually you could rearrange its elements in various ways. And we did do that. Eventually, however, we realized that there was a requirement for some kind of order. Frankly, we wanted to end up so that the film's images had a dramatic impact. And that's where Godfrey was able to rely on my experience in the theatre [mainly ballet and opera], where dramaturgical concerns underlie the structure of the work. So when we applied that concern to a non-verbal film, what we were looking for was some kind of dramatic shaping of the kind one would find in an opera or ballet.

As you look at the film from that point of view, you'll see an overall dramatic slope. It does have a quiet beginning as well as a crescendoing series of dramatic segments each with its own kind of visual energy and excitement. There's also a quiet ending, a long epilogue, which ends the film. So you can actually map out a dramatic structure along a curve if you want to. And, actually, this was done before I started with the music.

By both of you?
Yes, we did it together. In fact, what I brought to the film was a set of varied experiences in working in that kind of way. What Godfrey brought to the film was his own personal vision in terms of the particular subject matter. He knew what he wanted to say about "life out of balance," and how he wanted to present that in visual terms. He had what he called "different modes of viewing" which were achieved technically through extreme time-lapse sequences with greatly accelerated real-time movements; at the other end were the slow-motion sequences.[23] Part of his visual vocabulary involved going in and out of normal-time contexts. What we did together, then, was to work out the dramatic structure. Then I began to write music for the different subject-role sequences that were now in the proper order, but which were not yet edited. For example, we had planned for a ten-minute cloud sequence, but the individual shots weren't in any particular order. So I just wrote a ten-minute cloud piece, but without reference to any particular cloud images.

That seems a bit chancy, especially if the final cut for such a sequence turns out to be appreciably shorter, or, perhaps, even longer.

Well, this kind of process is actually my specialty. This is what I am best at, probably because I've been working in the theater for so many years, and also working with visual artists. I've learned to develop musical-visual interactions whether the context is balletic or operatic. I've even written music for sculpture. So this is one of the situations I'm very experienced with.

An important part of the process is becoming involved in the subject matter. But apart from that, I'm also learning that the music can play within the image in a number of strikingly different ways. Now, you know I'm not a theoretician about this, and haven't read any books about it. But as I work, I'm aware that the music can be placed in the image in various ways. It can be what I call "under the image," or it can be "on top of the image," or it can be right "next to the image." In a sense, we're talking about whether the music is essentially in the foreground or background.

Now sometimes people talk about going with the image or against the image. That's a much simpler idea because you can be in back of the image and still go against it, or you can be in front of the image and, again, go against it. In other words, it depends on where the music is placed in terms of what you're looking at.[24]

Sometimes the music is the subtext of what's on the screen. It forms the emotional viewpoint of what we're watching, but it doesn't necessarily sound like what we're looking at. For example, with the clouds in *Koyaanisqatsi*, I decided to use a fairly analogous or allegorical musical image to go with the clouds. I picked large, slow-moving clusters of brass that became, as I said, an allegorical visualization of what's on the screen. In this case, I was right on top of the image.

Can you specify what you mean by allegorical? And also your rationale for using brass rather than, say, reeds?

Well, this is part of the artistic process where you get to make your artistic choices. One artist will say, "clouds sound like brass to me." Another artist will say, "they sound like strings to me." But, still, that's an important issue to consider because it involves the ways in which we, as individuals, personalize these things. It's not really important that clouds sound like brass to me, but rather that I make the use of the brass a convincing artistic decision. That's what's important.

To me, the cloud music works well in giving the images a certain sense of majesty, perhaps even gravity.

Exactly. That, I think, underscores my perception of what Reggio was trying to get at . . . that awesome magnificence of nature. In a way, I regarded the clouds like I regarded the music, as a huge mass of forms which actually have no physical substance. And yet at times, the clouds as well as the music, did have a sense of artistic weight, and, as you suggest, gravity. By the way, some of those cloud images, though they appear as if they had been photographed from planes, actually were shot from mountain tops.

The scene with the take-off of the Boeing 747, at what I assume is LAX [Los Angeles International Airport], is another case where the music influences our "reading" or understanding of the scene.
That's right, it was LAX. And for that, I used voices. There, I was working somewhat differently. In a strange sort of way, the voices became an aspect of the plane. Not the whole plane, because the plane itself is a tremendously huge and massive machine. Still, one of a plane's interesting qualities is its lightness; at moments, it actually seems to be lighter than air. So, I took that special facet of a plane in flight, its lightness, and made it the basis of the musical image, in part, by using voices.

The image of the plane in Koyaanisqatsi *has a kind of ethereality because of Reggio's use of an extremely long telephoto lens which catches and distorts a welter of heatwaves undulating up from the runway. Consequently, the plane seems to shimmer and palpitate in almost organic fashion.*
Well, what interested me about that huge plane was its appearance of seeming to be lighter than air. I therefore decided to make the music about the quality of lightness, an aspect underlined by the voices. So, when we see the plane, we hear a very ephemeral vocal texture. In a way, it's a poetic metaphor. We could have looked at that plane in a very literal way. But, with music, there are many other ways of "looking" at a given object.

Can the film's conclusion also be regarded as exemplifying that kind of poetic metaphor?
You're talking about the scene shot in Harlem, I think in 1978, during the power blackout when all the electricity went off, and everyone was down in the street. Well, not exactly. Instead of being metaphoric, it's an example of a situation where the music is way down under the image. Here, the music is subtly commenting on what we're looking at; in fact, the words are the words of the [Hopi Indian] prophesies that we also hear

at the very end of the film. That's what the voices are articulating. So, I wasn't looking for a metaphor for the image, but rather a subtext for the image.

That's a fascinating point because the words are in the language of the Hopi Indians. And though the words have a specific, literal meaning for those fluent in Hopi, it's a meaning that goes right past the bulk of the film's audience who, of course, don't speak Hopi.

Well, Godfrey did place the words in translation on the screen at the very end of the film. Personally, I would not have done that. But I understand his thinking. Film, of all media that artists work with, is the most public. It has the broadest appeal and addresses itself to the widest spectrum of the population. Furthermore, Godfrey didn't want to create an atmosphere where the film would seem removed from anybody. So he literally translated the words.

Working on the operas I've done, I've learned that language can function in a variety of ways. There are, for example, situations where the words form a kind of subtext, but with musical rather than literary significance. In these cases, it's not really so important that audiences understand the text in a literal way. However, Godfrey, at least at the end, wanted the meanings to be clear, which I understood, again, given the public nature of the film medium.

The musical setting of the words was interesting because I had to study the phonetic, or vocal inflections of the Hopi language. As with all languages, a lot of the meaning is conveyed to us through the rhythms and inflections of the speech, the spoken language. You can learn the vocabulary and syntax of a language, but if you don't speak with the rhythms of a native speaker, you're not going to be understood. So, as far as possible, I studied the Hopi's speech patterns and then set those speech patterns into the music.

Later, when I recorded the score with a group of New York musicians, I sent a tape back to the Hopis in New Mexico to check with them to see whether the words were comprehensible. They said they were. So, I would hope that if a Hopi Indian should happen to be in the audience, he would understand the words in a literal sense.

Does it actually matter if the words are intelligible to a Hopi Indian?

Yes, I think it does, because if you take the kind of care we took with the language, it translates into a feeling of authenticity that most people can sense if not actually understand.

It seems as if you're talking about artistic integrity.
That's part of it because if you bring a high level of concentration to the work like a good actor, it helps convey that feeling of authenticity. And if you don't do it, if you're careless about it, or do it without really caring, invariably that lack of concentration or concern comes across.

But as you know, the relationship between music and image is a very complicated one. There are some filmmakers, for instance, who really know how to work with music, but then there are many more who really don't appreciate it. Paul Schrader, as I've said, is very intelligent about music. In our collaboration for *Mishima*, I discovered that Paul is very astute about combinations of images and music. He knows where to put it. He knows how to use it. He knows when it's needed.

For film, music, next to primary visual aspects like cinematography and color, is probably the most important element. Yet to those of us who are in the business of making movies, we act as if music is almost an afterthought. That, of course, is terrible. It's more than a mistake because it means that those who treat music as an afterthought have lost a powerful artistic ally.

People like Schrader, though, know how to use music as an ally, to bend it to the needs of the film. These are the people who are capable of letting the music add an extra dimension, an extra emotional and dramatic charge that less careful directors and producers simply do not have access to.

Has your work been influenced by any of the well-known filmmakers, composers or theorists who have speculated about the formal relationships between image and music? For example, the great collaborations between Soviet filmmaker Sergei Eisenstein and Soviet composer Sergei Prokofiev for Alexander Nevsky *and* Ivan the Terrible *spurred Eisenstein to write rather extensively about music's role in film. Eisenstein's notions on what he called "vertical montage" as well as his particularly close working relationship with Prokofiev seem to parallel many of the formal as well as interpersonal dynamics that arose in your own collaboration with Reggio for* Koyaanisqatsi, *as well as for the forthcoming* Powaqqatsi.[25]
Yes, I've heard about the Prokofiev scores for Eisenstein. But, actually, my information comes from a very different set of sources and experiences. As I mentioned, my basic background comes from theater.

You're including opera and ballet here?
Yes. For me, the two most important theatrical influences were working

with Julian Beck's Living Theater and then with John Cage and Merce Cunningham.[26] In those instances, we're talking about situations where the meanings arose from juxtapositions of image and music, *but* in a more spontaneous way. When I think of Cunningham and Cage, for instance, the meanings of their fusions of dance and music are essentially inferred; and inferred, generally speaking, by each individual viewer. Their work did not have implicit content of its own. In other words, it was a situation where individual members of the audience had to make up meanings for themselves.

Now I don't approach it in that way. Nor have I used random chance procedures like Cage in my work. But the lesson of including the viewer wasn't lost on me. So, for example, if you tell a tenth of a story, the audience will make up the other nine-tenths of the meaning, or narrative, or whatever the case may be. In fact, very little of the story needs to be told. Here, I'm essentially talking about telling some kind of narrative. But really, it's exactly the same as far as how things work in my own collaborations.

Early on in my work in the theater, I was encouraged to leave what I call a "space" between the image and the music. In fact, it is precisely that space which is required so that members of the audience have the necessary perspective or distance to create their own individual meanings. If you didn't have that space there, if the music were too close and therefore immediately on top of the image, there wouldn't be anywhere for the viewer to place himself. In that case, it's like what you end up with on commercials. That's why television commercials end up looking more like propaganda than art.

Really, I can't believe the music on most commercials. The music tells you exactly what to look at, at each and every second. It's as if the filmmaker and composer were taking their hands and actually guiding your eyes around the screen. And this is exactly what you get in propaganda. They're not allowing you to look. They're *making* you look. They don't allow you to see and react or think for yourself.

Now what I do, what I learned from the theater, is that the big space that you leave between the viewers and what they're looking at becomes the area where they personalize the work. We're all twentieth-century people and in various ways we've learned to look or visualize that way, whether we know it or not. We're not nineteenth-century people, we don't look the other way. What's funny, and really odd and thoughtless in a way, is that the world of music for film, television, and commercials hasn't made the move at all. Yet it's there in the world of dance and theater, especially the progressive world of experimental dance and theater, and also in the work of the more progressive people in film and video. But as it enters the mainstream world of media, it will change the way we use music in commercial film and video as well.

To me, one of the fascinating aspects about viewing Koyaanisqatsi *a second, third, or fourth time is the way in which the meanings or experiences evoked by the film modulate from screening to screening. Last night, for example, my experience of the film was quite different than it was several years ago when I last saw it.*
Exactly! You did notice that. Good. I, too, am very struck by that dimension. Four years ago, for example, we thought *Koyaanisqatsi* was a very political film. Now, it doesn't look that way at all to me.

Yes, I agree. Now the film's critique of modern society is almost secondary. The images of the 747s, the skyscrapers, even the traffic, have a vitality, and a sense of beauty, experiences that are more typical of the experimental film or the more poetic forms of the documentary.[27]
Yes, that's very accurate. We look at it differently now. Really, it's been very instructive for Godfrey to see how much it's changed. And, really, I think it's changed because we didn't apply too formulaic an approach to it, which has allowed the film to survive, to change with the times.

Let me shift the conversation from your relationship with Godfrey, to what we saw last night, "the live performance-screening" for want of a more felicitous phrase. What was the motivation for going out on the road with the Ensemble and the film?
Well, the idea came essentially from Tom Luddy, Francis Ford Coppola's director of creative services. Luddy had been involved with the presentation of Abel Gance's *Napoleon* with Coppola's father, Carmine, conducting a live symphonic score in a road-show tour of the film.

It was an incredible event. The performance in Kansas City is still one of the most vivid experiences of a film that I've ever had. There was Carmine Coppola's wonderful symphonic score, as well as the restored 35mm print of Gance's 1927 masterpiece. One index of the project's success is that Napoleon *was literally seen in a new light, a light which provoked many critics and scholars to reposition* Napoleon *as one of the unqualified landmarks of the silent era.*
It was immense! I saw immediately that the live music heightened the impact of the images. I also realized that this was a phenomenon from the

silent film days that we've lost track of. You and I weren't alive for it, but in the history of film, we've let that special dimension that live music provides get away. But when I saw that Tom had recaptured it with the *Napoleon* project, I realized that our own project was a candidate for that kind of presentation. Tom is a friend of mine, so we talked about how *Napoleon* was organized. I asked if such a venture could actually work in terms of being profitable. Tom said that they actually had made a lot of money with it.

Our project isn't that big of a money-maker, but it hasn't lost money either. Last night, for example, we had over 2000 people, which was rather impressive, I thought. And, they really seemed to like it. Also, it's nice to have the score breathing anew with each performance. I remember that when we finished the score and locked it into the sound track for *Koyaanisqatsi*'s first release, there was a part of me that regretted having to set it, so to speak, "into cement." Now, on this twenty-five city tour, the music is free and living each night.

How did you prepare the Ensemble for the job of synchronizing the score so that the "live" accompaniment would mesh with the images as tightly as the original recorded soundtrack had?
First, there was the task of transcribing what was originally a symphonic score down to a reduced score for a traveling ensemble of some ten musicians. Next was seeing if we could actually meet the challenge of performing the score live so that it synchronized with the images of Godfrey's film.[28] That's why it took several years to prepare. Then we had to go out and actually book the tour. What we're now discovering is that the music is actually becoming very alive and responsive to the film. For example, last night, we noticed that Michael [Riesman, the Ensemble's conductor], was creating dynamic shadings that weren't in the original score. And I thought, well, that's what we really wanted to happen.

Even though it constitutes a change in what you wrote for the original score?
Yes. It's actually a process we've never had an opportunity to explore. And Michael was responding in the way that any good musician would respond to a piece of music. If, for example, you were to give Michael, or any competent musician, a piano piece, after he'd had a chance to play it ten or fifteen times, he'd begin to personalize it. That's what you want from a sensitive interpreter. So, the conductor has to be the interpreter.

Since you're the Ensemble's leader as well as composer, why have you left the conducting chores to Michael?
First of all, when we made Michael the conductor, we did it because of his technical capabilities. He has a very precise sense of time, something that I just don't have. The fact is that with my sense of meter, there's a lot of drift. When I play, it's not at all metronomic. But Michael can do that. So it's a skill. And Michael is a very accurate musician and he's studied it. I haven't. I was spending a lot of time learning how to write the piece.

So Michael's time is metronomic, almost like a clock. He's the right person for the job. Now I don't know how well you know the film, but Michael was never more than a few frames off . . . only a fraction of a second from perfect synchronization. And when I say perfect sync, I mean the sync that we're accustomed to seeing in the film with the recorded soundtrack.

I understand that the conductor's score includes drawings that match up with key images in the film, which seems analogous to the story-boarding process which many filmmakers and animators use for pre-production planning purposes. Is that how the synchronization is maintained?
Yes, Michael does it visually. First, he took the score and memorized it. He knows what he's supposed to be seeing at any given moment. Then he put pictures on the score itself, in the margins. So he has visual cues which now function as reminders of key points in the synchronization. At this juncture, we're in city number twelve of a twenty-five city tour. Also, we rehearsed for about two weeks. In addition, Michael rehearsed with a video of the film and the score before we even rehearsed with the musicians. So I would say that Michael knows the film rather well. Now, it's all really quite tight.

When you were here two years ago with the Ensemble, there were some people who objected to what they perceived as volume levels that were excessive. Last night, though the music certainly had presence, I didn't hear a single complaint about the volume. With your battery of electronic keyboards and amplification equipment, how do you monitor volume levels?
Well, on this trip, it's much better because we have a mixer in the hall. Someone is actually out in the hall with the audience, which makes it much easier to control. Often we have a mixer on stage as well. So we're constantly trying to monitor the feedback from the mixer to get the volume right. But it's always a difficult challenge, and each hall has its own acoustic idiosyncracies. How was it last night?

Fine.

I thought it was excellent. And as you know, we only had a very short sound check because a plane had been canceled. But, we had played the room before, which was a big help.

One of the intriguing aspects about the "live music" Koyaanisqatsi, as well as the "live music" Napoleon, is that each performance, as you've suggested, seems to have an identity or signature all its own.

Well, the music acquires, say, a living relationship to the film. Actually, the problem with film, something I think even the most ardent film buff would agree with, is that it's frozen in time. It becomes a document. It can't be changed. I suppose you could go back and change some things, but that doesn't happen.

There's a story about a great French painter. When he was an old man, he'd often be found in the museums of Paris touching up his paintings! The guards, of course, would throw him out. But he was doing what any artist wants to do! He was trying to keep the piece alive! And that's very difficult to do with film.

In fact, when we look at a film, even a classic like *Citizen Kane*, what invariably happens is that we are forced to include an element of nostalgia about what we're looking at. It can't become new again. So that film, in a sense, has become history.[29]

Film becomes history more quickly than other arts because it doesn't have the means of adjusting to the flux of time. Of course, it's also true of painting, but at least paintings, and this is an odd way of putting it, deteriorate to a certain degree.[30] What bothers me about film is that, unlike the opera and ballet scores that I do, the film scores are set in cement so that I can't do anything about them. The exception, of course, is something like we're doing now with, as you put it, the "live music" *Koyaanisqatsi.*

In this case, I can see what happens with the film's score. The same thing applies to my concert music, as well as to the operas. When, say, an opera is revived, it's a different proposition, a different conceptualization, even though the score is followed exactly. It's similar to the contrast in how an actor will read Shakespeare when he's fifty, rather than when he's twenty-five. So, in film music there's virtually no opportunity to be an interpretive artist. But on our tour with *Koyaanisqatsi*, changes, as I mentioned, are taking place in the score. In the clouds sequence last night, for instance, I noticed a long crescendo-and-diminuendo in the brass that wasn't in the original score. Now, it's part of the music!

Last night, I was impressed with the totality of the experience—you and the members of the Ensemble just below the large screen, garbed in black, generating the music, thereby propping up Godfrey's amazing images exploding out at us. In a strange sort of way, it was reminiscent of Fritz Lang's Metropolis *[1926], with the Ensemble being the subterranean workers, Lang's symbolic "Hands"; the film on the screen the authoritarian agent of control, Lang's symbolic "Brains"; and, the music itself the great mediator Love, Lang's symbolic "Heart," the force of reconciliation.*

That's interesting. Actually, this configuration is something that's going to arise more frequently for me now that I've become generally less interested in concerts since I've done so many over the past twenty years. Now, I'm much more interested in theatrical extensions of the concert form which is why *Koyaanisqatsi* has been so fascinating for me. It's allowed me to get past the concert situation into larger audiences. Now, I'm starting to write works that will be more dramatic and theatrical in nature, works that will include the Ensemble.

Getting back to last night, did we remind you of the people in the new theater who change the sets around, the guys who dress in black and move the props? It's a little like that, though that wasn't intentional. I just happened to notice the other day that it resembled that new theater-like situation. But, we're wearing black mainly because we don't want to distract from the visual emphasis of the film. So there's, let's say, a rather self-effacing look that the Ensemble has. But, as you say, it is at the same time rather striking. You've got the instruments, all the equipment. It's very focused. And behind it you have, in this case, a rather splendid visual presentation.

Is the collaborative dimension also something that you'll continue to seek out?

Yes. With my roots in the Living Theater and with John Cage and Merce Cunningham, the group process is very important to me. So I'll continue to look for situations that involve the Ensemble, and situations that result from group visions where group authorship becomes a practical and comfortable way of working, a concept that's still quite new. *Koyaanisqatsi* is a good example. It's a joint work where the vision came from a group of artists working together, rather than from a single individual. It's a process that's actually quite idealistic, but one that's actually happening, and one that's on the rise. [31]

1. Further background on Glass can be found in Glass's own *Music by Philip Glass*, ed. by Robert T. Jones (New York: Harper & Row, 1987), described on the dust jacket as "The Professional Autobiography of the Most Acclaimed American Composer of Our Time," which includes a valuable "Music Catalog" of his compositions, as well as a complete "Discography." Also useful are Allan Kozinn's "Philip Glass," *Ovation* (February 1984): 12–16, and Robert T. Jones's "Philip Glass," in *Musical America*.

2. Concise overviews of cinema's auteur theory, a variant of the great man (and more recently, great woman) approach to historiography that can be found in virtually every area where humankind's endeavors have been chronicled, are presented by Dudley Andrew, "Valuation (of Genres and Auteurs)," in *Concepts of Film Theory* (New York: Oxford UP, 1984), 107–32; and by Gerald Mast and Marshall Cohen, eds. of *Film Theory and Criticism: Introductory Readings*, 2nd ed. (New York: Oxford UP, 1979), 637–91, whose section on "The Film Artist" includes such important position papers on the auteur theory as Andrew Sarris's "Notes on the Auteur Theory in 1962" (1963), Pauline Kael's "Circles and Squares" (1963), and Peter Wollen's "The Auteur Theory" (1972).

3. Philip Auslander, "Going with the Flow: Performance Art and Mass Culture," *The Drama Review* 33:2 (Summer 1983; T122): 119–136.

4. Auslander, 120.

5. Linda Frye Burnham, "High Performance Art, and Me," *The Drama Review* 30:2 (T122), 15–51, cited by Auslander, 122–123. The radically subversive element vis-à-vis mediated mass culture, which Burnham deems as requisite to truly counterhegemonic aesthetic forms, is one which has been vital to the anti-bourgeois, anti-establishment stances of twentieth-century vanguard artists from the European Dadas and Surrealists of the 1920s to, it could be argued, today's popular black rap music groups. Sarane Alexandrian's *Surrealist Art*, trans. Gordon Clough (New York: Praeger Publishers, 1969) and *Surrealism*, ed. Herbert Read (New York: Praeger Publishers, 1971) provide excellent overviews of the basic tenets of and interconnections between the Continental Dadas and Surrealists.

6. Auslander, 123, cites Tania Modleski's "The Terror of Pleasure: The Contemporary Horror Film and Postmodern Theory," in *Studies in Entertainment: Critical Approaches to Mass Culture*, ed. Tania Modleski (Bloomington: Indiana UP, 1986), which argues that slasher films are adversarial to the mainstream in their assaults on bourgeois institutions such as the family and the school.

7. See Raymond Williams, *Television: Technology and Cultural Form* (New York: Schocken Books, 1974), cited by Auslander, 124.

8. See Andreas Huyssen, *After the Great Divide: Modernism, Mass Culture, Postmodernism* (Bloomington: Indiana UP, 1986), cited by Auslander, 133.

9. Auslander, 132.

10. Several of the Kurtzweil electronic keyboards used by the Philip Glass Ensemble retail for $65,000 each, for example.

11. The quest for larger audiences is one that Glass discusses freely in the interview. That quest has also been manifest in such Glass projects as his composition of incidental music for the opening and closing ceremonies for the 1984 Summer Olympics in Los Angeles, as well as his album *Songs from Liquid Days* (CBS Masterworks, 1985), written and performed with lyricist/singers Laurie Anderson, David Byrne, Paul Simon, and Suzanne Vega.

12. Among other honors, Glass was selected as *Musical America*'s 1985 "Musician of the Year," and featured on the cover of the magazine's 25th-anniversary book-length special edition, *Musical America: 1985 International Directory of the Performing Arts.* Also, he is the composer of the successful operas *Einstein on the Beach* (1976), *Satyagraha* (1980), *Akhnaten* (1983), *the CIVIL warS: a tree is best measured when it is down* (1984), and, most recently, *The Fall of the House of Usher* (1988) and *The Making of the Representative for Planet 8* (1988), based on the novel by Doris Lessing; he also collaborated with Tony Award-winning playwright David Henry Hwang and designer Jerome Sirlin for the multimedia theater piece *1000 Airplanes on the Roof* (1988).

13. Even though Glass has been described as something of a recluse (see Jones), he nonetheless has appeared on *Saturday Night Live* and *Late Night with David Letterman*, a further indication of his celebrity-hood and, indeed, his acceptance by many popular music and rock fans as well as by devotees of so-called contemporary "serious music." Glass's status as a twentieth-century music top-gun is, however, not without controversy. Jones, for example, notes that Glass's penchants for arpeggiated repetitions and high volume levels of the kind so beloved by aficionados of rock are such that "Glass's music has been praised and hated, loved and damned, [and] has brought delight and occasioned fulmination. Whether he is a musical messiah or a sonic anti-Christ is a matter of conjecture, but his impact on the world of music cannot be denied."

14. Glass describes *Koyaanisqatsi* as "a reflection on nature, technology, and contemporary life, and it uses only images and music, no spoken dialogue, story line, or even actors," in *Music by Philip Glass*, 203.

15. Michael Dempsey, in "Qatsi Means Life: The Films of Godfrey Reggio," *Film Quarterly* (Spring 1989), 2–12, discusses the ambiguity of *Koyaanisqatsi*'s non-narrative structure vis-à-vis the multiple "readings" elicited by the film among both critics and audiences, a point elaborated upon by Glass himself in the interview.

16. *Koyaanisqatsi* was initially shown in September 1982 at Radio City Music Hall under the auspices of the New York Film Festival and the Film Society of Lincoln Center, largely because noted director Francis Ford Coppola agreed to attach his name to the production as "presenter." It then played at major film festivals in Berlin, Hong Kong, the Soviet Union, Tokyo, Havana, Cannes, Aspen and L.A.'s Filmex, as well as

garnering attention through a variety of benefit screenings for different environmental and disarmament groups, before opening around the country in select and limited engagements in the fall of 1983. The highly effective advertising campaign was directed by Cary Brokaw, who achieved his first notable success with the promotion of *The Rocky Horror Picture Show*. For further information on the selling of *Koyaanisqatsi*, see Karen Kreps, "The Marketing of *Koyaanisqatsi*: Market It? I Can't Even Pronounce It!," *Boxoffice* (December 1983), 68–70.

17. Adam Parfrey in "The Pre-Recorded Audience in Two Dimensions," *Performing Arts Journal* 9:2–3 (26–27), 213–218, discusses intertextual relationships between rock concerts and recordings, a situation in which the "original" performance, the live concert or the recording, becomes a matter of individual cases; Parfrey's discussion is expanded upon by Auslander, 128, who argues that when a recorded version provides an individual's first exposure to a work, the live performance can be regarded as a reification of the recording, since the recorded performance has become the referent of the live one.

18. "The Grid," a section from Glass's score for *Koyaanisqatsi*, has been performed in concert by the Philip Glass Ensemble since 1985.

19. Two years before its 1987 tour, *Koyaanisqatsi: Live* was presented in two sold-out performances at Avery Fisher Hall in New York City, in part as a kind of test-run to determine the feasibility of a national road-show production. The 1985 screenings were accompanied by the Philip Glass Ensemble, augmented by the Western Wind vocal group and a number of other musicians approximating the orchestral dimensions of the original soundtrack recording made in 1983. For the national tour of 1987, Glass scaled down the size of his musical group considerably by employing only the ten-piece Ensemble plus the pre-recorded vocal tapes of the Western Wind vocal ensemble and bass Albert de Ruiter.

20. Glass's curiosity was particularly piqued by the high level of theorizing on the use of music in the silent film; for further information, see Charles Merrell Berg, "Silent Film Principles and Techniques," *An Investigation of the Motives for and Realization of Music to Accompany the American Silent Film, 1896–1927* (New York: Arno Press, 1976), 170–237.

21. For another aspect of the collaborative dimension in the production of *Koyaanisqatsi*, see Ron Gold, "Untold Tales of *Koyaanisqatsi*," *American Cinematographer* (March 1984), 62–74, which chronicles the integral role of innovative cinematographer Ron Fricke.

22. The sequence and titles of the various subject roles as listed in the 1987 tour program for *Koyaanisqatsi: Live* are "Opening," "Organic," "Clouds," "Resource," "Vessels," "Pruit Igoe," "Clouds and Building/Stomo People," "The Grid," "Microchips," and "Prophesies—Closing."

23. Cinematographer Fricke must be mentioned again, for it was he who was as much responsible for *Koyaanisqatsi*'s visual style and "look" as director Reggio. See Gold.

24. The strategy of image-music counterpoint is one that has been discussed by a number of theorists, including Paolo Milano, "Music in the Film: Notes for a Morphology," *The Journal of Aesthetics and Arts Criticism* 91 (1941), 89–94, and, in an experimental study, Dominic A. Infante and Charles M. Berg, "The Impact of Music Modality on the Perception of Communication Situations in Video Sequences," *Communication Monographs* 46 (June 1979), 135–141.

25. *Powaqqatsi*, Part Two of Reggio's proposed trilogy (Part Three will be entitled *Naquoyqatsi*, if funding can be found), was released in 1988 to generally negative reviews, largely because of its thematic and stylistic similarities to *Koyaanisqatsi* and what was generally considered to be a lack of focus. John Powers, in "Kitschy Quatsi," *California* (June 1998), 126, panned Reggio's second film by noting that "Unlike the worst beer ad, *Powaqqatsi* doesn't know what it's selling, beyond some vaporous notion of the authentic life. Instead of illuminating life's complexity and diversity, Reggio reduces his themes to cheap iconography . . . *Powaqqatsi* juxtaposes images from all over the planet, yet it never shows us how anything connects except for tacit bromides about Spaceship Earth." For additional information on the Eisenstein-Prokofiev collaborations on *Alexander Nevsky* (1938), *Ivan the Terrible* Part I (1945) and *Ivan the Terrible* Part II (1946; released in 1958), see Yon Barna, *Eisenstein*, trans. Lise Hunter (Bloomington: Indiana UP, 1973). Also, Eisenstein wrote in detail on image-music relationships, using *Alexander Nevsky* as a case study, in "Form and Content: Practice," *The Film Sense*, trans. Jay Leyda (1942; reprinted New York: Meridian Books, 1967), 155–216.

26. For further background on Glass's early collaborations with the Living Theater of Julian Beck and Judith Malina, and John Cage and Merce Cunningham, see "Apprenticeship of Sorts," *Music by Philip Glass*, 3–24.

27. *Koyaanisqatsi*, though it has no dialogue or "story," can still be considered to have a narrative structure, as Glass clearly suggests. The film can also be placed under the rubrics of documentary and experimental. Louis Giannetti, in a chapter devoted to the documentary film in *Understanding Movies*, 4th ed. (Englewood Cliffs: Prentice Hall, 1987), 330, writes that "Documentaries and avant-garde films are generally thought to be on opposite ends of the stylistic spectrum, but there are exceptions to virtually every generalization about movies. *Koyaanisqatsi* is a strange hybrid that fuses these antithetical extremes. The haunting images (photographed by Ron Fricke) were taken from reality, but a reality that seems more surreal than a dream. They are accompanied only by a pulsating musical score by Philip Glass, which intensifies the film's weird sense of unreality."

28. Again, the "test-run" to check the feasibility of presenting *Koyaanisqatsi* with a live musical accompaniment came in 1985 with the two Avery Fisher Hall performances; see Note 19.

29. Here, I think, Glass's position is somewhat arbitrary. Indeed, *Citizen Kane* provides just as good an example of a film whose inherent narrative and cinematic powers continue to "speak" to contemporary audiences, regardless of whether individual specta-

tors are viewing the film for the first time or, instead, revisiting an "old friend" in a manner comparable to what happens when a connoisseur of classical music seeks out the familiar yet stimulating "companionship" of, say, Mozart's *Don Giovanni.*

30. Glass's argument vis-à-vis "deteriorization" as a process that assists in "adjusting" a painting to "the flux of time" is one that could be applied with at least equal force to film, a medium whose photochemical properties are actually far less stable than the gamut of physical materials employed by most painters; therefore one could, following Glass's proposition, contend that film actually is quite superior to painting in terms of such non-interventionist artistic "adjustments." For me, Glass's argument, though clever and useful for polemical purposes, stretches the bounds of the notion of the "living art work" beyond utility as a practical conceptual strategy.

31. As this article goes to press in mid-September 1990, Glass and the Ensemble are in the midst of planning another tour with the "live music" *Koyaanisqatsi* throughout the northeastern United States. In 1991, Glass and his Ensemble will tour major European venues with Reggio's sequel to *Koyaanisqatsi, Powaqqatsi/Live!* Both tours are further indicators of Glass's unique status as a high-profile, commercially viable performance artist; they also point up, I think, the equally unique and special attractiveness of the "live music film," itself a singular subspecies of the performance art phenomenon.

EINSTEIN ON THE BEACH (1977)

DAVID CUNNINGHAM

Einstein on the Beach has no narrative or conventional plot. Numerical and musical systems are heavily used throughout, but despite this, it is still a recognizable opera in the classical sense; the basic elements of music, decor and movement are present throughout the work.

STRUCTURE

There are three main elements present consistently during the opera; the train, the trial and the field (1, 2, and 3). Act one includes the train and the trial (1 + 2), act two includes the field and the train (3 + 1), act three includes the trial and the field (2 + 3), act four includes all three elements in transmuted form; the train becomes a building, the trial a bed, the field a machine. This gives the component parts of the acts an overall structure of nine parts, 123, 123, 123.

The transmutation process in act four requires some explanation. First the connection between train and building: the train is the most commonly used illustration of the relativity theory, showing the number of relative ways in which the relationship between two trains passing each other can present itself. So the train depicts the theory of relativity, the opera postulates that theory as a law, so the train becomes a building, fixed, established, and static. (Or is it?) This is the only explanation I can find for this imagery; it is certainly a tenuous proposition.

The process by which a trial becomes a bed (which itself appears to be a beam of light) escapes me. However, some points worth consideration are: that the bed is a constant element in all the trial scenes, that the French word for "trial" is *procès*, and that as a youth Einstein apparently speculated, "What would it be like to travel alongside a beam of light?" . . . a question he did not answer until he proposed the relativity theory.

The field becomes a machine, more precisely the scene described as field becomes the inside of a time machine which has been suspended above the stage during the first two field scenes. This is not a field as on a farm, but a field as in Einstein's unified field theory, again following the progression from weak to strong.

Before and after each act, there is a short scene called a "kneeplay," generally with choral accompaniment, which is set in the extreme right of the stage; these serve as a relief to the main action, which lasts for around five hours, and they also serve as a constant motif in the whole work.

There is a constant pattern of three sections to all the principal work in the opera. All the scenes are relative to three positionings on the stage: foreground, middle, and rear; Wilson calls these positions "portrait," "still life," and "landscape," respectively. Corresponding with these is a set of three "intensities" which have been created, I suppose, intuitively by Wilson, referring to the body: the parts being designated skin, flesh and bones.

The opera itself stems originally from drawings produced by Robert Wilson, to which Philip Glass wrote music; the drawings were revised; the music was then changed; and so on, up to the final version when contributions from the dancers and actors, as well as practical considerations, initiated further changes. One effect that this process of revision has had is an improvement in the overall placing of the pieces of music. Michael Nyman has criticized *Music in 12 Parts*, saying that the parts were obviously and unceremoniously played in the order they had been composed in, with no attempt made to arrange them in such a way as to hear each to its best advantage."[1] I think the music in *Einstein* has escaped this error both because of the strong overall structure and the numerical system inside the work.

The music for *Einstein on the Beach* is based on additive and subtractive process and on cyclical process. The innovation which forms a step forward for Glass is effectively a preview of his new (unfinished) work, *Another Look at Harmony*. This is a new structural idea which first appeared in *Music in 12 Parts*, where in part twelve, Glass states, "The

principal melodic figure is in fact two distinct harmonic and melodic fragments which follow in quick succession. Each develops separately within
the repeated figure."[2] In connection with *Einstein* he describes the music
as being based on the rethinking of cadential formulae which he is using
as a major structural part of *Another Look at Harmony*.

Philip Glass's ensemble is basically his working group from the
last two or three years, but there are some additions. The complete group
consists of Jon Gibson and Richard Landry, soprano saxophone, flute;
Richard Peck, tenor saxophone; Philip Glass, Michael Riesman and
George Adoniadis, electric organ; Joan La Barbara, voice; and Robert
Brown, violin. The most important addition is probably a twelve-person
chorus, featuring Joan La Barbara as soloist. The sung material is quite
unique . . .

"We're only singing numbers and solfège syllables. The whole piece
is made from them. The names of the notes or the rhythmic structures of
the music as represented by numbers are the only thing that is sung in the
piece. I've worked with numbers before, it's a lot of fun, isn't it?"[3]

Often the overall sound gives the impression that the chorus are
singing words and phrases. This illusion is contrary in nature to much of
the overall music and dance within *Einstein*, but it seems to be closely
aligned to the fragmented and convoluted narrative (?) imagery which
appears from time to time in the action. Glass, however, had no intention
to provide a specific illusion-orientated vocabulary for the voices. This can
be shown from the structure of the vocal parts and from a comment by
Glass: "One builds different meanings into it; one tends to put construc-
tions of meaning on things that aren't really there. That's more or less normal. We do that all the time."

This statement in particular could be applied as a preface to a consideration of the ideas behind and contained in *Einstein*.

THE OPERA

Einstein on the Beach begins with the first "knee-play," in which Lucinda
Childs and Sheryl Sutton sit at desks counting the numbers (one to eight)
of one of Glass's additive systems. The kneeplays take place in what is
really a cube of space in the bottom right-hand corner of the stage. This
spatial motif is recurring right through the opera and also in the supplementary graphic material, posters, and the book.[4] This device is an overall geometric reference to the direction of Einstein's work; the idea of the

fourth dimension and so on; on account of the cube's mathematical relationship to the full three-dimensional stage area, that is, the cube is x^3, Wilson and Glass are hinting that the stage area is a four-dimensional extension of this space constructed by pataphysical proposition. This illustrates one of a number of aspects of *Einstein*'s use of a statement by Apollinaire to the effect that artists should take the flavour of mathematics and science, and should not encumber themselves in the everyday practical problems or the strict interpretation of scientific formulae. This particular statement seems to have had quite an influence on the opera as a whole, and particularly on Wilson's contribution (insofar as this can be isolated).

Act one scene one starts at a very high level of activity which remains constant throughout the scene. The music appears to be loud but I would think this is due to the nature of the instrumentation and the piece, rather than simply due to amplification. Almost the full ensemble and choir launch into a very pretty, very simplistic, and very fast piece of music. Onstage, a boy, who would seem to be one of the recurring Einstein figures in the piece, stands at the top of a high open-construction gantry and periodically throws paper airplanes onto the stage. Lucinda Childs marches continuously forwards and backwards always in the same line from backdrop to stage front, in time with the music. This part of this scene is one of the most compelling experiences that this work contains; it provides for myself a similar experience to hearing a music of this texturally dense systems variety for the first time ever. This particular scene must contain the essence of quite a few very strong emotional triggers in its fairly sparse elements.

Other actors slowly come onstage, performing smaller scale cyclical activities in much the same way as Lucinda's action, and at the back a replica of an old American steam locomotive slowly travels onto the stage from the right. It is almost onto the stage when, about halfway through the scene, a bar of light draws its way down the center of the backdrop. A further, smaller backdrop of a picture of two trains passing is lowered; this image being the traditional explanatory image for the relativity theory. Then the scene reverts to the initial action again, with a few additions: a girl poses motionless with a large conch shell held to her ear, a man (another Einstein figure?) writes furiously on an imaginary blackboard, and the train draws its way slowly onto the stage again. The bar of light descends again and the scene ends.

At the age of sixteen, Einstein is said to have asked what it would be like if one could travel alongside a beam of light. His eventual development of the theory of relativity at the age of twenty-four was his answer to this early question. This stage of the opera is at the stage of asking the question and beginning the process of deduction and formulation. This is particularly relevant to the viewer at this point, as the only way that the viewer can[5] impose development on the work (because *Einstein* functions partly on the basis that information is supplied, perception by its existence alters the information perceived—perception is a form of change) is to actually deduce and formulate on one's own behalf. One interesting consequence of this action in relation to *Einstein* is that one can and perhaps must formulate in a fashion which bears very close resemblance to the pataphysical school of thinking, which itself generated many aspects of the opera. This kind of variation on logic as a method of working has a small but important connexion with Einstein himself; that he is thought in some circles to have been dyslexic, the result of which may have been to force him to acquire the ability to think in a more lateral fashion than was usual for his day and hence the important advances in his work.

The music completes its cyclical system at the two points where the descending bar of light occurs, and firstly as a break and secondly as end of scene, a very peculiar short piece of music is played and sung. It seems to be a scale with some of the notes left out and the remainder extended to fill the space. Then notes are slowly brought in and taken out, in much the same kind of way as in most of Glass's work, but here a lot more attention seems to have been paid to the basic material and the exact procedure by which it is treated. This is the piece which many of the reviews have compared to Bach or to church music.[6] It recurs throughout the opera in various ways with differing instrumentation, as a short internal break in a scene and as an end sequence, with the exception of act four scene three, where the piece becomes quite elaborate and extended. Here the basis of the piece can easily be seen to be rooted in a scale.

Act one scene two begins with the various characters coming on stage for the trial scene. The choir appears as the jury and stenographers, other actors sit opposite them. The stage centre is a large bed, behind it is the judges' table, loaded with books. The two judges come onstage, one is the boy who was on the gantry throughout the first scene, the other is an actor who, I am told, is 77 years of age, Samuel M. Johnson. They announce the sitting of the court, first in French, then in English, a number of times. There is then a slight overall change in the level of action and the music; Lucinda Childs sits on a high stool and recites one of the texts, Sheryl Sutton walks around the courtroom in slow motion, and slowly a gyroscope travels between the top right and bottom left corners of the stage. This is the first time one of the instrumental musicians appears in the lights (they are playing in the orchestra pit). Robert Brown sits up dressed as the most often seen representation of Einstein, as an old man with a white moustache, and plays a very even and rhythmic piece on violin, which is first accompanied by choir and later also flutes.

This scene also has a break in the middle, but instead of the visual action and symbolism of the previous scene, this break could be said to be almost literally self-referring. The performers go to the front of the stage and, with the exception of one woman who has been reading a book throughout the scene, they open brown paper bags and take out cups of coffee. They drink their coffee, look at their watches and return to their previous activities.

Philip Glass said about this break something that reflects on the relationship and interdependence of the music and action, that "it's structural in the music, and Bob [Wilson] picked that as an emotional break in the piece to correspond to the structure in the music . . . we didn't plan ahead of time to work towards the coffee break, as we call it, but once that break in the music was there, we were able to work with it in terms of the action."

The odd thing about this comment is the idea of an "emotional break" in the work. Obviously that kind of thinking came from Robert Wilson, but one wonders how much Glass merely accepts the idea and how much it has affected his own output. The most puzzling thing about this opera to many people who were acquainted with both artists' work was how they could work together. Even after the event this is unanswered except to say that they work together very well.

The next part of this scene is quite different in terms of focus, though most of the elements remain the same. Samuel M. Johnson delivers an impressive speech in badly articulated French on how young men and women in Paris pass the time. To illustrate his point, a very transparent front-drop of an unclothed lady is lowered for a few minutes. When it is raised the boy judge, Paul Mann, announces, "When, When I get . . ." and so on until he constructs the phrase, "When I get some wind for the sailboat."[7] The lights dim and the violin plays the end-of-scene music.

Kneeplay two follows, the choir singing very rapid 1-2-3- . . . structures. Lucinda Childs and Sheryl Sutton sit and lie on tables, stretch bend and turn.

Act two scene one is "field," the third in the series of three elements of the opera's main structure. It is announced as Berne, Switzerland.

The stage area is empty, except for the dancers dressed in white:

this is where they really come into their own. The choreography, by Andy de Groat, is composed of intertwined simplistic components, running, jumping movement forwards and backwards, turning, and kneeling.

"I chose simple movements which the dancers could make naturally, and structured them very rigorously."[8]

These structures which de Groat emphasizes here are mathematically based and in this piece are working from the musical structure, from addition, subtraction, and cyclic repetition.

The dancing is visually very attractive, the motion is almost always fast, like the music. The motions are always on the fringe of obvious relationship to each other, the relationship is implied but never forced, it appears natural and complex at the same time. The only way I can attempt to describe it is to picture two dancers running round each other in contrary motion relative to each other, and then extend the image to include two further dancers, each circling one of the first (also in motion) dancers in contrary motion. This is a fairly representative image of what some of the dancing looks like, although most of the dancing is much more dependent upon various kinds of interrelationship either between different structures ending and beginning, in time, or between other spatial relationships. It looks like phased dancing.

As the dance proceeds a large compass, suspended near the top of the stage area, slowly travels across, above the stage. This is half of the rather obscure "time machine," which Robert Wilson has developed through this work, referring to the properties of the "field."

The dance continues, the lights fade, the dance stops, and the music changes to act two scene two, the "train's" reappearance.

The train reappears as seen from the rear, still the old western train, one can see the rear compartment and the open platform bounded by a guard rail, at the very rear of the last carriage, in apparent motion away from the viewer. The stage is in darkness apart from the interior of the train and the backdrop, which depicts the night sky and an illuminated moon.

According to the relativity theory, time in the carriage, were it actually moving, would appear to be passing at an imperceptibly slower rate relative to the viewer's time, with even this rate getting slower as the train accelerates away from the viewer. This application of the theory is used by Wilson and Glass as the basis for this scene; they emphasize it by having the characters on the train move extremely slowly and finally cease to move at all.

There are two characters in the coach, a white man and a black woman both in more or less period costume (to go with the train), the women wearing a white dress, almost a bridal dress. Very slowly they move out through the rear door of the compartment, onto the outside platform, until they are both standing on the rearmost part of the train. Equally slowly they start to go inside again.

The woman raises a gun and points it at the man, all in slow motion. Then the moon above the scene is gradually eclipsed, while the action is motionless, and slowly the stage fades to darkness. When the moon re-emerges from its eclipse, and we see the train again lit up, it is smaller (physically smaller) as if in the distance and empty. Any shooting, if it took place, was unrestrained by light, that is, it could only appear to us to happen as the laws of physics in relation to the moving train dictate, but without light, (for Wilson hence without physics) things may change. Throughout this scene the music, in contrast to the action, has been full and fast, shifting through many themes and patterns, the choir singing both solfège syllables and numbers for, I think, the first time inside the same piece. The music sounds like a reiteration of many of the themes that have gone before.

Here in this scene the figure of the girl with the conch shell recurs; she stands center-left in the same position and pose as in the first scene in act one. Thus most of that scene's elements have reappeared, the train (the central element), the girl, and conceivably the man referrs to the Einstein figure. Slowly the transmutation process has begun: the train has already begun to solidify into the "building" of act four.

The third "kneeplay" follows now, this time being centred around a light panel which forms the rear of the kneeplay area. The panel is an eight foot square that contains, in changing lights, firstly two sets of two straight lines at right angles to each other, secondly two sets of two parallel diagonal lines. Then these two figures are both simultaneously illuminated, and a third figure, two concentric circles, lights up as well.

Once again the choir is in view, this time wearing headphones and singing numerals.[9] The headphones perform no function other than visual, another rather mysterious Wilson gesture. The actors Lucinda and Sheryl stand and move against the illuminated panel. The lights flash through the permutations of the pattern and the kneeplay ends.

Act three, scene one is the second trial scene. It opens with the two judges sitting in their place in the courtroom, as it slowly fills up with much the same personnel as in act one scene two. The bed in the centre of the court is still there, this time lit up from inside.

Lucinda Childs enters and takes up her place, now wearing a

white dress. The boy judge leaves, and by degrees the right-hand half of the scenery begins to move off stage. Some is pulled off by concealed cables; stagehands appear and remove the rest until the right-hand side is empty. A set of bars descends over that side so that the stage becomes half court, and half prison with prisoners.

The music has so far in this scene been a slow organ solo, now it changes to a rapid piece for choir and organ.[10]

Lucinda sits on the bed and delivers a monologue over the music about how she went into a supermarket, saw some bathing caps in different colours, and realised that she had been avoiding the beach. This is the first reference to the beach of the opera's title.

Still reciting, repeating the speech a number of times, she walks in front of the bars and changes into a dark suit, picks up a machine gun; poses with it, puts it down and picks up some handcuffs; again she poses with them, then she puts them down and leaves the stage. Sheryl Sutton then performs the same actions with the gun and handcuffs, and leaves the stage.

The music changes to a fast instrumental piece for a time, the other characters leave the stage.

When that music stops, Childs appears lit up behind a transparent front-drop behind the bars. Accompanied by violin and saxophone, she recites a text[11] by Christopher Knowles (one of the people Robert Wilson has worked with): "I feel the earth move . . . I feel the tumbling down tumbling down . . . " She repeats this text a number of times. It finishes with a listing of the times of the shows on radio station WABC [New York]. Throughout this scene the gyroscope has been moving across the stage as in act one, scene two. The lights dim.

This scene has been transmuted in a similar way to the train scene, most of the elements present, but with an apparent change of emphasis; away from the rigid ritual of the first court to the more emotive gestures and texts of the second: this is perhaps a development towards act four.

Act three scene two is the return to the "field" dance. The music is similar to the previous "field" scene, the dance is different; marching, shuffling, and standing still.

Here, there is an indeterminate element present, the choice of the dancers to move or remain motionless at certain points throughout the scene. It works well. There are about eight dancers, wearing colored t-shirts; they run, zigzag, and stop with a manner reminiscent of Brechtian theater; the fast-beating loud music and the poses.

As in act three scene one the compass passed overhead, here a clock slowly travels over the stage area. We have had space, this is time; next, the field will refer almost exclusively to these elements, and to the machines travelling across.

At the end of the dance, a front-drop depicting stars descends; the music changes to a twirl on organ into a scale-like piece which is then played by the violin. This leads into the fourth "kneeplay."

Lucinda and Sheryl lie and posture on transparent tables. Below the choir sings, accompanied by the violin. At one point the choir members all raise toothbrushes to their mouths as they sing. The music is systematic variations on the end-of-scene theme scale mentioned before. Directly the piece resolves, the ensembles launch into the music for act four scene one.

The long sustained notes from some instruments and voices sound very much like *Music with Changing Parts*, although the basic rhythmic music sounds different, more percussive. This percussive quality has a lot to do with the organ sound; the organs can be set to give a very sharp attack to the note. It is likely that this piece is very similar to the earlier piece, albeit with different instrumentation.

Onstage action is minimal and fairly casual. There is a backdrop depicting a large, tall, redbrick building, and through an opening high up (made up to be a window) one can see a man (another Einstein) writing on a blackboard, calculating and numerating. For some time nothing else happens. Then, gradually and without any obvious pattern people wander onto the stage; the black judge holding the boy by the hand, no longer dressed as judges, the girl who was reading through the first trial scene, still reading; and various others; dancers and actors.

They group together below the window and look up at the man working.

Then, just as casually, they begin to leave the stage, the girl reading is last to leave. After a short time the light at the window fades.

This is the tenuous extension of the train into the relativistic building. This transmutation is not chosen for scientific or logical reasons any more than it is chosen for emotional effect. The idea of cause/effect would appear to have little to do with this work, however; as noted earlier, both scientific and highly emotive material is presented here, but the flavour is stronger than the actuality.

Act four scene two is the transmutation of the trial into the bed. The phrase 'lit de justice' is used in French; the court is the bed of justice; we are left with the bed.

A strange bed it is, illuminated, it presents itself as a bar of light.

It lies on the floor of the stage, in darkness except for its own light. Step by step the left-hand side tilts up and the right-hand side centres itself on the stage, so that eventually the bed stands on end stage centre, presenting an image not unlike the bar of light in the first scene of the opera. Then it slowly lifts out of sight until the stage is in darkness.

The music for this scene is for solo organ and voice (some of the organ music is written out in the book). It is haunting and drifting; Joan La Barbara's voice is high, clear and note perfect. It's an obviously systemised and fairly complex piece, but it sounds quite unlike anything I've ever heard by Glass before.

Act four scene three is the final and most immediately impressive scene. This is the final transmutation of "field" to "machine."

The stage area is filled with a large construction of twelve eight-foot square panels, the bottom right one being the kneeplay area, and not used here. In front of the squares are suspended firstly, a compass on a large transparent container containing an actor, this assembly moves from left to right and back, about halfway up the stage area. Secondly a clock, which rises from a trapdoor in the stage and travels up and down, also mounted on a transparent box which also has an actor inside. Sitting at the edge of the top left panel is Philip Glass, who gets up and begins to play an organ installed in the set.

Slowly the panels begin to light up. Each one is the same as the panel in kneeplay three, having the same repertoire of lines, diagonals and circles. They start with lines, and more musicians climb up the side of the structure and take their places standing up in their squares. The light patterns switch to diagonals, a dancer dressed in black appears on the stage, dancing with lights in his/her hands. Two small transparent domes appear on the stage, actors and dancers are occupying the rest of the panels on the frame.

The music has been developing and getting more intense. A keyboard bass part is sounding very dynamic, sweeping up and down the scales which are being played. The music has an almost classical feel to it; on being asked about this, Glass said that he thought so, it reminded him of Berlioz. It also sounds very Glass, seeming to be a culmination of pieces heard throughout the opera.

At this point there is a brief visual interruption, as a front-drop of sky is lowered and a small rocket travels diagonally across the stage area.

This device lifts and the musicians are again revealed. The lights change to circular patterns. The music finally develops through scales into the churchlike piece heard intermittently throughout the opera, mostly at ends of scenes. The gradual buildup, although it is probably systematic, functions as a very dramatic climax.

The lights flash and change, and a dancer suspended on a deus ex machina device sweeps and hurtles across the stage.

Another front-drop is lowered depicting diagrammatically nuclear explosion, showing radiation, fallout zones, and the explosion itself.

The fifth and final kneeplay. The organ drones softly again and Lucinda and Sheryl crawl out from under the two transparent domes on the stage. The choir sings numbers at a slower tempo than the previous piece; and Lucinda recites another of Christopher Knowles's texts, "These are the Days." From the right a train emerges, a futuristic train, but in the driver's seat again is Samuel M. Johnson, who delivers another speech in his peculiar French, this time on lovers. He is joined by the violin. Both he, Lucinda, and the music stop. The lights go down.

*   *   *

At times I have viewed the opera as a normal illusory piece of theater, referring to "characters" and "actors." To some extent it is a work of this sort, but it is also anti-illusory, not so much as a contradiction as to contribute to a dialectic, to use anti-illusionistic devices, such as the empty stages, lack of narrative and the positively anti-narrative action, to explore the possibilities of *Einstein on the Beach*.

Various contributions from the minimal movements have been taken and reassembled to form a new kind of multi-media; now, because the history of those contributions has included structuralism and minimalism, they can no longer reassert the kinds of convenient medium/media functions which they previously had to assume.

It is probably rash to say how *Einstein* functions. Wilson has compared it to schizophrenia: the splitting of the atom and the splitting of the mind. This is certainly one clue to the function of the piece: the unrelatables, the transmutations. Wilson has had much experience of working with schizophrenics.

As to how the piece treats Einstein: "The style is the man." —Richard M. Nixon.

Various critics have seen the piece as "metaphysical transcendence" and a "mystical experience."[12] It is not about those qualities. Glass denied any involvement with that kind of thing, but did remark on the way people tended to regard the sense of time in his music: "My feeling is that composers have always had a different sense of time, isn't that so? That's true of Monteverdi, that's true of Palestrina . . . of Stravinsky—if you were listening to a Beethoven symphony and someone asked you how long a movement was, you might have an awfully hard time to figure it out. Music time and colloquial time are obviously very different. My music sets up its own kind of extreme in a way, but I think music structures itself in time as to create independent coordinates of its own. This business of metaphysical this and that—it's just a lot of words that don't mean anything. What happens is that one has an authentic experience of time that is different from the time that we normally live in."

One's experience of time in the whole opera is certainly remarkable. It felt like two hours at most, I was amazed to learn that it was five hours long. This feeling of diminished time was apparent even when I knew how long the piece would last when I saw it a second time.

Besides being very systematic, *Einstein* is also a very emotive work. Generally the visual element and the music mesh to provide the emotive experience; I think it rarely comes from the visuals alone, except in the first scene. I do think that both Glass and Wilson together ought to undertake a more systematic and thorough investigation of these particular effects. Glass commented on these phenomena: "One of the interesting things for me about it is that there is an emotional content to the music that seems to come spontaneously from the music itself. It's not planned in the sense that I'm trying to achieve an emotional effect. In making the pieces and writing the pieces I'm almost always thinking of practical items such as rhythmic structure, harmonic structure, and melodic structure; I'm thinking of the length of time of the piece and how it fits into the action on the stage and the decor that it's going with. I have never thought about the emotional content.

"What happens is that perhaps because of the way I work, or because of my own nature, or perhaps because of the results of all these processes, there comes into the music, I would say almost spontaneously, an emotional content of its own. I think it's because the music attains a reality of its own or say an individuation of its own, and once it achieves that it appears to have its own emotional dimensions."

I asked him how he attempted to cope with this:

"It never occurs to me to do anything with it, it's just there; it's like a chair or a door . . . I find that the music almost always has some emotional quality in it; it seems independent of my intentions."

Robert Wilson's contribution is almost impossible to evaluate. He works very much within his own terms; his work strikes some very interesting intuitive responses, as well as triggering all kinds of approaches on the part of the viewer. The facts he puts forward about Einstein are obscure at first sight, but meaningful in the context of the opera: that Einstein played the violin well (he apparently wrote a book on Mozart), Einstein's possible dyslexia, and his early life: Wilson works on all those sources.

The action and decor are dynamically loaded; they act as triggers to factors external to themselves.

Einstein on the Beach involves a large amount of people and equipment. The sound system is about as good as is available. Kurt Munkacsi, the balance engineer, carries out detailed analysis of each auditorium so that the speakers he installs in the theater will give a flat response over the whole frequency range. The whole system has to be quite complex to cope with the choir's moving from place to place, and the microphones on some of the performers.

Philip Glass: "We had to pay twenty people for four months to rehearse. Before we even pulled the first curtain we had spent 300,000 dollars. That money came from the French government, from the Italian government, partly from our government, from some private people in New York; they're listed in the book."

I was interested in finding the reason *Einstein* was not being performed in Britain. Glass told me: "It's totally economic. I went there for a week last Spring with Bob and we were invited to the National Theatre. . . . They said they invited us, but in effect it looked like they were renting us the theater. They wanted us to pay all the costs and, I mean, that's not a proper invitation. Here in France we got a fee and a theater . . . the fee pays our salaries and our transportation. In England we were offered a theater; they wanted us to pay the crew; they wanted us to take part of the box office. In effect we would have been the producers and we simply couldn't afford to do it."

He also said he regarded Britain as isolated basically because of the British attitude to public spending on the arts, and went on, "I think it's a decision that's been made on a bureaucratic level and the result has been for the last—up to ten years it's just been closed . . . It's not simply a question of money, because there's no money in Italy either, but we gave five performances of this piece in Venice and the Italians have no money at all. It's a question really of attitude. The Italians are very open, for all the problems they have, and they're very anxious to be in the mainstream of the most progressive movements. That's simply not the case in England.

On an individual person to person, artist to artist level that's not true; I'm talking about a bureaucratic level and that's what makes the problems."

In both Avignon and Paris *Einstein on the Beach* was playing to packed houses. There is a story told of Einstein's expulsion from his class at school. On questioning his schoolmaster as to why he was being moved when his marks were good he was told, "Your very presence disturbs the other pupils."

Notes

1. Michael Nyman, *Studio International*, Jan./Feb. 1976, page 64.

2. *Contact* 13, Spring 1976. Keith Potter and Dave Smith—an interview with Philip Glass.

3. This and further uncredited quotations by Glass are from an interview I did with him in October 1976.

4. The book *Einstein on the Beach* by Wilson and Glass, edited by Vicky Alliata. Published by E.O.S. Enterprises, New York.

5. I'm not saying that one must impose anything on this work simply that there are elements within the work that may otherwise escape the viewer/listener.

Perhaps not to actively investigate but to use it in a more passive way is firstly contrary to the anti-illusionistic spirit of much of the work and secondly comes close in attitude to a treatment of the work as a piece of "metaphysical transcendence," a description which Glass at least has refuted.

6. Clive Barnes, *The [New York] Times,* 27 Nov. 1976.

7. Christopher Knowles, in Wilson and Glass, *Einstein on the Beach.*

8. From an interview with Lise Brunel.

9. The score to this kneeplay is included in Wilson and Glass, *Einstein on the Beach.* This section contains the end-of-scene section referred to earlier.

10. Ibid.

11. Ibid.

12.*The Guardian,* 13 Aug. 1976; see also note 6.

LISTENING TO GLASS (1981)

JOSEPH RODDY

In this the next to last decade of the 20th century, the 1980 opera season began in New York with the *Anna Bolena* that Gaetano Donizetti finished composing at Bergamo in 1830. The season began in Philadelphia with the *Don Giovanni* that Wolfgang Amadeus Mozart finished in Prague in 1787. In Houston, it began with the *Trovatore* that Giuseppe Verdi finished in Rome in 1853. In San Francisco, it began with the *Samson et Dalila* that Camille Saint-Saëns finished in Paris in 1875.

The listing is not close to complete but altogether characteristic. It suggests the extent to which opera producers in the United States still limit themselves to a repertoire out of the last century from another continent on which no such limiting exists. In Europe, this year's opera season began in Rotterdam with the world's premiere of *Satyagraha*. Its composer, 44-year-old Philip Glass, a graduate of the University of Chicago, was born in Baltimore. He finished scoring *Satyagraha* last spring in his apartment on the Lower East Side of Manhattan. That was three years after he was commissioned to write it by the city of Rotterdam. Theatre buffs from all over Europe gathered in that Dutch seaport last fall to behold the latest stage piece by the composer who has mattered greatly to them ever since he wrote *Einstein on the Beach*.

Opera: Great or Grand?

During the fortnight after *Satyagraha*'s first performance, the *Frankfurter Allgemeine Zeitung*, the *Süddeutsche Zeitung*, the *Groene Amsterdammer*, and at least a half-dozen other important European dailies published *feuilletons* assessing the work. All of them were long, informed, and analytic, and while not one was unequivocally laudatory, all gave it the space and serious attention that marked it as an important work of art. The *New York Times*'s critic who flew to Holland for the performance wrote that the opera was "reminiscent in mood of Wagner's *Parsifal*."

Satyagraha is in three acts and depicts the young Mahatma Gandhi's first use of organized passive resistance against state-sanctioned race prejudice in South Africa from 1893 to 1914. Its libretto, sung in Sanskrit, is a set of texts culled from the Bhagavad-Gita sections of the ancient Hindu poem *Mahabharata*. With its words and plot paralleled or layered, instead of linked or interlocked as they are in other operas, *Satyagraha*'s libretto provides a moral commentary on the stage action without being a narrative part of the production. It is a libretto that caused some viewers in Holland to find *Satyagraha* more of a Hindu cantata celebrating a civic saint than a grand opera about Gandhi.

"I never know what opera really is anyway," Glass told one inquirer. "I just kind of push it around and say, 'Well, if it isn't an opera, what is it?' It's words throughout. It's singing throughout. It's a theatre piece in all those ways. Wagner didn't call his pieces operas, he called them music dramas.

"I know that would bother a regular subscriber to the Metropolitan Opera. You can change your orchestration, you can change anything, but if you deny them the love story or the narrative, that's a stumbling block."

And a saint walking around a stage is a stumbling block, too, as Bernard Shaw argued before introducing his Saint Joan. But Shaw's saint was a power-oriented maiden and more than five centuries out of sight, while Glass's holy man has hardly settled into his grave and still has friends in Asian politics. In one preliminary sketch of the work, *Satyagraha* had complementary Gandhis, one male and one female. The composer and the librettist had abandoned that androgynous approach long before they came to feel so burdened with even one Gandhi in their cast that they considered omitting him altogether by fashioning an opera about, but without, him. To learn more about their difficult subject from the best surviving sources, the composer, his librettist Constance DeJong, and their stage director Robert Israel traveled to New Delhi, Bombay, and the Sabarmati ashram in Ahmedabad and the Sevagram ashram in central India on a small grant from The Rockefeller Foundation. Later, when Glass had finished his work, the Foundation covered the costs of having the singers' and instrumentalists' parts copied from the full score.

For its first performance, *Satyagraha*'s running time was about three hours and 15 minutes. It required six soloists, a chorus of 40, and a pit orchestra of about 50 without brass or percussion. Any opera set in Dutch colonial South Africa might interest Hollanders enough to have them pack its Rotterdam performances as well as its follow-up ones at Utrecht, Scheveningen, and Amsterdam. But what made *Satyagraha* a cultural event that mattered to a lot of other Europeans is that they—in substantially larger numbers than the composer's countrymen—are seriously interested in the music of Philip Glass.

Short Course in Western Music

Of course, it also perplexes them. Maybe a thousand years back, Western music was melodically as one-lined as folk songs and metrically as free as prose. But by the middle of the 18th century, its metrics were as unyielding as the tickings of clocks while themes and their counterthemes in canons and fugues were threading together into the sonic textures known now as tonality.

From Pachelbel through Brahms and on into this century, the law of tonality ruled Western music as immutably as the law of gravity ruled terrestrial space. Mozart's *Don Giovanni* and Irving Berlin's *God Bless America* are equal in their observance of the law tonality. The single characteristic tonality was its do-re-mi-type eight-toned scale, the linearly organized arrangement of every composer's building materials. But by 1910, those materials had been declared obsolete by Arnold Schoenberg. He broke from tonality and later introduced serialism, his system of 12-toned sequences, arranged in whatever pattern pleased the composer, and therefor without linear order.

For all but a very few listeners, serialism was the great disorienter. It left even the acute-eared unable to recall what they had heard a bar back, and incapable of anticipating what would follow. Before Schoenberg struck, composers had left few harmonic anticipations unfulfilled; melodic reprisings and variations impressed themes on even their least attentive listeners.

But by the doctrines Schoenberg conferred on his followers, the repeatings and reworkings of themes were proscribed as crass caterings to those whose minds were wandering. Every new mix of serialism and snobbery succeeded in thinning the audience for music, the result being that ever since Schoenberg, composition has been a craft in perpetual angst, with most of its products of little interest even to other composers. After audience alienation ran its slightly fashionable course, the reaction set in. "We've had 70 years of pieces since Schoenberg that no one understands," Philip Glass noted a few weeks back when he was in an oversimplifying mood. "So there's nothing really wrong, is there, with a little contemporary music being appealing?"

After Nadia, What?

Glass came to that view close to 15 years ago. What he was hearing around him then were the intricate aridities of Schoenberg, the puckish adventuring of John Cage, and the neoclassical inclinations of his old mates and teachers from the Juilliard School whose road he was staring down, however reluctantly. It led, first, to Paris, where Aaron Copland, Roger Sessions, Virgil Thomson, and Marc Blitzstein before him had presented themselves for instruction to Nadia Boulanger. It was a kind of junior year abroad for right-thinking young American composers. She reviewed the fundamentals of harmony and counterpoint for Glass while her student who had been famously prolific back home composed just about no music. But between lessons, Glass fell into a Paris friendship and worked on a film score with the Indian composer and sitarist Ravi Shankar.

No Faustian struggle between his professor and his friend was joined for the soul of the young American composer. But when he thinks back on those Paris days now, he knows that in 1965 he was terrified by Boulanger and inspired by Shankar. Because of him, Glass moved out of whatever composer's cul-de-sac he was in and saw where he should go with his craft. Less by invitation than by intrusion, he wrote incidental music for a Left Bank production of the Samuel Beckett play *Comédie*. It was the first time the composer set a repetitive melody over a stable harmonic foundation to achieve what he now calls drone music without even a hint of self-censure.

"I took two soprano saxophones," he recalled a few weeks back, "and I gave each of them two notes to play against each other, in a constantly shifting pattern. What was heard was never exactly the same, but it never really changed very much. I wrote six or eight little sections like that and I put them on a tape with 45 seconds of music followed by 45 seconds of silence followed by the next section of music and so on." That tape would run all through the Beckett play in which the three characters are dead and each is telling his life story to the other two just as if they were alive.

Glass saw 15 to 20 performances of *Comédie* in Paris, and every time he would experience a catharsis, or epiphany, in a different spot in the play. "That struck me as very odd," he said. "I thought that if the play were really a classical tragedy, that big emotion should hit me at the same place every night. But it was always a different place. After a while, I came to understand that the catharsis or epiphany happened every night when I reached a certain awareness of the play, and of myself. And since that was subject to my own psychological instability, it happened in different places every night. Think of it this way: it happened whenever I was ready for it." In the middle of all that play-going, Glass came to the altruistic view that *Comédie* did not need his music, but that he had had his life in music changed by Beckett's play.

Don't Get Me Wrong

To explain the change, he talked first about Beethoven's music. "In the 19th century, we had what was called program music," he began. "Even Beethoven was responsible for that—Symphony no. 6, a walk in the country, the *Pastoral Symphony*. But you can see what I have in mind by program music even more clearly in the development of the violin concerto. There, the solo instrument becomes more and more the alter ego of the composer. And the listener identifies with it, too, as the instrument experiences happy moments and sad moments until there is a triumphal end."

If there was a little patronizing inflection in that, Glass wanted it corrected. "I'm not putting it down," he said. "I'm talking about a narrative mechanism in which the violin has a kind of identification with the story. And that's how we listen to a lot of program music. The music becomes a model of the real world. The musical happenings in any big piece are allegories of the events in the real world, and the musical time is an allegory of real world time. I call that colloquial time. Now colloquial time is the world you and I live in when we have our love affairs and our horses win at the races. A lot of music exists in colloquial time.

"One of the main things about my music is that it doesn't exist in colloquial time. And one of the first things that people perceive in my music is extended time, or loss of time, or no sense of time whatever. All that narrative structure of the Beethoven concerto is gone from my music. But instead of finding the music empty, they found quite a bit in it. What happens is that instead of identifying with the music and getting themselves mixed up with it, getting themselves actually confused with the violin in the concerto, they find that my music is all about something else.

"It is all about acknowledging a difference. My music is over there. They are over here. And then between the music and its listeners there arises another feeling which is spontaneous. It is a feeling that does not result from a direct manipulation of the music by them, or of them by the music. It is simply a result of the conjunction of them and the music." So what Beckett did to Glass with *Comédie* is what Glass did to many others with *Einstein on the Beach*.

The Einstein Formula

It is the intermissionless four-act opera he wrote with the variously gifted Robert Wilson, who also designed and directed the production. Or he ring-mastered it. It included paper airplanes sailed by a wild-eyed child, a train that turned into a cellblock, dancers in a glade, and a rocket ship in the stage-sky. All of them were kept in dramatic motion by the motoric throb of the music Glass wrote for a chorus that sang solfeggio and Arabic numbers, a small instrumental ensemble that included a sound engineer on an elaborate control panel, the composer on an electronic keyboard, and an aged violinist off to one side dressed as—of course—Professor Einstein.

The show's two sold-out performances in New York four years back were at the Metropolitan Opera House, whose administrators rented out their stage and seats to Glass and Wilson but had no part whatever in mounting their production. Among the critics in the audience was the *New Yorker* magazine's Andrew Porter, who published a guide for the understandably perplexed: "A listener to his music usually reaches a point, quite early on, of rebellion at the needle-stuck-in-the-groove quality, but a minute or two later he realizes that the needle has not stuck: something has happened. Once that point is passed, Glass's music—or so I find—becomes easy to listen to for hours on end. The mind may wander now and again, but it wanders within a new sound world that the composer has created. The simple harmonic foundations induce a feeling of security. . . . In an age when Erik Satie's *Vexations*, a few bars for solo piano, *très lent*, played over and over again for twenty-four hours, can find performances, when Stockhausen begins his *Piano Piece IX* with the same chord sounded two hundred and twenty-seven times and builds his *Stimmung* on one chord sustained for seventy-five minutes, audiences are readier than their fathers were to sit and savor slow-shifting, chronic experiences—hypnotized by repetition, stimulated by the observance of tiny changes, not bored. *Einstein* is busier, more active, than those pieces. Glass's score may be incantatory, but it is not lulling."

Thinking about Music

Abstracting, then? Yes, and, in a way, addicting. Ten years before he wrote *Satyagraha*, its composer had already settled into a writing style that seems more Indian than Western. When pressed, he undertakes to distinguish them. "In the West," he began, "we take a measure and divide it. Then we'll take a whole note and divide it into half notes and divide the half notes into quarter notes. We think of music in terms of dividing. The Indians think of it as adding. They'll take an eighth note and add a second or a third or take three and add two and another three and add two, and then take another three and add another two. They think of small units, and then of adding up the small units to make a long string of units. So theirs is a very different way of thinking about music. Even Stravinsky didn't think about music in additive ways."

Glass does, with results that seem simplistic only to the inattentive. "The difficulties in my music are in the metrics," he explained in a recent issue of *Contemporary Keyboard*. "You have to be able to play in five in one hand and four in the other. Or what regularly happens in my music is that I'll set up a recurring meter of three in one hand and a cycle of meters in the other, so that against the three you'll have nine, eight, six, five, four, three, four, five , six, eight, nine, and twelve all worked out so that they fit the basic cycle of three but nevertheless require a good rhythmic feeling to carry them off."

The composer can be seen carrying them off whenever he performs in a concert hall or a jazz club with his Philip Glass Ensemble, which consists of three woodwind players, two organists (one of them being the composer), a soprano voice soaring overhead like an indefatigable flute, and a sound engineer operating a battery of mixers and amplifiers whose part in the act is as central as the violinist's in the *Kreutzer*

Sonata. The Ensemble's few dozen appearances on university campuses can no more account for the popularity of Glass's music than his catalogues of published scores that ranges from early works titled *In Again Out Again for Jon Gibson, Strung, Piece in the Shape of a Square*, and *How Now* to such relatively recent ones as *Another Look at Harmony, Part 4, Lucinda's Dance, Geometry of Circles*, and, of course, *Einstein on the Beach*, which has been released by a small corporation beatifically titled Tomato Music Company Limited.

Oh, No, Nadia

Satyagraha may come to replace it, but *Einstein* remains among the Glass works of which the composer is still most proud. He thinks that it may well find a place beside Kurt Weill's *Threepenny Opera* on the very short list of stage works with music that will tell more than shelves of tomes about the 20th century. And when he talks about *Einstein*'s start, Glass gets set off on the most forthright revelations about himself.

At the first of *Einstein*'s performances at the Opéra-Comique in 1976, he kept looking up from his keyboard in the pit all the time to see if he might spot Mme. Boulanger in the audience. "Had she been there," he said, "I don't think I could have gotten through the performance. She had that way with her students. We either admired her or hated her, but, in any case, she exerted an authority over us that was unquestioned. And when I was writing *Einstein*, I wasn't willing to run it past her. Had she looked unfavorably at it, I might have survived, but survival would have been a lot more difficult. She was the only authority I recognized in that way. If Pierre Boulez thought my music was primitive, that didn't matter to me."

When Glass was a Boulanger student, Boulez was about as revered and feared by Europe's composers as Sartre was by its writers. The Boulez sphere of influence moved west in the '70s when he was installed as the music director of the New York Philharmonic. Since from that podium he would be conferring a measure of personal validation on any American music he chose to perform, he performed very little of it in Lincoln Center. The American composers that the French composer-conductor could abide he played downtown for audiences of Greenwich Villagers whose tolerance he took to be limitless. The concerts in the Village were called Prospective Encounters for an audience Boulez tried to draw uptown later to hear less-heady programs in Lincoln Center that he called Rug Concerts. In neither series was any Glass played.

"Those concerts were disasters," Glass said. "By giving them downtown, Boulez got off the hook. It was his way of writing a rubber check on American music. So I said, 'I don't need you to play my music downtown. I'm downtown already. And I don't need to be introduced at Loft Concerts. I invented them.'" Glass actually had, with some help from downtown friends in the arts—Sol LeWitt, Richard Serra, and Klaus Kertess. They would collect rugs from Village trash piles and lay them over greasy loft floors for the Sunday-afternoon concerts they gave on Bleecker Street for audiences paying anything they could part with to get in.

Up from the Floor

Most of those who did were musicians on the forward edge of an alternate avant-garde at the time. As he had them sized up, they were reacting to the overcomplicated and overintellectualized avant-garde experiences that Boulez was dispensing at his Encounters a few blocks away. "On Bleecker Street, we wanted simple experiences," Glass said, "but fair ones. By then, I was seeing that there were other classes of ideas that had to do with musical time and musical structure that were untapped and from which a whole vocabulary could be developed. And I began very systematically to go about building up that vocabulary and writing some of my early pieces for which I probably deserve the description of Minimalist Composer. I was making A,B,C's, block letters, for a vocabulary. That eventually led to *Einstein* and *Satyagraha*.

"But it's not that I am returning to an earlier harmonic language. Harmony, or the crisis of harmony, is not really an issue. Whether music is dissonant or consonant has become irrelevant. We can no longer say, 'Well, if it's consonant it is old-fashioned and if its dissonant it is modern.' That's what we could say back in the '30s. There is plenty of consonant music around now. Jazz is consonant. Rock is consonant. But what seems to appeal to my audiences is something else, the focus on structure rather than on theme. What's focus? It's the way some music has now of drawing people into a different world without time. And without boredom."

GLASS'S SATYAGRAHA (1986)

ALLAN KOZINN

"*Satyagraha*" (roughly, "firmness of truth") is a term coined by Mohandas Gandhi to describe an approach to civil disobedience he developed during his years as a young lawyer in South Africa. In its day, it proved an effective weapon in the Indian community's struggle for civil rights in the face of a relentlessly oppressive British regime. Philip Glass's opera of the same name is a meditation on the genesis of this form of peaceful persuasion; in fact, while Gandhi is its central character, the work is less about him than about the concept, one of his earliest and most crucial achievements in creative political thought.

The opera, completed in 1980, also marked a turning point for Glass, musically and dramatically. Except for some student compositions published in the early 1960s, this was his first piece using orchestral strings and winds instead of his own amplified ensemble; and it was his first in a recognizably traditional form, a three-act opera with an arching dramatic shape. The score, though replete with Glass's trademarks—concise melodic cells and frenetically whirling rhythmic figures, repeated by the hundreds—also contains elements of lyricism and expressivity not previously part of Glass's repetitive idiom. These he has retained and extended in his more recent works. notably his evocative soundtrack for Godfrey Reggio's film *Koyaanisqatsi* (1982), now available on laser video disc in digital stereo.

Perhaps it's too much to hope that the release of these recordings will lead Glass's detractors to reassess his work; after all, the scores have already been heard in performance, to no avail. The consternation his music arouses is itself an interesting phenomenon; indeed, few composers since Wagner have engendered such hot partisan debate. In New York, Glass's home, the musical press is clearly divided into two camps. John Rockwell, Gregory Sandow, Tim Page, Andrew Porter, and Alan Rich have written often and at length in praise of Glass and those who share his "minimalist" aesthetic. Others, though, find that aesthetic empty and fraudulent, an earwash of simplistic, reactionary, diatonic babble—self-indulgent '60s pop art posing as High Art.

Most disdain Glass on musical grounds. On his first encounter with Glass's music, in 1970, Peter G. Davis wrote in the *New York Times* that the insistently cycling rhythmic figures reminded him of "trying to pat your head and rub your stomach at the same time." More recent encounters have not changed his mind; in fact, reviewing a 1984 concert version of Glass's contribution to Robert Wilson's *the CIVIL warS*, Davis seemed almost nostalgic for the old days: "Glass," he wrote in *New York*, "has pretty much deserted the shifting mosaic patterns of his earlier style for great clumps of bald repetition, simple arpeggios, and scraps of banal melody that do nothing and go nowhere." Meanwhile, Donal Henahan, the *Times*'s senior critic, has complained that Glass's arpeggiations remind him of Hanon and Czerny exercises. And reviewing the composer's most recent opera, *Akhnaten*, he suggested that Glass's operas "stand to music as the sentence 'See Spot run' stands to literature."

The anti-Glass camp is also, it seems, fairly inflexible. No matter what changes and refinements accrue to his style from work to work, the criticism reads pretty much the same. So far, I've seen only one reviewer switch sides. In 1969, Robert T. Jones reviewed a Glass concert scathingly in the *Times*, calling a pair of early works "limited enough to be merely trivial" and "lacking even the sophistication to raise them into the class of the primitive." Twelve years later, in *Opera News*, he wrote that *Satyagraha* "shines with a luminous beauty that makes it the most sensuously appealing of all Glass's works." And in the New York City Opera's program book, at the time of *Akhnaten*'s premiere (1984), he wrote that "a Glass score presents a dauntingly bleak sight, with pages of what seem to be only bare scales and arpeggios; fully assembled, though, magic shines from the sparseness." Apparently a fan now, Jones contributes an excellent and concise historical essay on Gandhi's South African period to CBS's libretto booklet.

That Glass's repetitive, consonant scores ring false to critics who expect something else from music, or feel that Western tradition has passed beyond that, is certainly understandable. Unfortunately, the objections raised aren't entirely musical. A good deal of critical ink has been spilled decrying the composer's popularity, not only with the normal classical audience (or part of it), but with rock and jazz listeners as well, as if that were prima facie evidence of the music's valuelessness. Musing on the Brooklyn revival of *Einstein on the Beach* last winter, Harold C. Schonberg guessed (in the *Times*) that many who attended were pop fans, and that they were there so they could claim to have heard classical music without actually having to hear any. That theory misses the mark broadly, though, for most of the people he describes would have stayed away had they suspected Glass were considered classical in some quarters.

But the most virulently hostile response to Glass I've seen in print was Kenneth Furie's review, in *Keynote*, of *Satyagraha*—or more accurately, his review of Sandow's *Village Voice* review of the work. In an appalling abdication of critical responsibility, let alone sense, Furie insisted on calling the work *"Santawhatchit"*; and without having bothered to attend a performance, he ridiculed what he assumed to be the work's message, and excoriated Glass's audience for its susceptibility to trendiness. It angered Furie that an audience would "pay money to be clubbed with the revelations that a) Gandhi was good, b) oppression is bad, and c) there's some connection between Gandhi and Martin Luther King[, Jr.]." Of course, he'd have to have heard the work to know that said "clubbing" never happens. Still, his point is well taken: Why should opera audiences dwell on such trivialities when they could be grappling with deeper issues—for instance, the dilemma of a courtesan who abandons her lover at his father's request, and then dies?

For Furie, and for many other Glassophobes, the composer and his music seem to have materialized in an instantaneous marketing flash, like the hula hoop and the pet rock. This view, however, ignores three historical points:

First, Glass began his experiments with repetitive music in the mid-1960s, when his work held little prospect of acceptance into the mainstream, much less trendy success. Audiences were tiny and sometimes hostile, and the reviews, at least from the Uptown press, were consistently derisive. Through all this he persisted unwaveringly, and by the mid-1970s he had attracted a following on the fringes of the rock world and the art school crowd. Fully a decade of steadily developing work preceded his first grand popular and media success, *Einstein on the Beach*, in late 1976, and despite the full houses, even that production proved a serious financial setback. Whether one likes his music or not, he has followed his own path from the start with integrity. If he's pandering to his audience, there must be an easier way.

Second, Glass's work was neither isolated nor without sequel. He was hardly alone in feeling that the complexities of contemporary harmonic language had alienated much of the audience for concert music. Nor was he alone in searching for an alternative to contemporary harmony that would be more than a neoromantic turning-back of the clock to a point just before music "went wrong" at the dawn of serialism. Revolution was in the air, and Glass, along with several colleagues, opted for a thorough renovation and re-examination of musical thought. To achieve that, they stripped music to its three structural components (melody, harmony, rhythm) and scrutinized each through a repetitive process of slow variation. Eventually, they erected new edifices, quite different from those they had torn down, for in the process they had learned to manipulate and emphasize a fourth element, psychoacoustical illusion.

The list of other composers who thought along those lines in the mid-1960s is familiar enough, since most of them still pursue the course they embarked upon back then. Working in their separate garrets, Glass, Terry Riley, La Monte Young, and Steve Reich reassembled those musical building blocks differently, each developing a distinct and recognizable compositional voice. Moreover, younger composers, both in this country (John Adams, for example) and abroad (Arvo Pärt and László Melis), have combined some of the pioneer group's repetitive and cyclical techniques with other elements to produce allied but distinctive styles of their own. What we have here is not an isolated fluke, but a thriving, varied school of composers who want to reach an audience and have found the approved academic language insufficiently communicative.

Third, a point implicit in the others, Glass's music has developed steadily and logically in the twenty years he has been writing. Traceable development may not of itself indicate compositional greatness, but neither is it the hallmark of a flash-in-the-pan hoax. Compared to his current work, Glass's early music was primitive indeed. He preferred at the start to explore one element at a time. Thus, a work might begin with a short melodic fragment, repeated many times and then altered slightly by the addition or subtraction of a note or series of notes. The new version would be repeated numerous times before the next permutation—and so on. In a subsequent work, he might retain this "additive process," but gradually tamper with the rhythmic profile as well. Harmony was fairly static in these works, although as the notes in the individual voices shifted, so, naturally, would the general harmonic haze.

As Glass's ensemble grew, he gained access not only to a greater variety of textures, but also to more complex effects obtainable by overlapping voices undergoing additive process at different rates. He had so far concentrated on abstract music, and Glass now concedes (grudgingly) that this could be called his "minimal" period. Its culmination was the massive *Music in 12 Parts* (1971–74), a thorough compendium of the techniques he had developed by then, which some in the pro-Glass camp consider his best work to date, minimalism's *Art of Fugue*. But in his next major work, *Einstein*, he turned from abstract composition to representational music. I have trouble thinking of *Einstein* as an opera, primarily because it lacks a text, seemingly a crucial element in the genre's definition. Rather, it strikes me as a mime to music, or a dance piece, or a Philip Glass Ensemble concert with an ambitious (and compelling) stage show. Still, Glass considers it his first opera—indeed, the start of a trilogy about science (*Einstein*), politics (*Satyagraha*), and religion (*Akhnaten*).

In opera, Glass found a medium in which he could put his newly developed language to expressive use, and although he continues to write music for smaller forces, it appears that opera will become his form of choice. His contribution to Wilson's epic *CIVIL warS* is his fourth; he is currently at work on a fifth, *The Making of the Representative for Planet 8*, and contemplating a sixth, another joint venture with Wilson. He has also written the a cappella *Madrigal Opera*, and a children's opera, *The Juniper Tree*; and if *Einstein* counts as an opera in Glass's book, so perhaps should his "theater piece" *The Photographer*.

Glass's move to opera has wrought further changes in his musical style, most noticeably a less stagnant approach to harmony. Figures still repeat, at length, but they now outline chord progressions rather than static atmospheres. At the same time, Glass began to manipulate his textures and tonalities more abruptly, creating pictorial effects. Examples abound in the three operas, although his pictorial sense perhaps comes through most vigorously in *Koyaanisqatsi*, where the music perfectly mirrors the stream of images Reggio throws onto the screen.

*   *   *

The evolution Glass's style has undergone these past twenty years would become manifest if CBS were to issue a collected edition of his music. Fully produced master tapes already exist: The Glass Ensemble's sound-mixer,

Kurt Munkacsi, has recorded virtually every major score. Although some were fleetingly available on small labels—Shandar (France), Chatham Square, Virgin, Tomato, and CP²—most are now unavailable or extremely hard to find.

To its credit, CBS has reissued the old Tomato recording of *Einstein*, and has announced plans to do likewise with *Dance*. Yet despite the fanfare it accorded itself when it signed Glass—the first living composer added to its roster since Goddard Lieberson's days, as CBS's executives like to point out—the label has been a little weird about releasing his work. When it took him on, in 1981, *Satyagraha* was his current major opus; it had already enjoyed successful runs in the Netherlands and at Artpark, near Buffalo. Glass hoped CBS would record the opera when it came to the Brooklyn Academy that November for his inaugural offering on the label. But even as they invoked Lieberson's memory, CBS's executives declined to record the opera then, insisting instead on "Glassworks," an LP of uncharacteristically short pieces—some of which, ironically, were out-takes from another major work CBS's a&r staff had astonishingly rejected, *Koyaanisqatsi*.

During that tense early relationship, Glass raised the idea of a collected edition, with covers designed by Milton Glaser; CBS nixed it. Then, when the label's a&r department heard that Glass planned to include lyrics by rock songwriter Paul Simon on an LP of song settings, it tried to scotch that too, arguing that Glass should abandon Simon (who had left CBS for Warner Bros.) in favor of a more loyal (and much more trivial) CBS pop star, Billy Joel. On this point, Glass held his ground; in fact, part of his response was to contribute a brief coda, played by his ensemble, to the closing song on Simon's latest LP ("Hearts and Bones"). The saga's funniest moment, though, came at the start, when a CBS executive suggested in all seriousness that if the composer would only change the title of *Rubric*, in "Glassworks," to *Rubik*, a photo of Rubik's Cube could adorn the jacket—just the touch a composer fighting charges of faddism would have needed.

CBS and Glass seem now to have arrived at a more comfortable *modus operandi: The Photographer* was recorded and released without incident. And having belatedly agreed to take *Satyagraha*, CBS waited patiently as an attempt to record the piece in Stuttgart was scrapped in favor of New York sessions featuring most of the original Rotterdam/Artpark/Brooklyn cast, plus the orchestra and chorus of the New York City Opera (where the work will be mounted next season). The finished product, moreover, is presented in fitting style. Like *Einstein*, it appears on Masterworks proper, not the "FM" crossover label to which Glass's ensemble discs have been consigned; and like other CBS boxed sets, it benefits from an excellent Dutch pressing. The booklet contains two essays (history by Jones; Glass's style by Page), a note on the recording technique (by the ensemble's keyboardist and coproducer, Michael Riesman), and a libretto.

This libretto, in fact, is the first I've seen that juxtaposes the sung Sanskrit text with the English translation. (German and French are also given.) The published libretto, available in bookstores at the time of the Brooklyn performances (Constance DeJong and Philip Glass, *Satyagraha: M.K. Gandhi in South Africa. 1893–1914*, New York: Standard Editions, 1980), gave only the English translation. That allowed listeners to follow what was being sung in a general way, and to make the connections between text and stage action, but it didn't let them know when one verse ended and the next began. Even with CBS's libretto, it's not easy (or necessary) to follow the Sanskrit through all of Glass's repeats. But the transliteration makes the progression clearer, and thus casts considerably more light on his intentions—and on what turns out to be a sensitive approach to text setting.

*   *   *

Satyagraha is, in a way, two works in one. Its text derives from the Hindu epic *Bhagavad-Gita* (chapter and verse indications are given in the margin), and divorced from its staging and characters, it seems less an opera than a grand Hindu cantata. Much of the text, culled and arranged by DeJong, is platitudinous and prescriptive, yet it is also timeless, as it must be if it's to work in an operatic context. Glass and DeJong supply that context—as well as, at the start, a bridge between the ancient words and modern action—in their scenario, a sequence of tableaux depicting (in a kind of slow motion, as one might expect, and not in chronological order) several key incidents from Gandhi's South African years, signposts along the road to the effective deployment of *satyagraha*. They provide another sort of context, too, introducing three historical figures, each of whom silently presides over one act, almost as a form of ornamentation: Leo Tolstoy, whose work (particularly *The Kingdom of God Is Within You*) inspired Gandhi and whose letters encouraged him; Tagore, an Indian poet, whose moral authority Gandhi respected; and King, whose use of passive resistance in his own civil rights struggle was inspired by Gandhi's methods.

Glass ties together the Sanskrit text and modern action masterfully. The opening scene, for instance, is something of a mythological prologue, much like that in a Monteverdi opera, but with one foot firmly in the world the rest of the work inhabits. According to Glass's stage directions, the opera begins where the *Bhagavad-Gita* does, on the battlefield. In the epic, the opposing forces are those of Duryodhana and Arjuna, the latter a devotee of Krishna (described in commentaries as the Supreme Personality of Godhead—greater than man and demigod, but not quite God, who is pure consciousness). Arjuna surveys the armies and, seeing friends and relatives on both sides, asks Krishna why the battle, with its inevitable carnage, must occur. The bulk of the *Bhagavad-Gita* is Krishna's response, starting with a dissertation on duty and honor.

In *Satyagraha*, two armies face each other in silhouette. Duryodhana and Arjuna occupy chariots at center stage. Behind them is Krishna, between them Gandhi, who begins singing Arjuna's words, "I see them here assembled, ready to right, seeking to please the king's sinful son by waging war." Arjuna's response to the scene and his question to Krishna—"My very being is oppressed with compassion's harmful taint. With mind perplexed concerning right and wrong, I ask you which is the better course?"—are presented as a duet between Arjuna and Gandhi. Rather than having Krishna respond *to* them, Glass has him respond *through* them, in a trio setting of Krishna's injunction to stand resolute for the right that duty prescribes. As the intensity mounts, Gandhi, Arjuna, and Krishna are joined, in a text that jumps back and forth between a description of Arjuna's (and Gandhi's) moment of doubt and weakness and Krishna's answer, by choruses—the two armies which, when the lights come up, are shown to be Indian and European. From the choral climax, Gandhi's voice emerges, solo, with Krishna's words, "Hold pleasure and pain, profit and loss, victory and defeat to be the same, then brace yourself for the fight."

The music of this scene is cut from the standard Glassian fabric that some find so objectionable—scales, arpeggios, and seemingly simple diatonic tunes, all repeated often and varied slowly. But the use of this vocabulary is unabashedly Romantic. Verse by verse, Glass matches the shape and character of theme, tempo, and orchestration to the spirit of the text.

Thus, Gandhi's opening statement of Arjuna's dilemma is given a meditative theme, repetitive yet slowly expanding, its melancholy character underscored by the dark, arpeggiated cello accompaniment. At the description of Arjuna seeing his kinsmen fitted out to do battle, the accompaniment brightens with flutes momentarily. Then, when Arjuna joins Gandhi to seek Krishna's advice, the original figuration returns, but Gandhi's and Arjuna's vocal lines are impassioned extensions (ascending now) of Gandhi's first music. Though the tempo has increased only slightly, the vocal counterpoint creates the impression of much greater speed, and the entrance of the chorus and the rest of the orchestra brings the scene's tension to its height. Music of frustration, anger, and confusion, it beautifully evokes the conflicting emotions Arjuna and Gandhi grapple with while trying to resign themselves to Krishna's word. That Gandhi has ultimately succeeded becomes clear in the end, when the choral section abruptly stops, leaving Gandhi singing Krishna's command to the opening melody, at its original slower tempo and accompanied, at first, by cellos only.

That example should suffice to show the kind of close correspondence between music, text, and underlying emotion that Glass maintains throughout. But it is worth noting the incidents he has chosen to depict. Scene 2 portrays the 1910 establishment of Tolstoy Farm, the agrarian collective that served as headquarters and spiritual training ground for Gandhi's movement; Scene 3 represents the Indian community's solemn vow, taken at a public meeting in 1906 and drawn up as a resolution, to resist the British government's Black Act, which required Indians to carry registration certificates. This latter, a pledge to resist unto death, marked a turning point for the movement. The *Bhagavad-Gita* text begins with a verse from Chapter 18, "Whoever gives up a deed because it causes pain . . . follows the way of darkness," and ends with a similar one from Chapter 3, "So was the wheel set in motion, and who here fails to match his turning . . . lives out his life in vain."

The start of the second act goes back to 1896, when Gandhi returned to Durban after a visit to India, having drawn the world's attention to the plight of his countrymen who had come to South Africa as indentured workers. The British in South Africa, not happy with the picture he had painted of life there, accosted him as he made his way through town. His life was saved when the police superintendent's wife happened by and took him under her protection. Scene 2 shows the 1906 founding of *Indian Opinion*, the movement's weekly newspaper, set to the text "As witless fools perform their works . . . so with senses freed the wise man should act, longing to bring about the welfare and coherence of the world." Glass's staging included the assembly of a giant printing press and the printing and distribution of the paper. In Scene 3, the Satyagrahi meet again in 1908 to discuss the Black Act, which the British had failed to repeal despite a promise to do so. Recalling Krishna's injunction, they burn their registration cards in protest. The choral setting of this second-act finale is melodically simple but rhythmically intricate; its accompaniment quotes the opera's opening scene and adds a few of the quick chromatic "rocket ship" figures (à la Mannheim) Glass used throughout *Einstein*.

The whole of the third act is devoted to the Newcastle March of 1913, here set on the same mythological battlefield as the opening scene. Gandhi's plan was to persuade the miners to strike in protest of the government's new discriminatory immigration and tax laws. It was an inspired move: if confronted, the Satyagrahi were not to resist, and when arrested, they would flood the jails, creating logistical problems and expense for the government. If not challenged, they were to take the strikers to Tolstoy Farm and prolong the strike until the government gave in. The government came around after five weeks of this, and within a few months the Black Act and the tax law were repealed. In the opera, after the arrests, Gandhi remains alone on-stage but for King, looking on.

Gandhi's final aria is nothing more than an ascending Phrygian scale, repeated thirty times over a simple progression of minor chords; it's one of the opera's most touching moments, however, a suitably austere setting of a text that embodies the spirit of the entire work and explains Gandhi's final skyward glance at King. The words are Krishna's: "I have passed through many a birth and many have you. I know them all, but you do not. Unborn am I, changeless is my Self, of all contingent beings I am the Lord. Yet by my erosive energy, I consort with Nature and come to be in time. For whenever the law of righteousness withers away and lawlessness arises, then do I generate myself on earth. I come into being age after age and take a visible shape and move a man with men for the protection of good, thrusting the evil back and setting virtue on her seat again."

*   *   *

One might think that little need be said about the performance, since its principals are well practiced in their roles—Douglas Perry, in particular, sings Gandhi with grace and passion—and since it was overseen by the composer and his right-hand men, Munkacsi and Riesman. Yet a few points are worth raising. Glass's approach to recording is unique in the classical field. He believes that the studio is a tool that should be used to capacity. In Munkacsi and Riesman, he has producers who agree and, as members of his ensemble, know his music intimately. To them, the idea of hanging a microphone in front of an ensemble, turning on the machines, and capturing a "live" performance is unthinkably archaic. Instead, they work like pop producers, as Riesman describes in detail in his notes: Starting with a click track, a cue track, and a reference track containing a performance of the music on keyboards, they record the players and singers section by section, producing various lines to be assembled through overdubbing on a 3M thirty-two-track digital recorder.

On paper, it sounds all too mechanistic. How, one wonders, can a sense of ensemble be achieved if the players hear only their own parts, a click track, and a few cues to tell them when to stop repeating figure A and move on to figure B? What sort of fluidity can be obtained when the players are, in effect, chained by the ears to a metronome? And if the clicks and cues tell the performers what to play and when, where does that leave Christopher Keene listed as conductor?

Yet listening to the recording with these questions in mind and with a deeply ingrained feeling that orchestral music can't be recorded this way, I had to admit that it works. Years of practice seem to have given Glass's team the ability to manipulate click tracks in a way that simulates the tempo changes that occur live; and the composite mix does indeed give the impression of a full, interacting ensemble. As Riesman and Munkacsi would no doubt ask, is a performance assembled vertically, track by track, any less true to life than one assembled horizontally, in a series of takes edited together? Perhaps not. Where problems do occur here, they have less to do with the illusion of a performance than with what seems to have been a temptation to conduct at the console. One of my few regrets about the recording is the balance at the very start: in performance, the cello accompaniment is louder and has real bite. Here it's recessed, far behind Perry's voice, and somewhat less effective. Later, the flute parts seem unnaturally prominent. And at various places, a lighter hand on the studio echo might have yielded a somewhat more natural (or less artificial) sound. But these are minor, momentary problems. Overall, the recording does *Satyagraha* justice.

As for Keene's contribution, while this studio technique may have made him superfluous during the sessions, Riesman writes that he did participate at the stage where tempos and cuing points were decided—and of course, he has had an effect on the way the work is performed. Keene's connection with Glass goes back to the early 1970s, when the conductor invited Glass's ensemble to play at the Spoleto Festival, of which he was music director. That invitation apparently led to a sizable battle between

Keene and Spoleto's founder, Gian Carlo Menotti, who was appalled that his conductor would taint Spoleto with what he considered a rock band. Keene admired Glass's work, though, and championed it when he could. Glass, in turn, had selected him to conduct *Satyagraha*'s Rotterdam premiere in 1980, but illness forced him to bow out, and the assignment went to another young American, Bruce Ferden.

Perhaps it was a question of taking on a tough job on short notice, but I've heard a tape of one of those early Dutch performances, and it's pretty deadly. There, even without the supposed impediment of a click track, tempos were rigid and slow. When Keene took over for the first American performances, he molded the score into the much more dramatically vital entity it is here. (In fact, he gave a tenser, more exciting reading than Dennis Russell Davies would subsequently in Stuttgart.) His tempos were brisker overall, and they followed the impulse of both the text and the staged drama. Keene also played a slightly shorter score than Ferden, for in preparing the work for its American staging, he and Glass decided to make a few cuts.

Glass would in any case have prescribed cuts for the recording; he believes that a performance heard on disc is fundamentally different from a live one, where visual elements and atmosphere make repetition more effective. To trim his works for recording (as he has also done with *The Photographer* and *Einstein*), he cuts some repeats. I'm not sure it's necessary—after all, repetition is central in creating that psychoacoustical effect Glass strives for, and particularly now that his changes come more quickly anyway, elimination of the repeats makes the change in his style seem more radical than it really has been. On the other hand, some of the cuts in *Satyagraha* are for the better: At the Dutch premiere, for instance, the off-stage chorus at the start of Act III went on endlessly; pretty as it is, one wants to get past the introduction and into the fray.

Of course, this business of composer-directed cutting is bound to muddy the waters for future authenticity mavens, as are the numerous performance tapes that circulated among collectors of Glassiana during the years CBS was waffling about whether to record the work. Which most truly represents the composer's intentions: the tape of the world premiere—uncut, but so dull as to keep much of the score's beauty a mystery? The Brooklyn tapes—less complete and more incisive than Rotterdam, yet longer than the CBS set? Or the studio production—the most evocative performance, and the one over which Glass presumably exercised the most direct control, yet the most severely cut, and the one with the least natural instrumental balances?

Untangling all of that I will leave to some future reviewer.

The original production of *Satyagraha*, with Glass's staging and Robert Israel's sets, would have made for a gorgeous video presentation. Alas, the one video production that has been shown in this country so far (on Bravo, a cable arts channel) is not that version, but the travesty designed, produced, and reinterpreted by Achim Freyer, at the Stuttgart State Opera.

Things go wrong from the start. In place of Glass's mythological battlefield, with its pitched armies, Gandhi, and Arjuna and Duryodhana in Kathakali-like costumes, Freyer fills the stage with a veritable circus of superfluous characters and props. Gandhi appears carrying a huge barbell, weighted to the floor, and as he sings his opening aria, he trips about the stage with the weight. Lest the symbolism be lost, he thrusts the weight into the air with one arm at the scene's end, when he has accepted the task of taking up the fight. I do like Freyer's idea of presenting Gandhi, Arjuna, and Krishna on three levels, one above the other. Yet the persistent clutter of nonsense outweighs the scene's few bright notions.

This is the most outrageous of the scenarios, and some of the others come close to Glass's suggestions, with only a bit of stylized movement superimposed. But in the sublime third act, too, intermittent lunacy takes a devastating toll. It may not matter so much that Freyer chooses to portray Gandhi's later and more famous March to the Sea rather than the Newcastle March; at least the march itself is put forth soberly and with a sense of purpose. There are a few moments of odd charade before Gandhi's final aria, but fortunately that comes through unscathed. There is, however, no sign of Martin Luther King, Jr., other than his name in blue neon at the start, and a sort of blue electric showman with a dove over his head that comes wheeling in during Gandhi's final bars—hardly a fitting realization of Glass's intent. There are musical drawbacks, too—a Gandhi split among three tenors of varying timbre and quality; mediocre, lifeless orchestral sound; and a lethargic pace.

In short, this is not the production by which to judge the work. Given the unusual and nonnarrative aspects of the opera itself, this loony staging is more likely to alienate than convince newcomers to it. . . .

PHILIP GLASS: *THE PHOTOGRAPHER* (1984, revised 1996)

ROBERT C. MORGAN

In browsing through a collection of photographs by the late nineteenth-century zoopraxeologist Eadweard Muybridge, one is immediately struck by the logical association to the music of Philip Glass. The title of the book is simply *Animal Locomotion* (1887). Each sequence of photographs is constructed within a grid and constitutes a specialized study of either an adult male or female in the positions of walking, climbing, running, dressing, lifting, bathing, jumping, or performing a multitude of other mundane activities or chores. The figures are either partially clothed or naked. Occasionally, there are photographs of children as well—an infant crawling, a toddler running.

Were it not for the pretense of science, one might refer to these examinations in terms of an obsession. Apparently, there are hundreds—perhaps thousands—of these photographs taken by Muybridge from different angles, using different lenses, offering varied perspectives and points of view. Men and women posing and performing in front of the lens. They appears as pictograms of the culture of diurnal work and play. There is something fundamental about these photographs, some basic truth—an odd summation, perhaps, given their allegiance to Structuralism. Yet there is something ineluctably *moving* about these studies of the human animal. They are capable of eliciting an emotional response, a particular sensitivity. It is, perhaps, in this spirit that Philip Glass chose to work with these images as signifiers of time, specifically modular time, the kind of tempo that connects with a Structuralist sensibility or raison d'etre.

Indeed, the modularity of Muybridge's zoopraxeological photographs, taken in the latter part of his career, after the famous duel in which he shot and killed his wife's lover, is the formal affinity upon which the opera, *The Photographer: Far From the Truth*, was based. The production premiered at the Brooklyn Academy of Music on October 4, 1983 and was directed by JoAnn Akalaitis, choreographed by David Gordon, written by Robert Coe, and with set and costume designs by Santo Loquasto.

If one is to question why Glass decided to become involved in writing a score for *The Photographer*—based on the later career of Muybridge—it is clearly because he felt a connection with the Structuralist parameters inherent in the work. Glass has an association with advanced visual artists—particularly with Minimal Art and Structuralist film-making. For example, the playwright Richard Foreman, has compared the early music of Glass to that of the films of Canadian artist Michael Snow.

One might say of the later sixties in New York that the idea of structuring reality according to principles of modularity and repetition in a disinterested context was simply "in the air." There are numerous examples ranging from the sculptor Don Judd to the conceptual artist Sol LeWitt to the "white paintings" of Robert Ryman. The metaphor of Muybridge's visual taxonomy in relation to Glass's serial approach to music—as with other artists working in their respective mediums—suggests that the composer was not simply illustrating a dramaturgical event, but was engaged in these structured photographs on a deeper level.

It is interesting to examine Philip Glass's development as a composer and musician before and after the success of his first operatic piece, *Einstein on the Beach*, co-authored with Robert Wilson in 1976. In the late sixties and early seventies, the sound of Glass's music was closely aligned to Minimal Art. The building and repetition of phrases, the playing in unison, and the logical progression of sound textures were all made explicit and existed as key elements in his performances.

In recent years, Philip Glass has ostensibly expanded his idea of "process" or "phase music," as it was sometimes called, by taking it into more complex permutations. Glass's relationship to performance is still integral in his approach to composition; but at times the complex laying and diversity makes for an unevenness in the transition between passages. The cumbersome aspect of these transitions is uncharacteristic of Glass's earlier Structuralist works. This suggests that the music heard in a performance (that is also *seen*) has a different effect from the same passages heard on a recording. There are other interesting examples of this problematic as well, both related to operatic collaborations and to his recent film scores.

In his 1983 CBS recording, based on the life of the late nineteenth century zoopraxeologist and photographer, Eadweard Muybridge, Glass no longer adheres to the purely systematic progression of sequence. His phrases do not develop in a steady line. Instead they build for brief intervals and then shift abruptly into other modes of repetition. There are both vocal and instrumental components interacting in relation to one another. The structural device here is indeed more complex, but it holds less of the pervasive tonal evolution found in earlier works, such as *Music with Changing Parts* (1971) or *Music in Fifths* (1969).

In these earlier compositions, Glass's variations on a musical structure stress fundamental principles of composition that may be more radical as a truly innovative departure from traditional western music than the more operatic and cinematic works. One might consider that any radical departure in musical composition or, for that matter, any other art medium or intermedia structure, is not exempt from qualitative standards, even though it may significantly shift the criterion of evaluation to another level. The critical concern raised by *The Photographer* is the degree of significance this recording has when compared, for example, with one of the last pure Structuralist recordings like *Music in 12 Parts* (1974).

There are some exceptional moments, however, to be heard on the selections chosen by Glass for the recording of *The Photographer*. Occasionally the shifting structural lines really work and, when they do, they reveal some of the composer's most interesting work since *Einstein on the Beach*. One cannot help but acknowledge exhilarating and heightened moments in Glass's performance in *The Photographer* with or without the visual effects and set designs. The rhythmic momentum achieved in the instrumental section towards the end of Act II and the virtuoso violin by Paul Zukofsky in Act III are both exemplary in this way. In such passages the spectrum between Structuralist and Romantic music does not seem so wide. One gets the point of Glass's systemic rigor and overlayering complexities as bringing these two disparate antipodes together.

On Side One of *The Photographer*, there are two versions of a motif called "A Gentleman's Honor." The first is a vocal arrangement and the second is primarily instrumental. Glass's vocal section makes for difficult listening in that it splits the musical texture into two discrete components: a metaphorical narrative—that in its insistence appears forced—and a progressive modular and modulating structure. The problem is that the voices do not harmonize adequately within the system. This is true in parts of other works as well, including his recent soundtrack recording for the film, *Koyaanisqatsi*.

Where the vocals do succeed in *The Photographer* is when the libretto is purely phonetic as opposed to the generally failed attempts *to make meaning*. Even so, one senses a conflict in the vocal section of "A Gentleman's Honor," for example, where Glass tries to keep the lyrics "anonymous" and then uses repetition to instill somehow a metaphorical content within the theatrical event. By attempting to keep the vocals anonymous—as if to create a vocal counterpart to "systems aesthetics" (a term attributed to the critic Jack Burnham)—in the same way as the instrumentals, Glass overrides the possibility of lending an emotional ingredient to the score.

As previously suggested, the conflict is truly interesting when the hinge between the Structuralism and Romanticism do not go to opposite ends of the spectrum, but begin to do their overlay. This is one of the most original contributions offered by Glass, but does not appear fully developed until some years later. Put another way, the composer uses conflict within the score without forcing a resolution—specifically when it does not appear overdetermined as it does in the vocal section of "A Gentleman's Honor."

In following suit with Minimal Art, the early Philip Glass was apparently against any reference to subjectivity in music. It was more about the pragmatic structure. The problem of vocals had not entered in— not until *Einstein on the Beach* (1976). With *The Photographer* seven years later, the problem of emotional content in Glass's music was still unresolved. Yet, the tendency of moving more overtly toward the Romantics was clearly in place.

Glass's career since *The Photographer* has shown the composer's remarkable ability to transform the conflict, so profoundly felt within this work, into a more relaxed performance. One may even talk of two distinct approaches in the music of Philip Glass—that which works best as a recording, and that which needs to be heard in the context of a performance. This is the crux of the conflict in *The Photographer*.

*   *   *

Some of the remarks included in this essay first appeared in a review published in Domus, No. 648 (March 1984).

INTERVIEW WITH PHILIP GLASS (1984)

Editor's Note: The following typescript was found in Glass's archive. He doesn't remember the Yugoslav interviewer's name, nor is there a published version in the archive.

I would like to start by asking you how you perceive the current cultural context in which you work.

I tend to work as internationally as I can, in Western Europe, Japan, and North America. In America alone, I discovered that there wasn't enough work here. So, I do tours now—one tour in Europe every year, one tour in America with the ensemble—and the operas that I write are done more in Europe than in America. So, in terms of the social context, it is an international one. Although I am identified as an American, which is true because that is my background, I can't economically limit myself to America.

So the prime reason or motivation for your work being international is economic, or is there a deeper reason also?

I would have to say that the prime reason is economic. The first problem that an artist has is how to survive. I chose not to make my living teaching. I have no means of support apart from my work. Had I taken an academic route, then all these questions would have been different, because I would have had economic security. In fact, my goal has always been to support myself from the work that I do, and to do it from the work that I chose to do, so that it is not work that is responding to a commercial marketplace, but to an artistic one. I chose not to take an academic route or a commercial route.

Until I was forty-one I was not self-supporting as an artist. And I began writing music when I was fifteen, so that was over twenty-five years that I could not entirely support myself through the work that I wanted to do. So, the struggle for me to reach a point where my entire efforts could be only through music was important. And it was important that I do it under conditions that were acceptable to me. Neither academic nor commercial conditions were acceptable. So that meant that I had to do it independently, adhering closely to an artistic vision that seemed authentic to me.

Can you say a word about that vision?
Well, that is the hardest thing to talk about. You'll find that I will talk more easily about all the other things. The struggle to develop an artistic language, a personal voice, all these things—those are very personal ones, and I think those are problems that artists have always had. How they solve them may be very different.

It seems to me that over the past century an increasing trend in artistic work has been towards making a name for oneself. In some cases that led to a position where artists are at times very personal, even self-centered, and sometimes very esoteric. The counterpart to that, in my mind, is that artists are also relevant to their cultures and to their time, and as such need to have some sense of what their culture is or needs in order to serve it. I would be interested to know how you approach this.
The question of serving the needs is something that, well, to put it that way, it doesn't quite occur to me. For many years the work that I did did not have a large public. So, what are the reasons that I am doing it? The music that I was writing when I was writing *Music in 12 Parts* or even *Einstein on the Beach*—before that piece I really wasn't that well known, though I did many concerts starting in 1968. But it also comes down to what the artistic aims are. I am not a cultural historian, and I cannot speak to that so directly. I can't honestly say that I was serving the needs of society; it never occurred to me. I was mostly interested in writing music. The work that I am doing now that is recognizable as my work started around 1965, and the first piece that I considered a successful piece was around

'69. I had an ensemble that had been functioning for more than a year, and some of that work I am still performing today. So that I have a whole repertoire of work that I consider playable starting from that year. At that point I found myself, when I was thirty-two, with a showcase for the work that I was doing, with a language that in retrospect seems primitive in some ways, but was adequate to serve my artistic needs at that time. And I was able to write pieces that I cannot improve on now without totally reconceiving them. At that point, I had already reached the first level of what I consider to be a functioning artist. I knew that my best work was ahead of me, but I knew that I was no longer struggling for a voice. In other words, although I knew that the work would inevitably mature, I knew that I had a recognizable voice. There was another full ten years before there was an economic match to that artistic situation.

So, my struggle became one of surviving in order to do the work that I wanted to do. It happened that from a very early point there was a community, a very small community, that was very appreciative of this work. It centered in New York, and in the community of visual artists that lived in downtown New York City, theater artists, people in dance, some musicians (but not too many, really)—this became my first audience, in a way. You can say that in a sense, since I was also a performer, I was constantly playing for this audience. This was a real context for the music. Now, over the years, I have expanded way beyond that original audience. But it wasn't until I began working on large theater pieces that the large audiences became essential.

You see, you can hardly ever separate the economic reasons from the artistic ones. Because at the point where you begin to do a large theater work, which only a repertory opera company can do, perhaps, that requires maybe 200 persons to stage and maybe six weeks to rehearse, to build the decor maybe three or four months. You're talking very big-scale pieces. You cannot do big-scale pieces for audiences of fifty or sixty, which are the size audiences that I originally played for. It simply is not viable; no one will produce the work. Had I decided to remain with the ensemble alone, it wouldn't matter; I could continue playing for fifty or sixty people audiences forever. And in fact, from a composer's point of view, it is a completely satisfying relationship. It is not a question of numbers in that case. If you have fifty or 100 or 200 people who love the work, what's the difference? It's only a decimal point away from 2000. And it doesn't qualitatively make it any better, to have a bigger audience. From the point of view of the satisfaction that an artist feels, that can be gained very quickly from an authentic audience relationship.

You asked about society at large—it became important when I

began to do large-scale pieces, which became large social events. So, if I want to do an opera for the Stuttgart Opera, then it becomes something that everyone in that town knows about. And they do fifteen performances a year and they do it over a period of several years, and I would dare say that there is hardly anyone in that city who doesn't know that opera has taken place.

The image that you project is of an artist who is very much at the influence and at the mercy of currents of the society. What are other influences?
You have to remember that I also helped to shape the currents too, that the musical life of the city that I live and work in is very different now from 17 or 18 years ago. I am one of the people that made that happen.

Who in your mind are some others?
Well, there are many. Theater people, and other musicians; people in the theater like, originally, the Living Theater; and the Mabou Mines collective; but also Meredith Monk and Bob Wilson, they're painters; and sculptors like Richard Serra—those that create the artistic values that become the recognizable culture of that time. You can say in one way, then, that we're at the mercy of it; then, on the other hand, it is a relationship, because we're also performing it. In fact, I don't think that you can separate it one way or the other. We are both victims of it, and we are both the creators of it. So, our relationship is always more complex than that.

Now, I know what you are driving at, and eventually I'll get to it, but I think it is very important to see the social context that the artist works in. When I began to do my work, it was completely unacceptable in the music world at that time. At this point it is not only completely acceptable but I am now considered by some younger composers as if I had always been alive and working. Now to someone who is twenty and sees my work, to them I have always been there. So, their point of view is very different.

That must be very satisfying to you, as an artist.
To be satisfied is hardly the point. In fact, it is just the mechanism of the way it works. To take pleasure in that would be to rob it of the fatalism that it has. Do you see what I mean? It's not a personal issue; it's the way the world works. You can look at Berlioz and say the same thing. I don't mean to compare my work to his, but I look at it from a social point of view; or from the struggle that anyone has, from being a radical figure to

a person who becomes identified as one of the people of a generation that creates the culture of the times, to finally being considered one of its icons, perhaps. I'm too young for that, and we don't know whether it would ever happen, but that could even happen later. It's a mechanism. To say that I did it is to place myself in a position of power that I don't have.

Now, we want to talk about what is the real reason that I write the music. That's what you want to know. The reason I don't separate it is because that moment is never forgotten. Every day that I work, I come back to that point.

What is that "point"?
It's the point where I am alone with music. This is, I would say, the fundamental relationship. The reason I talk about these other things is that in the society where we are living—where are you from?

I was born in Yugoslavia.
I do not know how it is there, but I have to tell you that this society, in relationship to artists, is one of the most brutal societies that you can imagine. Although there are other classes in the society who are also treated very badly, old people, for example, and people who don't speak English well. You're safe by the color of your skin, but if you had the wrong skin color *and* the accent, then you're in trouble. We have a fairly narrow spectrum of acceptance, let's say, of "safe" groups of people in this country. By becoming an artist, you definitely fall out of that class.

I don't know an artist—and I've talked to many people, a visual theater artist or a music or performance artist—whose parents when they were young, asked them to become an artist. I don't know anyone who didn't on their own say, "I am going to be a painter," "I am going to be a sculptor." And so that later on when they say, "Well, I'm not doing well; I'm having a hard time," people say: "Who asked you to do it?" Or this is the reply: "If you want to spend time painting pictures, that's fine, but don't expect *us* to help you." This is the American life; this is the way we do it here.

That's why these questions come up. But we come back to why is it to begin with, in the face of this, that one will do it anyway? And in fact to the point that, in my opinion—I'm afraid to appear chauvinistic but— American artists are among the strongest in the world. For reasons that are not clear—maybe the heterogenous nature of the society, the extreme independence of the artist through survival, the lack of real tradition in the arts in this country—the many factors maybe make it so that we develop a very strong artistic personality in this country. To begin as an artist means to take on a life of struggle, so that at 41 you may finally be making a living as an artist. My European artist friends would say, "My gosh, it took you so long," but in this country you'd say, "You mean you did it so quickly?" It's because it can easily never happen.

So first of all, you have people who are very motivated. I can't speak for other people. I know some artists very well. I've lived with them, gone out with them, and I know that my case is not so different. I had a friend who once talked about his relationship to painting as a response to painting, in that he felt that he was responding on one level to all the paintings that have ever been made. And at a certain moment as a musician, there's a lot of music that brings you to a point where somehow you have to try to speak that language. That happened to me fairly late, because I was fifteen when I began writing. I began playing music when I was six, but didn't actually begin to write until nine years later.

Music is one of the few places, perhaps one of the only places, where we find the meeting of our intellectual life and our emotional life. The possibility of forming a perfect match can take place there. We can use our brains in one way and at the same time respond. I don't know of any other thing that does that, where the raw stuff of art becomes emotions in certain ways, which are captured through this strange and elaborate process of artistic technique. It's a very curious phenomenon. I think when one is struck by that, it can be at an early age, or sometimes later in life, but it can become the focus of all the energy that you have. In this way, being an artist is more like a vocation; it's more like a calling in that you can't be asked to do it, and you also can't be dissuaded from doing it. It sounds abstract, but it's also a daily process. If you work every day at it, it becomes very immediate, and there is a constant engagement with this. I think that's a primary motivation.

Now there are many others. I know for some people there are very much simpler things, things like money and power and fame and all those things too, the usual gamut of human gratification. Certainly there are few artists who don't have some elements of all of those things. But I would say that the primary one for me is that this is one area where this most intangible thing can be made almost as solid as a rock.

To what degree do you think of yourself as taking on a lineage of work?
I think very little about that. I had the curious experience of finishing my music studies in Paris after already having a very complete training here. I went to Paris when I was around twenty-four or -five, and I spent anoth-

er two to three years there. I was mostly struck by the enormous difference in the sense of history the European artist has in relation to the American artist. I remember Nadia Boulanger, who was my teacher, telling me one day, "You know, a great sadness for me is that you Americans have no sense of history."

Of course, any American would have told her that having no history can be a great gift and a great opportunity, but in fact she was exactly right. The European composers and the fellow students that I knew—there was a tremendous abyss between us in terms of our sense of history.

On the other hand, I feel that the history of music is my history too. It's rather my relationship to it that's different, so that if I think of an orchestration, I'll think about Shostakovich and Mahler and Berlioz. If I'm thinking about vocal writing, I'll think of Verdi and Monteverdi. They are my history too. I never would have believed that we could have been so different had I not lived in Europe and seen the European artists relate to their tradition very differently from the way that we do.

I've been looking around your room here, and there are two what I imagine are sacred scrolls. One looks Tibetan.
They're both Tibetan actually, one from Eastern Tibet and one from Central Tibet. And that's from Japan.

You're an American; you started in Europe. Seems to me that maybe the difference is one of being capable as an American to unplug yourself from a given culture and explore all these other cultures.
Well, the American identity is fairly recent in terms of cultural history. What are we talking about—200 to 300 years? And it's mostly a hodge-podge. My family is from Russia, but I can't say that I have any sense of being Russian at all. We are Russian Jews. That already is different from being Russian; it's not even being Russian, practically. I could have been Polish, possibly, depending on how you drew the map. My girlfriend's family is partly Chinese and partly Irish. Another friend who works very closely with me, his family is from Hungary. Within the close community of friends that I work with, if you go back only two generations, everyone was from Europe. I happen not to know any people whose ancestors came over on the Mayflower. I suppose those people exist. I've never met them. My black friends, their lineage is older in America than mine is.

There is a great difference also in what part in America you're from. You'll find that west coast artists, it seems, grow up looking west more than we on the east coast who are much closer to Europe do, not only geographically, but emotionally. John Cage was from California. If you're an American, you can be sensitive to that. From the point of view of Belgrade, we are all Americans, but if you're here, believe me, you can tell a difference.

Now in terms of the whole climate of the arts in general, we are moving towards a much more international feeling anyway. To give a specific example, when I studied in music school more than twenty-five years ago, there was no music taught that was not western music. Any music that was not considered western music, any music that was outside the western tradition was considered primitive music. This corresponded exactly to a general attitude of western culture *vis-à-vis* the rest of the world. This was the civilized world, and everything else was—now we have a euphemism, we call it the "developing world." Basically, it was the undeveloped, pre-industrial societies that could make no claim for sophistication of any kind, including the arts.

This idea was largely accepted by artists. The second world war brought us into much closer contact with the rest of the world on an international level. This was a growing awareness, and it happened in my generation, so that even with silly things like guitar players deciding they want to play the sitar, even that had a tremendous impact in terms of the culture of this country. By the '60s, as John Cage said in one of his books, America was just another part of the world, no more and no less, and there were several great traditions of music. The great traditions of music were the African tradition, the Indian tradition, the Balinese tradition, the Japanese tradition, and the Western tradition. They were parallel traditions that could claim no superiority over each other. This is something that actually happened within our time, and I see that you grew up seeing that too.

On the west coast, Lou Harrison is a very fine composer who has taken a great interest in the music from Bali. I have personally taken a great interest in music from south India. There are other composers who have taken great interest in music from Africa. I've heard it said that this is another case of colonization on another level. But if you've ever been to their countries, you see it's actually more complicated than that. When I go to India in fact, I hear that western music has now become part of Indian music. The influence is not just one way at all.

In the city like Madras there are certain techniques of playing that have been affected by guitar playing. There are people saying that this is the ruination of tradition, but on the other hand maybe that isn't. I don't know to what extent any of our traditions are going to be able to be totally separated. It's not just simply the west taking from the non-west; you see the non-west absorbing as rapidly as possible things from the west. Because we're the ones that can travel, it's easier for us to go there. There's not a lot of their music that can come here. So it's very one-sided from that point of view, but the music is everywhere.

Do you have a sense what the end result of all this cross-pollination will be?
The best people that I know in other countries wish to preserve the identity of their own culture. They also do not want to be left out of this great cross-culturalization that's going on, so there's a conflict. Can you have both? I don't know. Can you have the purity of traditional music and at the same time be open to the traditions of western repertory opera? I don't know. It's very hard to say whether the results will be good or bad. Probably they'll be both.

I've had the good luck to travel. That's been the best antidote—to go out and see what's happening. And you see all manner of things; you see things that are very negative, and you see things that can be very wonderful.

For example?
I think for example in film. You take someone like Satyajit Ray from Calcutta, who's a filmmaker, who clearly is a man who understands the history of film. The history of film did not develop in India. This is a western art form, and there is a master film maker from Calcutta who is working in a technique that is not Indian. So that's an example from that side—we tend to forget that is also possible. There are novelists who come from non-western countries, who are working in the tradition of the novel, which didn't exist in those countries before. Then on our side, I've been enriched by traditions that I met in my travels, first in Europe, then through north Africa, then through central Asia and India. The curious thing for me that I find very interesting is that I am told that my music sounds very American, and not only that but people in Europe will say, "Your music sounds not only American, your music is from New York." And if they live in New York, they even know what part of town it is from.

My predilection has been to participate in an aesthetic understanding of other traditions as much as I could. The way that it's been incorporated has been personal to the point where it's not that apparent. But in fact I could not be writing the music I'm writing today had I not traveled as widely as I have.

You mentioned before the image that music provides a synthesis between the intellectual and the emotional. Where does the spiritual side fit in your music or in your home?

You mean, in the trinity of the Father, the Son, and the Holy Ghost, where is the Holy Ghost? Well, you never see it, do you? [laughs] You explain it to me. I don't know where it is. Where is the ghost in the machine? I don't know. It's funny. There are mysteries even in technology that are fascinating to me.

We just recorded *Satyagraha*, an opera I wrote a few years ago about the early life of Mahatma Gandhi. We're working with very high technology, where the machinery is so complicated now that when something happens, we're not even sure why it happens. There may be a pop on the tape, for example, and we do not know where it came from. And so to look at that, you get to a point where you say, well, there's something that goes beyond the technical, the mechanical, the cultural. It's almost like the Hegelian idea that when there is enough quantitative change, you come to a qualitative change, the quantitative leads to the qualitative. Another factor is operating, and I don't know that we know what it is. There's a lot of mystery in this.

It seems to me, looking at your operas exploring the life of Gandhi and delving into Egyptian mysteries, there must be something that compels you about those things more than, say, the life of Eisenhower.

It would seem to be. I was just reading a book by a Japanese writer who quotes from *Brothers Karamazov* by Dostoyevsky about the mystery of beauty. It's a very striking passage, about how God has set this terrible mystery for man to unravel and that we'll never figure it out. And so you get into these questions.

I prefer to leave these questions out of my speculations. It's enough simply to master a technique or to even master economic survival, which is another level that I'm never unaware of, or to grasp some real idea of how our cultural life interacts with other peoples to form something that becomes the life of the late twentieth century. This is the ninth decade of the twentieth century; the ninth decade is now. And we're beginning to see that there seems to be something that could not be described as simply French or American or Bulgarian or Russian or Iranian or anything. So there is something that's peculiar to this moment in history, and these questions are the ones that, let's say, amuse me to think about. When you talk about the spiritual things, my God! I mean that becomes another—I can't even begin to think of it. I don't think I'm smart enough to do that. There are people that do, like Thomas Merton, who in modern times try to think about spiritual things. The Dalai Lama is another one and, you know, they're specialists just like the rest of us.

Yesterday I met with Paul Winter. I don't know if you know who he is. He's a jazz musician, and now he does music that incorporates sounds of animals, like whales or wolves. In talking with him, he's very concerned about ecological issues and the survival of the earth on that level. And in some ways he's saying, "My music will be a vehicle through which I express that concern." Do you have a similar dialogue going on?
No, I don't. I have a more fatalistic attitude.

How's that?
Well, we talk about survival, and of course, things are very difficult and of course, it seems things are going to happen in the worst way, but they never really will. But we have no assurances that they never really will. I don't have some kind of blurry confidence of it one way or the other.

But given that possibility that they may not work out, you do not feel compelled to engage yourself?
You mean I'm writing some kind of tombstone?

Do something to correct the situation?
You know in a way I have two answers to that question. In my words I will for the most part deny it, but in fact if I look at the work that I do, I have to admit that there seems to be some—there's a work about Gandhi, a work about Einstein, a work about Akhnaten—again, one of the watersheds of the development of human consciousness at the time. I don't know really historically whether that's true, but we've made it that.

The next major work that I'm doing is on a book by Doris Lessing, *The Making of the Representative for Planet 8*. It's the story of a whole planet that is freezing to death, and it's dying, the whole planet's dying.

Now why did you choose that from among many wonderful stories?
The questions she raises in the book are among the most interesting ones I can think of. Without giving away the story, *The Making of the Representative* is about how we face the possibility of not surviving. How do we face the possibility that no one is going to come and save us? The planet is dying, there's been a cosmological disaster, the heat has left the planet, the planet has moved out of its course. The people have been assured by their neighboring planet that they are going to be taken away

and all will be safe, and at some point they realize that their helpers are not going to come, that they're going to be left to deal with it all by themselves. What could be more the question of today?

So, for me this is the most interesting work I can do right now. On the one hand, as I speak, as I talk about the work I do and my intentions, my overt intentions are really not to polemicize. I don't feel that I'm an ideologue in that way, and I stay away from that. But in fact the work that I have done in the last eight or nine years is all about questions of this kind. So I must say that in spite of myself, or in truth to myself, I'm doing it anyway.

It takes two to three years to write an opera; you have to take on something that's going to last you that long, that will carry you through. The only works that interest me are ones that touch on those most fundamental issues, so in the end that's what I end up doing. Apart from the work itself, I rarely talk about these issues. My anxieties about the future of mankind, I never discuss that. I don't take part in panels about ecology. But on the other hand, on the truest level of where I'm working, I can't deny that this seems to be the sort of thing that I do. For myself I find it curious because I find myself unwilling to talk about it. On the other hand, I find myself unable to work in any other way.

Do you think that you're typical in that sense that, by necessity, artists, if they're really sensitive to what's going on in their world, must really consider these issues now?
Most of the artists that I know in some way or other deal with these problems, don't they? There are a few who do work in some kind of abstract aesthetic, whose work I admire, and whose work doesn't seem to be socially conscious in that way. In the theater arts where I spend a lot of my time, I find that many artists are doing that now, maybe more now than in the past. It's hard to say. I don't know what it must have been like to experience yourself as an individual in society 40 or 50 years ago; I've no way to know that. That the artist would also be a man or woman of social conscience seems to be more the norm now, doesn't it? Rarely will someone admit that they are not interested in these things. That would be interesting if someone would. It would be a different point of view. It would almost be interesting.

The reason why your name caught my attention was precisely your choice of topics. It seems that you are persistently dancing around something.

Who is it that said that we ooze self-betrayal? So finally, that is what you see. No matter what it is that we say or that appears in your book or what I may say in another interview about this or that, in fact if you look at the body of work, it points to a certain direction.

My reluctance to speak about it beyond that may be that I have almost nothing to say beyond the work itself. I have much more to say about the economic situation of the artist, the social situation of the artist. Those are easy things to talk about. On the larger view of the fate of the world, I mean, my God! I find that an unthinkable question.

Are you ever afraid of what might happen?
I tell you, fear doesn't enter into it. It's too abstract an idea. I can't imagine the world not existing, so that I have no fear of it not existing. On the other hand, I know for a fact that there are enough maniacs around capable of blowing the world up so that I have to say, well, my God, those guys might actually do it! But even as I say it part of me doesn't believe it's possible. But isn't this the comfort that we all have?

Where do you do most of your work?
I found a place in Nova Scotia, in Canada, far away from everyone, where hardly anyone I know is there, and I spend a month there—I used to spend two months, but now I spend about a month there. It's a fairly raw state of nature. I have a cabin in the woods that only got electricity very recently. The nearest house is a few hundred yards away. I'm in the woods, and that's where I work. I usually work with the door open, weather permitting, and a lot of the work seems to be sitting on the step outside the cabin and looking at the trees. So I must spend half my time looking outside, and the other half I spend writing.

There is quite a contrast between your cabin and this house on this busy and noisy corner here in New York.
You can't believe what a contrast it is. To come from that ground back to New York is always shocking; I never get over that.

You must like New York to be here.
Well, I made my peace with it certainly. Also, I thrive on the stimulation, and not just artistic stimulation, but the stimulation of people and events, especially this corner. This neighborhood I'm in is a particularly lively one, and I've chosen to live here for the last 15 years. All kinds of things happen here, which I find very interesting and very peculiar.

Last night I was outside my door. There was a blind man walking down the street. He had glasses, but only frames with no lenses. And he came across another vagrant—they were both vagrants—sitting on a box, and he pushed the stick and he hit this person. He took the stick and he broke it against the fence with a cry of complete rage, and then he said, "Where's my stick?" It was the strangest thing I've ever seen. The man sitting on the box was half-naked. His pants were down to his knees. I mean, you couldn't have written a stranger scene than this was. The blind man couldn't find the other end of his cane which he had destroyed, and the half-naked man couldn't get up, not because he was half-naked, but because he hadn't moved all day. The friend I was with went and got the other end of the cane and gave it to him. Now he had two pieces of cane that were broken, and what is that? I mean, what was that all about?

That's very different from sitting and looking at trees. I'm not saying that this was staged for my benefit. This is happening all the time. It's the damnedest thing you ever saw.

You must be curious enough to notice them, because somebody else might walk by and not pay any attention.
I'm noticing it all the time. The "human comedy," simply our life as you know it, I find it very interesting.

Your music revolves around repetition of a certain theme. Why is that?
Why did that language develop? Well, there are musical reasons for that. The period of music I grew up with was dominated by an avant-garde attitude about music, which had to do with an extreme development of a serial technique that was European-based originally. The important composers when I was a young man were people like Karlheinz Stockhausen, in this country Elliott Carter or Leon Kirchner. There are many others. As a young man, this was not the kind of music that was attractive to me. So I had to find a different language to work in, and I took a very extreme position. I reduced all the music that I knew to something that was based on the simplest materials of music that I could think of. It was in kind of opposition to this very evolved technique. Now, in fact over the last nineteen years, it has developed into another kind of technique, but it began from a very different place.

Also, one of the main interests of that time was the idea of rhythmic structure in music, which is an idea that came for me through non-western music. Almost any music that is non-western is involved in rhythmic structure, generally speaking. It sounds like an over-simplification, but it's amazingly consistently true. I saw this ideal rhythmic structure as a powerful technique that I could make into a personal vocabulary.

A lot of these rhythmic structures have to do with repetitive structures and, in the beginning, with very simple tonal relationships and a very slow evolution of material. That's developed a lot since 1965, but it is still recognizable in the music even now.

Sometimes the effect can be very hypnotic. Do you want to achieve that?
As a matter of fact it doesn't affect me that way at all. The idea of hypnotic seems like a form of sleeping, doesn't it? In fact my experience of it makes me very awake. So, I don't know. When I was young, I can remember going to hear a performance of Beethoven's *Ninth* and saw people sleeping in the audience. So what can I tell you? Some people wake up and some go to sleep whether it is Beethoven or whatever. When you say "to achieve an effect," to even put it in those terms supposes an intention that wasn't actually there.

Okay. Do you have any intention? For the people who come to your opera or concert, what would you like them to experience at the end of the event?
First of all, I would like them to have the same experience of music that I have. Well, of course, this is not achievable. It never really happens that way. When I write the music, I write it because it affects me in a certain way, and I hear the language of music as the most powerful way of achieving a specific response.

However, in fact, I'm aware that other people do hear very differently, so I long ago gave up the idea that they would hear it the way I did. On the other hand, there's enough similarity in the way they hear, it seems, that quite a consensus in an audience can take place. When you hear *Satyagraha*, towards the end of the opera, the very last thing that's sung are words that come from the *Bhagavad-Gita,* about how in every age a man is born to carry on the fight of good against evil. It's a very simple idea and this music at this moment is my response to this text. I think that it merges with the text in a way that makes a musical statement about it in a way. It seems that other people hear it that way as well, though I suppose that some people can hear it as trivial, or boring. Enough people hear it as uplifting, so that it's a very special moment that comes at the end of the opera. I've seen it performed many times and with many audiences, and I can feel that the audience is having a contact with the music and text that seems very consistent and seems appropriate to the material. So as a matter of fact, when I say that in a general way most everyone hears it differently, also in a general way there seems to be a possibility of having a consistent reception to the piece.

But I think the thing to remember is that the first listener is myself. I think for any artist this is true. For the painter, the first viewer is himself; for the poet, the first listener is oneself. If you're lucky it can be generally shared. There is some great work that is most difficult to communicate and that doesn't have a large audience. We also know that doesn't mean the work is less wonderful. There are great works of literature that I can't read; they're too difficult for me. I've never succeeded in reading *Ulysses*; I'm told it's a wonderful work of literature. I don't doubt that it's as great a work as it's claimed to be. I simply have never been able to read it. So there are works that are difficult; that does not make them less true.

The artist is a lucky one when the work communicates and is accessible, because it means that things happen, like someone will come to you on the street and say, "Your music is very important to me," or, "I heard this concert and I was very moved." And of course, it's an ancillary result of the work. It's one that no artist can fail to appreciate when that happens, but it's not in the cards that that's always going to happen. Some people it happens to and some people, it doesn't.

Do you ever concern yourself with invoking images of the future?
No, I'm free of any fantasies about the future. When I look into the future, I see a production of this new work in the spring or fall of '86 in Holland. I'm working on a film biography that will be released in the spring of '85. That's the future for me. Those are the things that I know. I have no fantasies beyond that. You'd be amazed about how little I speculate about the future, very, very, very little.

What about the larger future of the world?
Even less. I choose those words carefully when I say that I'm free of fantasies of the future. I'm truly free of it, nor did I have to conquer them. They don't come to me easily, and I never developed them or tried to evolve them. I have a very short-term view of the future, which is usually very, very specific—where we're going to eat dinner tonight, who will conduct this work next fall, when the tour will be to Europe—very, very specific things.

EDITOR'S PREFACE TO "PHILIP GLASS'S AKHNATEN" BY PAUL JOHN FRANDSEN (1993)

MARK SWED

The study of Philip Glass's opera *Akhnaten* by Paul John Frandsen comes from an unusual source for publication in an American journal of music, especially in that it concerns American opera. Mr. Frandsen is neither American nor a musical scholar, but he has singular qualifications. He is a Danish Egyptologist whose background in music comes through his father, who is a former general music director of The Royal Opera of Copenhagen. And Mr. Frandsen's musical literacy is such that, not having a score available from which to work, he took the musical examples down by dictation from the CBS Masterworks (now transferred to Sony) recording of the opera. The paper, first presented as a public lecture, was originally written in Danish for publication in *Papyrus*, a journal of the Danish Egyptological Society.

It is, to say the least, a quirky study. Mr. Frandsen's musical analytical methods are not particularly sophisticated. Nor, before examining *Akhnaten*, Mr. Frandsen admits, did he have much exposure to Minimalism. But finding such a nondoctrinaire approach toward what is surely the most controversial musical style of the past quarter century is precisely the attraction of this study for an American readership. Whatever its limitations, it brings a completely fresh perspective to an area of music so hotly debated that there seems little middle ground, a perspective that can not only shed light on the musical structure of the work, but also offer a unique inquiry into its historicity.

Mr. Frandsen's study comes at a propitious time. *Akhnaten*, Mr. Glass's third opera, is not a new opera, but there have been few serious investigations into Mr. Glass's operatic works, even though Mr. Glass is, by far, the most prominent American opera composer of our time. He has written some seven or eight more operas since *Akhnaten*. (It is not easy to count them; the composer is so prolific some have not yet been performed, and there is the further difficulty in distinguishing between the more general theater works [such as *1000 Airplanes on the Roof*] and full-fledged operas.) Mr. Glass, moreover, has been particularly on the minds of the American opera public lately, particularly in New York. His most musically elaborate opera, *The Voyage*, had its premiere at the Metropolitan Opera October 12, 1992, and was broadcast live nationally and overseas. . . .

Yet, American critics actually have little to go on when confronting a new opera by Mr. Glass. The operas have rarely been presented at their best (and some have hardly been presented at all) in the United States. One would have to go to Stuttgart, for instance, to see the finest productions and hear the best performances of *Satyagraha* and *Akhnaten*, those directed by Achim Freyer. Scores, published by Glass himself, have been, until only lately (now that G. Schirmer distributes them), nearly impossible to obtain except through the reticent composer, and none still have been published for sale (hence Mr. Frandsen's transcriptions from the recording).[1] This paucity may also, in part, account for the dearth of scholarly and analytical literature about Mr. Glass's work.

It is here that Mr. Frandsen's investigation has its value. Mr. Glass's music does have meaningful structure, and while Mr. Frandsen may not have much perspective on the background of Mr. Glass or Minimalism and relies primarily upon Mr. Glass's own chatty book for an understanding of the composer's intentions and style, he nevertheless demonstrates that the music is, indeed, readily analyzable if approached without prejudice.[2] Even more could be said about *The Voyage*. The "accompanimental" music on top, in the middle, and on bottom that Mr. Lipman objects to, may not be particularly interesting if so isolated, but the counterpoint and dramatic juxtapositions can be, and *The Voyage* is an opera of much structural intricacy and ingenuity if taken on its own non-narrative terms.

In the end, Mr. Frandsen comes to something of the same conclusion that Mr. Lipman does, finding Mr. Glass's technique not one that can really define character, though he does so sincerely and without automatic rejection of the music. Mr. Frandsen, himself, has other preconceptions—archeological ones. *Akhnaten*, *The Voyage* and Mr. Glass's other operas, however, will ultimately require a new critical vocabulary for dealing with non-narrative opera—Mr. Frandsen is only a little closer to the aesthetic than Mr. Lipman when he turns to Mussorgsky as a model. . . . Mr. Glass has little interest in Akhnaten or Columbus as historical or mythic figures; his is a late twentieth-century attitude of *demythologizing*, not so much to reveal or to revel in their foibles or failures, but rather to focus on the elemental where one can discover the essence through musical Minimalism, which restricts harmonic and melodic motion so that one can more thoroughly experience musical time. Glass's theater music represents, then, a process of questioning not of defining character, something that can be a problem for a traditional analytical approach based upon historical narrative process. Theater, dance, and film audiences seemingly have no problem with that. Mr. Frandsen, through his own cultural perspectives, has also some of those abilities to look at this work from at least a partially fresh angle, and he accomplishes something remarkable: he provides the justification for more analytical investigations of Mr. Glass's work while, at the same time, his own personal conclusions might comfort those who do not see the point in doing so.

Notes

1. Mr. Frandsen's transcriptions, while accurate, do not always follow the published versions, and have been corrected.

2. Philip Glass, *Music by Philip Glass*, ed. and with supplementary material by Robert T. Jones (New York: Harper & Row, 1987), 138.

PHILIP GLASS'S
AKHNATEN
(1993)

PAUL JOHN
FRANDSEN

As an Egyptologist, I am often asked to recommend a good book on ancient Egypt, and for many years I have suggested *Sinuhe, the Egyptian*, written in 1945 by Mika Waltari, the great Finnish writer.[1] The novel is based on research into Egyptological literature, and for its time it was remarkably accurate from a historical point of view. Today, however, it is a bit outdated, and many colleagues disapprove when I tell them that I do not recommend a book that reflects the present stage of research. But the hypothetical request mentioned above did not concern research as such; it had to do with what life in ancient Egypt *might* have been like, and the two do not necessarily coincide. Researchers have long since abandoned any pretence of establishing *wie es eigentlich gewesen* (how it really was), but there may be an alternative common goal that is less evident. The English historian, M. J. Oakeshott, says that "the historian begins with a homogeneous world of ideas, and his task is to transform (though not wholly transform) what is given into what is satisfactory."[2] Or, as the Norwegian historian S. Langholm says of historical research, "We seek to reconstruct a reality which will account for the sources."[3]

In fact, we are not just interested in "truth" but in intellectual constructs. Thus, the door is open to interpretations that are, for example, artistic, or not "strictly scientific." Furthermore, I believe that a good artistic interpretation can make a contribution to understanding and insight as valuable as any produced by scholars, and Waltari's book is an admirable example of this. The stage is set in the New Kingdom, more particularly during the years known as the Amarna Period (around 1350 B.C.). Through his fictional central character, the physician Sinuhe, Waltari paints a sensuous and detailed picture of life all through the Middle East. An "artistic reconstruction" may ultimately even reflect on the research in which it originated, and *Sinuhe, the Egyptian* is included in the Amarna bibliography of many Egyptologists.[4]

The Amarna Period has, in fact, attracted many different artists, and one of the latest is Philip Glass, with his third opera, *Akhnaten*.[5] As in Glass's two previous operas, *Einstein on the Beach* (1976) and the Gandhi portrait, *Satyagraha* (1980), which are all linked by a common musical "Trilogy" theme, *Akhnaten* represents an attitude toward history rather unlike Waltari's. To Glass, history is the history of "great spirits":

> to me, the entire history of humanity is a history of ideas, of culture. When I think of Ancient Greece, Rome, France, China, or wherever, what comes to my mind are poets, painters, writers, musicians, philosophers. I never think of generals and politicians. Except, perhaps, for Alexander the Great or Napoleon, that part of history is a story of faceless violence which, though it may be exciting to read about, adds little or nothing to the sum total of our humanity. And yet we often act as if the opposite were true, naming airports, highways and other public places after warriors and politicians who are barely remembered, and sometimes totally forgotten, by the next generation.[6]

We are, in fact, presented here with a somewhat old-fashioned view of history, and Glass hardly differs from most other composers or dramatists. But while working on *Akhnaten*, he realized that social, political, and religious ideas could be made to play a central part in a work if they are, as in the works of the standard repertoire, clad in flesh and blood. It remains, however, for Glass to turn this dramaturgic requirement into something more than a common banality.

That requirement also implies a more conventional musical language than had been found in earlier minimalism, in general, or in Glass's own principles of composition, in particular. In the earlier operas, systematic repeats dominated, both in the melodic technique of additive process and in the rhythmical principle of cyclic structure. These procedures led to very complex links between melody, rhythm, and harmony, with little attempt to wed them to conventional plot. In fact, *Einstein on the Beach* has no plot at all. *Akhnaten*, while too fragmentary to be termed a true epic opera, is, nonetheless, a step in that more conventional direction.[7] The chronological progress of the opera follows that of history and is probably no less coherent than *Boris Godunov.*

As a consequence of composing more conventional opera, Glass's musical language, in many respects, becomes more conventional as well. Thus, in *Akhnaten,* melody plays a much greater part than in his previous works, such that people actually find themselves humming tunes from the opera. Rhythm and harmony are also used more traditionally to convey dramatic situations. But the most decisive novelty is Glass's use of themes, timbres, and keys as leitmotivs in the epic/musical development.[8]

When we turn to the libretto—by Glass, Shalom Goldman, Robert Israel, and Richard Riddell—of the opera, however, we see at first glance that Glass hardly seems to consider the audience. With the exception of the Akhnaten's "Hymn to the Sun," all other texts are performed in the original languages, that is, in ancient Egyptian, Hebrew, or Babylonian. Glass does not wish the text to describe an action, and even less to provide a comment on it. If the listener does not understand the words, then the music must be granted even more explicit power of expression (though one may ask, Why then write an opera at all, and not a symphonic poem?). He also dismisses the intelligibility of the libretto with the argument that you can never understand opera singers' enunciations, no matter what the language. Still, Glass was unwilling to allow the text to bypass the audience totally, so he introduced a narrator, the scribe, whose recitation of largely supplementary texts functions in the contrapuntal manner that Glass allegedly disapproves of. It turns out to be a brilliant solution.

However, this decision raises questions about Glass's view of the relation between audience and composer. Glass has spent the majority of his adult life in the world of the theater. During a stay of several years in Paris in the mid-1960s, he was deeply influenced by Samuel Beckett, for whose drama, *Play,* he composed the music. Glass discovered that Beckett works in a way that incorporates the viewer into the work, thus providing the audience with an alternative option for interpreting or even completing the piece.[9] Glass, too, wants the listener to play an active, creative part.

We might perhaps conclude that Glass, as a composer, is in much the same situation as his main character, Akhnaten, the religious reformer. To make himself understood, Glass, like Akhnaten, has resorted to convention. Yet, in the context of the opera, they are, nonetheless, still revolutionary, and the ideas presented in the following pages may therefore be seen as one response to such a challenge.

Akhnaten begins with an instrumental prelude that consists of five sections, each divided into two subsections. The harmony of the first of the two subsections is characterized by alternating between A minor and F major, while every second subsection is identified by alternating between A minor and B-flat minor/B-flat major. The harmonic material is presented in the repeated arpeggios so characteristic of Glass, where three- or four-beat rhythms both interchange and contrast in an increasingly complex polyrhythmic pattern.

   Also in the first section we meet another familiar aspect of Glass's music—the extensive use of intervals of a second. Let us, as an example, examine more closely the first subsection of the first and second section (1, 1 and 2, 1). Over the alternating arpeggios in 1, 1, a theme gradually emerges, based on the aforementioned seconds. The theme, a quasi-ostinato figure, is made up of four groups, each of 32 notes. The first group, which may be regarded as a kind of introduction, consists of the note A repeated 32 times on a basis of pure A minor:

```
1. a a a a a a a a      a a a a a a a a
   a a a a a a a a      a a a a a a a a
```

Hereafter, the rest of the subsection looks like this:

```
      F major             A minor
2. f f f f g g f f     a a a a a a a a
   f f f f g g f f     a a a a b b a a
3. f f f f g g f f     a a a a b b a a
   f f f f g g f f     a b a b a b a b
4. f g f g g g f f     a b a b a b a b
   f g f g g g f f     a b a b a b a b
```

Similarly, in the second subsection of the first section, the A-minor chords still form the harmonic basis for an interchange between A and B, while the B-flat minor/B-flat major link produces a figure that only emerges fully as a theme in the fourth and fifth section (Ex. 1):

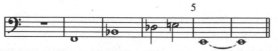

Example 1. All music from *Akhnaten* by Philip Glass, copyright 1984, Dunvagen Music Publishers, Inc. Used with permission.

According to Glass, the emergence of the theme lends the entire introduction an ominous air, but since the theme further appears in the epilogue as well as at the foundation ceremony (City/Dance) and the destruction of Akhetaten, he grants it a much more comprehensive significance. Its rise and abrupt fall is synonymous with Akhnaten's rise and fall, in that, at the same time, it creates "an uneasy harmonic ambiguity" (vacillating between B-flat major and B-flat minor); it can further be considered "as a musical metaphor for that part of Akhnaten's character that was so unusual and unsettling to the people of his time."[10]

Act 1.1: The Funeral

The first scene of Act 1 describes the funeral of Amenophis III. Glass has been fascinated by the traditional view of ancient Egypt as a civilization focusing on death, and in his opera, rituals of death therefore become the epitome of the old order—that is, of Egypt before Akhnaten and his attempted revolution. The theme of Scene 1 is thus traditional Egypt of the old order. Glass has looked at the general state of knowledge of Egyptian music and

> to judge from that evidence, Egyptian music was soft, lyrical stuff. About funeral music, no mention is made at all. Thus the music I designed for the funeral of Amenophis III in the opening scene of the opera does not resemble any funeral music I have ever heard before. The drumming that begins it, the flourishes for brass and winds and the emphatic entrance of the singing, give it a raw, primitive, quasi-military sound. In this music, coming as it does right after the prelude to Act I, my idea was to give an unmistakable and clear image of how, at least in part, "our" Egypt would be portrayed. By vividly portraying that world through the music, I hoped to set off the idealism of Akhnaten even more strongly. The blaring brass and pounding drums introduce the world into which Akhnaten was born.[11]

Glass, especially as far as his instrumentation of the funeral music is concerned, can be accused of indulging in the kind of "orientalism" that Western artists and scholars have often employed in their treatment of the

Orient. But by speaking of "our" Egypt, the composer makes it clear that he is not concerned with historical validity and is hardly attempting to compose history.[12]

We have already encountered the musical raw material for the first scene in the prelude, with its contrast between the notes A and B. This contrast will ultimately constitute the points of tension in the "plot" of the opera: the funeral of Amenophis III is set in B major, while the opposite pole of the opera, the Akhnaten's "Hymn to the Sun," is in A major.

Act 1.2: The Coronation

In the next scene, Amenophis IV is crowned as king of Egypt. The high priest of Amon, Aye, and Horemhab, along with the priests of Amon, sing a coronation anthem, and while the scribe reads aloud the official titulary of the king, the latter receives the double crown. Here we first meet Amenophis/Akhnaten. He is characterized as a potential revolutionary, but also as someone who is part of the old regime. The opera demonstrates this dual part by showing the king on stage, though he is left mute, not singing a single word. The music captures the situation in several ways, such as by creating new musical material out of old.

The first section of the coronation scene begins with a short repeat of the A/B contrast and the B-major tonality from the funeral scene, developing into a melodic phrase A-B-C-E (Ex. 2):

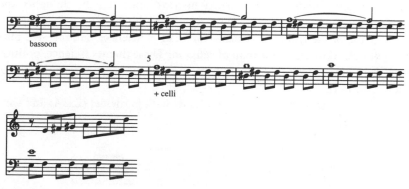

Example 2.

The A-B-C-E phrase is then incorporated in what Glass has termed the "Trilogy" theme because it occurs in all three operas (Ex. 3):

Example 3.

In its simplest form, the notes A-G-C, the "Trilogy" theme introduces *Einstein on the Beach*, and it may also appear in a number of variations. But the thematic role of the phrase is only seriously expressed by Glass in connection with its use in *Akhnaten*:

> This Trilogy theme, linked as it is to scenes in which essential aspects of Akhnaten's character are revealed, is strongly associated with Akhnaten himself. This is precisely how the Trilogy theme is used in *Satyagraha* and *Einstein* as well. In *Satyagraha*, it appears in the second scene when young Gandhi embarks upon his life's work, and again in the final scene at the penultimate moment of his political victory. The Trilogy theme occurs in all five Knee Plays of *Einstein*, scenes which represent the more intimate portraits of Einstein.[13]

The connection is even more clearly expressed in Glass's preface to the booklet accompanying the recording, where he calls Akhnaten, Gandhi, and Einstein "three men who revolutionized the thoughts and events of their times through the power of an inner vision. This, then, is the theme of the trilogy. Einstein—the man of science; Gandhi—the man of politics; Akhnaten—the man of religion. These themes (science, politics, religion) are, to an extent, shared by all three and they inform our ideological and real worlds."[14]

The first section of the scene ends with [a theme] (Ex. 4) and variations thereof.

Example 4.

This theme occurs several times in the opera, always as either an introduction to or an end of important moments in the opera. The theme usually appears with the A in the upper position, but at the end of the opera, this position is reversed and, combined with the "Trilogy" theme, the reversal causes the opera to conclude in the same mode in which it began, A minor, which, in a manner of speaking, represents ancient Egypt.[15]

The deep note E leads us to the second part of the coronation scene, producing a tonal system of contrasted A minor and E minor. If the "Trilogy" theme represents the religious, revolutionary King Akhnaten, E minor must represent Akhnaten, the human being. Given the close relationship between E minor and A minor, we are tempted to interpret its effect in the scene as Akhnaten's achieving liberation from his parent.

Act 1.3: The Window of Appearances

Here we are introduced to Nefertiti, Akhnaten's queen, and to Queen Tye, his mother. At once we are presented with a question that, strangely enough, I, as an Egyptologist, had never before asked myself: What did their voices sound like? Glass has made three choices—all unusual: Akhnaten is a countertenor, Nefertiti is sung by a mezzo-soprano, and Queen Tye by a light soprano.

To have the hero sung by a high, light voice may be in accordance with a tradition of centuries, but a countertenor is more than just a male voice that is higher than the tenor—especially when viewed from the end of the twentieth century. The sound of a countertenor to modern listeners is archaic. The voice has become more fashionable during the last two or three decades, especially in connection with performances aiming at historical fidelity, and if we are therefore to assume that Glass's choice of voices is to be judged within the conventional musical framework of appreciation, then Akhnaten must be viewed either as a conscious link with Baroque opera, or he must "represent" something archaic. However, this reading contradicts the message that the opera otherwise seeks to express; thus we shall have to search for a different set of values.

Glass, himself, maintains that he has chosen this particular voice in order to emphasize, in the strongest possible terms, that the main character is something out of the ordinary. "The effect of hearing a high, beautiful voice coming from the lips of a full-grown man can at first be very startling," Glass writes. "In one stroke, Akhnaten would be separated from everyone around him. It was a way of musically and dramatically indicating in the simplest possible way that here was a man unlike any who had come before."[16]

This "differentness" of Akhnaten also applies to his appearance— at least to the extent that it has been transmitted through statues and reliefs. In Amarna art, the rendering of man, and thus not just the kind and his family, is obviously different from representations of earlier periods, even to a modern observer. Therefore, it is not very likely that Glass should be right in saying that

> the art of the Amarna period may be the first period of conscious naturalism in the history of art. One of Akhnaten's dictums was "living in truth," and presumably he chose to be portrayed as he really appeared, not in the formal, idealized style of the pharaohs who preceded him. If this is true, then he certainly must have been an odd-looking character: swollen thighs, enlarged hips, breasts almost pendulous. At first glance he appears almost hermaphroditic.[17]

I would interpret the use of a countertenor somewhat differently. A hermaphrodite is a monster, the result of something that has gone wrong. Although at the present we are uncertain as to whether or not Akhnaten's mummy has, in fact, survived, and thus there is no possibility of testing the hypothesis of the androgyny syndrome, there is little probability that he should have been genetically "defective," as scholars in the 1930s believed. Nevertheless, the choice of a countertenor remains a congenial one. Scholars engaged in the research on the Amarna period during recent years do now largely agree that the famous colossi of Akhnaten represents the king as god of creation, and hence androgynous, containing both the male and the female creative principle. The iconography of Akhnaten is the visual rendering of a theological dogma, and the musical rendering could hardly find a more apt expression than a voice that is neither male nor female, the countertenor.

The light, high, female voice is a lyric soprano, a voice typically associated with youthful purity and innocence. It is naturally interesting that Glass depicts the mother figure in this way. According to Glass, Queen Tye supports her son as a participant in the attack on the temple, but at the same time, she represents the old regime. Thus, the revolution of Akhnaten contains a certain ambivalence. The king is all set for innovation, but in this urge there is a longing for the old, for established, ritual cosmography.

This interpretation may be supported by the implications of having Nefertiti turned into a mezzo-soprano. The deep female voice is reminiscent of darkness, danger, and sensuality, and Nefertiti, in this context, is seen as a temptress, a seductress representing reform and thus also allowing for love between man and woman, as opposed to the ritual love between mother and son.

Glass has justified his choice of voices by a reference to purely musical/technical considerations: "Normally the younger woman, in this case Akhnaten's wife, Nefertiti, would sing the higher part, but for musical reasons, I wanted the voices in the Act II duet between Akhnaten and Nefertiti to be as close as possible to the same range, to create a more intimate effect in their vocal intermingling."[18]

But elsewhere, both in the opera and in his book, Glass considers the royal couple's love. Referring to the depictions of the family, mentioned below, he says: "It is easy to imagine a tender romantic connection between these two. If this is so, then Akhnaten and Nefertiti are among the earliest, if not the earliest, romantic couple in recorded history, predating Antony and Cleopatra by many hundreds of years. It seemed, then, that we should at least give them a scene to themselves in the opera.[19] Besides, who could resist writing a love duet for such a pair?"[20] Indeed, one of the reasons the art of the Amarna period is revolutionary is that it introduces intimate family scenes into the official repertory of representation, and Glass's choice of just such a mezzo-soprano is admirably suited to Nefertiti.

Act 2

Act 2 takes us into the decade of revolution, from year five to year fifteen of Akhnaten's reign. During this period, Amon is overthrown and the new city is built: Akhetaten, the modern name of which is Amarna. Both are historical events that are included in *Akhnaten* in the first and third scenes of this act. Akhnaten's attempt to force upon Egypt the cult of one transcendent god, a god above time and space, makes up the climax of the act and of the opera in the fourth scene. The nature of love is characterized in the second scene.

Act 2.1: The Assault on the Temple

In this scene we witness how the priests adore Amon with a hymn. The text is performed by the priests, while the high priest invokes Amon

[Amen]: the hymn itself is one of the most moving pieces in the opera.[21] The attitude of Egyptologists towards hymns (and other Egyptian texts) is usually influenced by the problems of translating them, and this focus tends to make us forget that the hymns were performed—and that they were surely a pleasure to listen to. Glass's version is a beautiful piece of "orientalizing" music, with its abrupt transitions between A minor and A-flat major.

Toward the end of the hymn, the song changes character almost imperceptibly; the invoking adoration becomes a cry for help, achieved through the abrupt transition via the E-flat of the horns to A-flat major. When the hymn fades away, an A, in iambic rhythm in the basses, takes us into the next section of what sounds like the danger music so familiar from films. A descending bass line is heard at full blast, and the battle is on. The units consist largely of a shrill, plunging, syncopated sequence led by the solo trumpet. The conflict is widely dissonant, with violently syncopated rhythms (for example, the choir vocalizes on F and G). Queen Tye's voice intermingles with the choir, and the destruction assumes more barbaric, musical forms. Toward the end of the section another motif emerges (Ex. 5) that also appears in the other violent scene in the opera (Act 3.2):

Example 5.

Glass himself termed it a motif of destruction, but the entire theme—motif and key—seems now more complicated.[22] The motif is also almost identical to a later motif of a dance of joy, and it may well be ecstasy, a violent euphoria, that forms the nucleus of the motif, the kind of ecstasy that is related to endless rejoicing or mad delight in pure destruction. The fact that A-flat major is maintained throughout the scene may be interpreted as representing the restriction and rigidity that, according to the composer, is a structural feature of the old, ceremonial, established society that carries within itself the germ of its own destruction.

Musically, A (minor) is separated by half a tone from A-flat and B-flat, respectively. The key creates a balance between the potentially—and in this scene evidently—violent, on the one hand, and the "new and disturbing feature in Akhnaten," on the other. However, the revolution is not sufficiently profound and is doomed to failure. The borders can be stretched in both directions, and they are accordingly extended to include

G and B so that for a moment, G major is drawn into the harmonic pattern. But to no avail.

Act 2.2 Akhnaten and Nefertiti

As mentioned above, Glass sees Akhnaten and Nefertiti as the first lovers in history, and it is not difficult to follow him in this reasoning when you contemplate the reliefs of the royal couple or wonder in silent joy at the intimacy that radiates from the family scenes.[23] Akhnaten and Nefertiti had to have a duet, but instead of choosing a suitable phrase from some piece of Egyptian love lyric, Glass and his collaborators made a surprising choice: the text on the end piece of the golden coffin found in Tomb No. 55 in the Valley of the Kings—one of the most disputed monuments, not only from the Amarna period, but from pharaonic Egypt as a whole.[24] The most peculiar thing about the text on the coffin is that it was altered during the Amarna period itself. The sections of gold-leaf text that contained pronouns and proper names were largely cut out and replaced by other corresponding grammatical categories. The fact that texts were changed in ancient times is well-known, but the interesting point about this text is that it was altered from what was probably a prayer to Akhnaten on behalf of a woman, more than likely a queen, to a prayer by Akhnaten to the sun god.

To Egyptologists, the most fascinating aspect lies in the possibilities that philological and historical considerations concerning the text provide to solve one of the fundamental questions of the time: How did it end, and what happened to Akhnaten, Nefertiti, and Tye? But the opera uses this text in a totally different way. In the introductory phase of the scene, it is recited by the scribe, and the audience is led to believe that it is a prayer to a god. But then Akhnaten and Nefertiti sing the text to each other, and it becomes a love hymn. The translation has been "improved" somewhat, but the message is clear: in the universe of Akhnaten love is not atomized and labeled "love between man and woman," "love between parents and children," or "love of god." Glass, however, has taken the text at face value.

The scene opens with a soft theme in the violas in E minor, descends into A minor and returns to E minor as the key of the duet. The relation between A minor and E minor in Act 1.2 represents Akhnaten as a man torn between a vision of a new life and his roots in old, safe but locked, patterns, a schism exemplified in his ambivalent relationship with his mother.[25] When the duet settles down in pure E minor at the end, Akhnaten has finally left the old realm of Tye for the new love of Nefertiti.

Act 2.3: The City and the Dance

This scene concerns the foundation of Amarna, Akhnaten's new capital city, where Akhnaten transferred his residence in the fifth year of his reign. The city was originally named Akhetaten, or Horizon of the Sun. It is situated in Middle Egypt in a huge semicircular plain on the east bank of the Nile and surrounded by low mountains. The circumference of the city was marked out with boundary stelae, all inscribed with a lengthy foundation text. Egyptologists refer to two sets of stelae, an older and a younger set, but the two pieces of text recited by the scribe during the first unaccompanied part of the scene are both excerpts from the older text.[26] Earlier, certain passages of both boundary texts were interpreted as statements of the King's intention never to leave Amarna; he had put the world behind him and wished to spend the rest of his life in Horizon of the Sun. But the words say nothing of the kind. They are simply Akhnaten's vows never to let the city expand beyond the boundary—and thus into areas belonging to others. In the opera, the libretto for this part was taken from Breasted's *A History of Egypt*, and the scribe thus repeats the former interpretation of Akhnaten's intentions.

The inauguration of the city is celebrated by a wild dance, which, according to Glass, is to contrast with "the heavy traditional ritual of the temple scene" (Act 2.1).[27] The music is wonderfully supple and energetic, and the orchestra uses triangle, tambourine, and wood block. The key alternates between A minor, F major, and B-flat major/minor tonality, the same combination as in the prelude. Ultra-fast arpeggios and a motif in the high woodwinds are reminiscent of the motives that began the opera. In the bass (Ex. 6),

Example 6.

the sequence is strikingly reminiscent of the music (Ex. 7) for the violent destruction of the temple in the first scene of the act and it will return again in the other violent scene in the opera, the second scene of Act 3. For Glass, ecstatic jubilation and furious violence are the two sides of religious fervor.

Act 2.4: The Hymn

The last scene of the act is the most important one in the opera from an ideological, dramatic, and musical point of view. Here, Akhnaten is shown to us as our ancestor and contemporary in that his religious program, exemplified in his hymn, is seen as the true predecessor to our own Christianity. With Judaism as intermediary, the connection between the ancient Egyptian doctrine of Akhnaten and our faith is, of course, far from immediate. Glass and his co-librettists have adopted the older belief, according to which the author of the 104th *Psalm of David* allegedly was inspired by the *Sun Hymn* of Akhnaten, and the scene, therefore, concludes with the choir singing this psalm in Hebrew.[28]

The *Sun Hymn*, performed by Akhnaten, is justly famous. Even in translation it retains a poetic vigor that has appealed to many composers (for instance, as a setting by the Danish composer Vagn Holmboe).[29] The text, found in the tomb of Aye, was allegedly written by Akhnaten himself.[30] It praises the sun and light as creator of all life and emphasizes strongly the role of the king as intermediary between god and men. Scholars specializing in religion do not agree on how to interpret the doctrine of Akhnaten in relation to what preceded it, but what matters to Glass is that Akhnaten "changed his (and our) world through the force of his ideas and not through the force of arms."[31]

Although rendered in a textually corrupt version, the hymn (Ex. 7) is, nonetheless, given a musical shape of great beauty and meaning, and Glass instructs that it should be sung in the language of the country where the opera is performed. The tonal center is A major, thus counterbalancing the funeral of Amenophis III, as mentioned previously, symbolizing life versus death.

The music begins by a repeat of the coronation music (Ex. 2), and once more we encounter the Trilogy theme, which heralded the coming revolution. A few new phrases have been added (from Ex. 7), which, like the preceding music, serve as instrumental intervals between the two parts of the hymn and the *Psalm of David*. The hymn begins in F-sharp minor and, as usual, the melody is harmonized in a series of arpeggios. But this time their mutual relation differs. Glass is never much in favor of triads, and even in the hymn, where there are more thirds than anywhere else in the opera, we still find chords where the third has been omitted, sometimes obscuring cadential formulas. Indeed, one is left to consider why Glass uses the cadential formula at all. However, since the harmonizations of the transitions are abrupt and brutal in a pre-Baroque way, while the cadential formulas in the hymn are more conventional, suitable to its own

Example 7.

conventionality of being sung in an understandable language, we might guess that this more "advanced" harmonization of the setting serves to underscore the revolutionary nature of the hymn text.[32]

Lyrics in the musical score:
Thou dost ap-pear beau-ti-ful
On the ho-ri-zon of
heav-en Oh, liv-ing
A-ten He who was the first to
live

Example 7 (continued)

Act 3.1: The Family

As previously mentioned, representations of the royal family provide an important new motif in Amarna art. Glass's interpretation of the material made him view Akhnaten and Nefertiti as the first loving couple in history, and consequently he is justified in depicting the royal couple and their daughters as the archetypal family in this scene—a family unit sufficient in itself.

This interpretation is revealed musically in a simple and dramatic way. The scene opens with the music from the love scene between Akhnaten and Nefertiti played by the woodwinds and synthesizer, and this music remains the foundation of the monotonous and homophonic song of the family, which, briefly, consists of alternating E-minor and A-minor chords. The song is occasionally interrupted by an ominous E-flat major chord in the brass, but the family persists in its self-indulgence, musically expressed through a stream of E-minor scales, rolling up and down, first in the strings, but then in contrary motion in the woodwinds so that it grows to an increasingly complex cycle of scales. After the second cue, where the ominous E-flat major of the brass alternates with the quiet familial E minor, there is a sudden shift to F minor, the relative minor of the A-flat major of the temple scene. The scribe begins to read select passages of the Amarna letters.

These letters once formed part of what would in modern times be called the archives of the Egyptian Ministry of Foreign Affairs. Found toward the end of the nineteenth century, the texts were written on clay tablets in cuneiform writing. The letters are addressed to Amenophis III, Akhnaten, and Tutankhamun, the senders being the kings of Babylon, Assyria, Mitanni, and Hatti—the Hittites—and some of the minor Syrian kings whose city-states were under Egyptian suzerainty. The conventional interpretation of the letters from these minor kings is that they reflect Akhnaten's preoccupation with his religious reforms to the extent that he had lost interest in the fate of his vassals; they were left to quarrel among themselves without interference, and hence the Egyptian empire fell apart. Although recent research has begun to question such an interpretation, Glass follows it.[33]

The free excerpts of these lamentations used in the libretto are recited at a fervent pace (Ex. 8):

Example 8.

The enemies of the letter writers charge ahead amidst the roaring signals of their trumpets of victory: intervals of the fourth and sixth are here transformed into a gloomy theme in A-flat major, which has a deep sound below the aggressive and syncopated F-minor music. However, the impact fails. Through E-flat major, the E-minor music returns, the family music of Akhnaten and his two daughters (Ex. 9).

Example 9.

Although reminiscent of the phrase "Oh, living Aten, he who was the first" from Akhnaten's *Hymn to the Sun* and, at the same time, being a transformation of a trumpet signal, which in the temple scene (Act 2.1) heralded Akhnaten's revolution, everything has come to a standstill, and nothing can upset the circular world of the family.

Act 3.2: Attack and Defeat

It is not only in Syria and Palestine that the situation is critical. In Egypt, as well, a threat is looming from the opposition, that is, the old gang led by Horemheb, Aye, and the high priest of Amon. In this scene, they manage to complete a revolution in the palace. As a pretext, they use the loss of the city-states of the Levant, and in order to instigate an attack on the royal palace by the people, they sing an excerpt of an Amarna letter, which concludes with the words "All is lost." The end of the scene witnesses the crowds storming the palace.

The music is a direct tonal continuation of the previous scene. When Akhnaten and his two daughters have ended their song, the ominous E-flat major chord is heard again, and once more the music suddenly shifts to F minor, which is now clearly the key of violence. All musical elements in this scene refer to earlier parts of the opera.[34] The "all is lost" letter is sung as a scornful and distorted allusion to the *Coronation Anthem* (Ex. 10).

The tempo may be a little faster, the music has an obtrusive and exciting pulse rate, and the orchestration becomes even more savage with the addition of syncopated bass drum and cymbals. Nevertheless, the basic metrical resemblance remains unmistakable, and the same persons remain in action. From a melodic point of view, the situation is slightly different, for Glass combines the coronation anthem-like motif with the "ecstasy" motif, which this time appears in D-flat major (Ex. 11).

ye - nedj hra - ak   ye - mi em he - te - pu   ye - nedj hra - ak

ye - mi em he - te - pu   ye - nedj hra - ak   ye - nedj hra - ak

ye - mi - em he - te - pu   ye - nedj hra - ak   ye - mi em he - te - pu

ye - nedj hra - ak   ye - mi em he - te - pu

Example 10.

Example 11.

With the opening motif of the opera (Ex. 1) now set against the distorted coronation anthem motif, Akhnaten and all that he represents is about to fall.

Act 3.3: *The Ruins*

Akhnaten's regime has come to an end, as has his attempt at substituting Aten for Amon and having a sincere, creative dialogue with god replace the old relationship, where communication consisted in an exchange of material goods. History is back where it began. The music expresses this state of affairs through an abbreviated version of the music of the prelude, while the scribe recites excerpts from two texts, which together proclaim the "new" Old Order. The first text evokes Amon,[35] followed by an excerpt from the so-called restoration stela of Tutankhamun. The passage chosen by the authors concerns all the material riches offered to Amon and the doubling, tripling, even quadrupling of all temple income.

The Amarna period has come to an end. The sand has settled over the disintegrated city. Life goes on in the Nile Valley much as it did before Akhnaten, but the ancient Egyptian civilization is dead. Only the ruins remain, but they have been the subject of abundant attention on the part of scholars and travelers. Toward the end of the prelude music, the ruins of Akhetaten, now Tell el-Amarna, appear on stage. Tourists walk about taking pictures while their guide, the former scribe, reads from a *Guide of Egypt* describing how to get to Amarna and how ruined the monuments are.

Act 3.4: Epilogue

With this the opera could have come to an end, for ancient Egypt is no more. But Glass did not wish to reject the legacy of Egypt, and it is not surprising that the opera concludes with an epilogue that both emphasizes death as the foundation of all existence and refers to the integration into our "world" of Akhnaten's ideas, which was the starting point of the entire opera. The tourists leave Amarna at dusk, and as the city lies deserted at night, Akhnaten and the other characters of the opera appear as ghosts, moving about in their erstwhile capital. The funeral procession of Amenophis III is shown on the horizon, approaching heaven. Akhnaten and all the people "of his time," as the Egyptians would have said, take up their positions in a funeral procession in the footsteps of the above mentioned.

The music in this scene is the only part of the opera that Glass himself has described: "I designed the Epilogue to form a kind of restatement of all the important materials, this time forming a new, compressed series of musical events. The series repeats four times with a final resolution at the end."[36] The sequence consists of three motifs and an end. The first motif is the Trilogy theme; then follows Example 1, taken over by a gentle version of the "ecstasy" motif, which in Glass's words has "a lyrical, almost distant quality, as if death and the passage of centuries . . . have softened the violence of those moments, making them almost beautiful."[37] The end (Ex. 12) is similar to the concluding phrases in the *Sun Hymn*:

Example 12.

At the conclusion of the opera, Glass says, "The Trilogy theme becomes the key that turns the lock, setting the ending firmly in A minor, the 'relative minor' of C major, the key in which *Einstein* began."[38]

Let us now return to the question of the artistic path to understanding. Our starting point was a novel, a piece of fiction, and a claim considering the possibilities of fiction to depict reality. The Hungarian philosopher and literary theoretician Georg Lukács maintained that the most adequate representation of reality is fictional, that is, that reality is construed. According to Lukács, naturalistic authors, who allegedly seek to depict reality, do not achieve true insight because they mistake the typical for the average, a statistic median, by means of which they veil a true reality of contrasts.[39] Instead of persons who embody nothing but ideas, clichés, or slogans, Lukács prefers the kind of description of reality, realism, that introduces "the typical by concentrating the essential determinants of a great social trend, embodying them in the passionate strivings of individuals, and placing these personages into extreme situations, situations devised in such a way as to demonstrate the social trend in its extreme consequences and implications."[40] The core of realism thus becomes a dialectic relationship between individual and society, in which the individual, conscious of his own roots in a given society, seeks to alter the present situation of that very society.

Drama, conversely, must condense its rendering of life. It focuses on a conflict and arranges all matters of life to the effect that they are only experienced with this goal in mind. This concentration leads to necessary simplification.

> The portrayal is reduced to the typical representation of the most important and most characteristic attitudes of men, to what is indispensable to the dynamic working-out of the collision, to those social, human, and moral movements in men, therefore, out of which the collision arises and into which the collision dissolves. Any figure, any psychological feature of a fig-

ure, which goes beyond the dialectical necessity of this connection, of the dynamics of the collision, must be superfluous from the point of view of the drama.[41]

The important thing in these plays is that the inner social substance of the conflict makes of it a decisive event, historically and socially, and that the heroes of such plays have within themselves that combination of individual passion and social substance that characterizes the "world-historical individuals."[42]

Glass has chosen to write such an opera with a historical subject and with a number of world-historical individuals as characters, but he does not consciously aim for insight—"truth"—in the form of a dramatic, intellectual construct. Glass's opera has, instead, become a form of "singing archaeology," and, hence, he finds an easy way out. It is, of course, not a question of going straight to the raw material, since the opera has largely been gathered from nonprimary sources. It is, perhaps, a question of construction. On one hand, Glass speaks of "our Egypt," and he makes use of texts out of context. On the other hand, he uses original texts and has them sung in their original language. There is no meaningful reconstruction of a reality, nor has any attempt been made to place the opera in a context that goes beyond "the philosophy of a great spirit," which we referred to earlier. I do not think that Glass and his collaborators had a clear picture in their minds of what they were aiming for when they tackled this subject.

But Glass has obviously learnt from Bertolt Brecht, who opposed "dramatic opera" with "epic opera":[43]

DRAMATIC OPERA	EPIC OPERA
the music dishes up	the music communicates
music which heightens the text	music which sets forth the text
music which proclaims text	music which takes the text for granted
music which illustrates	music which takes up a position
music which paints the psychological situation	music which gives the attitude[44]

Glass seems to want opera to fit into Brecht's idea of epic drama. Brecht's aesthetics are firmly linked to his didactic aim: "Once the content becomes, technically speaking, an independent component, to which text, music, and setting 'adopt attitudes'; once illusion is sacrificed to free discussion; and once the spectator, instead of being enabled to have an experience, is forced as it were to cast his vote; then change has been launched which goes far beyond formal matters and begins, for the first time, to affect the theatre's social function."[45] The theater must provoke a debate, and, according to Brecht, so must opera if it is to survive.[46]

In many respects the dramatic structure of *Akhnaten* fits into Brecht's idea of epic opera. The music, however, does not appear to do the same. Take, for example, the music of the *Sun Hymn*: Does the music heighten and proclaim the text? Or does it set forth the text and take it for granted? Glass does not seem to be interested in creating truly dramatic situations, let alone meeting Lukács's demands.[47] The opera has many fine details, as I have sought to demonstrate, and it attempts a greater historical statement. But does it succeed in going beyond entertainment? I think it does not, in part because Glass has relied too much on a fragmentary, archaeological, and allegedly existing reality. In this way, it becomes almost irrelevant to the dramatic form whether the emphasis is on the dramatic or the epic form of theater. Like so many others, Glass has succumbed to the terribly conventional (twentieth-century?) opinion that only "true reality" is real.

But this is not so, neither in science nor in art. One of the clearest expressions of this apparent paradox can be found in a famous passage in a letter of 1876 from Verdi to Countess Maffei; it reads,

> I saw *Color del Tempo* in Genoa. There are great things in it, above all a quick-wittedness which is a particular gift of the French. But, *au fond*, there is little there. To copy truth may be a good thing, but to invent truth is better, much better. There may seem to be a contradiction in these words "to invent truth," but you ask Papa [i.e., Shakespeare]. It may be that Papa found Falstaff just as he was, but it would have been difficult for him to find a villain as villainous as Iago, and never, never such angels as Cordelia, Imogene, Desdemona, etc., etc. and yet they are so true! To copy the truth is a fine thing, but it is photography, not painting![48]

Akhnaten does not, I think, offer us much insight into the "reality" of ancient Egypt, as does a work like *Sinuhe, the Egyptian*. I shall probably have to admit such reservations because I am an Egyptologist and because the opera creates associations and ideas for me. Nonspecialists may not feel the same way. The "sound" of the music, its repetitive nature, the fascination with ancient Egypt, etc., do have their attractions, the same attractions that make opera lovers appreciate romantic Italian operas, in spite of their notorious story lines. But maybe, just as *Sinuhe* has helped popularize ancient Egypt far more than any scholar could, that is not such a bad thing.

Notes

1. This article is a more comprehensive version of a paper read during a theme day on this very novel, arranged by The Danish Egyptological Society, on 10 February 1990. Until I ventured into this project I had hardly any knowledge of minimalist music— and hence of Glass. Since then I have derived great pleasure from reading Jacob Levinsen's dissertation "Et nyt syn på harmoni—Philip Glass og den amerikanske minimalmusik" [Harmony in a New Light—Philip Glass and American Minimalist Music], Copenhagen, 1989. I am greatly indebted to my colleague, Jens Brincker, in the Department of Music, who drew my attention to Levinsen's work, read my article, and , above all, "proofread" my transcriptions of Glass, which saved me from a number of errors. I owe a debt of gratitude to my colleague Niels Martin Jensen, Department of Music, for having undertaken the time-consuming task of computerizing my musical examples. I also wish to thank Britta Munch for the excellent drawing. I am grateful to Lise Manniche for translating my Danish text and to the Faculty of Humanities, the University of Copenhagen, for sponsoring that translation. I thank William K. Simpson for advice on practical problems of publication. Finally I am indebted to my father, John Frandsen, for having "lent me his absolute pitch" when I was in doubt.

2. Michael J. Oakeshott, *Experience and Its Modes* (Cambridge: The University Press, 1933), 98.

3. S. Langholm, "Vi søger at rekonstruere en virkelighed some kan forklare kilderne," in *Historisk rekonstruksjon og begrunnelse* (Oslo: Dreyer, 1967), 17.

4. See, for example, also Claus Bjørn's remarks concerning the impact of the historical novels of B.S. Ingemann in "Kontinuitet og forandring i dansk historie" [Continuity and Change in Danish History], in *Over hegnet*, ed. M. Trolle Larsen (Copenhagen: 1990), 9.

5. I would also like to refer the reader to a fairly recent novel by the Egyptian Nobel Prize winner Naguib Mahfouz, ᶜ*Al- a'is fi I-haqiqa [Who Lives in Truth]* . I am indebted to Mohammed Abla for this reference.

6. Philip Glass, *Music by Philip Glass*, ed. and with supplementary material by Robert T. Jones (New York: Harper & Row, 1987), 138.

7. During a visit to the Cairo Museum, Glass experienced the Amarna room as a metaphor of the future opera, both because of its location in the museum building itself and because of its collection of fragmentary objects.

It seemed to me, at that moment, that we needed no more story than was already there, that the missing pieces, far from needing to be filled in or explained, actually added to the mystery and beauty of the subject. A theatrical approach, to be sure, but theater was what we were making. Back in New York, I explained my idea to Shalom [Goldman, an Orientalist and librettist]: an opera about Akhnaten based upon fragments with the missing bits intact as it were. His face lit up, and at the end he exclaimed, "Ah! Singing archaeology!" (Glass, *Music by Philip Glass,* 150)

8. Glass, 171.

9. Glass, 36.

10. Glass, 173.

11. Glass, 153.

12. Glass, 137.

13. Glass, 172–73.

14. Text booklet, CBS Masterworks M2K 42457, 11. In greater detail in Glass, 138–39.

15. Glass, 174–75.

16. Glass, 156.

17. Glass, 149. The quotation continues: "Medical analysis is not conclusive. Akhnaten's appearance could have been genetic in origin, or it may be the result of disease. In any case, he was biologically male and capable of fathering children."

18. Glass, 156.

19. Act 2.2. See below.

20. Glass, 151.

21. The text booklet of the record indicates that the text is taken from the article mentioned in endnote 24. This is not the case.

22. Glass, 173.

23. See, for example, the numerous depictions in Cyril Aldred, *Akhnaten and Nefertiti* (New York: Brooklyn Museum in association with the Viking Press, 1973). For no. 114 (Berlin/DDR 17813) see now especially Harris in *Acta Orientalia,* 35 (1973), 5–13.

24. See A. H. Gardiner, "The So-called Tomb of Queen Tiye," *Journal of Egyptian Archaeology* 43 (1957): 10–24, 17; G. Perepelkin, "The Secret of the Gold Coffin," *Nauka* (Moskva, 1978), 26–35.

25. See the discussion of Act 1, Scene 3, and also Glass's somewhat cryptic remark concerning "a veiled reference to the ambiguous sexual relationship of the three principals does remain in this aspect of the vocal writing" (170), where the reference is to the intermingling of voices in the ensembles.

26. Wolfgang Helck, *Urkunden der 18. Dynastie* (Berlin, 1958), 1968, 2–10, 14–17; 1972, 4; 1973, 6.

27. Glass, 185.

28. E. A. Wallis Budge, *A History of Egypt, vol. IV, Egypt and Her Asiatic Empire* (London: Books on Egypt and Chaldaea, 1902), 12: 125–26. Budge is the first scholar to suggest this hypothesis. The most elaborate discussion is in James Henry Breasted, *A History of Egypt*, 2nd ed. (London: Hodder & Stoughton, 1909), 371–77, where the following remarks occur:

> In the hymn the universalism of the empire finds full expression and the royal singer sweeps his eye from the far-off cataracts of the Nubian Nile to the remotest lands of Syria. These are not thoughts which we have been accustomed to attribute to the men of some fourteen hundred years before Christ. A new spirit has breathed upon the dry bones of traditionalism in Egypt, and he who reads these lines for the first time must be moved with involuntary admiration for the young king who in such an age found such thoughts in his heart. He grasped the idea of a world-dominator, as the creator of nature, in which the king saw revealed the creator's beneficent purpose for all his creatures, even the meanest; for the birds fluttering about in the lily-grown Nile marshes to him seemed to be uplifting their wings in adoration of their creator; and even the fish in the stream leaped up in praise to God. It is his voice that summons the blossoms and nourishes the chicklet or commands the mighty deluge of the Nile. He called Aton "the father and mother of all that he had made," and he saw in some degree the goodness of that All-universal sway of God upon his fatherly care of all men alike, irrespective of race or nationality, and to the proud and exclusive Egyptian he pointed to the all-embracing bounty of the common father of humanity, even placing Syria and Nubia before Egypt in his enumeration. It is this aspect of Ikhnaton's mind which is especially remarkable; he is the first prophet of history.

29. "Solhymne" (Copenhagen: Wilhelm Hansen Musikforlag, 1961). The text also exists in an English version, and the work had its first performance by the Dansk Korforening on June 3, 1961. Holmboe's text has also been abbreviated.

30. Norman de Garis Davies, *The Rock Tombs of El Amarna, Part IV* (London, 1908), 29–31 and plates XXVII & XLI.

31. Glass, 138.

32. Cf. Glass, 60.

33. See M. Liverani, "Contrasti e confluenze di concezioni politiche nell'eta di el-Amarna," *Revue d'Assyriologie* (1967), 41:1–18.

34. When, for example, the choir starts in on A minor, the pattern is identical to Example 10.

35. The text is allegedly taken from the tomb of Aye, but surely this must be a misunderstanding.

36. Glass, 172.

37. Glass, 173–74.

38. Glass, 175.

39. See, for example, his remarks on Emile Zola in *Studies in European Realism* (New York: Grosset & Dunlap, 1964), 91.

40. Georg Lukács, *Studies in European Realism*, 168.

41. Georg Lukács, *The Historical Novel* (Harmondsworth: Penguin, 1969), 108.

42. Lukács, *The Historical Novel*, 120. It is the absence of these elements that, according to Lukács, makes the majority of bourgeois and also "proletarian plays so banal, tedious, and insignificant." Furthermore, modern drama focuses on "the most prosaic moments of modern daily life. In this way the grey banality of life becomes the subject of representation, underlining those very sides of the material which are the least favorable for drama. Plays are written which dramatically are on a lower level than the life which they portray."

43. Bertolt Brecht is mentioned several times in Glass's book, and Glass's first experience in musical theater consisted of rehearsing Paul Dessau's music for a performance of *Mother Courage*. See Glass, 5.

44. Bertolt Brecht, "The Modern Theatre is Epic Theatre," in *Brecht on Theatre: The Development of an Aesthetic*, ed. and trans. by John Willett (London: Eyre Methuen, 1964), 38.

45. Brecht, 39.

46. Brecht's notes to the opera *Aufstieg und Fall der Stadt Mahagonny* "form part of a series of notes and essays labeled 'On a non-Aristotelian Drama,' which is scattered through Brecht's *Versuche* beginning in 1930." These papers were originally announced under the title "On a Dialectical Drama" (note by J. Willett, *op. cit*, 46).

47. Although Lukács (1885–1971) and Brecht (1898–1956) are contemporaries, they do not seem to make reference to each other; I should have thought that Brecht's works would pass muster with Lukács.

48. The letter is quoted in virtually all editions of Verdi's letters, here from Charles Osborne, *Letters of Giuseppe Verdi*, trans. and ed. from the COPIALETTERE (London: Gollancz, 1971), 200–201. See also the opening lines of *King Henry the Fifth*, a play with a "world-historical" subject, where Shakespeare himself has the Chorus make the same point:

O for a Muse of fire, that would ascend
The brightest heaven of invention,—
A kingdom for a stage, princes to act,
And monarchs to behold the swelling scene!
Then should the warlike Harry, like himself,
Assume the port of Mars; and at his heels,
Leash'd-in like hounds, should famine, sword, and fire,
Crouch for employment. But pardon, gentles all,
The flat unraised spirits that have dared
On this unworthy scaffold to bring forth
So great an object: can this cockpit hold
The vasty fields of France? Or may we cram
Within this wooden O the very casques
That did affright the air at Agincourt?
O, pardon! Since a crooked figure may
Attest in little place a million;
And let us, ciphers to this great accompt,
On your imaginary forces work.
Suppose within the girdle of these walls
Are now confin'd two mighty monarchies. . . . (Prologue, 1–20)

HYDROGEN JUKEBOX (1990)

THOMAS RAIN CROWE

I look forward to the Spoleto USA festival every year, not only because it affords me the opportunity to visit Charleston, South Carolina—one of my favorite American cities—but also because it allows me to witness, firsthand, new performances by some of the world's most talented and provocative artists. This year I was more enthusiastic than ever about my trip to Spoleto in late May, because I had arranged in advance to interview the contemporary American composer Philip Glass on the morning prior to the world premiere of his new music mini-opera, *Hydrogen Jukebox*, an event I was also eagerly anticipating.

Hydrogen Jukebox is a two-and-a-half-hour-long piece on which Glass collaborated with poet Allen Ginsberg and visual artist/designer Jerome Sirlin. The title comes from a line in Ginsberg's book-length poem, *Howl*, which became a manifesto for a whole generation in the late 1950s and early '60s.

One of the world's most celebrated "new music" composers, Philip Glass is one of the founding fathers of the minimalist movement in contemporary music. Having written for opera, orchestra, film, theatre, dance, chorus, and his own group, the Philip Glass Ensemble, he is probably best known for his trilogy of "portrait" operas, including *Einstein on the Beach*, *Akhnaten* and *Satyagraha* (which deals with the younger years of Mohandas K. Gandhi). He has also worked on major collaborative pieces with such filmmakers, writers and choreographers as Godfrey Reggio (*Koyaanisqatsi, Powaqqatsi*), Errol Morris (*The Thin Blue Line*), Doris Lessing (*The Making of the Representative for Planet 8*), David Hwang (*1000 Airplanes on the Roof*), Twyla Tharp and Jerome Robbins. As a prolific recording artist, Glass is perhaps best known to the general public for his recording, *Songs from Liquid Days* (1985), which features lyrics by Paul Simon, David Byrne, Laurie Anderson and Suzanne Vega, as well as vocals by Linda Ronstadt.

Allen Ginsberg, who is both *puer aeternus* and *pater familias* of the Beat Generation, is best known for his book *Howl*, which rocked the post-World-War-II literary world with its 1957 obscenity trial (won by Ginsberg and his publisher, City Lights Books), and which is still, a generation later, considered a classic by activists, intellectuals, environmentalists and younger writers who are "fighting the good fight." A strong, internationally respected voice for freedom of speech and civil and human rights, Ginsberg is still—as he has been for the better part of 35 years—at the forefront of the major issues of our time.

Jerome Sirlin, who has created stage and scenographic designs for a wide range of productions in theatre, opera, dance and film, has been described as a master of dazzling three-dimensional effects "who can transform the stage into a veritable landscape of the imagination." His innovative concepts were a major force behind *1000 Airplanes on the Roof*, the sci-fi music drama which he co-authored with Philip Glass and David Hwang, as well as Madonna's "Who's That Girl?" 1987 World Tour. Along with his extensive work in collaboration with other artists over the years, he has taught architecture, interior design and photography at Cornell University and Antioch College.

Although billed as an opera, *Hydrogen Jukebox* is essentially a loosely-woven exploration of interconnected themes (war, sexual freedom, the struggle against authority, censorship, free speech, reverence for nature, truth), based on 21 poems drawn from Ginsberg's life works—each set to Glass' musical score and Sirlin's high-tech stage design, and brought to life on a human scale by a talented chorus of six vocalists (three men, three women). Without a real plot or any specific characters, the piece nevertheless has dramatic shape and a thematic direction which keeps its audience on course as it free-forms its way from the not-so-distant past into an unknown and yet prophetic future. In essence it is a visual/musical surrealist poem consisting of segments with leaping images that are non-linear and/or spatial yet somehow connected and meaningful. These are the "eye-songs" of the atomic age—orchestrated embodiments of America waking, simultaneously, from both its conscious and its unconscious sleep.

In the morning before the May 26 evening premiere, Glass and I sat down together and spoke at length about his music and his work with theatre and opera, the state of the present creative universe and the future. As a result of my quality time spent that morning with the composer, and then later that evening at the performance, I arrived at a very clear picture of just how this piece on the premiere would have to be written. In the spirit of *Hydrogen Jukebox*, I chose to use a repetitive structure similar to Glass's own compositional techniques. I decided to collaborate, in effect, with Glass and Ginsberg, combining the three aspects of my total experience of the performance that seemed most essential and most familiar—my own spontaneous notes taken in the dark of Sottile Theater during the performance; sections lifted from Ginsberg's libretto that most powerfully represent the thematic progression and lyrical procession of the piece; and excerpts from my interview with Glass that seem to best suit the sentiments of the libretto sections, the visual sequences and my own observations and impressions of the performance. Following this introduction, then, my notes appear in the regular type as is used here, while passages from Ginsberg's poetry appear in boldface type and Glass's comments recorded during our interviews appear in italics.

Before leaving North Carolina for Spoleto-enthused Charleston, I spent hours listening to all the Philip Glass recordings I had accumulated over the years. In the final few moments before departing, I wrote a consolidated statement I thought best described my feeling for his music—a statement which, now, seems a fitting prologue for what follows:

"If ever the term 'future primitive' applied, it applies to the music of Philip Glass, in his portrayal of urban paralysis of rhythmic ecstasy, repetition and the insinuation of ritual. Glass's musical vision seems to be an intuition of modern mass insanity, driven by the hopeful memory of our deepest archetypal past grounded in the complex yet simplistic heartbeat of the earth."

*　　*　　*

Sheet-lightning, silhouettes, apocalypse. . . . Figures dressed in camouflage watching the sky—Principal cast members: priest, policewoman, laborer, maid, majorette, businessman—a cross-section of American sensibility. Sad, dirgeladen, blue-violet sky. The music of aftermath, or the precognition of aftermath—an apocalyptic blues. . . .

SONG #1

Lightning's blue glare fills Oklahoma plains,
the train rolls east
     casting yellow shadow on grass
          Twenty years ago
approaching Texas
     I saw
         sheet lightning
            cover Heaven's corners
       Apocalypse prophesied—
the Fall of America
      signaled from Heaven—
An old man catching fireflies on the porch at night
watched the Herd Boy cross the Milky Way
        to meet the Weaving Girl . . .
      How can we war against that?
      How can we war against that?

"Music with subject matter is the way I work. There are some composers who work with music in abstract ways. These kind of composers are inspired by the language of music itself, and their own development of that language. Then, there are others for whom the inspiration for writing music has nothing, really, to do with music—or at least that is how it would appear—where subject inspires and dictates the direction of any new music. Something in subject, for instance, like 'social change through non-violence' or 'an ecologically balanced environment.' It's a rather small number of composers among the whole general run of composers who are attracted to subject matter. I happen to be one of those.

"It was really when I began working on my own pieces in the mid-'70s, beginning with Einstein on the Beach, *that I really began to think seriously about just what the pieces were about. Or, to put it another way, when you start to write an opera, or even a piece like* Hydrogen Jukebox—*which is a small opera—it can take about a year and a half to do a small piece, and a large piece may take as long as two to three years. So, for me to spend that much time working on a project, it has to be about something that's important to me.*

"It seems to have intensified as I've gotten older—this need to find a point of departure for the work, a point of departure which springs from

a concern for the world I live in in a very ordinary way. The ordinary world that we ordinary people live in in an ordinary way—all those things. The ordinary world we wake up in and to, and what's happening to it.

"Hydrogen Jukebox, of course, was an ideal project in that way. Allen Ginsberg's work has ranged and roamed over these subjects for 35 years. There's no one who has been more at the center of the major issues of our time than Allen—to the point that things that seemed so radical in the '60s almost now seem like mainstream issues. Though Allen is as feisty as ever!"

. . . labyrinths of buildings, beams, bold geometry of 3-D. A girdered prison of construction, expansion, sharp-cornered design—Man amidst the beamed paradox of his own making. Megalopolis. The loneliness of voluntary captivity. . . .

SONG #2

> *Who's the enemy, year after year?*
> *War after war, who's the enemy?*
> *What's the weapon, battle after battle?*
> *What's the news, defeat after defeat?*
> *What's the picture, decade after decade?*

"Art and culture are invented. We make them up. Otherwise, they don't exist. We live with our culture so closely we think of art as something that has its own natural, independent existence. But, obviously, it does not. I have no doubt that if I lived alone long enough, I would stop making art, because art has to do with people. But of course no one lives totally alone, isolated from the society around them. Even a hermit carries society with him in his extreme solitude, and art, as we often say, is a form of human communication. Human society and culture consist of things people create together, and this is truer of art than of anything else.

"People talk about criminals being the result of their environment, but they seldom speak about artists being victims of their environment, though in fact they are. When things go well, we take all the credit; when things go bad, we blame 'society.' Rarely does an artist give credit to society, but all too often society gets the credit for our failures."

. . . Glass's quick, repetitive musical refrains become balanced with slower, softer, more tactile rhythms. An unexpected and more melodic music from this prince of the avant-garde. . . .

SONG #4

CONSULTING I CHING SMOKING POT LISTENING TO THE FUGS SING BLAKE

"In the film Koyaanisqatsi—*which is a film in images (without words or characters) presented as a portrait of America, specifically, as it experiences the impact of a new high-tech society, of a new high-tech culture—there were scenes where the music and the images act on each other to activate different aspects of each other without actually complementing each other or reinforcing each other. For instance, early on in the film there is a scene where you see these huge airplanes floating down onto the runway, floating in the air. This is directly followed by scenes dominated by tanks, warplanes and cars. This was a section of the film we called 'vessels'—meaning things that you travel in, like a boat. Writing the music to go with the visual images of the planes, the tanks, and the cars, I decided to concentrate on one aspect of those things. Looking at the planes, I took the idea of 'lightness,' and I set it for voices. So, in the finished product, the opening scene with the montage of the airplanes is done to six-part a cappella choir. So I took one aspect of the image, which was the image of floating, and created a musical sound that, to me, insinuated floating. But I could have done it in many different ways. There are other places in the film where I reinforced the images directly. Later on in the piece there is a whole segment of rapid movement of a variety of things. Here, I used a very rapidly moving music. A very simple one-on-one association was used in this case—a musical technique mirroring a visual technique. There is a way to reinforce something by similarity, and there is also a way to reinforce something by dissimilarity. In other words, you can go against the image or you can go with the image. So, you can work against something as a way of reinforcing it. In* Hydrogen Jukebox *we used this technique quite a bit. In fact, very seldom did we use the complementary approach in combining all three elements of the piece."*

. . . 30, maybe 40 minutes have gone by . . . I keep waiting for a bomb to go off, musically; waiting for a dramatic denouement to break the balanced river of sound which has, so far, predominated the performance.

Becoming too comfortable with the wonderful difference of the integration of compositions, one following the other—But "bombs" are not
Glass's way—he lulls you into a mood, like sleep, then lets the time-
released ambiance work its magic!. . . .

. . . "the whitewashed room, roof" set, and Sirlin takes us literally through
a multi-dimensional window—like a telescopic opening out from the solitude that produces thoughts and the memory of Baudelaire, into the eternity of Calcutta at Christmas symbolized by an Orange Crush. . . .

SONG #6

The whitewashed room, roof
of a third-rate Mohammedan hotel,
two beds, blurred fan
whirling over yr brown guitar
knapsack open on floor, towel
hanging from chair, Orange Crush,
brown paper manuscript packages,
Tibetan tankas, Gandhi pajamas,
Ramakrishna Gospel, bright umbrella
a mess on a rickety wooden stand,
the yellow wall-bulb lights up
this scene Calcutta for the thirtieth night—

"When we began with the idea of Hydrogen Jukebox, *Allen might*
have come up to me and asked, 'Why do you want to take my poetry and
set it to music?' This is a good question. In fact, Doris Lessing did say this
to me. In her case it was: 'Why do you want to take my novel (The
Making of the Representative for Planet 8) *and make it into an opera?'*
What both Doris and Allen are asking is: 'What are you doing for the
work?' What I said to Doris in response to her question was: 'I can do
things in the music you can't do in the words. I can describe things your
words describe, but I can do it in a way the words can't do it.' In terms of
Allen's poetry—I am reminded of a writer by the name of Edward T. Cone
whose books I just recently finished. In his book on 'words and music' he
says when you set words to music you are making one interpretation of
all the possible interpretations. And so in a certain way, by doing this you
are limiting it. You have defined it in a way. But on the other hand, he goes
on to say—and this is the point I wanted to get to—that what you get
instead is a vivid *presentation. Something more vivid than either the music*

or the text would have by itself. The word 'vivid' is central to the appropriate response to this question. It comes from the root word 'vive,' meaning: to live; liveliness."

. . . I keep hearing echoes from *Einstein on the Beach, Koyaanisqatsi, Songs from Liquid Days*—Glass inside this *Hydrogen Jukebox* has hit his stride, has found the balance, musically, between too much of too little and too little of too much. Tonight, there are deeper bass rhythms and percussion that are not only conduit and ground for the electric firestorm of the extended familiar, but, in fact, grounding for how his music takes us almost without permission out of body and into space—softening the concrete with a little dirt along the way. . . .

. . . the performance has become a three-dimensional film . . . a visual feast for the eyes! Sirlin, the ringmaster, the weaver, wefting and sleying together layer upon layer of transparent drops—like a deeply yet lightly textured nightgown of dreams upon which are projected rumors from Hell, the sensual mind of the future, the awesome idiosyncrasies of the heart of a weeping machine. . . .

> SONG #8
>
> *. . . And the vast starry space—*
> *If the brain changes matter breathes*
> *fearfully back on man—But now*
> *the great crash of buildings and planets*
> *breaks thru the walls of language and drowns*
> *me under its Ganges heaviness forever.*
> *No escape but thru Bangkok and New York death.*

"My work, generally speaking, is collaborative. So I'm working with other artists all the time. With dance, design, literary sources—as well as, quite literally, with light in the form of lighting techniques. All the music theatre work I have done up to this point includes all these things. My personal view of all this is that very often these things are but contributing aspects to a total work, and that by themselves they don't really 'do it.' What we look for in a theatre piece when we bring these together is something that is more than the sum of its parts. In that sense very often we're not looking to reinforce things. In other words, I don't look for a visual complement that reinforces a musical statement. I'm usually looking for something that is different. That actually heightens the music and

heightens the image at the same time, because they are different and not the same. This happens in film all the time."

. . . Glassbomb goes off! Camouflaged sung lyrics are unmasked and take on face(s) of clear lyric with Ginsberg's recorded voice. "Wichita Vortex Sutra" to Glass's electronic requiem of praise! Transfixed becomes transfigured. Like a perfect-pitched high note in the middle of a storm: the voice of Blake. A sensual love poem turned into a Whitmanesque 21st-century Bill-of-Rites. . . .

> *. . . To Wichita where McClure's mind*
> *burst into animal beauty*
> *drunk, getting laid in a car*
> *in a neon misted street*
> *15 years ago—*
> *to Independence where the old man's still alive*
> *who loosed the bomb that's slaved all human consciousness*
> *and made the body universe a place of fear—*
> *Now, speeding along the empty plain,*
> *no giant demon machine*
> *visible on the horizon*
> *but tiny human trees and wooden houses at the sky's edge*
> *I claim my birthright! Joy*
> *reborn after the vast sadness of War Gods!*
> *A lone man talking to myself, no house in the brown vastness to hear,*
> *imagining the throng of Selves*
> *that make this nation one body of Prophecy*
> *languaged by Declaration as Pursuit of Happiness!*
> *Come to my lone presence*
> *into this Vortex named Kansas,*
> *I lift my voice aloud,*
> *make Mantra of American language now,*
> *I here declare the end of the War!*

"Epiphanies are rare birds—not flying into the room every day! I've had a few artistic ones, and I've talked to Allen, and he's had some. Most artists, in fact, will tell you about epiphanies they've had—realizations that have come out of a heightened experience, a heightened emotional experience. And the vividness of that can sometimes lead to an artistic insight, or even to an artistic quest that may last as long as 20 or 30 years. You, on the other hand, may try and create through your own

*art form an epiphany you had when you were a child. Actually, that's lit-
erally what happened to Allen—he had an epiphany, a vision, in his
early twenties and he says much of his writing is an attempt to recreate
that."*

END PART ONE

. . . Ginsberg, Glass and Sirlin come out into second act with both barrels
blazing! "Moloch" section from *Howl.* The Ginsberg libretto being
matched stride-for-stride by the dynamic complementary fireworks of
Glass's music in a Bach-meets-Mozart-meets-Wagner-meets-God crescen-
do that is the most exciting piece of "new music" (including Reich and
Anderson) I've heard yet! With Sirlin's "Moloch" reproduced to huge
scale on projected backdrop and the off-and-on tympani of electronic
thunder to the provocative and impassioned lyric from *Howl,* the second
half of the program begins right where it left off, just prior to intermission,
with "Wichita Vortex Sutra." . . .

> *. . . Moloch! Moloch! Nightmare of Moloch! Moloch the
>   loveless! Mental Moloch!
>   Moloch the heavy judger of men!
> Moloch the incomprehensible prison! Moloch the cross
>   bone soulless jailhouse and Congress of sorrows!
>   Moloch whose buildings are judgment!
>   Moloch the vast stone of war! Moloch the stunned
>   governments!
> Moloch whose mind is pure machinery! Moloch whose
>   blood is running money! Moloch whose fingers are
>   ten armies! Moloch whose breast is a cannibal
>   dynamo! Moloch whose ear is a smoking tomb!
> Moloch whose eyes are a thousand blind windows!
>   Moloch whose skyscrapers stand in the long streets
>   like endless Jehovahs! Moloch whose factories
>   dream and croak in the fog! Moloch whose
>   smokestacks and antennae crown the cities!
> Moloch whose love is endless oil and stone! Moloch
>   whose soul is electricity and banks! Moloch whose
>   poverty is the specter of genius! Moloch whose fate is
>   a cloud of sexless hydrogen! Moloch whose name is
>   the Mind!*

Hydrogen Jukebox *(1990)*

"We—and when I use the word 'we' I mean my generation—we're not against the old operas. Some of them are very beautiful. It's just that at this point and time there doesn't seem any point in doing them like that anymore. I don't think we're interested in that. In terms of process whereas collaboration is concerned, a lot of it has to do with technology. The new technology has allowed us, somewhat paradoxically, to bring the arts together in a way we could have never done before. Hydrogen Jukebox is a perfect example of this, with its amplified stage projects, images, amplified music, vocal music. During the process of making this piece, I have often wondered how, in fact, we could have even put on this piece 200 years ago. Not only couldn't we have, but we wouldn't have even thought of it! The technology available to us now gives us that opportunity. It allows us this possibility.

"I don't think that you can underestimate the effect of technology on artists today. It's literally opening up and determining new ways of working. I don't think that we'll ever go back. And in truth you can't ever go back to old forms. I think, instead, we're pushing more and more towards something which for us has become an ideal—which is manifest as a kind of collective work, where art and technology are finally working hand-in-hand. And through the labor of all these people working together, a piece like Hydrogen Jukebox is possible even though it takes an enormous amount of collective and individual talent. It's impossible to conceive of doing something like this in any other way."

. . . end-of-police-state retreat to the mountains. To and into Nature. To a relaxed piece of meditation-music sounding like the resurrection song of the woods. Proscenium stage in a state of haiku (high coup) consciousness—a light year's leap from what came before and what is to follow. . . .

SONG #14

Sitting on a tree stump with half cup of tea,
sun down behind mountains—
Nothing to do.
In the half-light of dawn
A few birds warble
under the pleiades.

SONG #16

> *. . . for we can see together*
> *the beauty of souls*
> *hidden like diamonds*
> *in the clock of the world . . .*

"I think maybe it's important to say here that I am, also, in the same position as a listener. I'm not that different from the listener. In other words, what I am exposing to myself can very often be new to me. I'm not proceeding from a position of knowledge I am giving to other people. I'm proceeding from a position of ignorance, which I am overcoming like everyone else. When Godfrey Reggio and I went around for a time talking to people about the film Koyaanisqatsi, people were always asking him what he meant by this and what he meant by that, referring to the film. He was always careful to respond to these questions by saying, 'Well, you know, the question is really more important than the answer. I can frame the question, but I don't know the answer.'

"Although he saw some of the problems of the impact of a high-tech culture on contemporary society, he was quick to say he didn't have any answers to these questions, was very careful not to set himself up as some sort of Messiah. And I think we try and do that in this culture to our heroes—we think they know more than they can reasonably be expected to. I think that kind of modesty is appropriate as an honest assessment of where we both were in relation to the making of the film.

"So, to get back to your idea about the 'calm' or centeredness in my music and whether or not that is meant to be a sign to other people—as I say, the music doesn't proceed from the idea of the sharing of a great spiritual insight. It doesn't. I'm in the same position as everyone else in that I am trying to break through my own limitations. And what you are seeing in Einstein on the Beach, Koyaanisqatsi or Hydrogen Jukebox is me doing that."

. . . American flags everywhere! The sky: a flag. Flags on all sides. Large flags. Small flags. Flags in pockets as handkerchiefs. Current issues of flag-burning, censorship of the arts, the blind leading the blind of politics being addressed here! Powerful use of fog-machine implying nerve-gas, artistically consuming the stage like deathly etheric piece of floating sculpture. . . .

SONG #17

Richard Secord and Oliver North
Hated Sandinistas whatever they were worth
They peddled for the Contras to ease their pain
They couldn't sell Congress so Contras sold Cocaine

They discovered Noriega only yesterday
Nancy Reagan & the CIA

Ramon Millan Rodriguez of Medallin Cartel
Laundered their dollars he did it very well
Hundreds of billions through US banks
Till he got busted and sang in the tank

It was buried in the papers only yesterday
When Bush was Drug Czar, USA

"Right now so much of what's disturbing to artists is the issue of the enemies of the National Endowment and free expression in the arts. In our community and in our society we have people who are very much afraid to 'go beyond themselves.' When artists like Mapplethorpe or Ginsberg start to work along the frontiers of what these people consider acceptable, they consider it very threatening. They have a hard time understanding what these breakthrough artists are doing. They think these artists are actually trying to destroy the world they're living in, and in a certain sense, they're not far wrong. Because what someone like Ginsberg or Burroughs or Mapplethorpe are trying to do is to move the center to a different place. And this does mean breaking down the invisible borders of our minds. But here the important thing to remember is that, first of all, these people, these artists, are challenging themselves. It turns out what they are doing may challenge other people, too. But the history of art has always been that way.

"So, we have in our culture the people who don't want to change it and are afraid of the change. It's threatening. It's disturbing. They can barely hang onto what they've got, and here's some jackass come along who's trying to turn everything upside down. And in a certain way you can have a certain sympathy for that kind of attitude, because not everyone has the capability of absorbing these kinds of changes. Even so, this kind of attitude is anathema to the artist, as it is a direct threat to the *lifeblood idea of going beyond ourselves, or what we expect of ourselves. These kinds of attitudes not only are hurdles but can become actual walls or barriers to our attempts at overcoming our own ignorance, at exploring the unknown."*

. . . lighting and visuals (old Alwin Nikolais dance-theater effect) projected onto chorus members dressed in white coveralls to create apocalyptic ambiance. Walking radioactive corpses: the leftover living legacy of failed politics and the nuclear age. Followed by a landscape hinting strongly of nuclear winter complete with in-house clouds and falling snow! Sensitive power of all three collaborative elements—shocking! Sirlin contribution is a continuous kaleidoscope of stunning visual effects and environments! Here, to Ginsberg's "plutonium, UFOs, and a desecrated rain forest." . . .

SONG #18

I walked outside & the bomb'd
        dropped lots of plutonium
        all over the Lower East Side
There weren't any buildings left just
            iron skeletons
groceries burned, potholes open to
        stinking sewer waters

There were people starving and crawling
        across the desert
the Martian UFOs with blue
        Light destroyer rays
passed over and dried up all the
        waters

Charred Amazon palmtrees for
            hundreds of miles on both sides
        of the river

"Things in general look pretty bad. But Allen, I think, is more pessimistic than I. I hold out a little hope—hope based mainly on examples of things that are getting better. In terms of environmental issues there are examples such as Lake Michigan, where after years of such bad pollution that nothing could live in that body of water, recently there is evidence

again of fish life. Closer to home for me, in the Hudson River, the water quality has improved to a point where there are fish again living in this river. These are just two examples, and there are other examples of improvements on the environmental front. These small examples, as minor as they are in the overall drama of things in general, are still indications to me that things can be turned around and past mistakes rectified.

"*Despite these signs of recovery, the overall picture is grim, I admit, but at least some of these issues—which have been the center of Allen's work all along—are beginning to be addressed in large-scale serious kinds of ways. Or at least that's what we are being led to believe. One can only hope that this, in fact, is what is happening. We'll see.*"

SONG #19

*When the red pond fills fish appear
When the red pond dries fish disappear.
Everything built on the desert crumbles to dust.
One rain turns red dust green with leaves.
One raindrop begins the universe
When the raindrop dries, worlds come to their end.*

. . . "among the stars" and a backdrop of starry night sky like pinholes into the promise of a lighted infinity. After world destruction, we return to the stars, or at least to gaze at the stars for a last time eliciting comfort. Again the calming effect of Glass's musical sensitivity (reminiscent of *Piano Solos*), Ginsberg's Blakeian Buddha lyrics and Sirlin's out-of-character (in this case) use of stunning simplicity (a handful of fairydust stolen from Glass's minimalist cache and Akhnaten's tomb). . . .

SONG #20

"*Out! Out! into the Buddhafields, among stars to wander
forever, weightless without a headline, without
thought, without newspapers to read by the light
of the Galaxies.*"

"*When I was younger, it was the visual arts that caught my attention. I was mostly inspired by painters and sculptors. Later by dancers. Now, I'm actually more interested in writers, I'm coming around to writers—to people like Allen Ginsberg and Doris Lessing, and even some younger writers. I'm discovering a new magic in poetry and language is*

*finding its way into my music. For the last couple of years I've been work-
ing almost exclusively with writers on major collaborative pieces. This
past year, for example, Allen and I have been traveling around the country performing as something of a sideline to this larger work we have been
working on called* Hydrogen Jukebox. *I'm beginning to find it's true, at
least for me, that music and language are inherently similar and compati-
ble in ways that are not only interesting but inspiring. And so this is the
direction my work has taken."*

. . . *Hydrogen Jukebox* began with shadowed silhouettes of figures standing in lines, looking into the purple haze of nowhere, and ends with law-
and-order, the church, the proletarian masses, Little Miss America, the
racial caste system, and George Washington as Donald Trump, all in a
human circle. Spokes of a human wheel, facing outward like E. T. calling
home—"Daddy, I'm coming home." Hints of a return to godliness. A
"kaddish" of music, lyric, and visuals. The accepted embrace of eternity
in the moment of death.

    *"What I do and the way I go about it has to do with my own per-
ceptions about such things as the social issues addressed in* Hydrogen
Jukebox *as well as the ones we have spoken of here. Luckily, I would say
a lot of people are also interested in things I get interested in and so are
attracted to my work, and in this way some of my pieces may synchronis-
tically become kind of teaching vehicles in some way for some people. But
what music can do in a general way is to heighten our emotional sensibility and awareness. And when applied to a particular subject, it can bring
that heightened perception to the subject itself. So, if I set a poem of
Allen's to music, from that point on you, as the listener, might remember
that poem more easily because it may have a whole emotional world
attached to it, now, through the music. And let's not forget, after all, that
theater (or opera) is a species of poetry. It is our confidence in the validity of artistic truths that gives courage to our efforts."*

> **Genius Death your art is done**
> **Lover Death your body's gone**
> **Father Death I'm coming home**
>
> **Guru Death your words are true**
> **Teacher Death I do thank you**
> **For inspiring me to sing this Blues**

INTERVIEW ON OPERAS (1990)

JOHN KOOPMAN

Philip Glass is a gentle-mannered, soft-spoken person who doesn't concern himself much with formalities. Today he is on a day trip to a small city in the American Midwest, to deliver an address at the university there. That he has arrived late is not his fault; his plane was delayed. Still, no provision has been made for such an eventuality, and the university audience has long been assembled by the time Glass arrives. Led to the stage by a visibly relieved official, Glass wears a relaxed, slightly tousled appearance, blue jeans and a colorful flannel shirt quite innocent of a necktie. He delivers himself of an informal, rambling explanation of his musical style and intentions.

Later, when the formalities of the day have been completed, he clearly welcomes our interview as an opportunity to just sit down, have some coffee—he prefers hot cider, thanks—and chat for a bit.

How did you learn to write for the voice, and what is it that makes music vocal?
What great questions! I sometimes say that I became an opera composer by accident, because when Bob [Robert Wilson] and I did *Einstein on the Beach* it was only technically an opera, because the only place you could do it was an opera house—you needed an orchestra pit and you needed fly space and wing space. I really had little intention of becoming an opera composer and yet the writing I did in the first few operas—*Satyagraha*, for

example—did, in fact, turn out to be suitable for the voice. But it's what I learned from singing in a chorus, what I knew about choral singing that helped me. As a young man, in the Juilliard School, we had to sing in the chorus. We did the *Missa Solemnis*, the Verdi *Requiem*, and a lot of the standards. I learned these works by singing in the bass section, and it was a good form of instruction. By the way, if you study *Satyagraha* you'll see that it's really a choral work.

It was the Swiss-French composer, Arthur Honegger, who pointed out that most Puccini and Verdi arias—which many take to be superb vocal writing—lose little when they are played by a violin, suggesting, at least to him, that they do not epitomize a pure, true vocal style.
You know, George Bernard Shaw disliked Verdi's vocal writing. Shaw considered Handel the ultimate vocal composer, and there's a lot to be said for that. He thought that Handel best understood the voice and knew how to exercise it, realizing that it had to go through its whole range to stay fresh. Getting back to my own experience; after *Satyagraha* I began a series of large-scale vocal works and some smaller works, and I would say I spent the last fifteen years learning about the voice. I look back at *Satyagraha* now, and think that I was remarkably lucky! I was very lucky! I didn't deserve to have written so well for the voice as I did at the time. I know much more about the voice now, and think I write better for it now. It's something you spend your life doing. Now I listen to vocal writing in a very different way than I used to. I work with singers and I know singers; I think of their physical instrument, the breathing involved, how the *tessitura* has to change, and I know about all this because I ask them.

You're not saying you tailor our music to a specific singer—as the Baroque composers did—but that you consult with your singers on vocal questions?
What I say to them is, "How does this lay on your voice? How does it seem to you?" And that's how I learned of the break in the tenor voice. I didn't know about that. And when I asked Doug [Douglas Perry, the creator of the role of Gandhi in *Satyagraha*] about that, he said, "Well, the break in my voice is here." And so I discovered that tenors have a break! In point of fact, *Satyagraha* lies in his middle voice, as he calls it, and it did not really test him. Later, I wrote a piece called *the CIVIL warS*, in which I ventured into the upper part of the tenor voice, and I wrote a very difficult piece. It is a very dramatic and nice piece in many ways, and it was at that point that I began addressing more realistically what the voice can do.

You often write for unconventional instruments and use untraditional structural ideas in your music, but your vocal writing sounds rather orthodox. Is that intentional?

Yes, I would say so. When you say unconventional, I must point out that I don't ask my players to play things that aren't on their instruments. That's an important point. Don't forget, just a generation before me, some very inventive and interesting composers—people like Berio, Nono, Carter and others—were testing the limits of instruments in many ways. I grew up studying that music, and I know it well. And I asked myself, okay, we have had these explorations and now have these new findings, these new orchestral sounds, but what does it mean for me? Does it behoove me to find new ones? Or have they, in fact, found more than I am actually interested in? That turned out to be my response. Their work is interesting. When I hear that kind of writing, I *always* think it is interesting. But does it serve *me* as a composer? I found that it didn't. That was true of the vocal writing as well. I found that I was looking for a performance manner that would serve the music, rather than the other way around.

Is there a place for vocal virtuosity in your writing?

I've written a coloratura part in my new opera, *The Voyage*, and have just lately begun to think about that. Maybe it's because I finally began to feel more comfortable and more assured about my vocal writing that I'm more able to do that now. It's funny to say that and I realize that I must sound like a very conservative composer to you, and in many ways I am. I feel that I've been misunderstood in a certain way. I certainly never set out to change the musical world. I've just been trying to find a line that suited my particular needs.

Let me correct something I said about your vocal writing. It is unusual in one way: you don't use vocal feats—powerful high notes, virtuoso runs, that sort of thing—to convey dramatic intensity. Debussy is the only other composer I think of who shares such a trait.

Well, this is the zig-zag theory. I hear everyone zigging, so I zag! I *hear* everyone else writing that way, so my response is to avoid doing it. There is no distinction in doing it. I find no distinction for myself in it.

And distinction is a reasonable pursuit?

Well, I think having a voice of my own is something I've earned, in a way. I've earned it and I cultivate it. I don't think it's a false voice. I think it's an authentic one and that I'm entitled to its confirmation.

I haven't had the opportunity to see one of your scores. Do you edit them heavily with performance instructions? If so, are you afraid of precluding what some interpreter of genius might bring to them?

It's a problem. In *Satyagraha* you'll see very light editing. But I have learned that it's a good idea to indicate what you have in mind. The conductor will do plenty of his own interpreting! I've learned a lot about editing since I began, and it simply saves everyone a lot of time if I put in ritenutos and diminuendos where I mean to have them. I just had a work done with Robert Shaw in Atlanta, *Itaipu* (for chorus and orchestra—based on South American Indian legends), and we came to a place between chorus one and chorus two, when I was at the rehearsals, and Shaw said, "Philip, I find that you need a *ritenuto* here." And he was right! When I listened to it, it was good that way. Then the question was, do I write that into the score? I decided not to. Now it was true that Shaw needed that *ritenuto*, because of his overall musical interpretation, and he made good use of it. But I decided not to put it in, because another conductor might not need it. I guess I would see my scores as having late-Romantic type editing; and I don't use Italian descriptive terms, I use the equivalent. I make my metronome markings pretty accurate. But that doesn't mean they're always going to be followed! I was just recently looking at a piano piece of Babbitt, because a friend of mine is playing it. And I said, "Just what is one left free to do?" and he said, "Oh, there's a lot left to do." And he played it for me and showed me how much in the phrasing and playing there was still left for him. But as you look at the score, you think, my gosh, there's nothing left for the performer's imagination here. But, you know [he leans forward, as if to convey a well-kept secret], performers don't follow the signs. [We both laugh knowingly.] Well, they don't. And in fact, someone like Elliott Carter or Milton Babbitt might not even require it. I don't know about Pierre Boulez. He seems a little different.

Perhaps a composer would do well to emulate Wagner and create a cadre of favored conductors, to carry his performance ideas onward?

I have actually begun to do that. I consider Dennis Russell Davies a very authoritative one. Bruce Ferden and Paul Daniels, an English conductor, are others. There are half a dozen or so I really like. There's a brilliant young conductor, Carl St. Clair, who did a work of mine last summer, and he was wonderful. There are other conductors whose approach I don't like and I simply don't respond to their inquiries. Of course, with good luck, all this will go beyond my ability to monitor it, and there is something

interesting that happens when music gets beyond the grasp of the composer. I was talking to Dennis about this recently, and he said, "Isn't it
interesting when somebody does it in a way you would never have thought
of!" And that's true.

The same thing can be said of producers. I remember once asking
a producer why he had given a certain dramatic treatment to my
Akhnaten. His response was, "That's the way you wrote it!" I thought
about that answer for a long time.

*It seems you avoid setting the English language. Is it more difficult to set
than other languages?*
Our language has a problem with final consonants. It doesn't exist in
French or Italian. Take the word "star" for example. In a long phrase it
could be "start" or "stark" or something else, and you don't *know* what
it is until you hear the end of the phrase. So you have [he sings],
"Star . . . . .t!" It is surprising to me that it isn't even more of a
problem in German. It's there, but it's not as bothersome somehow. So
much of the *meaning* of words—in English—is tied up in the consonants,
and *they* are what is hard to put across, vocally. So there's the problem.

What about the Sanskrit text of Satyagraha *and the ancient Egyptian in*
Akhnaten?
Well, there it really didn't matter, did it?

You really didn't expect the audience to understand those languages?
I was aware that few would ever understand those texts. Now, every once
in a while someone will come up and say they understood it. But it's once
in a blue moon and I don't worry about it very much. Basically, I was
using those languages as an exotic medium and even played on their
exoticness in *Akhnaten.* I wanted the exoticness of the language to give it
an esoteric sound. You're hearing languages you've never heard and it
adds to the glamor of the piece in a way. But I don't expect anyone to
understand it.

The solfège *syllables you used in* Einstein on the Beach *are another
example.*
Ah, yes, in a way. Well, I had fun with it for some time. I also used the
Hopi Indian language similarly in one work. But I could hardly continue
avoiding English forever, and after *Akhnaten* I felt I just couldn't avoid the
problem any longer. I would have if I could, but after all it is a conun-

drum—not to use one's native tongue. And Benjamin Britten had figured out something, though I'm not so sure he was all that successful with it. It became a burning issue for me and I just felt I had to address the question: how could English serve me, and how could my music serve the language? And I began working with heavy duty authors! I mean, David Hwang, who's a well known author . . .

Pardon me for interrupting, but isn't it the singers, rather than the authors, where the problem resides?
You end up beating your head against the wall with singers on this. No matter where you begin—even with *very* articulate singers—you have to beat them up about enunciation. Let me tell you of my piece *Hydrogen Jukebox*. It is written in colloquial English, so it is a case in point. Now the author, Allen Ginsberg, is nothing if he's not a poet! And he's a poet for *everybody* . . . a poet whose words we *must* understand. And taking him on, as a librettist so to speak, setting his songs, setting his words to music, I felt I really had to preserve those words as best I could. It was very difficult, and finally I just had to accept that in passages of choral writing there would be words that would not be understood. So I would say that, in *Hydrogen Jukebox*, my hope would be that, given a good performance, you would understand 70 to 80 percent of it, which I think would be *great*! I've been to operas where I hardly understood 40 percent.

I went to *The House of the Dead*, the Janacek opera, not long ago. They used supertitles even though they sang it in English, and I thought I might have understood the words anyway. I have just one quibble with supertitles: I thought I was looking at the titles more than I needed to. I was looking at the titles to check my comprehension, to see if what I had heard was correct! I don't think I really needed that, but the fact that they were there inevitably drew my eye to the top of the stage. Well, I don't know. Since opera is a populist institution—and I think it *is* a populist art form—apart from a few 20th-century experiments (and not unsuccessful ones), *Lulu* and *Wozzeck*, the operas that we end up listening to and performing do not require heavy academic background to understand. By its nature, opera is a populist art form. Your European readers will know that there they have a tradition of performing very difficult operas, and even though few really understand them, they get performed anyway! I'm not sure what to make of it.

I'm told you have completed the opera, The Voyage, *that the Met commissioned for the 500th anniversary of Columbus' discovery of America.*

Will you tell us something of it?

I'm trying to keep some of it under wraps, but I'll tell you a little bit. I want it to be something of a surprise. Columbus *is* in it. He is in it, yet the major theme is Discovery.

Does it extend your trilogy?

No, no. It's a work unto itself. The trilogy is completed. *Voyage* is an historical fact-and-fiction fantasy. A clue to it is that my librettist is David Henry Hwang, who is a Chinese-American who grew up in America in a highly visible and distinct minority: people of Chinese ancestry. And David's work has always been extremely aware of and sensitive to the non-white part of American culture. It wasn't until I finished writing the opera—and there's *nothing* like writing an opera to help you really understand a libretto—that I really understood what it was about—even though David wrote the libretto based on a story idea of mine! So I called David, and said, "I've finished the opera, and I've discovered something." He said, "What's that?" and I answered, "You didn't like Columbus!" He laughed, and said, "Well, I gave him a few good lines." But the point is, that the arrival in the America is not an event of universal rejoicing. And you will see in 1992 that there will be anti-celebrations, just as in Australia. When the Australians celebrated their arrival there, the native peoples celebrated a day of mourning. I don't know to what extent the native Americans will take it, but without any doubt, Columbus's feet of clay are going to turn out to be very much clay indeed.

I, myself, have many interesting perspectives to bring to the Columbus story: growing up in multi-ethnic Baltimore; my own grandparents only came to this country less than a century ago. My grandparents were born in Russia. They were Jewish Russian people who came here in 1905, and we were also kind of a minority, not in the music world, but otherwise. And working with people like David Henry Hwang; and my association with musicians from India and Africa.

And what was interesting about Columbus? Was he a devil? Was he a saint? Obviously he was an unusual man: highly motivated, and a man of tremendous courage and conviction. At the same time, he was a man of his time. He was no worse and he certainly was no better. And *that* was the problem: he was no better. Not that Vasco da Gama was any better either! I mean, the sorrows of the natives started with such men and have never really stopped—witness the events this last summer in Montreal! It's shocking that this could still be going on, but it is. And now we're talking about five hundred years later, for God's sake!

Okay, so we treat Columbus's arrival here—we never call it a "discovery"—as a most interesting event, but not as a cause for universal joy for the people of North America. Nor is the opera entirely about Columbus. He is part of a larger story, and that story is one of discovery. And the question I ask myself is, "What is it that motivates most of us to leave our homes, our secure foundations, our secure upbringings, and to cast off in unknown places? Whether it's physically in a boat, or we simply do it with our minds, or with our religions? What motivates us to leave the security of the known? What *propels* us into the unknown?

Did knowing that you were writing for the Met affect the work, knowing what the facilities are, the roster, and so forth? Has the premiere date been set?
Yes, a date has been set: Columbus Day [October 12] 1992. I really question if its being for the Met affected my writing. Certainly, I was well served by the fact that it was not my first or second opera; it was my eighth or ninth. Had it been my first or second or third, I think I would have gotten damn nervous! But as it was, I was in rather a different position. I could go talk to them about the orchestration—what size orchestra I wanted. I could talk about the stage structure, the conductor I wanted, about when I wanted to use the chorus. The basic tools of the opera composer are in my grasp now, and when they spoke with me, it was not as though I was a novice. That helped a lot.

What having it performed at the Met means to me is that this is a work that everyone is going to pay attention to. I don't have to worry about whether it's going to be noticed or not. It meant that I had to try to buckle down and write the best thing I could. Did that concern me? Sure, and it made me work harder. Did it make me hold back in some way or push forward though? I don't know that it made me work any differently. Actually, I have to say that I've never been far from the spotlight, and I can't say that any work of mine has ever really been unnoticed. So I can't say that this is going to be new. Maybe we make too much over these big American commissions! Certainly the ones in Europe can be just as important.

Have you any projects coming up, specific to Europe?
I'm working an a new work with Bob [Robert Wilson]. It has been commissioned by an organization in Lisbon, Portugal, and the subject, by a strange coincidence, is: Vasco da Gama! The premiere date will be June of 1992, so we're going to have a Vasco da Gama opera in the spring and a

Christopher Columbus opera in the fall! How's *that* for a double shot! The people in Portugal asked me if I would do a da Gama opera, and I had just finished *The Voyage*, and I thought, "I don't want to do another one just now." But they persisted, and invited me to come. And finally I said, "If Bob would do this with me, then I'll do it," because then I would have a co-author and I felt that the burden of authorship would then be shared with someone who, theatrically, is my equal, my comrade, and my colleague. So I called Bob, who was working in Frankfurt at the time, and he said, "Please come over and we'll talk." So I went to see him, and he agreed! We set up our first working session, in Lisbon, last September. Bob has submitted the first preliminary designs; I have received a text from a Portuguese writer, and I begin working on the music very soon. Incidentally, Bob has such good connections in Germany—we both do—I would be surprised if it doesn't got performed there as well as in Portugal.

Your mention of Germany reminds me of a question: What is the proper performance order of your trilogy? It seemed to me as though the performances in Stuttgart last spring were out of order.
It seemed that way to me, too. They were written, and should have been performed, *Einstein-Satyagraha-Akhnaten*. In any case, *Satyagraha* in the middle. They reversed the outer two, and played *Akhnaten* first.

At least that presents the historical characters in the correct order.
Yes, but the *musical* chronology isn't correct! But in defense of what they did, it had to do with the considerable problem of fitting the sequence into the ongoing mechanics of their season and repertoire. They had practical problems to consider—orchestra calls and chorus calls—that sort of thing. And I can understand why an opera house might well want to do *Einstein* last, because they could then release the orchestra for that night. Performing it in the ideal order runs against the economics of opera houses, and I think it is going to be difficult to ever get it performed that way.

MIDTOWN AVANT-GARDIST (1992)

KYLE GANN

As his reputation has it, Philip Glass writes "going nowhere" music. His music sure seems like it's going somewhere to me: to the Metropolitan Opera first, then Brooklyn Academy of Music, the Joyce Theater, and the Public Theater. Once upon a time Glass electrified the Soho loft scene with his virtuoso ensemble's austere, multilinear process pieces, which pioneered breathtaking approaches to superfast, irregular rhythm. Then in the '80s, he seemed to retire into the mainstream (yawn), forever to churn out predictable reams of arpeggios and scales in 4/4 meter (in a wild moment, maybe 6/8). Suddenly, he's back. The "'70s composer" we had forgotten about is all over New York, inescapable. Why Glass? Why now?

Maybe it's music's version of the Perot phenomenon. If neither Uptown nor Down has much use for Glass at the moment, that may show how out-of-touch both parties are. Musicologist Susan McClary, in her recent book *Feminine Endings*, cites Glass as a victim of the business's macho bias. Since his music avoids forward motion or climax, she argues, it flouts the expectations of our traditionally patriarchal sense of form. Twelve-toners dismiss it as theoretically wimpy; improvisers concur that it's not "kickass" enough. General audiences don't necessarily give a damn. They want it to sound good.

But is Glass an audience's composer or an impresario's composer?

The latter may love him for a nonmusical reason, his meticulous professionalism. Commissioned by the Met to write a Columbus opera, *The Voyage*, he turned in the score, parts, and piano-vocal score to the Met library months early, July of '91, for this month's premiere. "The Met's not used to doing new composers," Glass explains in the kitchen of his East Village brownstone, "and I thought it would do everyone a favor to have the music in early. The choral director might like to start rehearsing in the spring, I didn't know. It's a great reputation to have. People know they can count on you." If you were a producer risking millions on a new opera, isn't that attitude the first thing you'd want in a composer? (In 1986 the Met canceled Jacob Druckman's opera because he was so far behind schedule.)

One of the savviest and most articulate musicians I've ever met, Glass realizes that even his best fans tend to like only half his output. Admitting to a split between his "lyrical" and "rigorous" sides, he notes that hardcore new-music types lament his downhill slide after his 1974 classic *Music in 12 Parts*. Others prefer the lyricism in *Songs from Liquid Days* and *Hydrogen Jukebox*. Glass has emphasized the lyrical in recent years, and now he's betting that *The Voyage* will bring some "rigorous" listeners back to the fold. Premiering on the 500th Columbus Day, *The Voyage* is an oblique Columbus portrait, with a libretto by David Henry Hwang of *M. Butterfly* fame, who previously worked with Glass on *1000 Airplanes on the Roof*.

Glass's operas have never favored realism. *The Voyage* takes Columbus as one in a series of exploration metaphors. In Act I a spaceship lands on earth in 50,000 B.C., and in Act III scientists receive signals from outer space. "We play on the cultural confrontation which has been on everyone's minds," explains Glass, "in an allegorical rather than literal way. When you deal with a subject allegorically you bring less baggage and can think more clearly. Columbus and the Indians is such an emotional issue, it's hard to get anybody to disagree about it. Everyone knows he didn't behave very well. But if you can't go beyond that, you get stuck in Indians and us and white people and black people.

"At the end of Act I David wrote a beautiful scene where the commander, who's a woman, meets the natives. She does an aria in which she talks about, 'I wonder what they expect from me, what do they think I'm going to do for them, who do they think I am?' Then the chorus sings the same words back to her. It becomes evident that there is no objective way for cultures to see each other, that every point of view will be subjective. It's a statement we might not have come to had we dealt with Columbus and the Indians per se. David is first-generation Chinese American, and doesn't write from that white European male viewpoint that we now know we've suffered under."

In Act II, Columbus appears, but "never arrives. It's not the 33rd day at sea, it's the 32nd day. In fact, our opera takes place October 11. I may not have told the people at the Met that." The opera's prologue contains a character based on Stephen Hawking. "What interested me was a scientist who does it in a wheelchair, who travels to the very edge of the universe. Explorers are not necessarily Indiana Jones characters. They can be artists or scientists, the explorations can be spiritual, mental, or physical. I wanted to extend the range of the opera that way. The second act is Columbus as Noah, Ulysses, the Flying Dutchman, people who *have* to find courage because they are so alone, whose only resource becomes themselves. I'm interested in courage, and in doubt. They go together."

Act III jumps to the year 2092, with two scientists looking for life in outer space. They discover crystals that, when put together, amplify radio signals, and begin receiving messages from another solar system. In a humorous scene with cheerleaders, a band, and the chorus as spectators, astronauts leave to seek the source of the signals. "As the astronauts say goodbye, David made a nice point I wouldn't have noticed: every time we leave, we're leaving somebody behind. This is the side of discovery that we forget about, that it's about parting. We have a final scene with Columbus in 1506. He's dying, Isabella's already dead, but he has one last duet with her, and finally explains himself."

Musically, what's new? *The Voyage* isn't enough of a departure to convert inveterate Glass-haters, but its subtle advances in complexity are pervasive. Rhythm is once again a big issue. The score relies heavily on syncopating 3/4 meter as 6/8—no big deal in itself—but Glass milks that tic further than you'd think. The growling, whirlwind prologue keeps several rhythmic levels going at once, setting up nice tempo tensions of three against four. Elsewhere, phrase lengths expand from 7/8 to 9/8, melodies repeat in intricate cycles of 49 beats, in the jumpy way of Glass's early process pieces such as *Music in Similar Motion* and *Music with Changing Parts*. "The ideas I concentrate on gradually become secondary," says Glass, "background instead of foreground. Certain kinds of additive rhythm I've used a lot are still there, but instead of being the subject of the work, they create the context for other things. If you listen carefully you'll say, 'Oh yeah, that's five plus four plus three, Glass always does that.' But it goes by so fast that you'd have to know my music to be aware of it. Whereas, in *Music in Similar Motion*, that would be the whole piece."

Such details are linked to the structure of the story. "The only way music can be profoundly successful," Glass contends, "is if the musical language is part of the *argument* of the piece. The argument of *The Voyage* is sketchy and a little abstract, but there's enough of one. Finding a way of working on a musical idea *through* the dramatic idea is the key to doing opera." For instance, *Einstein on the Beach* of 1976 is about combining a functional harmony and a rhythmic structure into a unified entity; that's most audible in the "spaceship" scene. *Satyagraha* of 1981 is a series of seven chaconnes, the chaconne being a Baroque-era form of continuous variation over a repeating harmonic progression. Robert Ashley has also based operas on the chaconne, with dissimilar results; it's natural, Glass notes, that "my generation, which is interested in repetition, is drawn to a formal device in early music also based on repetition."

Glass calls *Akhnaten* (1983) his first experiment in polytonality, the music being in several keys at once. "What I was trying to do in *Akhnaten* was to make the perception of the harmony ambivalent. You could analyze a particular number in several keys, but not two at the same time. It was like an optical illusion, such as in [the paintings of Josef] Albers, where you could look at it two ways, but not both ways at once; it can't resolve itself. It was my first extension out of a triadic harmonic language that had been fairly simple up until then."

The Voyage, his ninth opera, extends *Akhnaten*'s polytonality into a metaphor of coexisting cultures that can't blend. The entire work is based on a familiar but theoretically problematic chord: the augmented triad (C, E, G-sharp). "The piece is an exploration of what an augmented triad really is. The sound of the crystals is the augmented triad. It's never out of earshot for long. People say a right angle doesn't exist in nature; in a certain way, an augmented triad doesn't exist in nature. It's an invented, conceptual chord. And by the time I wrote the epilogue, I finally saw what it is. We find it in polytonal music. It can be explained as a natural result of an extended diatonicism towards bitonality. That made me feel good, because I found a new way of thinking about music through thinking through this process."

Got that? In this respect Glass is no different from Schoenberg, who wrote his Chamber Symphony No. 1 to try out all possible resolutions to a chord made of stacked perfect-fourth intervals. Such thinking can make Glass's music thrilling. For example, the clash of A-flat major and E minor in the Epilogue to *Akhnaten*: those incommensurate keys won't blend, and their repeating seesawing finally balances them in your ear like two plausible but contradictory thoughts. This is why his music still requires repetition, and why, at its best, it repays attention to subtle relationships of harmony and voice-leading (the melodic ways in which harmonies connect). One thing Glass learned from studying with Nadia Boulanger—the century's most famous composition teacher, who also taught Copland, Barber, and other celebrated Americans—was to be meticulous about voice-leading. Nestle an A-flat major triad inside an E-minor one, and you can see where that influence survives.

The Voyage goes even further. In its opening moments, the lower strings spin out E-minor scales while the chorus repeatedly enters on an *E-flat major* triad. That's a common Glass contrast, but rarely if ever has he held the dissonance in such a sustained way. As it repeats, that gritty effect sounds more and more transparent, and key clashes related to it color the opera. (If you're looking for the augmented triad, take the E-flat from the E-flat major triad, the B of the E-minor triad, and their common note G.) In the final scene, as Columbus dies in a monastery, Dominican monks sing a flowing chant that rolls into a thread the chord relationships we've been hearing all evening.

Glass felt freer to write such dissonant choral parts and rhythmic difficulties because of the Met's expert forces. "The Met's such an ideal situation," he sighs. "Most opera orchestras aren't that good. You write difficult music for them at your peril; especially the kind I write, where there's no place to hide, you can hear everything. With most orchestras I've held back, with this orchestra I didn't. And they're working very hard." It's the audience who *doesn't* have to work hard, because after three hours those chord clashes have been turned through every possible perspective in slow motion. Envious composers complain that Glass's music is diluted by repetition, but it lays out complex information at a pace listeners can take in comfortably.

In fact, Glass's music is not only going somewhere, it's on a route no one else is taking. From *Music in Fifths* through *The Voyage*, Glass has retraced the history of musical materials from Gregorian chant to impressionism, getting a little more complex with each major work. After all, he came to John Cage's influence not from the more common direction of Ives and Schoenberg, but via Boulanger and Darius Milhaud; not from a chromatic, complex tradition, but from a tonal, diatonic one. His is a *conservative* background, not even uptown but midtown, diffracted through the '60s avant-garde, and there aren't many other examples. (It's a kick to run across, in music libraries, the Coplandish scores Glass published before his conversion.) When Glass talks history, you hear names other composers don't mention. One of Glass's profs, Vincent Persichetti, wrote a book on polytonal harmony, but Glass traces his interest in polytonality to Milhaud, whom he studied with one summer at Aspen and admires profoundly. "He made a subtle contribution to 20th century music. We tend to concentrate on the biggies, like Boulez, Stockhausen, Bartók, and forget other influences that may be subtler but more lasting. Like Debussy. I think about him more now than I ever did." Not a popular idea.

"History's curious, because our interests change, and as they change, our evaluation of the past changes. There were 20 years where no one listened to Bartók. Now we're hearing him again. There's no final judgment of history, because we judge music from the point of view of the present, and the present will always be new." This season, the present is Glass, and as *The Voyage* plays, history seems to shift uneasily. Adventurer in a wheelchair, or maybe an armchair, is a good image, for he's slowly exploring music's microcosm.

STAR DREK (1992)

PETER G. DAVIS

For those who feared that Philip Glass and the Metropolitan Opera might prove incompatible, the world-premiere production of *The Voyage* will be reassuring. The master of minimalism and our principal purveyor of grand-opera maximalism turn out to have more in common than one might think.

Commissioned by the Met to commemorate the 500th anniversary of Christopher Columbus's arrival in the New World, Glass's latest creation may sound characteristically minimal, but the visual aspects eagerly invite lavish treatment. And the Met has obliged. Even this exacting composer, who by now has seen his operas handsomely produced the world over, must have been pleased by the company's unparalleled facilities, which provide him with all the extravagant stage effects and mechanical marvels he requires. As an operatic reformer, Glass has been hailed as today's equivalent of Wagner and Gluck, but seeing his work at the Met puts that questionable claim into perspective. Produced with such splendor and in a house where the weight of tradition is heavy, *The Voyage* suggests that Glass has far more in common with Giacomo Meyerbeer, whose cleverly packaged but hollow historical spectacles dominated European opera stages for a time in the nineteenth century.

The story idea for *The Voyage* originated with Glass, who asked

David Henry Hwang to write the libretto. Like many of the composer's other music-theater pieces, his new opera is best described as a pageant of abstractions and moods rather than a plotted drama in which action is propelled by music. A prologue sets the tone: a celebration of exploration and discovery personified by a scientist, his body confined to a wheelchair but his mind and imagination floating in the cosmos. Act I takes place on a spaceship that hurtles out of control and crashes to Earth; the crew survives, and each member chooses to enter one of earthly society's exploratory callings. Act II presents a vision of Columbus en route to the New World: his doubts, fears, love for Queen Isabella, and rapturous first sight of land. Act III takes place in the year 2092, and the focus is on a united-nations gathering as it prepares a space launch to inspect a newly discovered planet. The epilogue brings back Columbus, now making his final journey on his deathbed, which rises to the stars.

Given a generous budget, few designers would not gleefully lay hands on a scenario with such display potential, and Robert Israel has responded enthusiastically. A room assembles and flies apart, singers and heavenly bodies float over the stage, Isabella's elaborate court dissolves into a ship at sea, a rocket soars from the head of Miss Liberty, soft drinks tumble from a cosmic Coke machine—there's never a dull moment, at least for the eye. No doubt other suggestions came from David Pountney, whose crisp direction faithfully serves the piece and helps clarify several more obscure Glass-Hwang fancies. Dance also plays a prominent part. The Act I finale invites native earthlings to indulge in a wild boogie devised by Quinny Sacks, whose eclectic choreography spans the centuries but seems inspired mainly by Busby Berkeley.

The premiere performance of *The Voyage* was broadcast, and I wonder what radio listeners, unable to see all this, made of the bare music. Bruce Ferden, who conducted the opera, has spoken of Glass's new harmonic adventurousness and use of pronounced dissonance. I suppose he is right, if such "innovations" are measured within the narrow context of the composer's style: the locomotive rhythms, wispy melodies, arpeggiated chords, primitive syncopations, and his other familiar mannerisms, all present here in abundance. But to my ears, as Glass loosens miminalistic disciplines and adopts more conventional procedures, his music sounds only increasingly fatigued and commonplace. *The Voyage* continues the process, a score of stupefying banality.

Beyond that, Glass writes clumsily for the voice. The opera's characters have virtually nothing of interest to sing, while the awkward prosody and gummy orchestrations ensure that scarcely a word will be understood. It's small wonder that the performances of Timothy Noble (Columbus), Tatiana Troyanos (Isabella), Patricia Schuman (Commander), and Douglas Perry (Scientist/First Mate) hardly register at all. Mostly the singers seem like additional bits of scenic decoration, inanimate objects to be manipulated by a pretentious, passionless, repellent piece of musical machinery.

Seeing *The Voyage* so expensively produced at the Met, though, did suggest an interesting paradox. Glass has traveled far since his cab-driving days, and he has definitely arrived. But, unlike Columbus, he has journeyed in the opposite direction: from the adventurous new world of downtown experimentation to the comfortable old world of Met Opera conformity. Even the composer's most ardent early supporters might admit that this particular voyage has been characterized mainly by diminishing musical innovation and creative vigor.

STYLE & SOUL: INTERVIEW (1992)

DAVID WALTERS

PHILIP GLASS: I am a theatre composer. They are very different people from people that write concert music. Concert music writers write in the world of abstract music; theatre writers work from subject matter. So I usually begin with a subject. It could be Columbus, a story by Doris Lessing, Edgar Allen Poe or it could be Einstein. Before I start writing I get an idea of what the stage presentation is going to be like. Is it a large piece or small piece? Who is the director? Who is the designer? Finally I have to select the writer for the piece, if there is going to be one.

Then I take a longish period of time—often a year—with this group of people and we meet and develop the dramatic concept of the piece. This sometimes results in a finished libretto or very often at least a first or second draft of the libretto. Sometimes I'm working with drawings or, in the case of a film, it might be film images.

At the end of this I have an outline of the piece, in terms of its length and time, the forces involved, what kind of text or visual material will be involved. Then I begin to write the music.

Do you write on your own?

I'll get an idea for a piece, concerto, opera or theatre piece. The next process is to find someone to commission it. So the ideas usually start with me. I get together my team of collaborators, then, very important to us is to find a producer—in American parlance, a person who puts up the organisational stuff, money, etc. I then find someone who will present and bill the work and pay and underwrite the expenses: that's the hard part. To persuade, cajole and intimidate—in any way you can—someone to put on a work is a big effort! But without that assurance of a production of some kind, with someone picking up the expenses of the work, I'm very reluctant to begin working. That is very clear in my mind.

Does that affect your writing?
Not really. I'm usually at work on one piece, doing the actual composing and I will have a second piece in rehearsal and a third piece that is more speculative. If I finish an opera and only then begin working on my next opera, I may have to wait 2 years before I'm back at work. That's not practical so I keep a time in the day for writing and other times when I'm involved in production and planning for new pieces.

When I write, I work at the keyboard *and* direct to manuscript. I find the keyboard is the only way I can keep track of how rapidly the music passes. I may find that it is longer or shorter than I perceived and sometimes the length of a piece can be crucial. In planning a dramatic work we are often working towards time periods. So at some point during the day I usually play through, at the keyboard, all the music I have written.

Sometimes ideas originate from that situation; sometimes the nicest ideas come when I'm sitting at a desk and can write them down, but then I check them at the piano, in terms of the tempo and the rhythm. With vocal lines you often can't do them in your head: they have to be sung.

I mostly use formal notation and, on occasions, a shorthand; if I'm writing very quickly it is too much trouble to write the whole thing out. I tend to write full orchestral scores and not piano scores, as some composers do. I'll do a short score—maybe notate very quickly what a harmonic passage might be—and I'll sketch out the melodic and instrumental material at the same time. Within 2 or 3 hours I'll write it up completely. Shorthand is good for getting things done quickly but, if I leave it too long, I can lose track of what I was doing.

Over the years—and I didn't expect it—this process has changed. Pieces I wrote 10 or 15 years ago were only written once. Now I find I spend much more time re-writing and re-thinking things, maybe because a certain complexity has appeared in the music in recent years and I simply can't let it go on such an easy basis as I did before. I also find that, in re-writing, I can make my biggest improvements.

As you get older as a composer, you bring more to the music: you have more experience; your technique becomes more supple. But it isn't all downhill! I've been writing music for, would you believe it, 40 years! I started when I was 15. I finished pieces with great difficulty until I was 25. Things picked up and I changed my style very much at that age until, by the age of 30, I began to get a fluency, because of the sheer amount of practice I'd had—at that point I'd written close to 75 or 80 pieces. I maintained that fluency for about 15 years and then at 45 I began slowing down again. I didn't lose the fluency but I began to be more critical of what I was doing.

I don't get stuck very often when writing, probably because I write a large quantity of music: I don't have the time! Getting stuck for me is a kind of self-indulgence. I just don't tolerate it. If I don't like the way something is going I'll just throw it away. If I find I'm in a place where things aren't going well, I simply start from another place and sometimes that will do the trick.

Do you reflect back on pieces?
Never! Mainly because I'm too busy doing a new piece. The other thing is that I'm not sure that we improve things when we go back to an early piece. This is the problem: pieces I wrote in '69 or '70 had a complete set of musical and aesthetic ideas that were consonant with the music I was writing at that time. When I come back to them, 20 years later, I can't recapture the frame of mind I was in at the time. It is impossible. So you go back to these earlier pieces as a stranger. Whether you're really making improvements or simply editing, I would be reluctant to say.

Do you do things outside of writing?
I do. Going to rehearsals, working with singers and I have an active life as a performer: I'm involved with about 50 or 60 concerts a year. That is a very stimulating process and one I recommend to every composer. It keeps the music in that vital connection with the public, which I think is crucial if the music is to maintain a high degree of communicativeness.

When I was young my teachers discouraged performance. They thought that you gave the music to the instrumental specialists because they were better performers than the composer. This was true. I was at a very good music school in New York and some of our country's finest instrumentalists have come out of there. I actually stopped playing for 5 or 10 years. I think that was a mistake and very bad advice.

I also cook to relax. It's very like music and it's also a social activity. The way I do it is to have 2 or 3 friends over and we all cook together. Musicians can be a very social lot.

I associate myself with other kinds of artists—dancers and painters and theatre people in general. It is not so far away from what I do. Going to the theatre is kind of a busman's holiday but all this external stimulus feeds into my work. In terms of casual reading I tend to read history and biographies and try to find a way to make almost everything a part of what I do.

The artistic personality is something we rarely talk about in music schools. What we look for in a composer is that singular personality that comes out of the *soul* of the person—the creativity which, I'm afraid, cannot be taught. We sometimes think and worry that we smother it or heap technical things over it and that it doesn't have a chance to breathe. I'm not sure that is a problem. A strong creative personality will find its way. To tell you the truth I don't think there's much you can do about it.

So where is your soul?
This is the most interesting thing. Why is it that a composer sounds the way he does? It was one of the things I learnt when I studied with Nadia Boulanger, who was a great, great teacher. . . . What she was teaching about was style. Style is a special case of technique. Technique is a general thing we can all learn; the style we bring to a piece is the way we use a technique. So that, in one measure of any composer, you can immediately recognise who they are and this predilection for working in a certain way becomes identified with the personality and soul of a composer.

What I also learned is that a personal style is impossible without a technique to begin with. The style comes from the deepest aspects of the composer's being and those are the parts that we can't really develop. But we *can* create an opportunity for the personality to express itself. In a music school you're creating the conditions for the soul of the composer to emerge. Without those conditions it will never come out.

So what conditions are best for you?
This is inspiration. I got involved with the life of Gandhi after reading about him and I found his life very inspiring and moving. It became the inspiration for an opera. We don't use that word "inspiration" much but it is that interaction between you and anything which fires your imagination. I went to South America once and saw a great hydroelectric dam and it inspired me to write a cantata. It can be just a movement that you see in a dance studio. This is something we can cultivate: we can learn to be responsive to inspiration and take it seriously.

What would you pass on about composing?

There are some things about composing that are essential: although it is tedious, there is nothing to replace a solid technique in music fundamentals. I'm afraid to pass on this bad news to young composers, but years of counterpoint, harmony and analysis, I have to say, seem unavoidable!

It's not all bad news, however. I would certainly be involved with the new computer technology, software, etc. Those kinds of writing have to be looked into. They shouldn't, however, replace the basic music fundamentals that have stood us well for hundreds of years.

The other thing is not to be overly concerned about individuality at a young age. The sound of your own "voice" *will* appear. It may take a few years to happen and I think young people sometimes get very anxious about that. What most of us do in the early years is to imitate the people we like, and that can go on for 10 years, easily. I am known for having a very individual style, easily recognisable—a very strong signature, people have said. In fact I only acquired my own compositional voice when I was about 29, after I had been writing for 14 or 15 years.

The last thing I would say is to take pleasure in what you're doing—for many years that may be the only reward you're going to get! If you don't rejoice in it you are going to have a very hard time. You can't count on quick success in this business; I wasn't able to support myself from my music until I was 41—until then I still had "day jobs." But I took great pleasure in writing and playing music all through the difficult years and never felt badly about it.

The impulse that brings us to music is one of rejoicing. I think that is the great, profound pleasure of a life in music and is something that we can cherish for all our life. Something not to be forgotten.

THE SOUND OF MINIMALISM: PHILIP GLASS IN CONCERT AND ON RECORD (1987)

AARON M. SHATZMAN

I. Minimalism Inherent Contradictions

Philip Glass enjoys popular recognition and critical acclaim as a minimalist, creating music which one commentator has described by suggesting that it reminds him of a record on which the cartridge stylus has become permanently stuck in one groove. For some reason I failed to react to the recordings with the impatience, annoyance, anger, or boredom implicit in that reviewer's remark. Rather, my first encounters with the music as a serious and attentive listener, using a high definition system, as opposed to merely taking note of sounds heard through boom boxes in an environment full of distractions (my record shop acquaintance), proved seductive. The music had an energy, and created a tension (almost an irritation), which captured my interest, and which also entertained. Not all the music, to be sure, for some of it was far less intriguing, inducing at "best" a tendency to become reflective, and at "worst" seeming tedious. But, in general, if this was musical minimalism, then I found I liked minimalism.

The recordings *qua* recordings, especially *Glassworks* and *The Photographer*, were also interesting—sonically superior productions from a company, CBS, which has not recently distinguished itself in that respect. Not only was the quality of sound very good, but even more enticing, the records provided a terrific stereo image—a sense of dimensional space—which attracted, then held my attention. There was, I discovered, a lot to listen to in these records.

I approached the Glass Ensemble's performance, therefore, with genuine anticipation. I knew beforehand . . . that we were about to hear musicians in a hall designed to provide an acoustically ideal setting for the performance of live unamplified music; who, nevertheless, would communicate with their audience through microphones, amplifiers, a mixing console, and loudspeakers. The philosophical questions thus raised about the relationship between the live versus the reproduced musical experience intrigued me. But I was especially eager, given my interest in audio equipment which provides "true" or "natural" sound, to be forced to consider the question of just what that standard ought to be when the performers use electronic devices to help create the original, genuine, actual sounds of the music we hear.

The Ensemble's program consisted of excerpts from a number of longer works composed during the past several years. The first half of the concert was devoted to music which I surmised to be minimalism at its most minimal, for even heard live and amplified to a level far louder than I would have chosen to play it in my music room at home, the pieces failed to seize my attention. Perhaps the presence of the performers, or the crowd in the hall, distracted me. But Viky reported between numbers that she was bored. And Karen said during intermission that though she "liked" the music, her thoughts had wandered to the final exam she was preparing for her pediatrics students—that the Glass Ensemble had provided nice background music as she focused her attention on other matters.

In the days following the concert I mulled over this aspect of Glass's compositions, which, under some circumstances, can take on the quality of background music, becoming part of the environment in which we think or act, rather than the primary focus of our attention. Could that characteristic, I wondered, actually be a feature Glass has attempted to incorporate, a goal he has striven to accomplish and which, therefore, dominates certain works and marks segments of others? I recalled how often over the previous several years I had encountered that music in public places, yet had failed to respond by *listening* as opposed to merely being vaguely aware of its presence, and continuing to go about my business. Has Glass attempted to create music which aims to induce a thoughtful, perhaps meditative state of mind in the listener, music whose specific purpose is to stimulate contemplation or reflection, and which encourages such responses by adding a supportive or suggestive sonic element to one's environment?

I know of a couple who, with severely restricted assets, have built a great collection of minimalist visual art. Their apartment is so small, and their discretionary income so limited, that they have chosen to forgo buying furniture, which would occupy precious space needed to display their acquisitions, and whose purchase would diminish resources which might be allocated to adding to the collection. Instead, at a few key locations in their home, simple covered or carpeted platforms fulfill their sitting or serving needs. More than a few times, sophisticated visitors, ranging from museum directors, to fellow collectors, to prominent art dealers, to minimalist artists, have entered these rooms and spent hours looking both at the art and for a place to sit, for invariably, guests find it impossible to distinguish those forms or objects which are important examples of minimalist art from those which simply are part of the background designed to display the collection.

Similarly, I recall a morning I spent in the Museum of Modern Art a decade ago, during which I entertained myself by watching visitors confront one of the sculptor Larry Bell's minimalist creations—a clear glass cube. I sympathized with the reaction of all those who mistook the sculpture, the work of art itself, for a display case from which a work by the artist had been removed, for, of course, my own initial response to the piece would have been identical had I not been told beforehand that Bell had donated one of his cubes to the museum.

But more than a few of the art lovers who encountered that Bell sculpture, and the other examples of minimalist art then on display, once having determined that the work under scrutiny was in fact the artist's creation, responded not merely by looking at the cube, but by *studying* it— devoting to it a level of attention that amazed me, searching for qualities I fear it could not possibly have possessed. In fact, it occurred to me that the artist was, at some level, engaged in playing a great joke on all of us, and that MOMA was a perhaps unwitting collaborator in his game. Now I realize that those gallery visitors were, quite possibly, influenced by their surroundings—after all, this was a MOMA exhibition gallery and, by definition, any work on display had been certified as "worthy" by the curatorial staff. Yet I suspect that at least some were responding to other influences as they engrossed themselves in that simple transparent box, that their committed, impassioned scrutiny was merely a manifestation of rather normal human characteristics—traits which practitioners of minimalism both relied on and manipulated in order to capture an audience, then hold its interest.

What I am trying to describe here is what may be a universal tendency to give more dedicated attention to that which is small, quiet, subtle, unclear, obscure, partially hidden, than to that which intrudes upon us by blatantly announcing its presence. Are we not predisposed to respond with disfavor to that which is too obvious, to that which reveals its secrets too easily? Conversely, do we not tend to derive satisfaction from the process of discovery, from engagement in a kind of dialogue with some external stimulus during which we must exert intellectual, perhaps emotional effort in order to comprehend it? Are not such encounters invariably more fulfilling than those in which one serves merely as a passive recipient, as a kind of sponge deemed worthy only to absorb what is proclaimed by another human, or by a work of art surrogate? Is there anyone who fails to feel offended, patronized, or demeaned when placed in that position?

It occurred to me, as I pondered my positive response to Glass's minimal, sometimes seemingly endlessly repetitive music, that at least part of the attraction derived from the way his music *forced* me to be attentive if I wished to appreciate its subtle variations. Since such nuances might not be audible in the public, congested, noisy places where, in the past, I had heard the music, I realized (or rationalized) that my previous disregard for music I now really enjoyed might simply have resulted from the specific circumstances under which it had been heard.

We all know that understatement is a useful strategy for arousing interest. Overstatement, conversely, simply repels, or undermines credibility. Most of us have learned that we can command a greater level of attention if we whisper than if we shout, for a lowered voice compels the listener to concentrate. Recall the classic story about Fritz Reiner's response to his orchestra when the players manifested their resentment to his imperious, even cruel leadership by disorderly, undisciplined, imprecise unsynchronized playing—by intentionally failing to follow his direction. Of course, Reiner knew exactly what the musicians were doing and, as he conducted, gradually reduced the movement of his baton, ultimately making only minuscule, barely visible motions. Needless to say, the rebellion dissolved, for each member of the orchestra was forced to concentrate more dutifully than ever on Reiner's every tiny motion as his movements became increasingly less easy to see, or to ignore. I suspect that minimal art seizes our attention, whether we see it on a wall or hear it in performance, because we react to it the way Reiner's resentful orchestra players responded to his barely perceptible baton movements.

Thus Glass's music, because of its very minimalism, exhibits contradictory qualities. The music can seem so endlessly repetitive, so unvarying, that it becomes either mind-numbing, or is transformed into part of the background in which we act, ceasing to exist as an entity separate from the environment, worthy of interest. Yet it is precisely those same characteristics which can work to rivet our attention, making the music seem at once compelling, fascinating, and entertaining.

II. Minimalism Sonic Contradictions

Since my weeks of listening to his records led me to focus on the subtle, evolutionary, sometimes even delicate nature of his work, imagine my surprise (shock more accurately describes my reaction) when I discovered that the decibel level at which Glass intends his music to be heard is simply ear-shattering. (I assume Philip Glass wishes his music to be heard at the volume at which he played it.) Jeff Coggin of TAS attended a Glass Ensemble concert in New York last year, and he had advised me that the music had been performed at sound levels he found uncomfortable. Yet in spite of that preparation, I never anticipated the actual live concert volume, or the intellectual tension created by hearing music noted for its subtlety performed at sound levels which belied that quality. It was as if Larry Bell's transparent glass cube had been painted an unrelenting day-glo orange, and could be viewed only in the confines of a tiny booth in which uncomfortable eye contact could not be averted.

Before attending the concert I had recognized that the same quality in Glass's music which caused it to blend unobtrusively into the background could also work to make it impossible to ignore. Now the juxtaposition of minimal music with maximal sound suggested that perhaps the essence of this music was its inherently self-contradictory nature—that Glass's compositions might well be approached, and best comprehended, by finding other manifestations of such opposing tendencies in his work.

I had come to the concert prepared to address the issue of how the standard of music heard live in a hall performed by real musicians, which serves as my reference when I encounter recorded music, would be affected when the musicians placed electronic devices between themselves and their audience. That circumstance raises a number of nice philosophical questions, and anyone who remembers the film *Blow Up*, knows how intriguing a consideration of the big question "What Is Real?" can be. Yet the actual sound I heard at the live performance was so utterly "mechanical"—so obviously "false"—that questions about the relationship of live or natural to recorded or amplified sound immediately seemed wholly irrelevant.

Now maybe all those musicians, Philip Glass included, simply cannot hear. Or perhaps on stage they have no idea what their music sounds like out in the hall. But I doubt it. I suspect that just as a primitive artist knows that his or her paintings lack characteristics which might lead some observers to remark how "real" or "lifelike" they look, and strives to create exactly the abstracted, stylized image which appears on the canvas, that Philip Glass both knows how his music sounds to someone sitting out in row Q, and that he has worked very hard to get it to sound just the way it does.

The main question I brought with me to the concert, therefore, turned out to be the wrong one to ask, for within only minutes as a member of the audience I realized that Glass never intended to use microphones, amplifiers, and loudspeakers to help the crowd to hear the natural sound of human voices or acoustical instruments more clearly or perfectly—to assist in conveying their intrinsic qualities to people dispersed throughout a large hall. If his recordings are intended to reflect the quality of sound heard in actual performance (or vice versa, as I am about to suggest), then to evaluate them by investigating the degree to which the recorded saxophone or soprano sound like their counterparts heard unamplified in a different musical context is to miss one of the points Glass seems to be trying to make. Only after hearing Glass in actual performance does one begin to understand how to listen to his records, for what has seemed unnatural in those recordings may be less the result of inept engineering, inferior monitoring equipment, improper microphone placement, or careless processing than a wonderfully faithful portrayal of the artist's genuine intentions, similar in critical respects to the sound of his music heard live, performed by the composer. In fact, it has occurred to me that the true, the essential, the pure, the ultimately valid sound of Philip Glass is what we hear when we play one of his records—that the medium which most faithfully conveys the sonic fabric he seeks to create is the vinyl disc (or tape). There is reason to believe that in live performance the Glass Ensemble attempts to recreate the sound engraved into the grooves of a record, which may well represent a more perfect realization of his goals than he is able to achieve outside the studio.

For much to my surprise the live performance sounded, if anything, less "natural" than most of the Glass recordings I have auditioned. The dominating presence of huge loudspeaker towers, combined with the occupation of center stage front by the sound engineer seated at his mixing console, gave the audience visual clues about the nature of the sound which could not be ignored. But in spite of their physical prominence, these symbols of the artificial, the manipulated, the contrived, only reinforced perceptions which would have been inevitable even had the speakers, amplifiers, and control booth been discreetly camouflaged. That they were not hidden, of course, is ample evidence that Glass's primary sonic goal has little to do with insuring that individual instruments retain their inherent qualities. It is less important, for example, that a soprano sound like a human than that her voice serve as the source of a specific sound Glass needs in order to complete his composition.

What most forcefully suggested itself to me at the concert was the artificial, electrical, mechanical nature of the sound the Glass Ensemble created for its audience. The quality of synthesization pervaded every aspect of the performance, dominating both what we saw and what we heard. Let me relate two examples which come to mind. During my preconcert self-immersion into Glass's music, I frequently heard sounds on his records which I understood to be humans chanting in unison. I was shocked to discover that those sounds are, in fact, produced by one of the keyboards. Second, periodically throughout the concert the person charged with controlling the live sound mix, seated at his console in the position on stage usually occupied by the conductor, would check the accuracy of the sound in order to determine if adjustments to the mix were necessary. He did this not by listening as a member of the audience, but rather by taking a set of headphones from a rack, and placing them over his ears, in effect isolating himself from the hall and from the sound being heard there.

Out in the hall we heard the results of the musicians' efforts only after they had been processed for us by electrical devices which imposed their own mark on the sound. I am accustomed, for example, when listening to a soprano in a concert hall in performance with instrumental players, to hear her voice float out over the orchestra riding on a cushion of air. (I shall never forget Kathleen Battle's voice gently emerging as distinct from the chorus, then rising, then soaring out into Powell Hall during performances of the Mahler Second in St. Louis several years ago—my own reference standard whenever I hear other singers with other orchestras in other halls.) The Glass Ensemble soprano's voice not only failed to float into the hall, blaring instead from a loudspeaker driver, but it took on a harsh shrillness that effectively deprived it of its human qualities. The other instruments, as well, had many of their distinctive characteristics bleached away by the amplification system. Even more telling, virtually every spatial clue which informs a listener that a number of individual players dispersed about a stage are performing, vanished from the live performance, as the sound system blended discrete contributions from different parts of the stage into an indistinct synthesized whole which emerged from either the far left or the far right of the stage, where the speaker systems had been erected. The physical individuality of the players thus disappeared sonically, a rather unnerving consequence since they were, of course, clearly visible as individuals separated by space, distributed both left to right and front to back, producing sounds which could not be related to their specific locations on stage.

Needless to say, I found all this fascinating and provocative. Seeing and hearing Glass perform his music in concert turned out to be a kind of seminal experience which forced me to reconsider any number of assumptions about the relationship between live and recorded music which previously had seemed to me to be almost self-evidently valid. To the degree art exists to stimulate thought, to provide a basis for intelligent discourse, then Glass's achievement is both striking and formidable. That his music also touches both the spirit with its rhythmic energy, and the emotions with its melodic content, is simply remarkable. So too, of course, is its ability to attract an audience composed of individuals who, in all likelihood, share few other musical or cultural attachments. Those who have, as I had, avoided Glass's work, or ignored his contribution to contemporary music, ought at minimum to sample one of his recordings, if for no other reason than to determine what all the noise has been about. And if an opportunity to see and hear the Glass Ensemble perform in concert presents itself, those who seek fuel for their cerebral fires need to be in the audience.

PHILIP GLASS (1986)
R I C H A R D   S E R R A

Philip Glass: I was just up at the Guggenheim. Did you see the Richard Long piece?

Richard Serra: No, I would love to see it. I haven't seen it. Good?

Yeah. Yeah.

I like Richard Long.

Oh yeah. I remember when, around 1973–1974, he used to be walking around. He looked like a young hiker. A young English hiker.

Yeah, yeah.

We said, "Richard, what are you doing?" He said, "I am just walking around."

Yeah, yeah.

That's what he was doing. I liked him though. I always liked him. But the pieces, they look very formal and they seem very composed now in a way and in a way that's not so nice. But there were some drawings from '74—there were some drawings of the pieces from the time that we first knew him and they were very remarkable.

I think there is a big difference between what he does outside and what he does inside. And what he does outside in relation to the context makes some sense and when he brings it inside and artificially imposes it, it looks a little heavy-handed.

I wanted to ask you about that, actually, because you just brought something up. This is a good time to ask you about it because the machine is on anyway.

Oh, the machine is on.

You said something. I thought, well, I'll let it pass and I shouldn't have, but you said that I was interested in the culture in a way that you weren't.

Interested in what?

In the general culture in a way that you weren't. And then I thought, "How can that guy say that?" Here you are making public sculpture and public sculpture is the most perfect kind of sculpture you can do.

Okay.

In fact, it is a very provocative and interesting thing for an artist to do, because very few artists are actually known in this society and yet you've had pieces on the front page of *The New York Times*. Okay, let me take it a different way. I think that you are in an area where the product that you make has the possibility of reaching the mass culture as a duplicate.

Oh, that's fine.

And that really changes your relation to the audience in terms of the product, I think. It's a different limitation.

Are you talking about the uniqueness of a big piece like the one

I'm saying in this society usually the people who make the decisions about what becomes popular, those people don't make, necessarily, those decisions on the needs of either the artist or the needs of the public.

True. But that's not the point.

No, it is the point. Because I think mass-produced things become commercialized to satisfy needs that basically, usually, are the invented needs of the media, the manufactured needs.

Yeah, that's right.

And I think if you are into making individual pieces, even if they happen to appear in public, you're not subject to that same

appearance. There is another interesting thing that happens to public sculpture, that happens to no other art that I know. It has the capability of becoming almost symbolic in a way. It becomes almost a visual symbol. For example, I'll give you a stupid example, the Eiffel Tower or the St. Louis Arch or things like that where things become an actuality. They become tremendous, huge symbols for a place. And don't you think this could happen to something that you've done?

Yeah, but I think that

Not that I'm contemplating it. But it is certainly not impossible.

Let me go back to something you said earlier. I think that the first time we spoke you said that you had no history.

Did I say that?

Yeah, yeah. It struck me really funny. And I thought, certainly you have your own personal history.

Well, that wasn't certainly what I meant.

No, but then you also have the history of the people who came immediately before you.

Yeah, but they also have their histories. Their histories are very slight as well.

But whether you

Slight. Their history is very slight as well.

Yeah, but then you have your history of other histories. And even if you were with it or against it, in order really to make your first original work, the work probably can't be traced back to those histories, if that's what you meant.

Yeah, I think that may be true.

Okay, now the sculpture. If it enters the public domain and it has no antecedents in terms of the continuity of histories like, say, your first work that really broke with the history of music. You said, "I have no history because I did this music and whatever." Right? Whatever piece you think was a didactic opening piece for you. If that happens in the public sector and nobody else can make those connections and you are asking people to make a connection in seemingly an original work that breaks with that tradition, then they become symbolic. People feed a lot of things into them. This wouldn't be the case if it were an equestrian rider, nor would it be the case if it took other conventional forms. Then we would have the continuity of history. I was interested in what you said when you said you had no history, because I think you probably think, and maybe rightfully so, that you have discontinuity with a break. But only with the acknowledgment of history—that's the only way we know it's that break.

Yes. That's true, that's true.

I think what is difficult about people in public is that they don't understand that that's why they are taken aback. That's why they are startled. I think my

Why do you think people are startled by your piece?

I think because it revealed that place in a way that

You mean that space?

That space in a place.

That's where I lost it.

On my part?

Oh yes.

That statement?

Yes.

I didn't qualify how it revealed it. I just said it revealed it.

But you don't actually think they were looking at the whole thing.

I think the piece makes you see yourself in relation to that space, which most of those people don't do. Basically what they do is use that space as a transit. You walk from the stairs into the building. And usually you watch them with their heads down. I think that piece forces them, in not a very dictatorial way, but in just a normal-attention way, to look at the sweep of that plaza and to make all those connections that they would never make. Now the, some people may even find it oppressive. That's not the intention of it. A lot of people find it lyrical.

Yes.

I mean, what it comes down to is the people who know more about receiving language perceptually see it in a way that people who don't do not. And I think it is very simple of this public to say, well, "Keep those works in the museums but don't put them in the public." See, that would mean that you would always have to be in the concert hall.

Yes.

See, the difference is, I put one piece out there. You have the possibility of putting lots of records out there. And I think to put lots of records out there—here's where it comes to the difference in audiences. It's hard to put lots of records out there with something that is initially disjunctive.

That's right.

Right?

Actually, it's hard even to continue to put them in concert halls sometimes.

Okay.

You know, I'll tell you, the interesting thing that people aren't aware of is that there is still a very, very stiff resistance to the kind of work that I do in a lot of theaters. I can't get an offer from the West Coast, for example.

Let me go back to this record thing because I think the audience question is different. Is it possible to make a record where no one is going to deduce from that record anything that came before it?

Well, there have been some attempts to do that, actually.

With a regular, standard, conventional record?

No, they aren't regular, standard, conventional records. No one will buy them. You can make them, but you can't get anyone to buy them.

You can't, you can't get anyone to buy them? Okay, so there are other things that come. Now here is what I think happened here, right? You can't get anyone to buy a piece like that, right?

Right!

Now, I've got the city of Paris to buy one and I'm getting a few other people to buy one, but it took the kind of note out there. People had to hear of it. By comparison, it would be as if you produced a disjunctive record.

So you think it is because it already has a history?

Yes.

By the time you'd done the second piece you've already

Yes, then I'm working out of my history. Yes, I have the history of these curved pieces.

So the difficulty is the first piece. But you know, I can actually remember that very clearly when we did the Amsterdam piece. When we were splashing light on the side of the Stedelijk Museum and people got very pissed-off.

Yeah.

Actually, that wasn't the first time.

Actually, I saw [the Stedelijk Museum director] de Wilde and he recently reminded me of you throwing the piece. No, you and Fiore and me throwing the guy out of the Stedelijk when you were doing your concert.

Yes, yes. Well, actually, I don't remember you being there. I thought that you—you finally threw the guy out but let him cause quite a ruckus first.

I was sitting too far back. Fiore got to him first and I was very amazed that you confronted him the way that you did. But I don't think we ought to go on with that topic.

No, no. But that is interesting. Do you have any nostalgia for those pieces?

Nostalgia? No. No, I think I was first forced to get into all of that by doing a retrospective but I'm not very nostalgic in that way.

No, I'm not either actually.

And what happens is I don't see if you do a twenty-year body of work, I don't really see it as being older, newer. I see it as one whole.

Yeah. Well that's the way we

Let me ask you something. Because I'm thinking about what to do with this project. Is there a way that by defining different architectures, that the way they are structured will actually control the kind of sound in that space? By the kind of sound I mean there must be different wave length reflections in different spaces.

Sure. Sure.

Can you use—can you use that sound?

Oh yeah. This is what the acoustics in concert halls are all about in a certain way. And you become very sensitive to that when you are playing. For example, a room that is made all of glass or something versus a room that is lined with cork.

Let me just ask you—not even about that—does the particular shape of the room

And the shape does it too.

But does the shape do it so it either reinforces and reflects the sound?

Sure, absolutely.

Then contrary to that, does it do it so it diffuses the sound?

Yeah, you can do it that way too.

What would account for that? Different planes, different

Exactly. The more irregular the surfaces are, the more broken up the sound waves are.

Oh, so the sound waves run in a particular pattern?

You will get a live sound if there is a reflective surface, a live sound without a lot of echo, which is what the ideal is.

When the sound is more—I'm not sure of the terminology—but the sound is either more reflective, say, or more diffused, we'll say, or more

Well, that is actually, we call it—what do you say—a dry sound. A dry sound is very absorbed like [claps hands]. There is no reverb, you know.

But, then, are there sounds that in a reflective surface drop out, that diminish because the surface is reflective?

No, no.

What is an overtone?

Oh, that is a different matter entirely. That's a natural function of sound to divide itself in a series of overtones starting with a fundamental pitch, to have byproducts at specific points. Like an octave, two octaves, a fifth, and so forth. So for example, when you take a string and divide it in half, it will be an octave higher. If you divide it a third, it will then be a fifth higher.

Okay.

Now, this too is what overtones are: When a sound vibrates it sets up other vibrations above its natural, fundamental sound. See, this is what La Monte Young was very concerned about.

Well, I'm just asking whether—was he very concerned about that?

Very concerned about it.

I'm not quite sure. He didn't go about constructing spaces.

No, he didn't. He constructed scales. Now, on the other hand, he was very careful about where he played. You try to be careful but sometimes you can't be.

Could you start with the wavelength and then make the space that would be correct for that wavelength?

Yeah. You can do that. Yeah.

You could start with the wavelength.

You could decide whether you wanted to have a sound that was—by the wavelength? I'm not sure.

Or do you have to do it the other way around? Do you have to take the wavelength from the given measure of the volume of space?

That's usually, of course, what we do.

But can you do it the other way? In this room can you say, "Four hundred and twenty whatever."

You see, they don't really do it precisely. What they do is put up all kinds of variables in a hall that you can manipulate. And then they move them around until they get them the way they want. Because, it's still, as a science, it's not so

precise?

It's not so precise at the moment. Tuning a hall is what you are talking about. You can go in a hall and certain pitches in that hall will be reinforced by the hall itself.

That's what I am talking about. That's what I am talking about. If we go to the space in Ohio, it's going to have its own sound.

We can do that. We have equipment to go in and analyze that sound.

Okay. That's what I'm interested in. I think just for openers, I'd be interested in that. Does that interest you in any way?

Well, what I'd have to do—yeah, that can be. Yeah, because we are never in a position to do this. We're very often aware of what fundamentals in the hall are the pronounced ones.

Um hum.

And since I can't rewrite the pieces for the hall, what I then do is I even-out our equalization of the mix to match the house.

Oh, I see. So you do it electronically.

I do it electronically. Whereas ideally what I would do is say, "Oh, this hall has a very—it reinforces a low F." So that would give me an F and a C above that and I can go on from that.

But what is that called? The different octave. Do they have a name for that?

Those are called overtones.

Just overtones?

And also undertones, too. But what I could do then is, say, I'll write a piece that would be reinforced by the hall. But since I never do that, what I really do is just re-equalize the music to fit the hall.

Okay. Now if you are going to write a piece that is reinforced by the hall and I am interested in, say, the resonances of the space

You could work in an abstract way and then I could go out and see what you produced.

Okay, let's say

That's much more difficult to be predictive about it

To be?

Predictive. To say I'm going to make this hall do this.

Uh, let's just say, for instance, that I made a diagonal ramp that went from the bottom of the corner of the floor to the height of the ceiling at the other end of the room. So there were two spaces divided into equal triangular volumes. Now would they—because one's low and one's high—would they have different oscillation factors and different kinds of sounds?

We could go ahead and figure that out.

We could figure that out without building it?

No. We'd have to go and try it. That's the damned trouble. You'd have to build it and then we'd have to do it.

Uh huh. Uh huh. But we'd originally get at least something back on the whole space.

Oh sure. Oh sure. The thing you have to remember is when you divide a room, you can't predict it. That's why they have so much trouble with concert halls. That's why they are always rebuilding them. Like Avery Fisher Hall was a mess for years.

Let me ask you something.

Some things we do know about in terms of material and shape.

In order to find out what that oscillation is or whatever that sound is—that wavelength—how do you test that? Do you have to test that with a sound?

Yes. It is called white noise or pink noise.

And what

I knew you would get around to that. I could see this coming!

And what is that?

I think this is very, very interesting. I thought you'd be interested in this. What it is is a machine that broadcasts—that plays, so to speak, a full spectrum of sound. It is called pink noise. It just sounds like, oh, it sounds like you were hearing static, only from very low to very high.

Could you compose a piece out of pink noise?

You could.

Has anyone?

No. But we could do it. But this work is interesting.

Would you even compose?

Oh sure. And I would do it. I would do it. You see, there would be a way to do it. There is a way to do it but you would have to accept certain things as they were.

Would the conditions—various conditions of shapes of spaces

No. It would be very interesting to do because what you could do—you could use other parameters of rhythm and, let's say, range. Let's say you used range. Let's say you took the spectrum and made it narrow and made it wide, so that would replace the idea of melody, if you will. And then on and off is a form of rhythm, you know, stop and go.

Yeah, Yeah.

So you can work melodically and rhythmically with that. Now the interesting thing about that is that then we can get beyond something that is just didactic and pedagogic. Which is not so interesting.

Well, now wait. Isn't the sound that you are getting with this noise a condition of the place? Right?

Yes, that's right.

What I want to know is this: One may just be very phenomeno-logical. You test this and you get that.

Yeah.

And I'm saying, can you use that sound? You said, "Yeah. And there is an interesting way to use it if we do this and that to it. We just stop it now and then or whatever."

I would do something. I would make a piece out of it .

Would you continue to? Arbitrarily we have decided to use the physical conditions of the volume of space to define what the wavelength will be. Now you are saying you're going to make a piece out of it. Then you are going to do something else to it. Right?

Yes, that's right.

Then the something else that you do to it—does that rely on old ways that you structured music or does it rely on other ways you structure music or can we still even go into the condition of the architecture further?

You might be able to, but I'm not sure.

Let me ask you this. Let's just say one shape is star-shaped and one shape really is a shape that will amplify back a simple tone so there is a lot of [claps hands]. Right?

Yeah.

If you then take those two and overlay those two, that means it is still coming from the spaces?

Yes. And I don't know what the result would be.

Is it interesting enough to pursue?

Well, I think, this is the kind of thing

You don't know?

I don't know.

You have no inkling of knowing?

No.

See, what do you think about the spaces if on one hand the sound comes back and on the other it diffuses? What drops out when it diffuses? If it means it diffuses?

Well, different things can, depending on the space and the like.

Now can you make something out of what you have lost?

That's the thing you can't do, I don't think. It is just not there.

But you must know what it was, because you had—well maybe you don't.

Sometimes you need a machine to tell you.

Oh, I see.

It can be so subtle. In fact what happens is that I'm in the hall and I see Dan talking to Kurt [Munkacsi] and Dan is saying, "Boost the 400 cycle. We are shy at 400 cycles."

Now, has he tested to know that?

Yeah.

Oh, I see.

To a point you can also do it by ear. Michael [Riesman] will go out in a hall and he'll say, "Roll off 10K." You can hear that.

Ah hah.

Because we've had a lot of experience in the halls, we don't always measure it. We can do it that way until we get the hall sounding the way we want to.

I'm trying to figure out what kinds of spaces would make the probing of the sound of the architecture either one way or the other. Either more diffused or more reflective.

Probably what we would do is this. If you were going to do that, I would probably work out, let's say, a theoretical piece before I got there. I would write a piece, the sound of which I didn't exactly know. Then we would go into that space with the equipment that we have and we might spend a couple of days in it

Okay. okay.

deciding on what sound we wanted in that space when we were done. And then I would take that composed piece and I would run the sound through that piece.

What makes it composed?

You mean, why have it composed to begin with?

I just don't know.

That's an interesting question.

Yeah.

Because it gives you something to listen to.

See, I don't know. Now what is it? Is it the interval? Is it the rhythm?

In my case, it would be both. Like the early pieces I did. And I still think this is true with the music I am doing now, although I think, in some different ways. I think that what I am doing now is writing music that you can listen to or you listen to the music. It's a form of

Does that mean, like, hear it?

It is like a center. It's like an attention center in a way.

Isn't that just a matter of a condition?

I don't think so. I think the condition in which

That you're conditioned to hear the music while you are listening to the music because it is a redundant reinforcement.

Now, let's put it this way. If you went into that room and all you heard was the pink noise, you wouldn't listen to it for very long.

Could you be trained to listen to the intervals or whatever of the pink noise?

Yes. But most people who are going to walk into that room are not going to be.

That's where you get back to *Tilted Arc*.

Yeah. They're not going to be.

But that doesn't mean the investigation itself is not interesting?

No, no. But after all we're not doing it in our studio. We're doing it in a public space.

You mean we have an obligation to the people who happen to walk into this room?

Well, that's how I look at it, Richard. But I'm more of a performer than you are.

Well, maybe, maybe. I mean some obligation.

Otherwise we don't need to do it there.

But wouldn't you say we have also an obligation to curiosity, inquisitiveness, and knowledge?

Well, you do them both at the same time.

What?

Hopefully you do them both at the same time. That's having a cake and eating it.

You know, I think that if you are investigating something and if you

I don't think it precludes it being interesting, at all.

Yeah, I think

I think that we could do the investigation and you could also

You can say that you can use an ensemble there too. Or you can say you can do a lot of things. But that seems like coming back and composing the music.

But Richard, you do that all the time when you make sculpture. I mean, you pick a particular—I've seen the drawings, I've seen the ideas, you have explained the ideas to me. But why do you use a certain surface? Why do you pick a certain height? There are a lot of subjective aesthetics.

The surfaces I pretty much take as I get.

Oh, sure. But you pick materials that you happen to like.

No. I just pick them the way that they are really made by the industry. I happen to know them. Probably that's why I pick them.

Yeah, but I remember when

I try not to tamper with them too much.

I remember when we were working with lead years and years ago. You were very conscious of what it looked like.

I also didn't do anything to make it look any different.

I know. I know. But the selection of the material—even going back to neon pieces and the rubber pieces—I mean, the whole process of selection is something that is based on an aesthetic.

Okay. Then could we do something that isn't about the need to invent a new material condition in the space? Or is that—that's really one of the things you cannot omit. If you have to do that.

That's hard to do. That's the hard thing. It's like saying, "Can we leave our bodies?" How are we going to do it?

Because basically we're saying, "Let's find new ways of putting material together."

Is that what we said?

Well, I think that's what it is leading toward.

Well, I think it's another way to express it also. You can say, "Putting materials together in a way that make you aware of them in a different way."

Is that the only option you have?

Well, see, there are two ways of looking at it. Operating procedurally or perceptually. I think they are different.

In terms of perception, I really base it on walking and looking and here I'm not going to base it on walking and looking. So the problem we have

Well, I will. Because the way we are setting it up is that if you do the space first, I'd say I'm in a better position than you are because I then walk into the space and then I do the piece.

Yeah.

Unfortunately

See, I don't think in this instance

you could do it another way.

I don't think in this instance I'm going to be involved with making sculpture. I am going to be involved with dividing spaces.

We could do it the other way. But it would mean if I set up a sound it would be much more expensive and longer for you to reconstruct the wall to fit the sound that you wanted. It's easier for me to move the music around. Just the way material is. That's the way material is.

Yeah.

I mean, if you had the flexibility with materials that I have with the sound

Yeah.

we could do that.

Yeah.

We could actually go in there with the stuff

Yeah.

and spend a day or two together

hanging it up, putting it down

You could actually install it.

Does it make a difference—and it must—where you put speakers in relation to the architecture?

Sure.

Like on the ceiling or on the floor or on the walls or wherever?

Sure.

Now does that have to be figured out while we are doing this also?

I think that what we could do is go with enough flexible material. And I would have to talk to Kurt [Munkacsi, Glass's audio engineer] about this and Michael and they would have to be involved in this on that level.

So we'd have to just show up there, decide that we are going to put three days of experimentation or whatever into that space.

Well, yeah. If we had that time to do it.

Yeah, okay.

Yeah.

Yeah.

I'd have to see how much time. I'd have to look and see if we left that time to do it, if we left two days ahead or three days or whatever.

Then I would have to come to some conclusion about what I thought that material was.

Yeah, in terms of material. We'd have to go there with the stuff.

Yeah, okay. Or get the stuff out there.

Yeah. Yeah, we would really be making the piece right in the place and I suspect that I would try to come up with some idea. I doubt whether I would just leave the sound as a pure sound. I probably would do it in a compositional way. But then I think you would too.

I don't know. I think it probably has to come from an experimentation that one would want to reinforce.

It's certainly the most interesting way to do it. We would just start early in the day and just figure it out. I'm sure in a couple of days we will have figured it out.

Or would have some way of probing what it is we wanted to get at.

Jonathan [Greene, director of the Ohio State University Gallery of Fine Arts, Columbus] will end up with a piece one way or the other.

Yeah.

And probably knowing the way you and I have worked together in the past we'll probably get real interested in it. And we'll probably do something we like.

Yeah. Well, I think we are talking about going there and building a piece.

Either building a piece or experimenting for two or three days so at least we know—if the piece hasn't been brought to a finalized form and we don't conclude it then—how to proceed.

I don't think we need to go out there twice. See, what we are talking about is an introduction to the materials and sound.

Yeah. It probably just means getting material and hanging it from floor to ceiling and then hanging it off the wall horizontally or hanging it off the wall diagonally

or in front of the speakers

or in front of the speakers and find out what happens.

You know the thing that we could do, what I would be in favor of working out, would be that you and I would work together here in New

York. Maybe we could spend two or three days here and then we can go out. Then we can go out with an idea of what we are going to do with the materials just before the show and install it. And it doesn't matter exactly what the space is. It will be whatever we do.

You see as soon as you said that you were thinking of also applying integral stopping and starting.

Yeah.

That's something that you don't do in a given musical score that you write.

No. Not necessarily.

I mean not to that degree?

No, that's right. And I think that

Do you think you could use any of the feedback possibilities other than just the sound of the shape of the space? Other than that, you wouldn't use anything else that would come into that? No, you're not going to record people walking around there or whatever?

No, I don't think so. I don't think so. You see the thing

Could you conceive of using the language as an idea?

Yeah, except it probably doesn't have the sonic possibilities that a full range of a pink noise spectrum would have.

Could we use both?

Yeah. But then we get into collage and you know how we feel about collage.

Now wait. Could we use both where they weren't collage? Where each one is as independent as the other.

Yes. Yes, I think that's possible.

But how? Because I'm not sure.

I think you'd have to do it by locating it in ways so that it can vary from isolated to interactive.

Oh, okay. Like an isolated word to interacting with the range of the sound.

No. I was thinking in terms of the space.

Where the word is isolated in one space and is interacting with

Yeah. And you have gradations of that. That has to do with juxtaposition rather than collage.

Yeah.

Yeah. So I think that's another way to do it. I think we can use that.

Is there a way that it could also be grafted on but not collage?

I'm not sure.

And by grafting on and not collaging it always seems to me

A number of people have done some very interesting things that were just taking words. Alvin Lucier has done this. Where they will take speech and use it as a basis, use it as a sound source to make a composition from. So this is not exactly new. It is not uninteresting just because they've done it. I'm sure we would do it differently. But there is already a history of that.

Did they use it as a physical, separate entity or did they use it

In the case of Alvin and Cage, Cage became the sound source himself, his speaking became the piece. Alvin used his speech as the initial element in a long overall musical structure.

But he recorded his speech and played it back in the other room.

That's right. I think those are both interesting things.

But there must be another way of dealing with it.

I'm sure. Remember they were looking at it very much from the point of view of the Cage tradition. And I don't think we would.

No.

It would be interesting to find a way to do that. You know, in a funny way, that's what you do when you write opera.

Oh explain that. I'm not sure what that means.

Well, what's interesting about opera is that you have words and you have music. And the trick is to get them to work together.

But do you write them with one in mind of each other?

Well, it's interesting. It depends on how you do it. Then the next question is: Do the words mean anything or not? Because you can also use the words as pure sound without any connotative meaning. And I've done that, as you know. I've done a lot of that. But then when you decide the words are going to have a connotative meaning, in other words, the words also have a

subjective meaning?

linguistic meaning like

"it's going to rain"

or "the spaceship is leaving the planet" or something like that. Actually, I just had to set words like that. It has a very precise linguistic meaning at the same time you are setting it to a musical context. It's very, very interesting. Because you have two—you have the emotional content of the words and you have the emotional content of the music. It's just like any of these things that happen together, you have to decide whether they are going to reinforce each other or are they going to work against each other. Whether they are going to be indifferent to each other, whether one is going to proceed as if the other is not happening, or they are going to become partners in it.

I always am very suspicious of what is called the emotional contents of sounds and languages.

Well that's interesting. I'll tell you, it is worth looking into.

It seems to be

Let me just try

psychologically based, crying, laughing.

There is something in music we call the "cycle of fifths." It comes up in cadences.

What's it called?

Cycle of fifths.

Cycle of fifths?

They're formulas that are conditional, but we treat them as if they are universal.

Yes.

Now, is that very different from [Josef] Albers's color theory?

Albers only gets to—and really late in his life—the notion of wet and dry. He has really no emotional resonances for red or black. Zero. He never talks about it. Only talks about the interaction of the two next to each other and how they'll enlarge or pale, but he never talks about

They usually don't actually talk about it that way. But they use it as if it does. And it is my impression that painters use color

I think, obviously, Matisse did.

Yeah. That is my impression.

There is a given harmonics to color.

And you look at van Gogh and you can't miss it.

I'm still very suspicious of it because I think

But how do you get away with it? Because you don't use it? Is that it?

No. Because I think it finally comes down to how you use it. It is an open material to anyone.

Absolutely.

And you can have

Actually, I took a very ordinary sequence and it became the basis of *Einstein on the Beach*. It's very ordinary but by the time I get done with it you don't hear it that way. In other words, one of the things that I have done is I have taken rather ordinary formulas and made them sound in a different way.

Rather than starting with something that would conjure up an emotional response?

Yes, that's right. Well, I've taken things that are supposed to have specific meanings and I've used them rather differently. But the point is that in music it is hard

Let me ask you something about that. Did that happen in *Songs from Liquid Days*? The fact that we recognize those voices changes how we listen to the music.

I think it probably does.

Not that it works for or against, but does that also have something to do with a kind of recognition?

It is interesting when a particular singer brings more to a song than I thought he would. That is a big surprise for me actually.

Style!

Yeah. I didn't know that was going to happen.

I think that's why I'm suspicious of it.

Yeah. I actually didn't know that was going to happen.

So the music then becomes some sort of backdrop for the style. The style overlays the music.

That can happen.

And I think probably you had the idea that wouldn't happen. That there would be a new kind of mesh.

That's right. And so what happened is another factor entered into the process.

The recognition of those voices.

Yeah, that was unanticipated. There was no way I could have known that. I never did it before.

Really? I think probably one would have assumed that that's what you were, in one way, hoping would happen.

No, I didn't know it was going to happen at all.

Well, you probably assume that if you get people who sing well that they are going to

I thought they would make the music sound good and that would be the end of it. I didn't realize that they would be in the music. That they become the source of the color of the music.

Ah hah.

But I didn't know it was going to happen.

Ah hah, ah hah.

That was a big surprise, actually.

Do you have any anticipation of what kinds of sound—and this would all be theoretical

we would use in

Yeah. I mean, just if you are taking this for a source, this pink noise? But I might not.

But if you do. If you do.

That's not so interesting but it might be possible. See, we have other ways of doing it. I have other kinds of sound sources. I can even use my own music for example

Mm hum. Mm hum

as a source. I might in fact—what's more interesting to me would be to do a series of sounds, some of which were my music and some of which were speech and some were abstract sounds, and to use them all.

Mm hum.

That becomes a composition too.

Yeah.

I would be inclined to think that way. But that already is compositional, isn't it? You see I think the way you work and the way I work— I don't like to speak for you—but I have a hard time not working compositionally.

Yeah, I don't think about it too much. I usually try to resolve other problems first.

I know. But that doesn't matter .

No. No. But it does matter in that the composition is a consequence of other things that condition what I'm going to do.

Well, that happens to me too. On the other hand I'm always watching it happen. I can't pretend I don't notice that it's happening.

I decide things like height and length and placement on people's paths.

How people walk and look.

Yeah.

But that doesn't mean I start with an initial idea about composition. I start with an initial attitude

Yeah, I don't know

about people's behavior.

Yeah, it's difficult. It's hard to know sometimes, isn't it? I just finished this opera with Doris Lessing and I'm still not quite sure what it sounds like. I've listened to it a number of times. We made a recording. It's very hard. I wasn't working after an effect either. In other words, if I was working after an effect I could have listened and said, "Oh, yeah. That's what I wanted." Well, obviously, that wasn't what happened. In fact something very different happens. I finish a piece, I listen to it. I listen to it very carefully to see what the piece did.

But then if you are working in relation to an image or in relation to language and it has an emotional content to it and you said—to a degree—that you were writing the music to

I don't always know what's going to happen.

You don't know?

No. I really don't.

So you write to language not to image?

No, no. That's not exactly true either. Actually what I'm thinking of is far different from that and it's actually something that you'll be able to understand. I'm actually thinking about musical language.

Oh. Okay.

I'm thinking about something much more.

Okay, okay. Now, if I am working with sculpture, I think about sculptural language.

I'm thinking about musical language. I'm thinking about harmonic sequences. I'm thinking about orchestration. I'm thinking about dynamics. I'm thinking strictly—the way I'm really thinking—is the language of music.

The internal constructs of music?

That's right.

Okay.

That's why I say I have to hear what has happened because I don't always know. And on the other hand I have certain dramaturgical devices that can aid me, for example, libretto. I have divided my opera into scenes and acts. I know there is a story. I know certain people have certain things happen at certain times. With *Einstein on the Beach* I wrote a finale. Obviously, I knew I was going to write a big piece at that moment. But those are things that make it work in the theater.

Does it have anything to do with the choreographing, how the people move in the scene?

No, that comes later. I have nothing to do with that.

You have nothing to do with that?

No. I could, but I have chosen not to because it is just a nightmare. What if now I had to go and stage it? I just don't want to do it. It would take another year of my life to do that and I don't want to do that. I've always worked with directors and choreographers. And also I have never shown any particular skill in that direction. So there is no reason to think I would do it particularly well.

But aren't there people who do do that? Like, "the horses enter." So then the scene goes and is written that way.

Yeah, some people do it that way. I don't do it that way. If you look at the script you can see that people are in it, where people actually speak. When I do a piece with Bob Wilson, I don't tell Bob what's he's going to do. Like the piece you're going to see, *the CIVIL warS*. That was a very interesting piece. It was very interesting how we did that. Well, Bob did this piece. He wrote a script that is not really a script. It's a collection of letters and memories and fragments of people's speech. And we called that a libretto. Then we went to Rome and we staged it as if it were a play. And I timed it. And we had everyone speak very slowly because words when you sing them take longer. It couldn't be done in song because I could never get it all in. So people spoke much more slowly in order for me to fit the words in a melodic line. I timed everything. And then I went back and I took the timings and I wrote a piece of music exactly for the times. And I was within about twenty seconds of the piece. It's a two-hour piece!

Uh hum, uh hum.

So that was tactically a technical problem.

How to write the composition

Yeah, yeah.

to fit the structure of the time?

Right, right. And very often things like that lead into very interesting things. When they listen to it most people think I wrote the music and Bob staged it. But that didn't happen at all. It didn't happen at all. I knew that one minute and thirty seconds into the piece some character was saying "morte" and that ten seconds later someone said "morte" and then twenty seconds later someone else said it. That's all I knew and I had to fit that into the music. It was very interesting. So in a way you get involved with technical language in a certain way. But that's not what we usually talk about. In terms of the piece that we're talking about, what people will see is probably not what we're talking about. Because we're talking about the piece in terms of the language of the piece. Isn't that right? The interactive language of the piece. That's the word we've been using.

Yeah, I'm not sure. We might reach a point where we don't know how to conclude. I guess you'll know what to do. I'm not sure how. It seems very open-ended to me. What you did there, when you said you wrote a finale—you knew. In this case there is no

Well, yes. I had a theatrical shape. Here we have something quite different.

How do you know what

Well, here the whole situation is more casual. People come and go as they like.

I know. So does that mean there is a given sound and it is looped?

No. I think that we can be indifferent to that. I think that inter-facing between public observation and what we do is something we don't need to take account of.

Well, I mean, the piece has to have a given length.

I don't think it needs to. I think it might or it might not. I mean, I don't think it needs to, do you think?

Well, I don't know. How one's going to

It is not a performance.

But someone comes in. How do they know when the piece is over? Or, how do they know when it started?

Yeah, I know. I think that to those questions I'm terribly indiffer-ent. I am not concerned at all. Are you concerned about that? See, to me it is a non-performance situation.

Okay. No, I'm not concerned about it. But I want to know what the shape of it is. To a degree I would like to know what the shape of it is.

Well, we could do that. In other words, ask the gallery if it has a six-hour shift. It could be a six-hour nonrepeating piece. We could do that.

Well, I don't think that those

And then some nut is going to sit there for six hours to check it out.

I don't know. They watch Wilson a long time.

I know. I mean that's one way to do it. I don't think that's what's interesting.

I'm not saying for you to write a six-hour piece.

No. I understand. What I'm interested in is seeing if we can get into a really interactive aesthetic. Therefore it becomes a joint piece.

Okay.

In other words, a truly joint piece would be a piece that neither of us could have made alone.

That's right. That's right. And it's probably something neither of us would have done alone.

Definitely. The way this conversation is going! You know what I was thinking about—I don't know why—remember that piece we did for that woman, Esmond? You did that rolled piece And I had to cut a hun-dred of them. God, do you remember that piece? The more I thought about this one. We must have met somewhere long ago.

That interests me. Can you with the synthesizer—can you make any artificial sound you want?

Well, in principle.

There are sounds I hear every day in a shipyard or a steel mill

Yeah. In principle.

which are fairly bizarre. Can you make those sounds?

I can put them on the keyboard, yeah. I can do something that is even more interesting. I can record them, digitally, and then I can put them on the keyboard. I can play the sounds of motorcycles.

But does that interest you?

It is interesting in a way. The difficulty right now is there is a glut of that.

What would that be like? Realism? Found object sound?

Yeah. But what it really is when you get right down to it—it could be that, but in fact it is more or less a demonstration of how the equipment works, unfortunately.

Uh huh. See what we can do with it?

So that's not so interesting. I think that's the stage where we are working at now. But I use the same equipment. We've got something called sampling. We have sampling keyboards that can do that. I can put voices on it. I can put violins on it. I can put birds on it.

Totally fabricated?

No. The current way that is being done is very interesting. A digital recording will be made of the natural sound and that sound will then be put onto a floppy disk and then it will come out on the keyboard. Or I could then work it into a computer program that would make it part of my music. The difficulty is that there is such a glut of that right now and the technology is changing so rapidly that it is hard to use it. You are almost more in the position of doing demonstrations of technology than making art at the moment. I don't think it will always be like that. But right now that is less interesting to me than language. Right now we haven't gotten to the language of the aesthetic because we are still working with the technology. Technology and language are not identical, obviously.

Does that actually mean you could take Edith Piaf or whoever you want and do her again?

I can take Isaac Stern and put him on my violin concerto and he can't say a damned thing about it.

It's funny because that appropriation is going on in all the arts. It's not going on in music—or is it going on heavily in music?

It's going on in music. It goes on a lot in pop music, more than in my field.

That means some kid goes in and says, "Hey listen. I heard this yesterday and I'd like to put it in here. Can you put it in here?" And they do it.

Yeah.

But isn't that what makes music—a lot of pop music— similar to fashion in that it changes onion skin by onion skin with every little eclectic bit you overlay on it.

Right. Because the thing about language is that language is always more personal and therefore it takes longer to develop. It is more interesting.

More original you mean?

Yeah. The trouble with technology is that—I mean, I use a lot of technology, I've got a room full of technology, I am not against technology, obviously—but the difficulty with it is that to make technology into a personal language would be a real achievement. Now some people have done it. But it is rather peculiar technology.

Who has done it? Give me an example. Who has done it?

There is a guy named [Conlon] Nancarrow.

I don't know who he is.

He took piano rolls from the player piano.

Yeah.

This is a very simple example. And he saw how this worked. That normally you would play a piece and the piano would punch the holes into the roll. Then you took the roll and put it back in the player piano and it played the piece back. What Nancarrow did is take the roll and began making abstract patterns, making music out of placement of holes. So, in other words, he took the technology of the piano roll and made something very personal and interesting out of it.

Did he know—did he have an idea what holes would make what?

After forty years he did it very well.

You mean he started randomly, you think?

He learned to do it. It took him a long time. He began thirty or forty years ago.

Ah ha.

So he started with the technology and he developed a language to fit the technology.

Do you think, oftentimes, it is just an arbitrary source that is a way of interfacing or interrupting or making an intervention into technology? Oftentimes it seems to me that those kinds of inventions come out of something sheerly arbitrary for the sake of doing something arbitrary.

Yes, I think that may be true. And they fall from other kinds of activities. There is a lot of space age technology that is in the studio. Especially the same technology that sends things to the moon. The first thing that happens is that they use it for *Star Wars* or whatever and then the next thing that happens is they use it for medicine. Then the next thing that happens is that they use it in the music business. Or they use it in the business world. Gradually microchip technology was really built.

So the spin-off of those technologies

It's all defense technology. But the thing that is interesting is that you get someone like Bruce Nauman or yourself or someone who is interested in technology. In my opinion, when the poet uses technology, the poet is always there.

You mean when scientists use it, the technology is there.

That's right. When the poet does it, the poet is there. And that's one of the marvelous things about it. We were talking about photography. That happens with photography a lot. You and I were both very interested in Nauman since he was one of the first people who

who dealt in private language.

That's right. Private language was public material. Isn't that true?

Well, that could be a problem when you get to large-scale sculpture.

Well, I don't think it is. I think that your pieces are extremely identifiable and very emotive and all those things. I think they look just like Michelangelo's, actually. I think they're the same thing.

But the problem is that the source is probably private. If I say, "Look, I walk along the beach and the beach is on one side and I walk for four miles. Then, when I turn around and walk the other way, it is a different experience. And I am interested in that experience in relation to a plane." People think you are talking about something that is esoteric. But it's not.

No, no of course it isn't.

But for someone who uses technology there may be no private language to begin with, so there is no way for it to get into the work. This is maybe the most distressing thing about it for that particular person.

You mean the person doesn't have that language?

Exactly.

He's not the source of that language?

He can't be!

Technology is a tool he doesn't know how to use.

Well, he can use it, but he can't

He hammers the nail the way it is given.

Yeah. In that sense that would be tantamount to saying that the artist or the poet is born in a certain way. I don't know if I want to be stuck with that. But in many ways I think that may be true.

Often what happens is if you misuse the technology or you don't understand the technology

you may get something interesting out of it.

A lot of times when I've taught—and I haven't done it in a while—the students who seem to be the best were the students who misinterpreted problems.

Well, I remember when I was working with you years ago. You were always trying to do these pieces that I was sure weren't going to work.

Yeah, that's what the engineer thought, too.

Yeah. I was sure and you would say, "Come on, let's try." And I would say, "No, Richard, it will never work that way." And most of the times it didn't work but sometimes it did.

Yeah.

Most of the times it didn't. But sometimes it did!

Yeah.

And that made interesting times.

We have plates standing up right now and we have this plate 52 feet long and 12 feet high. It's standing up and it is leaning. It's in the shipyard and these people work there every day and they see a lot of big things go by and they're into the rocket industry now and they are into building a Navy for America down there. And they stand the piece up, right? And then they put these braces up that don't touch it. In case it would fall it would catch it. Now the piece is never going to fall. Now it shows that these people who watch it every day still aren't sure.

But don't they know how it is built.

Oh sure. They've built it. They've built it.

Well. There is the power of the emotion of your work.

They've built it. They've built it. And it's engineered to the millimeter.

Doesn't that show that

The braces don't touch it. They've built it and they've engineered it. And yet they are still concerned that the tendency of overturn is outside of their perception. They don't think it impossible, yet, when they stand it up they put braces nearby in case it falls over. It's not ever going to fall over.

Don't you think that it speaks somehow to the emotional language of the work?

What?

Don't you think that that addresses itself to the emotional language of the work?

Emotional language?

Yeah.

I guess I never think of it as emotional language.

I know but other people do.

I would say they get startled, if that's an emotion.

Well, I think it may be more than that.

You mean a haptic psychological

I think there's an interfacing

Oh. You think I'm interfacing with anguish and dread?

Well, it could be joy and elation.

Yeah. It could be lyrical like a feather standing up. I mean, there's a lot of ways of looking at that.

Yeah. They happened to choose that way. And maybe in the end other people will look at it differently.

Actually, it's the first group of people who I've been working with continuously who are so far into the problem that they are getting a great deal of satisfaction out of making the work. And that hasn't happened in this country. That's happened in Germany.

I'll have to give you a tape of this thing I did on *The Making of the Representative for Planet 8*. It was interesting because I took the book and then I wrote the piece of music using the book. And it was very interesting because there are two things going on. There's the language of the book and there's the language of the music. They go together in a way. And in another way the result is unpredictable.

You know I gave a problem once in architectural school where I said, why don't we take this plan, let's say it's a Frank Lloyd Wright plan, and why don't we take this other plan which is a Corbusier plan. And I laid one right on top of the other—same kind of site plans—and said, build it. Now that could be a collage but you get spaces

that wouldn't have happened.

that wouldn't have happened. And you get people really

Can't you just do computer models of that?

Well, students didn't do that. I really wanted them to get into building the models.

building the models and seeing what they thought. What they thought Wright was and what they thought Corbusier was. And then seeing what the difference really is. When I put them together they came up with a different hybrid. Have you ever thought that there is a possibility in music of doing overlays like that? What if you took two pieces and just decided, "I'm going to sink one right on top of the other."

Well, lots of people have done that, you know.

Oh. They have?

Yes. You know Ives did that.

Oh. He did?

Yeah, but maybe not in such a radical way. We can do it in music more easily than you can do it in sculpture, clearly.

I don't do superimpositions. You can do it in film.

I can put a string quartet in this corner and I can put—in fact I was just in Peru—and you've seen this too—I was just in Peru a month or so ago and I was in a small little churchyard and there were two bands. And they decided to try to outplay each other.

Oh yeah. Yeah. Yeah.

And what you hear is two pieces of music right at each other.

You don't hear a third thing which is both of them together?

You can. It's hard to, but you can.

Is that interesting? Is there something interesting there?

That third piece. It's hard to hear the third piece.

Is that collage?

Ives was able

But if you took your own music which has the same kind of orchestration

and put two pieces together?

Not interesting?

Well, it would be hard for me to do it.

Would there be something in that where you can pick out the tune or the song, but where there would be something that was the mean, that would be another language that you could then use?

I don't know.

Would there be a certain progression or disjunction that you couldn't have foreseen? You put those together and in listening to it all you think, "I don't need that." But there's thirty seconds in there that is a way of restructuring

Yeah, that could be.

another piece of music. Basically, what I wanted these students to do was put a curve and a straight line together. And you can't tell them that until they see it.

Oh. Could they do it?

Well, they start doing their own things and obviously they start using curves and straight lines.

What happened? Anything good come out of it?

Students are students. You present them problems. The reason I brought up that architectural analogy is that it is the first time I've seen an overlay happen where I didn't think it was collage. Because it was two different structures from two different people.

You end up with a resultant form.

Yes. It was just like a graph which I don't think is exactly like a collage.

But at the end it was new information?

Yeah. It's a new structuring. If you put your own music on your own music I think it's a different thing. You might put your early piece on a late piece. It's one of those ideas that sounds like an esoteric idea but it could yield something in its probing that you couldn't have foreseen.

Yeah, yeah, that's right. That's about language too. It's about making the language produce something else

that your disposition

Well, you see, that's what Cage tried to do in a way, I think. He tried to defeat his own—this is a funny word to use—his own mediocrity. A kind of sameness. I think he tries to defeat that. He devises strategies to produce unexpected things. Don't you think?

Yeah, to some degree. But isn't that what everyone did initially when they broke their first work?

Yes. It's still going on.

I'd have to apply the word *radical* to that idea in some sense.

Well, the guy is 75 and he is still doing it.

I think we're a little more further along today than we were.

Oh yeah. I think this is interesting. I actually think this is interesting. Tell Jonathan [Greene] not to worry about it. Because the real point is it's more interesting for us to have a methodology of working and figuring out what we're doing than to go and look at the space.

FIRST LESSON, BEST LESSON (1992)

TRICYCLE

In 1966, Philip Glass made the first of many trips to India. His Buddhist study and meditation practice began at that time. This interview was conducted for *Tricycle* by Helen Tworkov together with Robert Coe, author, critic, and playwright.

Tricycle: As your Buddhist studies followed an interest in yoga, let's start there. That puts us back in 1962, when even a yoga teacher was hard to come by.
Philip Glass: I found one in the Yellow Pages, under the Y's. For the next three years I studied with Indian yoga teachers, including one who started me being a vegetarian.

And did yoga put you under some kind of Eastern umbrella that extended to Buddhism?
I never heard anything about Buddhism through my yoga teachers. It was through John Cage that I knew anything at all, through his book *Silence*. And just a year or two before that, the first really good edition of the *I Ching* came out, which I knew about through an English painter who had joined the Native American Church and was a peyote eater. Throughout the late Fifties and early Sixties the painters were the most adventurous people in the arts, the ones most committed to searching out new ideas.

So it's not surprising that I would know of the *I Ching* through a painter. And then John Cage. I certainly did not learn about him at music school. He was not considered a serious musical influence at that time. Certainly not by the people at Juilliard. Then in *Silence* there were all these references to Zen koans. But the big explosion in the culture happened in 1968 when the Beatles went to India to study with the Maharishi. They brought back Indian culture. Only after that did people like Ravi Shankar begin performing in large concert halls—and filling them. George Harrison made Ravi Shankar a household name. But when I started out, any kind of Eastern interest was still pretty marginal.

What were you reading?
Well, there was an odd assortment of things like Marco Pallis's *Peaks and Lamas*, and then the yoga books by Theos Bernard. But he also wrote about Tibet. Bernard had gone to Tibet in the late Thirties. But see, from reading Bernard and from reading Charles Waddell, I figured out that one of the gateways to Tibet was the Darjeeling district. It was still a thriving, culturally intact Tibetan community, not yet disrupted by the Tibetan refugees that came soon after. Another interesting person I read at that time was Arthur Avalon. He had another name: Sir John George Woodruffe. He wrote the *Serpent Power* and several other books. He concentrated on the yoga that developed in the Bengali parts of India, and that led me to Ramakrishna. But I didn't get to India until 1965.

After working with Ravi Shankar in Paris?
Yes. I had received a fellowship to study in Paris with Nadia Boulanger in 1964. For extra money, I took a job transcribing music for Ravi Shankar. He had been invited to Paris by Conrad Rook to write the score for the film *Chappaqua*.

Had you worked with Indian music before?
I had never even *heard* Indian music before! Funny, isn't it?

Yes. Because in another two years it was on everybody's transistor radios.
It seemed to have happened overnight. But in order to find a way of notating the music, I made my first on-the-spot analysis of how Indian music was put together.

How did you notate it?
The trick, of course, was to take a medium that was based on a different principle of organization and to write it in a language developed for

Western music. Western notation was developed for music that is organized along Western lines.

*There has been criticism of the interpretation you made of Indian music
at that time. And haven't you yourself referred to your own music of the
late Sixties as having grown from mistakes that you made about the
structure of Indian music?*
I'm not sure it was a mistake. But it was a very narrow reading.

*Wasn't there a real misunderstanding of the structure? That the central
technique of Indian music is additive?*
That's what I thought it was. And that was a misapprehension. I thought
I was listening to music that was built in an additive way, but it turned out
it really wasn't. It is built in a cyclic way. And that turned out to be very
useful, because the misunderstanding, the use of an additive process,
became, in fact, the way I began to write music.

Did you get to India through Ravi Shankar?
No. Through Swami Satchidananda. I had met him in Paris when he was
en route to New York. He had a yoga ashram in Sri Lanka, that is, in
Ceylon, and he invited me to study there. This was in the fall of 1966. I
was married to JoAnne Akalaitis then, and we went off to India overland,
the classic route: through Turkey by train, through Iran and Afghanistan
by bus, and into Pakistan through the Khyber Pass, and then into the
Punjab. When I got to New Delhi there was a letter waiting for me from
Swami Satchidananda: "Dear Student: You'll be happy to know that I
have had a tremendous reception in New York and have started a school
here, so there is no reason to go to Ceylon. Please come back to New
York. You can study with me here." Well, I had no intention of returning
before seeing India, and because of the Bernard books, we ended up in
Darjeeling, but with Kalimpong as our goal.

Were you deliberately in search of a teacher?
I was interested in something more exotic than studying yoga in New
York. I was ready for an experience in India in a way that, for example,
Bernard had had. My question was whether the teachers who appeared in
those books were still around and, more specifically, were the teachings
that I had read about just book learning, or were they practiced?

*By 1967 you were back in New York, fresh from India and doing begin-
ning meditation practices; and your minimalist compositions of the years*

1967, 1968, and 1969 to some extent evolved out of the work you did with Ravi Shankar. Yet you have denied a common assumption that this music was influenced by meditation practice, and you have also been quick to disclaim any association between your work and so-called meditation music.

At the time, there were a lot of composers doing similar experiments with composition, and they hadn't been to India. They didn't have Buddhist teachers, and they hadn't been studying yoga since 1961.

By around 1968, there were articles on the "new meditation music" that referred to you, Terry Riley, La Mont Young, and Steve Reich.

I have always considered that a misconception.

Let's clarify something: meditation music does not imply that meditation is the inspiration for the music, or that the music comes from the experience of meditation, but that the music itself promotes—or induces—a contemplative state of mind. A mind that is encouraged to find its own resting place rather than get jerked around by auditory emotive buttons.

If you go to any of these float tanks or new-age spas, what's the music that they play? They don't play Terry or La Mont or me. They have "new-age" music, which doesn't sound the same. The music that the critics thought was that music hadn't even been written yet. It came later.

Was there no common source for the minimal music that was written in the late Sixties?

What's confusing here is that by 1968 North America was awash with ideas of a new culture, and the associations are inescapable.

Is it completely coincidental that at the same time as meditation practice enters North America in a big way, a movement in music appears with obvious parallels to meditation—music that, for example, denies habitual patterns of expectation, breaks the convention of beginnings and endings, eliminates crescendos, and dissolves the dualities of peaks and valleys?

There are other sources.

Such as?

Samuel Beckett. Don't forget that I was working with the Mabou Mines Theater at the time. And in those days we were all completely involved with Beckett.

How does Beckett's influence translate in musical terms?
Nonnarrative theater or nonnarrative art is not based on theme and development but on a different structure. The influences are not Indian alone. Beckett was a big influence. So was Brecht. Genet, too.

Can you say something about the parallels to the dharma?
These writers took the subject out of the narrative. They broke the pattern of the reader identifying with the main character.

How is that accomplished?
Brecht does it with irony, as in *Mother Courage*. Beckett does it through fragmentation, as in the theater piece *Play*. And Genet does it through transcendent vision. *Miracle of the Rose* is an example.

Is it the detachment from character identification that apprehends a dharmic sensibility?
It has to do with the self-grasping or self-cherishing mind. Brecht is the obvious example of trying to go beyond the self-cherishing mind. But in each case, the attempt is the basis for defining the artist as avant-garde.

What accounts for this?
World War I saw the end of a nineteenth-century Romantic idealism. These men came after that. They had lived through that disillusionment, and it produced an attitude that was freshly and newly critical of the Western tradition that landed the world in such a mess. Then, of course, it is even more intense for the generation after World War II. That's us. By the Sixties, coincidences of cultural ideas were going on. On the one hand, you have an explosion of Indian culture, and on the other, a reaction to nineteenth- and twentieth-century narrative art. These two cross-currents tended to reinforce each other. When I came back from that first trip to India, I started looking at paintings by Frank Stella and Jasper Johns, and again I saw work based on a different kind of thinking, work that was as different from abstract expressionism as abstract art was from the post-Dadaists. Genet and Beckett were two of the most important people in this respect, and you can trace that back to Duchamp, if you like.

That's an interesting crossroad, because the Duchamp-Cage-Zen connection is probably both the quietest and the most effective Buddhist influence in this culture. And if you really want to get into Western Buddhist genealogies, you can connect Cage and Genet to Artaud and to Bali.

I'm not trying to deny the Indian connection. But the base of it was much broader.

Well, it's curious. At a certain point there is the Indian explosion and what the press is calling "minimal meditation music." Yet throughout all of your interviews, you have always said, "No, they've got it all wrong." Yet the parallel remains; but unlike your contemporaries, there has been an aspect of your music—that obsessive, compulsive, driven dimension—that, shall we say, is even "Faustian." This seems to be about a Western sense of control. And one could see, in retrospect, how that would lead you back to a Western tradition.

I think that's accurate. And another dimension to this is that the word *minimalist* was originally applied to visual artists that I knew quite well—Sol LeWitt, Don Judd, and Robert Morris. If you spoke with them, they would probably not make any reference to the Indian influence at all. There was a cultural change of mind that was happening in the Sixties that embraced all of these art forms and drew from many sources: European as well as Far Eastern, Indian as well as American. Yet within all these influences and changes, it never occurred to me that my music was about meditation. The theater was an important source for me. A lot of my work came out of a need to evolve a musical language that could be married to the theatrical language that was going on around me.

And this musical language had no concrete reference.
That's right. It was a self-referential musical language that was, in essence, abstract.

Did that commitment to an abstract language also set you apart from your peers at the time?
In the late Sixties, any number of people were doing music based directly or indirectly on Indian influences. It was not uncommon to see Western musicians dressed in Indian clothes and lighting incense on stage. What I was doing was far, far away from that. I was quite content to let other people light the incense.

There are perhaps other ways of talking about your music and your own Buddhist meditation practice, but it's tricky, because the newness of Buddhism in the United States fosters an irksome imperialistic tendency to co-opt ideas, people, or music, for that matter, as "Buddhist" when they are not really so. Yet in spite of this, there seem to be recognizable

interconnections between your music and your studies in Buddhism.
Certainly. But not in the music itself. The real impact of Buddhist practice affects how you live your life on a daily basis, not how you do your art. How you live day by day, moment by moment. The impact of Buddhism is not theoretical, as in how you paint or how you write a novel. That's hardly as interesting as how you live on a daily basis, don't you think? Aspects of Buddhist studies, such as the development of compassion and equanimity and mindfulness, are the practical aspects of daily life.

This is a big departure from the exoticism you pursued in India thirty years ago.
You start out pursuing the exotic, and it brings you around to the most basic daily activities. Also, the music world encourages such an exhausting and compulsive way of living that it is important to balance your life against the demands of that kind of career.

It took a generation to discover that it's about how you put your shoes on in the morning.
But that's what turns out to be the most interesting thing. That's why I de-emphasize the impact on the actual music itself.

Even though certain aspects of the Buddhist path may have unexpectedly routed you from the exotic to the mundane, other aspects of Buddhist meditation practice complement the classical training of a Western musician: discipline, rigor, the relationship between formal structure and personal creativity, between discipline and playfulness.
That's what you learned from a teacher like Nadia Boulanger. Though actually, I was already pretty disciplined by the time I got to her. Ane Pema Chodron (from Gampo Abbey) gave me a pin with the abbey's motto, which is the Tibetan word for "discipline." And I said, "Pema, this is the pin I don't need!"

The late Zen teacher Maurine Stuart studied piano with Boulanger some fifteen years before you did, and she often spoke of Boulanger in the same terms that one might speak of a spiritual teacher.
I can understand that. Before I went to Paris I had acquired very good work habits, which in itself is a discipline. But Boulanger carried the idea of discipline to another level. She added something that I became familiar with later through Tibetan practice, something that I can only describe as a devotional aspect of music study, and anyone who studied with her could talk about that.

Were you inspired by Boulanger's devotion?
Boulanger set herself up as an incomparable model of discipline and dedication, and she expected you to be just like her. And that was almost impossible, because she seemed beyond what any human being could really hope to be. Yet, she did it in a very simple way—I would not say gracious, no one ever said that Boulanger was gracious—but she did it in a simple, clear way. When I studied with her, for example, the only way to live up to her standards and to turn out the amount of work she expected every week was to get up between 6 and 7 in the morning and work all day long. And, if I did that every day, I would turn up at my lesson and Boulanger gave me the impression that I had done just about the very minimum.

You have also referred to Boulanger as a monster.
In the sense that she was a relentless, unwavering example that she expected you to follow. One day I came to a harmony lesson. She saw an error in something called "hidden parallel fifths." She studied the page in silence and then turned toward me. With a look of understanding and compassion she asked how I was feeling. I said, "I'm feeling fine, Mademoiselle." She asked, "Do you have a fever? Do you have a headache?" And I didn't get what was going on. "I know of a good psychiatrist. Seeing a therapist can be very confidential, and one need not be embarrassed at all." I explained that I didn't need that kind of help. Finally, she said, "Well I don't understand." And I said, "You don't understand what?" And she said, 'This!" Then she wheeled around and pointed at the mistake I had made. "How else do you explain the state of mind that produced this error? You're so distracted, so out of touch with reality; if you were really conscious of what you were doing, this could not have happened. How can you live such a distracted, unconscious life that you would bring this in here?" That was Mademoiselle Boulanger.

What effect did that have?
I decided to find a way of guaranteeing without fail that the lessons would be perfect. I devised a system that entailed a mathematical analysis for each notation so that visually the page took on a completely different look. For the next year and a half every exercise that I brought to her had that analysis, and she never made any comment about it. Amazing.

What were the aspects of her teaching that became more clear to you through Buddhist practice?
Her insistence on conscious living, on what you might call "self-remem-

bering," though she certainly did not use that term. Her conviction that attention to detail was not just an exercise but a state of mind that reflected the quality of your life.

Were there aspects of meditation practice that were familiar to you through music practice?

Boulanger concentrated on three things, and they were, in a way, a preparation for working with dharma teachers: first, the basics—the fundamentals of harmony and counterpoint; the second was paying attention, and this was her hardest lesson (and, of course, so much of meditation practice is about paying attention); the third point, which she never stopped talking about, was "making an effort." And that's something else that we hear from our dharma teachers. At the beginning, middle, and end of every lesson, her mantra was, "You must make an effort!"

Paying attention, making an effort, and always the basics—I did that for two years. If you learn only that, you can go a long way. In dharma, too, the first lessons are the best lessons.

What you can learn from both kinds of practice is patience. You learn that what we want to accomplish is going to take time and demand patience. You do the same thing over and over again. Maybe you get a little better at it—slowly. And then, also, the revelation that the teaching is in the practice. You practice the piano not in order to perform but for the sake of practicing the piano. With music, you don't practice and then one day become a concert pianist. You *are* that. Practice is as much an expression of that as of practice itself. There's another thing that happens to me now, too. I've been doing a piano recital for the last year and a half, the same recital, and I've done it about forty times. And people say, "How can you keep doing it? Doesn't it get boring?" Part of the practice is learning how to play the same recital and find it interesting every time.

Can you apply that to your meditation also? Meditation, too, can become boring.

You have to figure out how it isn't boring. Right now I'm practicing for a concert that I won't even do for two months. In a certain way, I'm playing the concert. It won't be different.

With enough attention, you can eliminate the gap between the present and the future?

But you don't postpone life, with the result that your practice for life and your real life are the same. Rubinstein was playing Chopin at the end of his life as if he had just discovered him. Bernstein played the music of Mahler as if it had just been written. This happens to musicians all the time, and if it doesn't, you have nothing to give. You have to play each piece as if it were new. I do that now with music I wrote twelve years ago. I'm not pretending it's new. It has to *be* new. You can't fake it. To Boulanger, Mozart was a contemporary composer; Bach was totally alive.

Have there ever been conflicts between Tibetan practice and making music?
My Tibetan friends have always encouraged my music practice. I've been encouraged to devote myself entirely to music. There is some kind of recognition on their part, I think, that music is a kind of "practice," too—that this is practice in their terms. This is a practice of a kind that need not be profane or self-cherishing.

And then, too, you did a series of operas with overt social themes.
I did three operas about social change through nonviolence. It started with *Einstein on the Beach*, which I did with Bob Wilson, though at the time I didn't know what I was doing and would not have seen it that way. But with the next one, *Satyagraha* (in which Mahatma Gandhi was the main character), I was consciously thinking about a religious revolutionary. Again with *Ahknaten* and with his impact on the social order—in terms of the society as a whole or the individual in society. In my own work, those polarities went from *The Making of the Representative for Planet Eight* by Doris Lessing, which is about the transcendence of a whole society, to a personal hallucination such as Poe's *The Fall of the House of Usher*. That's the range, and the concern reflects Buddhist practice.

How deliberately did that enter your music?
At a certain point, I wanted the music to reflect my feelings of social responsibility. Take the image of the artist as someone cut off from society. We learn from dharma teachers that this separateness is an illusion, and things begin to shift—we begin to see ourselves as connected.

In the opera trilogy Einstein on the Beach, Satyagraha, *and* Ahknaten *(about the Egyptian king), the agents of these revolutions (of physics, politics, and religion) were all individual great men. The movements that followed would have been impossible without these three individuals, and yet all three of them ended in some kind of disaster or failure along with great triumph. From Einstein, we get Hiroshima . . .*

Not only Hiroshima, but also the paradox of quantum mechanics, which was a terrible failure that Einstein himself never recovered from. Gandhi lived to see the India that he had fought for torn all apart by religious war and division. And Ahknaten, after seventeen years of reign, was almost forgotten. He was eliminated from the list of kings.

Still, there is a deified dimension to these heroes as you present them here.
Is that a paradox? In Buddhism, we see the deification of the teachers all the time, although the teachings themselves point us in a different direction.

In both your version of Gandhi and in Richard Attenborough's film, we see an exclusively deified portrait of Gandhi—air-brushed in terms of what we know about his personal life.
I did not idealize Gandhi. That is, I never worked with the real Gandhi, and I took poetic license or artistic liberty to do that. As long as we are going to read every day about wars and rapes and mayhem, let's read about that, too. It was just a tiny bit of balancing. The Satyagraha movement and Gandhi himself have been kept alive by politicians, particularly by Martin Luther King, Jr., but also by artists. There is scarcely a political movement of the twentieth century that doesn't go back to Gandhi.

Nothing that Gandhi wanted to do worked. Not one thing he tried succeeded. For a monumental failure, he is definitely one of the great men of our time. It's easy to be an idealist when you're twenty. Try being one when you're fifty. Or when you're seventy, as he was. I never went to the "real" man as a source for the opera. I idealized the existing myth.

So addressing the illusion of a separate self, for example, or taking on a social issue for the benefit of society, justifies liberal artistic interpretation?
The artist who does that, in being a purveyor of the idea, becomes partly the teacher. I was not that ambitious. I never felt that I knew that much. All I knew was that there was something mysterious and interesting and wonderful about Gandhi. And I really didn't try to explicate it anymore than that.

In the Glass opera Satyagraha, *there is an Indian subject and an Indian story line about a great secular saint of our times. The sets are very dis-*

*tilled and stylized, and everything, from linguistic content, to sound—
voices, pitch, rhythm—to the sets, communicates great holiness.*
The music does not sound Indian.

*No. But there is an overt transcendence to the music that we had been
hearing for several years before* Satyagraha.
But it's also true that *Satyagraha* makes a very big statement. I think that
the occasion of an opera about Gandhi inspired that "transcendent" quality to go to another level.

*And are we still getting it all wrong to make associations between this
music and a personal spiritual evolution?*
In 1979, when I wrote *Satyagraha*, I was forty-two, just entering my middle age, so to speak. And that's what we have come to expect from artists,
with or without a spiritual practice. The late works of Beethoven are transcendent, and so are the late works of Shostakovich. You can see that with
some visual artists, too. There are changes, I think, that you can find in
the work of any artist who has seriously plied his trade for a solid twenty
years and where the intention of the work has been honorable. So this is
not personal to me. But you know, the most beautiful part of *Satyagraha*,
to me, is in the very last scene, when Lord Krishna says to Arjuna, "I have
known many a birth and you have not; and I have come to be reborn to
move and act with men and to set virtue on her seat again." That's what
he's saying. That is the Bodhisattva Vow: "I've come back on earth to
move with men and to place virtue on her seat again." I'm not certain, but
I wouldn't want to deny that the music is inspired by the text. Because of
my interests, I do use texts and materials that inspire transcendence in
some pieces. But not in others. But still, I would have to say, Buddhism has
affected my life more directly than my work.

How you put on your shoes?
There is a kind of ordinariness, a kind of ordinary thinking—is there such
a thing as high ordinary?—I mean, there is a way of thinking about ordinary life in a distinctly Buddhist way; and I think that's the real practice.
Funny, isn't it? It turns out that the pie in the sky is the same pie that's in
your refrigerator.

Part Four
Endgame

BIBLIOGRAPHY

Few contemporary composers have been as widely reviewed as Glass. The last time I checked the CD-Rom of the *Music Index* (beginning in the early 1980s), the number of citations approached four hundred. Extended essays, by contrast, have been remarkably few. Most are reprinted in the preceding pages. Others are listed alphabetically below:

Borden, Lizzie. "The New Dialectic," *Artforum* (March 1974).

Brecht, Stefan. *The Theatre of Visions: Robert Wilson.* Frankfurt: Suhrkamp, 1978.

Kertess, Klaus. "Gandhi in Choral Perspective," *Artforum* (October 1980).

Mertens, Wim. *American Minimal Music.* London: Kahn and Averill, 1983.

Oestreich, James R. "A Persistent Voyager Lands at the Met," *New York Times Magazine* (11 October 1992).

Porter, Andrew. "Many-Colored Glass," *Music of Three Seasons.* New York: Farrar, Straus & Giroux, 1978.

Queenan, Joe. "Braking Glass," *American Spectator* (April 1989).

Rockwell, John. "The Orient, the Visual Arts and the Evolution of Minimalism," *All-American Music.* New York: Knopf, 1984.

Schafer, John. *New Sounds.* New York: Harper & Row, 1987.

Schwarz, K. Robert. "Glass Plus," *Opera News* (October 1992).

Smith, Dave. "Phil Glass," *Contact* 11 (Summer 1975).

Truman, James. "New York Glass," *The Face* 22 (February 1982).

Among the major essays on the American "minimal" composers as a group are Edward Strickland's *Minimalism: Origins* (Indiana University, 1993); H. Wiley Hitchcock's "Minimalism in Art and Music: Origins and Esthetics," a 1988 lecture published in Richard Kostelanetz & Joseph Darby, editors, *Classic Essays on Twentieth-Century Music* (Schirmer, 1996); and Jonathan Bernard's "The Minimalist Aesthetic in the Plastic Arts and Music," *Perspectives of New Music* (1993). Among the extended interviews not reprinted here are Bruce Bebb's in *The L.A. Reader* VIII/3 (1 November 1985), Andrew Timar and Miguel Frasconi's in *Musicworks* 13 (Fall 1980), William Duckworth's in *Talking Music* (Schirmer, 1995), Edward Strickland's in *American Composers* (Indiana University, 1991), Keith Potter's in *Contact* 12 (1976), Walter Zimmermann's in *Desert Plants* (Beginner, 1976), and Cole Gagne and Tracy Caras's in *Soundpieces: Interviews with American Composers* (Scarecrow, 1982). Glass joined Virgil Thomson in a symposium moderated by Gregory Sandow, "The Composer and Performer and Other Matters," *American Music* (Summer 1989).

WORKS BY
PHILIP GLASS

Since 1965

Note: PGE denotes works written for the Philip Glass Ensemble

1965

Music for *Play* (Beckett)
For two soprano saxophones.

Music for Ensemble and Two Actresses
For wind sextet and two speakers.

Piece for Chamber Orchestra

1966

String Quartet

1967

Strung Out
For solo amplified violin.

Music in the Shape of a Square
For two flutes.

In Again Out Again
For two pianos.

One Plus One
For amplified tabletop.

1968

Two Pages
For electric keyboards (later, PGE).

Music for the Red Horse Animation (Breuer)
For the Mabou Mines Theater.

Gradus
For solo soprano saxophone.

How Now
For piano or ensemble.

1969

Music in Contrary Motion (PGE)

Music in Fifths (PGE)

Music in Similar Motion (PGE)

Music in Eight Parts (PGE)

1970

Music for Voices
For the Mabou Mines Theater.

Music with Changing Parts (PGE)

1971–1974

Music in 12 Parts (PGE)

1975

Another Look at Harmony, Parts One & Two (PGE)

Music for The Lost Ones (Beckett)
For the Mabou Mines Theater.

Music for The Saint and the Football Player (Thibeau & Breuer)
For the Mabou Mines Theater.

1975–1976

Einstein on the Beach

An opera in four acts.

For PGE, vocal soloists, and chorus. Created with Robert Wilson.

Premiered at the Avignon Festival in France.

1977

Dressed Like an Egg
Directed by Joanne Akalaitis; based on writings of Colette.

For the Mabou Mines Theater.

Fourth Series Part One
For chorus and organ.

Commissioned jointly by the Holland Festival and Festival Saint-Denis, Paris.

North Star
Music for the documentary film *Mark Di Suvero, Sculptor* by Francois de Menil and Barbara Rose.

1978

Fourth Series Part Two
For solo organ [same as Dance #2 from *Dance*, 1979].

Fourth Series Part Three
For violin and clarinet.

Written for the radio adaptation of Constance DeJong's
novel *Modern Love*.

Modern Love Waltz
For Piano.

Written for Constance DeJong's performance from her
novel *Modern Love*.

Chamber ensemble arrangement by Robert Moran.

1979

Fourth Series Part Four
For solo organ.

Commissioned by Bremen Radio. (Later adapted by
Lucinda Childs for her dance company and renamed *Mad
Rush*.)

Dance (PGE)
In five parts, combining film, live music, and recorded music.

A collaboration with choreographer Lucinda Childs and
sculptor/painter Sol LeWitt.

1980

Satyagraha
An opera in three acts for orchestra, chorus, and soloists.

Commissioned by the city of Rotterdam for the
Netherlands Opera.

A Madrigal Opera
For six voices, violin, and viola.

Commissioned by the Holland Festival, 1980.

1981

Music in Similar Motion
New orchestration for chamber orchestra.

Glassworks
Recording for CBS Masterworks.

1982

Habeve Song
For soprano, clarinet, and bassoon.

Koyaanisqatsi
For the Western Wind Ensemble (Albert de Ruiter, solo bass), chorus, and orchestra. A film produced and directed by Godfrey Reggio for the Institute for Regional Education.

The Photographer
Originally for chamber orchestra; later, PGE.

A music theater piece written with director/author Rob Malasch and commissioned by the Holland Festival, 1982.

1983

the CIVIL warS (Rome Section)
An opera with prologue and three scenes, with Robert Wilson. Commissioned by the Cologne State Theater.

Music for *Pages from Cold Harbor* (Worsley and Raymond). Tape. For the Mabou Mines Theater.

Glass Pieces
For orchestra.

Ballet choreographed by Jerome Robbins for the New York City Ballet from existing music.

1984

Akhnaten
An opera in three acts for orchestra, chorus, and soloists.

Commissioned by the Stuttgart State Opera.

Music for *Company* (Beckett).
(*String Quartet #2*)

For string quartet or string orchestra. Commissioned by the Mabou Mines Theater.

the CIVIL warS (Cologne Section) with Robert Wilson.
Commissioned by the Cologne State Theater.

Mishima
A film written by Paul and Leonard Schrader, directed by Paul Schrader.

The Olympian: The Lighting of the Torch
For chorus and orchestra.

Commissioned by the 1984 Olympic Committee for the ceremonies of the Summer Olympics, in Los Angeles.

The Juniper Tree
An opera in two acts for chamber orchestra, small chorus and soloists. Based on the tale by the Brothers Grimm.

A collaboration with composer Robert Moran and author Arthur Yorinks. Commissioned by the American Repertory Theatre, Cambridge, Massachusetts.

1985

Songs from Liquid Days
Song cycle recorded for CBS Masterworks, written with lyricists Laurie Anderson, David Byrne, Paul Simon, and Suzanne Vega.

A Descent into the Maelstrom (PGE).
Dance/theater work based on the story by Edgar Allan Poe, with writer/director Matthew Maguire and choreographer Molissa Fenley. Commissioned for the Australian Dance Theater by the Adelaide Festival.

Mishima Quartet
For string Quartet. Extracted from *Mishima* film score.

1986

The Making of the Representative for Planet 8
An opera in three acts, for orchestra, chorus, and soloists. Written with author Doris Lessing and based on her novel of the same name.

Commissioned by Houston Grand Opera.

In the Upper Room
A dance work written for and commissioned by Twyla Tharp.

Phaedra
A ballet score based on the *Mishima* film music. Conceived and choreographed by Flemming Flindt and commissioned by the Dallas Ballet.

1987

Pink Noise
A collaborative acoustic installation with Richard Serra.

For the Ohio State University Gallery of Fine Arts, Wexner Center, Columbus, Ohio.

Concerto for Violin and Orchestra
Written for Paul Zukofsky and Dennis Russell Davies.

Commissioned by the American Composers' Orchestra.

Premiered at Carnegie Hall (4 April 1987).

Hamburger Hill
Music for the film.

Cadenzas for Mozart's *Piano Concerto No. 21* (K. 467)

Commissioned by Rudolf Firkusny.

Powaqqatsi
A film directed and produced by Godfrey Reggio for the
Institute for Regional Education.

1988

1000 Airplanes on the Roof, opera (PGE)
Commissioned by The Donau Festival Niederösterreich,
the American Music Theater Festival, Philadelphia, and
Berlin, 1988 Cultural City of Europe.

Premiere at the Vienna International Airport, Hanger #3
(15 July 1988).

The Fall of the House of Usher, opera
Commissioned by the American Repertory Theatre,
Cambridge with the Kentucky Opera.

Premiere in Cambridge (18 May 1988).

The Thin Blue Line
Music for the Errol Morris film.

1989

Itaipu
For orchestra. Commissioned by the Atlanta Symphony
Orchestra.

The Canyon
For orchestra.

String Quartet #4
Commissioned by Geoffrey Hendricks.

Metamorphosis for Piano

1990

The Screens
Music for the Play.

Commissioned by the Guthrie Theater.

Hydrogen Jukebox, opera (PGE)
A collaboration with poet Allen Ginsberg.

Commissioned by the Spoleto Festival U.S.A., Charleston,
S.C. and the American Music Theater Festival,
Philadelphia, Pa.

Passages
A collaboration with Ravi Shankar.

Mindwalk
Music for the Bernt Kapra film.

1991

Music for Cymbeline (Shakespeare)
Commissioned by the New York Shakespeare Festival.

Music for Mysteries and *What's So Funny*
Written by David Gordon.

Commissioned by the Spoleto Festival U.S.A., Charleston,
S.C. and Lincoln Center's Serious Fun! Festival, New York.

String Quartet #5
Commissioned for the Kronos Quartet by David A. and
Evelyne T. Lennette, San Francisco.

The White Raven
An opera for soloists, chorus, and orchestra.

Commissioned by the Committee for Discoveries, Lisbon, Portugal.

1992

Compassion in Exile
A film about the Dalai Lama, directed by Micky Lemle.

The Voyage, opera
For soloists, chorus, and orchestra.

Commissioned by the Metropolitan Opera, New York.

Anima Mundi
Music for the film directed and produced by Godfrey Reggio for the Institute for Regional Education.

A Brief History of Time
Music for the Errol Morris film.

Henry IV, Parts One and Two (Shakespeare)
Music for the play production at the Public Theater.
Commissioned by the New York Shakespeare Festival.

Low Symphony
Commissioned by the Brooklyn Philharmonic.

Concerto Grosso
Commissioned by the city of Bonn, Germany, for the Bonn Museum of Art.

1993

In the Summer House
Music for the play by Jane Bowles.

Commissioned by the Vivian Beaumont Theater, Lincoln Center, New York.

Woyzeck (Büchner)
Music for the play.

Commissioned by the Public Theater, New York.

Orphée
An opera based on the Jean Cocteau film.

Commissioned by the American Repertory Theatre,
Boston, Massachusetts.

1994

Symphony #2
Commissioned by the Brooklyn Philharmonic.

Premiered at the Brooklyn Academy of Music (14
October 1994).

Etudes for Piano
Written for Dennis Russell Davies and Achim Freyer.

T.S.E.
A performance installation by Robert Wilson.

Commissioned by the Relâche Ensemble.

Premiered at the Annenberg Center, Philadelphia.

La Belle et la Bête, opera
For ensemble and film. Based on the Jean Cocteau screenplay.

1995

Symphony #3
Commissioned by the Würtch Foundation for the
Stuttgart Orchestra
Premiered in Stuttgart (3 February 1995)

Evidence
Music for the short 35 mm film by Godfrey Reggio.

Jenipapo
Soundtrack for the Brazilian film by Monique Gardenberg.

Le Streghe di Venezia
Ballet by Beni Montressor and choreographer Mauro Bigonzetti.
Commissioned by Teatro alla Scalla.

Candyman 2
Music for the Bill Condon film.

Concerto for Saxophone Quartet and Orchestra
Composed for the Rascher Saxophone Quartet.
Premiered on July 31st.

1996

Les Enfants Terribles
Dance opera in 27 scenes for ensemble, soloists and dancers.
A collaboration with choreographer Susan Marshall.
Libretto by Philip Glass based on the novel of the same name
by Jean Cocteau.
Premiered in Zug, Switzerland on May 18th.

Joseph Conrad's *The Secret Agent.*
Soundtrack for the film by Christopher Hampton.

Call to the Nations
Collaboration with percussionists Mickey Hart and
Zakir Hussain.
Premiered by one hundred percussionists during the opening
ceremony of the 1996 Atlanta Olympic Games on July 19th.

After Eros
Music for the play by David Henry Hwang.
Premiered in New York on December 21st.

1997

Heroes
Symphony based on the 1977 album by David Bowie and
Brian Eno.

Recorded by the American Composers Orchestra directed by Dennis Russell Davies.

The Marriages between Zones Three, Four and Five
Opera in two acts for orchestra, chorus and soloists.
Libretto by Doris Lessing based on her novel of the same name.
Commissioned by the State Goverment of Baden-Wurttemburg and the Cement Corporation of Heidelberg.
Premiered in Heidelberg on May 10th.

Kundun
Soundtrack for the Martin Scorsese film.
Conducted by Michael Riesman.

Songs of Milarepa for baritone and chamber orchestra
Commissioned by Sagra Musicale Umbra.
Premiered by Roberto Abbondanza and The Symphonic Orchestra of the Sagra Musicale Umbra conducted by Marcello Panni on September 13th in Perugia.

1998

Monsters of Grace
Digital opera in three dimensions.
For ensemble and soloists in collaboration with Robert Wilson.
The libretto is based on fourteen poems by the 13th century Sufi poet Jalaluddin Rumi.
Co-commissioned by the UCLA Center for the Performing Arts, Los Angeles, California (USA); Barbican Centre, London (UK); Festival of Peralada, Catalunya (Spain); Wolftrap Festival, Vienna, Virginia (USA); Het Muziektheater, Amsterdam (Netherlands); Change Performing Arts/Festival sul Novecento, Palermo (Italy); The Brooklyn Academy of Music, Brooklyn, New York (USA); The Society for the Performing Arts, Houston, Texas (USA); and Arizona State University Public Events, Tempe, Arizona (USA). It premiered in Los Angeles on April 15th, 1998.

Numerous dance works have been based on Glass's music. Here is a partial list, including the choreographer; where the Glass composition is known, its name is given:

DANCE TITLE	CHOREOGRAPHER	GLASS WORK	DATE
Trio in Unison	Judy Padow	Victor's Lament (North Star)	1977
North Star	Lar Lubovitch	North Star	1978
Songs Against the Wind III	Ansis Rutentals		1978?
Mad Rush	Lucinda Childs	Fourth Series Part Three	1979
Daily Rushes	Rita Jaroslow	Music with Changing Parts	1980
Doors Are Closing	Sabrina Peck		198?
Sounds of Sand	Milton Myers	North Star	1984
Glassworks	David Gordon	Glassworks	1984
Memories	Roger Tolle		1985
As It Is In Texas	Jo Harvey Allen		1986
Geologic Moments	Molissa Fenley		1986
Quartz	Wil Swanson		1986
Another Lecture	Claire Porter		1987
Life Out of Balance	Steve Gross	Koyaanisqatsi	1988
Installations	Roger Tolle		1988
Partners Who Touch, Partners Who Don't Touch	Sara Pearson		1989
Metamorphosis	Molissa Fenley	Metamorphosis 3-5	1989
Malambo del Sol	Deidre Towers/ Brenda Chambers	Powaqqatsi	1990
Draupadi (Multitudinous Trio)	Ananya Chatterjee	Passages	1990?
Intramuros	Laura Rocha		1991
Amazed in Burning Dreams	Kirk Peterson	Mishima	1993

DISCOGRAPHY

PGE denotes the Philip Glass Ensemble
Not all of the recordings are currently in print
Dates in parentheses indicate year of recording release

1000 Airplanes on the Roof
PGE, Linda Ronstadt (1989)
Virgin V2-86106

Akhnaten
Dennis Russell Davies, Stuttgart State Opera Orchestra & Chorus (1987)
Sony Masterworks M2K 42457

Akhnaten: Funeral Music
(1987)
CBS MK 39539

Anima Mundi
soundtrack: Michael Riesman, conductor (1993)
Elektra/Nonesuch 79239-2

Ao Meu Redor (Brass and Strings Arrangements)
Marisa Monte "Rose and Charcoal" (1994) EMI 8 30080

Atmospheres
(1984)
CBS AL 42313

The Ballad of the Skeletons (with Allen Ginsberg & Paul McCartney)
Allen Ginsberg "The Ballad of the Skeletons" (1996)
Mercury 697120101

La Belle et la Bête
PGE, etc. (1995)
Elektra/Nonesuch 79347

The Canyon
Robert Shaw, Atlanta Symphony Orchestra (1993)
Sony Masterworks 46352

Company (arranged as String Quartet #2 or for string orchestra)
Kronos Quartet (1986) Elektra/Nonesuch 79111-2
Kronos Quartet (1995) Elektra/Nonesuch 79356-2

Christopher Warren-Green, London Chamber Orchestra
Ultraviolet/Virgin Classics CUV 61121

Contrary Motion see Music in Contrary Motion

Dance Nos. 1–5
PGE (1988)
Sony Masterworks M2K 44765

Dance Nos. 1 & 3
PGE (1980)
Tomato TOM-8029
reissue (1987)
CBS MK 39539

Dance Nos. 2 & 4
Donald Joyce, organ (1993)
Catalyst/BMG 09026-61825-2

Dance No. 4
Christopher Bowers-Broadbent, organ (1988)
ECM New Series 21431

Dressed Like an Egg
(1981)
Soho News SH 001

Einstein on the Beach
PGE, etc. (1979)
Tomato TOM-4-2901
(reissue, 1984)
Sony Masterworks M4K 38875
PGE, etc. (1993)
Elektra/Nonesuch 79323-2

Einstein on the Beach (excerpts)
PGE, etc. (1978)
Tomato TOM-101

Einstein on the Beach: violin music
Gregory Fulkerson (solo; 1981)
New World 80313-2

Einstein on the Beach Highlights
(1996)
Elektra/Nonesuch 79435-9

The Essential Philip Glass
(1993)
Sony Masterworks SK 64133

Façades (arranged for flute & strings)
Ransom Wilson "Reich, Glass & Becker" (1982)
Angel DS 537340

Façades (Mark Burgess Version)
Mark Burgess and the Sons of God "Zima Junction" (1993)
Pinnacle PIK3

Film Works
(1995)
Elektra/Nonesuch 79377

#2 for Gaia (with Kitaro & Mickey Hart)
The Gyuto Monks "Freedom Chants from the Roof of the World"
(1989)
Rykodisc RCD 20113

Glass Masters
(1997)
Sony SM3K 62960

Glass Organ Works
(1993)
Catalyst 61825

Glass Pieces (based on excerpts from *Akhnaten* and *Satyagraha)*
PGE; Michael Riesman (1987)
Sony Masterworks MK 39539

Glassworks
PGE; Michael Riesman (1982)
Sony Masterworks MK 37265

Glassworks: Façades
Jon Harle, Christopher Warren-Green, London Chamber Orchestra
Ultraviolet/Virgin CUV 61121
Jon Gibson, PGE
CBS MK 39539
Ransom Wilson
Angel DS-37340

Heroes: Symphony
Dennis Russell Davies, Michael Reisman,
American Composers Orchestra
(1997)
Point Music 454388

Heroes: Remix (Aphex Twin Version)
Aphex Twin "Heroes Remix" (1997)
Point Music SADP-5

Hydrogen Jukebox (excerpts)
PGE; Martin Goldray (1993)
Elektra/Nonesuch 79286-2

Hydrogen Jukebox: Wichita Sutra Vortex
Philip Glass, piano (1989)
CBS MK 45576
Elinor Bennett, harp (arrangement)
Lorelt LNT 105

Icct Hedral (Orchestration)
Aphex Twin "Donkey Rhubarb" (1995)
Warp WAP 63CD

Icct Hedral Mix (Laurent Garnier Version)
Laurent Garnier "Laboratoire Mix" (1996)
React CD 87

In the Upper Room (excerpts)
PGE; Michael Riesman (1987)
CBS MK 39539

An Interview with Philip Glass Featuring Selections from *Glassworks*
(1982)
CBS FM 37265

Introduced by Philip Glass
(1993)
Elektra/Nonesuch 79377

Itaipu
Robert Shaw, Atlanta Symphony Orchestra & Chorus (1993)
Sony Masterworks SK 46352

Koyaanisqatsi
soundtrack (1983)
Antilles/Island 422-814042-2

Kundun
soundtrack, conducted by Michael Riesman (1997)
Elektra/Nonesuch 79460

"Low" Symphony
Dennis Russell Davies, Brooklyn Philharmonic (1993)
Point Music/Polygram 438 150-2

Mad Rush (Fourth Series Part Four)
(1981) Soho News SH 001
Donald Joyce, organ (1993)
Catalyst/BMG 09026-61825-2
Philip Glass, piano
(1989) CBS MK 45576

Merci La Vie
Arno / Glass (1991)
Virgin France 30844

Metamorphosis 1–5
Philip Glass, piano (1989)
CBS MK 45576

Metamorphosis 2
Elinor Bennett, harp (arrangement)
Lorelt LNT 105

Mishima
soundtrack (1985)
Elektra/Nonesuch 79113-2

Modern Love Waltz
The Waltz Project: 17 Contemporary Waltzes for Piano (1981)
Elektra/Nonesuch D-79011

Modern Love Waltz (Arranged for Chamber Ensemble)
Da Capo Chamber Players "10th Anniversary Celebration" (1981)
CRI SD 441

Modern Love Waltz (Transcribed for toy pianos)
Margaret Leng Tan "The Art of the Toy Piano" (1997)
Point Music 456345

[Music in] Contrary Motion
Philip Glass, organ (1975)
Shandar 83515
reissue (1994)
Elektra/Nonesuch 79326-2
Donald Joyce, organ
(1993) Catalyst/BMG 09026-61825-2

Music in Fifths
PGE (1973)
Chatham Square 1003
reissue (1994)
Elektra/Nonesuch 79326-2

Music in Similar Motion
PGE (1973)
Chatham Square 1003
reissue (1994)
Elektra/Nonesuch 79326-2

Music in Twelve Parts
PGE (1988, UK) Venture/Virgin 802768995
reissue (1989, USA)
Virgin 91311-2
reissue (1994)
Elektra/Nonesuch 79324-2
Music in Twelve Parts (Parts 1 & 2)
PGE (1974)
Caroline/Virgin CA2010

Music with Changing Parts
PGE (1971)
Chatham Square 1001/2
reissue (1994)
Elektra/Nonesuch 79325-2

North Star
PGE (1977)
Virgin 91013

North Star (excerpts; arranged)
Michael Oldfield: *Platinum*
Blue Plate CAROL-1856-2

Obras Maestras
(1995)
Sony Spain SM2k 69264

The Official Music of the XXIIIrd Olympiad,
Los Angeles 1984: The Lighting of the Torch
(1984)
CBS 7464-39322-1

Passages (with Ravi Shankar)
(1990)
Private Music/BMG 2074-2-P

The Photographer
Paul Zukofsky, PGE, etc. (1983) Sony Masterworks MK 37849

Piano Two
(1987) Private Music/BMG 2027-1-P

Powaqqatsi
soundtrack (1988)
Elektra/Nonesuch 79192-2

Satyagraha
PGE, etc. (1985)
Sony Masterworks M3K 39672

Satyagraha (excerpts)
PGE, etc. (1988)
Sony Masterworks MAS 2202

Satyagraha: Act III, conclusion
Christopher Bowers-Broadbent, organ (1988)
ECM New Series 78118-21431-2
Donald Joyce, organ (1993)
Catalyst/BMG 09026-61825-2

The Screens (with Foday Musa Suso)
(1992)
Point Music/Polygram 432966-2 PH

The Secret Agent
Soundtrack (1996)
Michael Riesman, Harry Rabinowitz, The English Chamber Orchestra
Elektra/Nonesuch 79442

Sextet for Brass
Christopher Larkin, London Gabrieli Brass Ensemble
Hyperion CDA 66517

Solo Music
(1975)
Shandar 83515

Solo Piano
(1989)
Sony Masterworks MK 45576

Songs from Liquid Days
PGE, etc. (1986)
CBS MK 39564

Songs from the Trilogy (Einstein on the Beach, Satyagraha, Akhnaten)
PGE, etc. (1989)
Sony Masterworks MK 45580

Spring Waterfall (with Foday Musa Suso)
Jali Kunda "Griots of West Africa & Beyond" (1996)
Ellipsis Arts CD3510

String Quartet #2 see Company

String Quartet #3 ("Mishima")
Kronos Quartet (1995)
Elektra/Nonesuch 79356

String Quartet #4 ("Buczak")
Kronos Quartet (1995)
Elektra/Nonesuch 79356

String Quartet #5
Kronos Quartet (1995)
Elektra/Nonesuch 79356

Strung Out
Paul Zukofsky (1976)
CP² 108

The Thin Blue Line
soundtrack (1989)
Elektra/Nonesuch 79209-2

Two Pages
Philip Glass, Michael Riesman (1975; first printing only)
Folkways FTS 33902
reissue (1975)
Shandar 83515
reissue (1994)
Elektra/Nonesuch 79326-2

Violin Concerto
Gidon Kremer, Christoph von Dohnanyi, Vienna Philharmonic Orchestra
(1993)
Deutsche Grammophon 437 091-2

ACKNOWLEDGMENTS

In alphabetical order

Charles Merrell Berg: "Philip Glass on Composing for Film and Other Forms," reprinted from *Journal of Dramatic Theory and Criticism* V/1 (Fall 1990) by permission of the author.

Thomas Rain Crowe: "Hydrogen Jukebox," reprinted from *The Arts Journal* V/10 (July 1990) by permission of the author.

David Cunningham: "Einstein on the Beach," reprinted from *Musics* 12 (May 1977) by permission of the author; "Music in Twelve Parts, Parts 1 & 2," reprinted by permission of the author. Copyright ©1997 by David Cunningham.

Peter G. Davis: "Star Drek," reprinted from *New York* (26 October 1992) by permission of the author.

Richard Foreman: "Glass and Snow," reprinted from *Arts Magazine* (February 1970) by permission of the author.

Paul John Frandsen: "Philip Glass's *Akhnaten*," reprinted from *Musical Quarterly* LXXIX/3 (July1993) by permission of the publisher.

Kyle Gann: "Midtown Avant-Gardist," reprinted from *Village Voice* (17 October 1992) by permission of the author.

Tricycle interview reprinted from *Tricycle: The Buddhist Review* (Winter 1991) by permission of the publisher Helen Tworkov.

David Walters: Interview reprinted from *Yes* 13 (Autumn Term, 1992) by permission of the publisher.

Wes York: "Form and Process," reprinted from *Sonus* I/2 (1981) by permission of the author and publisher.

Among the authors who would have been here, had their publishers made their work more available, are Lizzie Borden, Klaus Kertess, Doris Lessing, Andrew Porter, Joe Queenan, John Rockwell, and John Schaefer. There were no replies from *American Music, Interview, Avalanche, Musicworks, The Baltimore Sun*, Stefan Brecht, Constance DeJong, and K. Robert Schwarz, among others. James Truman, a former contributor to the British magazine *The Face*, now the editorial director of Conde Nast in New York, asked that his 1982 article on Glass not be reprinted.

Every effort has been made to identify the sources of original publication of the preceding selections and make full acknowledgments of their use. If any error or omission has occurred, it will be rectified in future editions, provided that appropriate notification is submitted in writing to the publisher or editor (P.O. Box 444, Prince St., New York, NY 10012-0008).

BIOGRAPHICAL
NOTES

Charles Merrell Berg is Professor of Film Studies in the Department of Theater and Film, University of Kansas, Lawrence. He also plays saxophones in a midwestern jazz ensemble known as Chuck Berg and Friends.

Cover was published in New York by Judith Aminoff, now residing in Paris, in the early 1980s. It has no connection to a later New York magazine similar in name.

Thomas Rain Crowe, born in 1951, is a poet and Native-American activist living and teaching in Cullohee, N.C.

David Cunningham, born in 1954, has worked since 1982 as the producer of Michael Nyman's music for Peter Greenaway's films. *The Listening Room* is a 1994 live sound installation, "a continuous piece of music over three days," also available as a CD.

Peter G. Davis has long been the music critic of the weekly magazine *New York*.

Richard Foreman, the distinguished American playwright, born like Glass in 1937, wrote the first extended essay on his work. The most recent collection of Foreman's performance scripts is *My Head Was a Sledgehammer* (1995).

Paul John Frandsen is an egyptologist teaching in Denmark.

Kyle Gann is currently the music critic of the *Village Voice* and a composer. He has published a book about Conlon Nancarrow.

Ev Grimes took a doctorate in music education and has since produced numerous radio programs on music, mostly for American public stations.

John Howell has worked in editorial positions at various magazines, including *Elle* and *High Times*.

Tom Johnson, born in 1939 and educated at Yale University, was during the 1970s the principal music critic for the *Village Voice*; his reviews there were collected in *The Voice of New Music* (1989). Moving to France in the mid-1980s, he now works primarily in Europe. He ranks among the most inventive contemporary composers.

John Koopman is Professor Emeritus of Music at Lawrence University in Appleton, Wis., where he continues to live.

Allan Kozinn has worked at the *New York Times* since 1977. *The Beatles* (1995) is his comprehensive introduction to their work.

Joan La Barbara is a distinguished performer/composer presently living in Santa Fe, N.M. *Music for Voice and Instruments by Morton Feldman* and *John Cage at Summerstage* are recent recordings featuring her voice.

Art Lange is a poet and music writer who lives in Chicago. During the late 1980s he was the editor of the jazz magazine *downbeat*.

Robert C. Morgan is a New York artist and arts critic who also teaches at the Rochester Institute of Technology.

Tim Page, long a music critic at *New York Newsday*, now holds a similar position at the *Washington Post*.

Joseph Roddy is a veteran musical journalist living in New York.

Semiotexte is a New York-based magazine now published by Autonomedia.

Richard Serra is commonly acknowledged as one of the major sculptors of the Western world.

Aaron M. Shatzman contributes to *Fanfare*, a quarterly journal of record reviews.

Edward Strickland wrote *American Composers: Dialogues on Contemporary Music* (1991) and *Minimalism: Origins* (1993). The latter is perhaps the richest critical essay on its interdisciplinary-arts subject.

Mark Swed, an editor of the *Musical Quarterly*, contributes music reviews prolifically to magazines around the world. He is completing a biography of John Cage.

Tricycle: The Buddhist Review is a New York magazine edited by Helen Tworkov.

David Walters is the director of the Coda Music Centre in southern Britain and co-editor of the Yamaha Education Supplement (YES).

Wes York is a composer and music writer living in New York. He has recorded a CD of his music (New World) and published a book on Morton Feldman (Greenwood).

INDEX

————THE EDITOR

Richard Kostelanetz is an electroacoustic composer and polymathic writer who has written and edited many books about contemporary music, including *Nicolas Slonimsky: The First 100 Years* (Schirmer, 1994), *Fillmore East: Recollections of Rock Theater* (Schirmer, 1995), *A Portable Baker's Biographical Dictionary of Musicians* (Schirmer, 1995), and *John Cage (ex)plain(ed)* (Schirmer, 1996). In addition to compiling a *B. B. King Companion* (1997) and *Frank Zappa Companion* (1997) for Schirmer Books, he is currently editing a series of individual volumes of *American Composers in Their Own Words* for Schirmer.